Marriage, Sexuality, and Gender

D1598410

Initiations: Sex and Gender in Contemporary Perspective
Laurie Shrage, Series Editor

BOOKS IN THE SERIES:

Marriage, Sexuality, and Gender
by Robin West

Marriage, Sexuality, and Gender

Robin West

Paradigm Publishers

Boulder • London

Paradigm Publishers is committed to preserving ancient forests and natural resources. We elected to print *Marriage, Sexuality and Gender* on 50% post consumer recycled paper, processed chlorine free. As a result, for this printing, we have saved:

10 Trees (40' tall and 6-8" diameter)
4,019 Gallons of Wastewater
1,616 Kilowatt Hours of Electricity
443 Pounds of Solid Waste
870 Pounds of Greenhouse Gases

Paradigm Publishers made this paper choice because our printer, Thomson-Shore, Inc., is a member of Green Press Initiative, a nonprofit program dedicated to supporting authors, publishers, and suppliers in their efforts to reduce their use of fiber obtained from endangered forests.

For more information, visit www.greenpressinitiative.org

Copyright © 2007 Paradigm Publishers

Published in the United States by Paradigm Publishers, 3360 Mitchell Lane Suite E, Boulder, CO 80301 USA.

Paradigm Publishers is the trade name of Birkenkamp & Company, LLC, Dean Birkenkamp, President and Publisher.

Library of Congress Cataloging-in-Publication Data

West, Robin, 1954–
   Marriage, sexuality and gender / Robin West.
      p. cm. — (Initiations: sex and gender in contemporary perspective)
   Includes bibliographical references and index.
   ISBN 978-1-59451-389-3 (hc)
1. Marriage—United States.   2. Marriage law—United States.   I. Title.
   HQ536.W44   2007
   306.810973'090511—dc22

                                                                          2007015266

Printed and bound in the United States of America on acid-free paper that meets the standards of the American National Standard for Permanence of Paper for Printed Library Materials.
Designed and Typeset by Straight Creek Bookmakers.

11 10 09 08 07   1 2 3 4 5

Contents

Introduction

There was a time, not long ago, when the questions that college and high school students would typically pose about marriage were almost entirely self-referential. Should I marry him? Is she the one for me? Do I really love her, or will this too pass? Sometimes, a potential bride, or groom, would take a longer view. Should I marry now, or should I wait until I'm finished with high school, or college, or graduate school? For some young people in this same generation, these questions were of a decidedly more agonized cast: Will he marry me, so that the baby I'm carrying will have a father? Or, should I marry her, because she is pregnant with my child? For a relative few, the questions were both agonizing and deeply alienating: Should I marry, so that I might one day develop heterosexual appetites? Should I marry, not for intimacy, but for its opposite, so that I might better disguise myself? And for many others—the bachelors, bachelorettes, playboys, swinging singles, doting uncles, and old maids of mid-century—the marriage market was a muddle: for inarticulate reasons, just not an option, or, perhaps, just not their cup of tea.

But for all, for both participants and outsiders, there was little doubt, at this mid-twentieth-century mark, about what "marriage" meant. Marriage meant a lifelong union, sanctioned by state, community, and faith, between a man and a woman that hopefully would be blessed with children. Likewise, there was little doubt about what it meant to be married. A man contemplating marriage would expect to take on the responsibility of being the head of a household. He would be responsible for the economic support of his dependents, including his wife, and he would be charged with the duty of making major decisions on behalf of his family—such as where to live, how to invest or spend their income, how best to develop their joint assets, and how to direct their children's educations. A woman contemplating marriage would expect to enjoy her husband's economic support, and would be charged with the daily tasks of raising their children, as well as the domestic chores involved in maintaining a household. They both would expect lifelong, monogamous sexual intimacy and affection from the other. Both husband and wife, if this pact were honored, would achieve considerable social acceptance from their larger community in the process.

The "value" of marriage—the point of the enterprise—was also well understood by all, participants and nonparticipants alike. The purported value, or point, or promise of marriage—meaning, the promise made by society to participants, regarding the value of the institution of marriage itself—in the middle of the twentieth century, was nothing less than a good, ordered, and meaningful life. A married life, everyone more or less understood, would require sacrifice, but it would be enlivened by the love, companionship, and nurturance of one's spouse, and deepened by the responsibilities that marital role bestows: the responsibility to one's family as well as oneself to achieve a financially secure future, the responsibility for a well-ordered and pleasing home so as to enrich the lives of one's intimates, and not only oneself, and above all, the absolute duty to guarantee the well-being of one's children, and to put their well-being above one's own. There would also be benefits—not just responsibilities—that would accrue to the individual. The burdens of life for which we are all bound would be significantly lessened for those individuals who lived out their lives within marriage. Old age would be rendered less worrisome when accompanied by the care and companionship of a loving mate. The vicissitudes and arrows of fate we're all destined to experience, to some degree, throughout adulthood, would no doubt bring hardship and heartache, but in marriage, they would be leavened by the appreciation that shared struggle can yield, of the deepest capacities of the human heart. Marriage would provide comfort when need be, and provide real safeguards, physical and financial, against personal and economic hardship, or physical calamity. And marriage, it was understood, would ward off chaos. Marriage would anchor one; it would lend a measure of predictability, and security, and reliability to one's emotional, financial, and physical future. It might bring a deep and abiding happiness. But even if not that, it would bring some assurance of a fruitful, orderly passage through adult life, as well as a relatively comfortable, and companionate, old age. Such was the promise of marriage, at the mid-twentieth-century mark.

Between the 1950s and today, just over half a century later, something quite important has happened: neither the meaning nor the promise of marriage are particularly robust, or even well understood. It is no longer so clear, to participants, nonparticipants, advocates, and critics alike, what we mean by marriage, what it means to be married, or what might be the point of this institution. Start with definitions. Is marriage really "for life"? The law here is a good guide to our definitional confusion. In the fifties, divorce could only be had if one spouse was innocent of wrongdoing and the other was "at fault"—meaning that one or the other had committed a quite serious moral, and often criminal, offense.[1] There was, we can now see, a good deal of fraud and collusion among married couples who wished to divorce but who did not wish to charge each other with criminal or immoral activity. Parties did get divorced, even in the absence of adultery and the like, with the help of collusive perjury and lawyers willing to facilitate it.[2] Nevertheless, the law of marriage—divorce only for cause, meaning only for fault—was quite clear, and hypocrisy notwithstanding, it well reflected expectation and social understanding both. Marriage was for life, and divorce was accordingly thought of as something of a scandal. The difference, today, is stark. The divorce rate for first marriages is at around 50 percent, where it has lodged for three decades.[3] Divorce, remarriage, the serial monogamy it sanctifies, and the blended families that result, are all acceptable and common.[4] By law, in all states save New York, unilateral, no-fault divorce is now available "without regard to fault"—couples can marry, divorce, and remarry at will, and they can do so at any point in the marriage.[5] Prenuptial and postnuptial agreements that settle the distribution of property in the event of divorce, signed by each individual prior to or at some point during the marriage, are not only acceptable, but advisable. Couples in the throes of "premarital passions" might think that the "statistics don't apply to them" and that "their marriage will last forever." Wiser heads advise them that in point of fact their marriage may not, and to seek counsel and execute contracts accordingly, particularly if they have substantial assets that a marriage might put at risk.[6]

This only seemingly straightforward change in our law—from a fault-based to a no-fault-based theory of divorce—largely reflects, but also to some degree may have caused, a deep change in our cultural as well as legal understanding of what marriage is. Today, marriage is less often perceived to be a permanent state into which one enters, with the transformation of self that permanence implies. It is, rather, increasingly perceived as a choice one makes, and then remakes throughout the course of the marriage. "Should I stay in this marriage or should I get out? Is this no longer a good deal for me?" One's "choosing self" remains intact during this self-interrogation, perfectly capable, even while married, of reassessing, re-negotiating, and terminating the marriage, should its value to the intact choosing self change. That one enters marriage knowing that one can legally exit virtually "at will" transforms the nature of the institution and the participants within it. That I can leave a marriage, relatively costlessly, directly implies that the ongoing value of the marriage—is this still a good deal for me?—is always a live question, always on the table, always something I can, and should, negotiate, and reevaluate, again and again, with my spouse or without. Marriage understood as a "union" but only until one of the two partners unilaterally decides to disunite, only while it is in effect a good deal for both individuals, is a very different sort of thing than marriage understood as a union for better and for worse, and for life.[7]

And, what of "hopefully blessed with children"? Whatever it once was, marriage is no longer a civil and religious door that parties walk through, and by that act, knowingly open themselves up to the joyous possibility of having children. Children are no longer necessarily fated by god's will to either happen or not happen as a result of marital sex. Rather, a couple, once married, can now decide not to conceive a child at all, and opt instead for contracepted, affective, pleasurable sex, with no significant risk of conceiving children, for their entire adult lives, should that seem the right choice for them. Or, a couple might decide to conceive a child at some agreed upon time, or stage, in their marriage—"after college, after we buy our first house, after I get my raise"—a very different thing from being always open to the possibility of conception. Then, the couple might facilitate that decision by a further quite conscious decision to quit using the pill, or to quit inserting the diaphragm, or to take out the IUD. These are conscious, sometimes elaborately planned decisions to take some willed action so as to have uncontracepted intercourse, and they are decisions that occur quite apart from the decision to marry. Marriage is not the event that creates the possibility of children born to a religiously and civilly sanctified union. The invention of reliable birth control, coupled shortly thereafter with a Supreme Court decision that articulated a constitutional right to use it within marriage,[8] severed the connection. Couples can choose to live in marriage without children,[9] and indeed they have a constitutionally protected right to do so. The decision to marry, and the decision to procreate, are now completely severable, and widely severed.

Finally, what about "between a man and a woman"? More dramatically, certainly with far greater fanfare than the no-fault revolution that effectively, if quietly, eroded our understanding of marriage "for life," and the birth control movement that undermined the causal and social connection between marriage and the conception of new life, it is no longer universally true that marriage is a union of a man and a woman. In Massachusetts,[10] in Spain,[11] in the Netherlands,[12] and in a smattering of other countries as well,[13] two men or two women may marry each other, and in a number of municipalities and states here and countries abroad, gay men and lesbians can enter into "civil unions" or "domestic partnerships" that carry many of the legal benefits of marriage, and much of the emotional and psychic meaning as well.[14] Mainstream Protestant churches as well as reform Judaic synagogues likewise now increasingly bestow the religious or spiritual meaning, and celebration, of commitment ceremonies on same-sex couples who wish to so sanctify their union.

This last change, albeit thus far limited in breadth, is by far the most significant. I will expand on its significance later in the chapters that follow, but let me suggest one of the most important, although perhaps least obvious, of its implications here. Surely, and as critics of "same-sex marriage" repeatedly point out, the availability of same-sex marriage or civil union does more than simply correct for an old-fashioned irrational societal and legal discrimination against gays and lesbians: an inability to see the relevant similarities between gay and straight couples wishing to marry. The existence of such irrational discrimination against gays and lesbians may be—generally is—a major premise of the legal and constitutional argument for extending the legal institution of marriage to same-sex couples.[15] (In the same way that the existence of irrational discrimination against African Americans was one premise of the Supreme Court's argument, when it found miscegenation laws unconstitutional, in the 1960s.)[16] In the logic of law, it is undoubtedly true that the best argument for gay marriage, and hence for the unconstitutionality of bans on gay marriage, is that the exclusion of gays and lesbians from marriage is nothing but an irrational oversight, borne of homophobia or, more mildly, just unthinking discrimination, and in either event, correctable by the stroke of a Supreme Court justice's pen. Remove the irrationality, refuse to honor the homophobia, and gays and lesbians, just like straight men and women, can also enjoy marital rights, responsibilities, and protection. The logic of legal argument, however, does not always cover or even contemplate the lived consequences of the conclusions of those arguments, and this is clearly true here. The extension of marriage to same sex-couples does more than eradicate one consequence of a particular form of invidious discrimination. It has already done more, in the one state and the few countries that have embraced it, and promises to do more, even if that eradication of discrimination was and is all that was legally contemplated by the advocates, jurists, legislative assemblies, or mayors, that undertook this cause, or hope to do so in the future.[17]

Rather, the extension of marriage to same-sex couples undermines the connection, pervasive in popular as well as some strands of religious and scholarly thought on the topic, between the institutions of civil marriage on the one hand and a very particular understanding of the requirements of what is now widely called "natural law" on the other. By natural law is meant a "law of nature," with its roots in Christian and Catholic theology, but no longer so limited, that dictates not only the purported moral superiority of heterosexuality over deviant homosexuality, but also dictates what we might call (borrowing from any number of sources) a "natural order of things": an order of things, knowable by man through his faculty for natural reason, guided by his experience and his capacity for logical thought, in contemplation of his given nature. Marriage, according to this understanding of the requirements of natural law, and as revealed to us through the exercise of our natural reason in contemplation of what our nature requires, is a coming together of sexual opposites, in a union blessed by God and state both, *so as to* produce, nurture, and raise children.[18] Coincident to this bringing together of sexual opposites, is the blending in union of masculine and feminine ways of being in the world, including the natural inclination of men to rule and women to serve, of men to work, act, discipline, and aggress, and of women to domesticate and nurture. Marriage so understood, according not only to Catholic religious authority,[19] but also according to the Supreme Court of the United States until well into the beginning of the twentieth century,[20] is not incident to, and is certainly not a construction of, but rather is a foundation of and condition for the social order we call civil society. It is older and deeper and more natural than the social contract itself. Traditional marriage and family, on this view, is a *condition* of statehood, not a result of it. It is a foundation on which states rest. It is *not* a creation of the state. It is a precondition for the existence of the state itself.

The societal redefinition of legal marriage as involving *anything* other than man-woman union toward the end of child-raising renders this natural understanding of traditional marriage—this view of marriage as rooted in nature and natural necessity rather than in state action—*nonobligatory*. A state, or a community, or a legal system, might recognize it, might honor it, or might just tolerate it, but it is not obligated to endorse it. "Civil marriage," as a consequence, becomes all the more sharply delineated from "religious marriage."[21] Civil marriage is what the state defines, constructs, controls, and regulates; religious marriage, by contrast, is what communities of faith embrace, and the two don't have to mirror each other. State legislators are not obligated to accept the natural lawyer's understanding of marriage, when codifying, legislating, and passing its marriage statute. A civil marriage, apparently, can quite literally be whatever the state says it is. The natural law understanding is nonobligatory: states are not obligated to embrace it. A state might if it so wishes—and most U.S. states clearly do. But it need not—and at least a few don't.

The same-sex marriage debate, the Massachusetts's Supreme Court's justly famous decision in *Goodridge* striking the State of Massachusetts's ban on same-sex marriage as unconstitutional, Ontario's definition of marriage, marriage in Spain and in the Netherlands, and of course the same-sex marriages themselves have collectively driven this point home, and have done so far more emphatically than either the no-fault revolution or the invention of reliable birth control that preceded it. That is what the movement toward "same-sex marriage" does, and has already done, above and beyond the removal from a couple states' and a few countries' laws of a particular kind of irrational discrimination. Civil marriage, once redefined in law as anything at all other than man-woman union, the point of which is reproduction and in a social form that is widely understood to be a condition of civil society itself, is suddenly—abruptly—no longer the same thing as "traditional marriage." Rather, "civil marriage" becomes an institution that both is and is perceived to be chosen by a polity, through its constructed legal system, rather than a necessary way of being, dictated by God or nature, and the necessary natural precondition for the maintenance of civil society.[22] Marriage as an institution, and not just its definition, becomes contingent, chosen, and changeable.

And once that happens, "traditional marriage" becomes quite literally terminable at will—the will of the sovereign, that is—and in a way that strikingly mirrors, on a large scale, the sense in which no-fault renders the continuation of any particular marriage terminable at will by the couples themselves. "Should we end our marriage, or should we plow on through? Let's discuss it, and decide." Likewise, as citizens, we now ask a question unthinkable in the 1950s: "Should we end traditional marriage, as a legal institution? Should we keep the form, but pour something very different back into it? Should we put this to a vote, or make it a ballot referendum? Should we litigate the question in court, or should we pass a constitutional amendment? Let's discuss it, and then decide." The moment marriage is subjected to democratic lawmaking, and remaking, its contingency is laid bare. Just as individuals can opt to continue a marriage, or terminate it, at any point in their married life, likewise, a society can, apparently, *opt for*—or against—opposite-sex marriage, same-sex marriage, contract marriage, covenant marriage, polygamous marriage, multiamorous marriage, or any other socially sanctified ordering of intimate affairs, calling any of that "marriage" if they so wish, and not commit social suicide by so doing. We chose this institution, somewhere along the line, in its present form. We can choose to change it, apparently at will. The institution of marriage, not long ago, had a quite specific social, cultural, and moral meaning: man-woman, for life, and in order to conceive, birth, and nurture children. That ground beneath us has shifted.

It is not only definitions, however, that have shifted. It is also no longer so clear, today, what it means, or what it should mean, *to be* married: what a man and woman contemplating marriage can and should expect, by virtue of becoming husband and wife. Is there, today, a predetermined role, or status, reinforced by public law, social consensus, or economic life, for those men and women who become husbands and wives, to assume? Maybe not: it is not so clear, as it once was, that by marrying one assumes a role, the contours of which are delineated, conferred, and sanctioned by society, rather than by individual choice. If you are married as you read this, ask yourself: What does it mean to you to be a "wife"? What does being a "husband" require of you? For many of us answering that question, and surely including those of us who take the fact of our own marriage and its obligations very seriously, the short answer is that those words mean "partner," or "spouse," or "lifelong companion." And, for many of us, whatever *else* it might mean—whatever "wife" might mean, to the couple or the woman who embrace it, other than "partner"—it has that meaning, because that is what the couple has negotiated, or agreed to, or just willy-nilly slipped into. In other words, what it means to be a husband or wife, today, much less than fifty or sixty years ago, is what the husband and wife or husband- and wife-to-be, agree it *ought* to mean, or what it will mean *to them.*

That is just as significant a change, as the changes listed above in our basic definitions. Because of the latter, the institution of marriage has become one that not just a few of us, but many—perhaps most of us—view as socially constructed, in the most literal sense: we, meaning all of us acting as citizens, through our most straightforward forms of political action, can change it, preserve it, or, it's not so crazy to think, we could just end it. We can defend it, mend it, or end it. The same is true, on the individual plane, of the content of our marital roles. We can, individually, within our own marriages, defend them, mend them, or end them as well. We can remake them, we can inherit the old-fashioned roles, or we can just drop the idea of marital role entirely, as we write, declare, and stay true to our individual vows. Marital roles are something less than "roles," when they are so utterly disposable. Social roles restrain our individual choices, and hence our behavior, but only if the roles themselves emanate from some place outside of our individual selves. When they don't—when we make up the roles as we go—they are indistinguishable from our choices. They can't possibly control us if we create them, individually, and can uncreate them at will. They don't constrain our choices, if they are choices themselves.

Now, why, and when, did this happen? Why, and when, did the role of "wife" and "husband" become so malleable? Put differently, when did those roles basically lose their meaning? As I will discuss in more detail in Chapter One below, a part of the reason for the increased malleability of marital roles—perhaps even the major reason for it—might have less to do with marriage law per se, than with a major change in our employment law, and underlying that change, a radical shift in our notions of what justice, fairness, federal and state law, and the U.S. Constitution, taken collectively, require of our work lives. Thus, by virtue of our law of the workplace—*not* by virtue of changes within family law—women are now entitled to compete on fair terms for the work once reserved for men.[23] In fact, they have a quasi-constitutionally protected right to compete as equals for those jobs—and they have a clear legal entitlement for equal compensation should they win them.[24] This was not true in the 1950s, and the reason it was not true, as we'll see in the first chapter below, had at least as much to do with the continuing power of a late nineteenth-century understanding of women's role in the home, as with worries regarding their competencies in the labor market.[25] But it is true today. Women cannot be discriminated against in the workplace, meaning, women cannot be refused employment, or fired, or treated less well once employed, solely by virtue of sex.[26] Cultural mores, furthermore, have for the most part followed suit. It is widely regarded as unfair and wrong when this norm is violated.

What is not so well understood is that this fundamental change in our understanding of workplace fairness has brought about a shift as well in our understanding of what it means to be a "wife," or a "husband." In fact, the extension of our basic antidiscrimination workplace law from its place of origin—race discrimination—to sex discrimination, brought on, indirectly and for some no doubt unintentionally, but nevertheless inexorably, a revolution in our understanding of marital roles at home. If women are expected to marry and become wives, but women are also entitled both by law and our sense of fairness to equal treatment in the workplace, then it no longer is so clear that husbands are supposed to be the breadwinners and wives are supposed to be homemakers. Apparently, both law and morality demand that "wives" are equally entitled as their husbands to be income earners, and hence "breadwinners," and hence responsible for their families' financial well-being. That women are entitled by law and fairness to work for equal wages in the paid labor market, given that some women are wives, implies that wives are so entitled as well. That equal wage, furthermore, by law, is not "pin money"—it is not the negligible earnings doled out to girls behind soda fountains and in department stores toward the end of enhancing their looks, and hence value, on the marriage market. It must, by law, be the equal to men's wages for the same work, and hence it is reasonable to assume that that equal wage is expected to contribute to the wife's family. The "wife," by virtue of being a woman entitled to equal and fair employment, becomes a potential breadwinner—which makes her a "husband," which of course, makes the roles implode.

There is a second way as well that our shift to equal employment on the basis of sex undermined traditional marital roles. That women cannot by law be barred from employment "on the basis of their sex" rests, in our legal culture, on the assumption that there is no rational reason to do so. Rather, women, our law instructs us all to now assume, are equally capable as men of doing this work of reshaping the natural world for human cohabitation. Women and men are "the same" in this respect: any task you can name that a man can be presumed to do, a woman can likewise, assuming the two individuals have equal qualifications aside from their sex. To assume otherwise, we now say, is to indulge in "stereotypical" thinking, and that stereotypical thinking is the uncontested target of antidiscrimination law.[27] This fundamental premise of the "sameness" of men and women with respect to their public selves is explicit not only in our federal law banning gender-based workplace discrimination, but in no less than two dozen Supreme Court cases addressing gender discrimination in other domains of social and public life as well, from jury deliberation, to estate administration. With only a very few narrowly defined exceptions,[28] a woman can do what a man can do in public life. It is a mistake to believe otherwise and flatly illegal to make employment or public sphere decisions on stereotypical judgments to the contrary.

But, as go foundational beliefs bolstering different roles and responsibilities of men and women in the workplace and public sphere, so go the underpinnings of so-called separate spheres ideology—the cluster of beliefs regarding home life that jointly justified relegating wives to unpaid domestic work and dependent status, and husbands to paid workforce labor—as well. If there is no rational reason to assume that women are less well suited than men for paid employment, public service, combat and leadership roles in the military, and so on, then inexorably, if only implicitly, there is no rational reason to assume that women are more suited than men for domestic chores, child-raising, economic dependency, obedience, or servitude in the private. And if that's right, then why assume that this is *women's* work, or that women will cheerfully acquiesce in their assigned role to do it, and that they will continue to cheerfully so acquiesce, furthermore, whether or not they're pulling equal weight in the public world? Increasingly, we don't so assume, and increasingly, women don't cheerfully do it.

With the "rational" basis for the general fit between women's nature, and the role of the wife, and men's nature, and the role of the husband, undermined, there is no longer, in short, any good reason to assign the wifely role to the woman, or the husbandly role to the man. Why not, if there are no natural differences, assign the wife's role to the man and the husband's to the woman? Let the man be the wife, and keep house and raise the children, and let the woman be the husband—earn the income and make the major decisions on behalf of the family. Or, why not split both jobs fifty-fifty, right down the middle? If it seems rational to retain the coherence of the role, but not its assignation to one sex or the other, why not simply assign each role to he or she that prefers it? And, if that doesn't seem fair, or if lo and behold neither party particularly likes one or the other of these roles, why not just flip a coin, or why not trade off every few months or years? If we take very seriously the premise of our sex discrimination law, there really is just no good reason not to do any of this. We can, and should, make these roles a function of individual choice, rather than a status derived from a social consensus regarding the different endowments of the two sexes.

And, increasingly, couples do so regard their roles. Whether a woman or man assumes the role once called wife, or the role once called husband, today, is largely up for personal deliberation, joint negotiation, and individual choice. Thus—the absence of the social role. When women and men decide to become wives and husbands, they do not assume a social role, so much, as negotiate one. That is a very different thing. The upshot is that "husband" and "wife," no less than "marriage," have lost a good bit of the social, cultural, and moral meaning they once quite unambiguously had. What it means to be a husband, what it means to be a wife, and what it means to be married, is up to the individuals involved to negotiate. It was not always thus.

And finally, what has happened to the once widespread consensus on the point, or moral good, or what I will sometimes call the "promise," of marriage? Begin with the purported point of marriage, or its promise, as suggested by marriage traditionalists: that within marriage, and only within marriage, a man and woman can have intimate sexual relations that are sanctioned by God, and thereby conceive religiously blessed and civilly legitimate children.[29] Perhaps this or something like it was once widely regarded as the point of marriage, at least for most Christians and Jews in mainline Protestant, Jewish, and Catholic faith traditions, and for some it still is. Marriage, on this view, is a way to consecrate and legitimate (and, no small point, cabin) adult heterosexual behavior. Sex outside of marriage is disruptive, disorderly, sinful, and leads to children who will be a drain on the public purse, while sex within marriage is not any of that: it is not terribly disorderly, it is not a sin, it is not a public problem, it does not threaten chaos and illegitimacy and public degeneration; it is in fact not wrongful in any way. Quite the contrary: so long as the marital sexual partners are "open" to the possibility of conception, marital sex is a positive good. Civil marriage, as understood by traditionalists, basically mirrors, or perhaps echoes, this fundamentally religious understanding. Civil marriage legitimates heterosexuality, as religious marriage blesses it, and it does so by underscoring its connection to the responsible, rather than reckless, creation of new life.

Clearly, though, whatever may be true of the religious vision of marriage on which this rests, this understanding of the point of civil marriage has been limited by both technological and legal events in the past half century. As noted above, married partners now can and often do decide whether or not to have a child, and when, and how many; they do not, by virtue of the marriage, open themselves up to a possibility—with the possibility becoming an actuality only by will of nature, God, or fate—to become parents. Becoming parents is a matter of choice, not a matter of marital status and God's grace—just as the decision to stay in the marriage is now dictated by choice, not marital status and state law. Married couples can choose when and if to parent: married partners who decide to have nothing but contracepted sex are just as married as those who view marriage as requiring them to be open to the possibility of new life.[30] Whatever the fate of *Roe v. Wade*,[31] furthermore, this fundamental right to birth control, and to the sexual freedom from reproduction that it signals, is not significantly threatened by any conservative legal or social movement of the last twenty years, including the changing political instincts of the current Supreme Court. Indeed, that right to individual freedom in the intimate sphere, and the specific right to birth control it entails, arguably has become just as central to our concept of freedom and liberty, as the more textually explicit rights to speech, press, assembly, and so forth.[32]

Is the point of the institution of marriage, if not to sanctify and regulate the conception of children and the sex that leads to it, rather, to encourage the creation, by the marital partners, of a stable environment in which to raise them? This looks more promising; it at least squares with some facts and a good bit of ordinary understanding. As best as can be tested, marriage is very good for children. As we will see, a solid body of empirical evidence supports the conventional wisdom that children of intact marriages are healthier, better educated, happier, and, eventually, wealthier than children of either broken marriages or single parents.[33] States, furthermore, have an undeniable interest in the well-being of children. If the institution of marriage is generally good for children, this would give the state a good, straightforward reason—and a secular one at that—to continue to take an interest in the intimate affairs of citizens, and a good reason to continue to promote marriage as providing the best guarantor of children's interests. The state exists, in part, to protect the interests and well-being of the vulnerable, and children are if nothing else vulnerable. Perhaps the way a state might best support them is through supporting the institution of marriage. We might say, then, that the point of marriage, as a secular or civil institution (whatever may be the point of religious marriage), is the promotion and protection of the well-being of children.

On the other hand, if that's right—if the well-being of children is the point of marriage—then it seems as though a good deal of rethinking, redefining, and reprioritizing might be in order. If it is the well-being of children that is the source of the state's concern with the institution of marriage, there may be other ways, and better ways, of ensuring children's well-being than the indirect path of protecting an institution that protects that interest only secondarily—even if it does so fairly well. "Marriage," in short, looks like both an over- and underinclusive target of the state's solicitude, if the interest the state is protecting is the well-being of children. Many marriages do not involve children, and many children are born outside of marriage. We could of course cure both problems through redefining marriage to better "fit" the target rationale, as has been suggested by a surprisingly broad range (politically) of theorists and family law and policy advocates. We could, for example, define the "marriage" that the state has an interest in protecting as unions of *parents*—thus avoiding the overinclusiveness of extending unnecessary and perhaps unwanted regulation, as well as not irrationally resented privileges and protections, to nonparenting marital partners as well. We could then better define, and more narrowly target, the state's interest in those unions, and perhaps draft better and more rational laws in the process.

If we go this route, though, we could and perhaps should go further. Why limit "marriage," if it's all about the kids, to only those heterosexual couples that raise them? We could, and perhaps should, simply define the "marriage" that the state has an interest in protecting, as *any* permanent or semipermanent adult relationship involving any sexes and any number of participants, wherever all the participating adults are seriously invested in the upbringing and well-being of children (or in the care for other dependents, such as aged parents). That would take care of at least some of the underinclusiveness. Putting these proposals together, we might define marriage as an intentional long-term adult relationship that contemplates the raising of children, or, more broadly, the caring for dependents, as its central focus. We could then focus our marriage policy and law on the desirable end of strengthening, where needed, those adult relationships that centrally involve the support and nurturance of dependents. As a number of commentators have now noted, were we to do all of this, we could take the word "marriage" out of the equation altogether, and focus our attention instead on "families" and their needs—whatever might be the family's configuration.[34] If the point of marriage is the well-being of children, we could, and perhaps should, call those marriages that centrally involve the raising of children "families," and go about the urgent work of supporting them. We could leave civil marriage on the legislative cutting room floor. It looks as though, if we go this commonsensical route of defining the state's interest in marriage as centrally concerned with the children, the end result will be that civil marriage as we know it will be on the road to extinction.

Perhaps, though, marriage has a point that includes, but is not limited to, the well-being of children. Let's take the focus off the kids, and focus just on the marital partners themselves. As things now stand, surely those marital couples who do not have children, either by choice or not, are no less married than those who do. Just as clearly, those who do have children are no less married during the extended and ever more extended parts of their lives that occur after those grown children have left home. What is the point of these marriages? Maybe the point, the good, or the promise of marriage is to secure, and for a lifetime, the companionship, intimacy, lifelong mature love, and whatever enhancement of value such intimacy might bring. This account too fits common understanding, and is broad enough to encompass our communal concern for the well-being of children but not be limited to it.

But here, there are problems of a different sort. Maybe the point of marriage is to provide state approval and sanctuary to relationships that enhance happiness in this way, but it is not all that obvious that marriage, as we understand it, is well suited to the end, or how it is suited to that end. Does marriage really make you happy? Married partners often find themselves drifting apart, not together, as a marriage matures. It is not at all clear that marriage enhances rather than undercuts emotional intimacy. Maybe it does, for some couples, but surely not for all. For many people, the assumption that one will remain permanently with a partner may well undercut rather than further intimacy; it might perversely reduce incentives to engage in the work required of one or both partners to deepen or extend an intimacy over time. Marriage, and the assumption of permanence it entails, might not promote true intimacy in the way that marriage celebrants commonly presuppose. Perhaps the monotony of it all just makes us emotionally dull.

Furthermore, in intimate relationships that somehow actually do remain genuinely intimate—and lively—over the better part of an adult lifetime, it isn't clear what the institution of civil marriage adds to the personal choice of each partner to stay united in this felicitous way. What's *marriage* got to do with it? And even more pointedly, what has the *state* got to do with it? Obviously, mature, longlasting intimacy can be achieved with or without marriage. As countless country music songs will tell you, if what you're seeking is lifelong love, companionship, and lust, you'll find it in the heart, head, and groins, not at city hall. Likewise, if the point of marriage is the pleasures, happiness, or emotional security that may follow from sworn vows of sexual fidelity, there's no reason to think these promises can't be made, honored, breached, and lied about entirely privately, or with a public bash but without the involvement of the state. Two people can proclaim undying love for each other, in front of friends and family, in their backyard garden or on a patch of private beachfront, with the blessing of a religious or spiritual guide if they so wish, followed by any manner of celebration, party, and honeymoon, and then either stick to it or not, and they can do all of that regardless of whether or not we involve the clerk of the city court. Civil marriage alone isn't going to guarantee fidelity between intimates. Again, it just isn't clear what it adds.

Here's another possibility: perhaps the point, promise, or good of marriage is not only to oversee or regulate the raising of children, and not only to promote love and sexual fidelity between adults (it might do both of those) but also to further participants' financial security, overall health, and general well-being, particularly when facing the risks and inevitable declines of age. Civil marriage might exist, in part, so as to minimize and privatize the fallout from financial disarray, or to put it more positively, to help us render somewhat more secure our individual financial futures, and thereby reduce the burden on the state to do just that. Briefly—civil marriage is in essence a publicly supported private hedge against risk. If that's the point of the whole thing—and if legally regulated marriage in fact does a pretty good job of it—then that might explain why the state has such an interest in this institution. And, as I will argue below,[35] this may indeed be a large part of it. The civil institution of state-supported marriage might have much more to do with striking a halfway measure between a fully socialized Social Security and public health system and a fully individualized system of self-reliance for old age, than anything at all to do with emotional intimacy or sexual fidelity, or even with children.

If that's right, though, then even if marriage does help individuals do a pretty good job of meeting these utilitarian ends, compared with currently constructed alternatives (of remaining single, of divorcing, of living communally, of raising children outside of marriage, etc.), that doesn't mean it does a good job compared with alternatives for securing these ends that are yet untried. If we got over our myopic fixation on the fact that marriage is the optimal way of securing the welfarist ends of individuals as contrasted with presently constructed alternatives, we might be able to think more clearheadedly about even better ways—or, at least, of complementary ways—of doing so, for those for whom marriage is not an option. We do this on an individual level all the time—for example, we remind ourselves and counsel our children that even the laudable ends of health, welfare, and financial security do not collectively constitute good reasons to marry, if love is wanting. Health, welfare, and financial security might, on an individual level, depending upon circumstance, be better achieved with a decent education, a good job, and a pension plan. On a societal level as well, it might not be advisable to put so much faith in marriage as the best hedge against risk. It might also be strikingly unfair, and unjust, to rely on the institution of marriage as the vehicle by which we discharge our communal obligation to care for the old, poor, and infirm. Some of us, after all, will not be able to marry, no matter how hard we might set our minds to it. For others, and particularly for many poor women, the probability that financial security might be enhanced by potential marriage partners might in fact be negligible: in some communities, marriage might pose a greater risk of increased financial insecurity, domestic violence, or both.[36] Some of us furthermore just might not be temperamentally well-suited for marriage, but nevertheless also in need of economic supports. For any of these reasons, many of us might be better cared for, when old age hits or should poverty strike, by a community of friends, caring neighbors, or even strangers, than by one, struggling, go-it-alone partner. If our ongoing commitment to marriage rests on nothing but a desire to partially privatize social services, and to do so through partially subsidizing marital unions, we need to rethink it. How fairly does it do so? How efficiently? How humanely? How compassionately?

Look briefly at another possibility. Perhaps the point, or promise, or good of marriage is related to all of the above but with a slightly different hue. Perhaps the point is to allow individuals, through mutual promises, to secure for themselves some sort of predictability, and hence peace of mind, with respect to major life decisions, or future moments of crisis—moments we can now only dimly foresee and only abstractly dread. This too looks like a promising response. We could all use a buddy—our own personal bodyguard—when facing the unknown. If we know, with drop-dead certainty, who that person will be, as we move through our unpredictable futures, we reduce to that degree our own uncertainty, and we thereby enhance, perhaps, our sense of psychic security, and, therefore, our well-being. There are problems, however, with this response as well. If the reduction of future uncertainty, or unpredictability, is the point of marriage, then, as any competent family law attorney will tell you (particularly if he or she specializes in ordering the financial affairs of gay and lesbian couples), the same ends can be achieved, and often more efficiently, through private contract. Powers of attorney, partnership agreements, dissolution agreements, medical care proxies, joint tenancy agreements with respect to property in community property states, community property agreements with respect to property in joint tenancy states, and the like, can all be vehicles for arranging ones' affairs in such a way as to ward off the risks of future uncertainty. Such is the function of *all* contracts, and it is the function of contract law, in general, to render these agreements all the more secure. Contract law, furthermore, has proven itself to be a flexible, highly usable tool toward just such an end. Contract law could easily expand, were it called upon to do so, to include the same ends that individuals achieve through civil marriage, at least to the extent that those ends are related to the minimization of future risk.

But maybe that sense of security against risk central to the institution of civil marriage transcends anything that could (or should) be captured by contract. Maybe the point of marriage, purely and simply, bottom line, is that it gives to individual life a desirable "Rock of Gibraltar"–like stability it would otherwise lack. Maybe the point of the institution is to give its participants a rootedness in a community of two—concededly a rather small community—that is larger than our precious individual selves. Maybe the point to marriage, as a number of communitarians and virtue theorists now argue, is just that it allows us—encourages us—to enter a permanent relationship that will be *resistant* to our ever-present instinct to act on our fleeting and changing individual desires, whims, and preferences, and thereby hold off the chaos and the bewilderment that comes on the heels of too much choice. Maybe the entire point is to give us a sense of self that is not exhausted by our presentist, atomistic, consumerist, and ever-changing preferences. We could call this other kind of self that marriage might promote a "relational self" as opposed to the self-centered self that rules like a sovereign over so much of our public, work-oriented, commercial, and even ethical lives. The point of marriage, then, might be to encourage, nurture, and promote the relational, rather than self-centered, self.

Maybe all of this is so—it strikes me that it is so. But if it is so, we've got some work to do. We need to figure out why that "relational self" is a good self to nurture, and whether the institution of marriage, as presently configured, is really the best way to do it. In other spheres of life we celebrate choice and change, seemingly above all else: consumer choice, free agency, Netflix, cable channels, I-tunes and I-pods, term limits, transportable health insurance, choice in the labor market, and the constitutionally guaranteed freedom to move from place to place. What has rootedness, stability, and the Rock of Gibraltar got to offer, in the intimate sphere, if we so disdain it in the public and economic? Why use marriage as the delivery vehicle for it, assuming it's such a good thing?

Marriage is a conceptual muddle, to put it mildly. Let me sum up the tension between contemporary mores, and the institution of marriage we've inherited, in this way. We live in an era that officially eschews separate spheres ideology. We deny the relevance and perhaps the existence of just those differences between the genders that would imply both the sensibility and the justice of different lives for each, in home and work. This disavowal of separate spheres, and the broad array of beliefs on which that disavowal rests, is not some subcultural, subterranean fringe doctrine held only by a relative few. Rather, it is a cornerstone of our modern public law, including our constitutional law. It is at the heart, not on the periphery, of the "law of the land." It permeates our mainstream educational curricula. It is part of our public pronouncements of what it means to be an American; it is part of our sense of America's virtue. It is deeply embedded in the ideals and the promises we routinely make to our daughters as well as our sons. "You can be anything you set your mind to be," we reiterate, again and again, in Sally Ride moments, year after year, as they grow to maturity. And yet, this proud disavowal of "separate spheres ideology," and our passionate attachment to a very different understanding of our human nature, is precisely what undermines the rationale for distinct social roles for "husbands" and "wives" to fill, and with it, accordingly, much of our understanding of the point and meaning of marriage. Let's face it: our gender egalitarianism, embraced and promulgated by both liberal and conservative Supreme Court justices over the last half century, and pushed by educators at all levels of both private and public school instruction, makes a hash of traditional marriage.

Just as emphatically, we live in an era that embraces an extreme form of individualism. We locate the creation of value—and not just economic value—with that magical moment of individual choice. We valorize the free individual. Today, we valorize the freely choosing *sexual* individual, as well, no less than the freely choosing consumer, buyer, producer, or laborer. We valorize the freely choosing sexual individual so much, in fact, that we have taken the extraordinary step of constitutionalizing an individualized right to sexual intimacy, choice, and pleasure. That right, in turn, has the fully intended effect of protecting against moralistic state intrusion on an individual or a couple's decision to engage in marital or nonmarital sexual practices free of any possibility of reproductive consequences.[37] At the risk of undue repetition, the point needs to be stressed: not only have we turned our backs on the traditional understanding of marriage as sanctifying reproductive intercourse, and accordingly of intercourse as only sanctified if both marital and reproductive. We have created an individualized constitutional *right* to that nonmarital and nonreproductive sexual pleasure. This is as complete a renunciation of this traditional triad of marriage, sex, and gender as one could possibly imagine. And who did this? Not the free love advocates of the late nineteenth or early twentieth century, not feminists of any era, and not the sex radicals of the 1960s or the 1990s. Rather, the Supreme Court of the United States, in a series of cases, by both Republican- and Democratic-appointed justices, spanning the last four decades, did it—prompted by, no doubt guided by, perhaps inspired by, but by no means bound by, changing political and social views of the polity as they did so.

Now, put our gender egalitarianism and our radical individualism together, and contrast them with the values and virtues once viewed as inherent in our understanding of traditional marriage. We eschew natural sex difference, we disdain social role, we rebel against natural hierarchy, we have turned our backs completely on the supposed virtue of wifely obedience, and we do all we can to minimize the role of either fate or God's will in our lives, each of us preferring, oh so vastly, to be captains of our own ships. We affirm, in place of this traditional set of virtues and values, the sharply contrasting virtues of contract, individualism, choice, self-determination, autonomy, personal liberty, and freedom. The consequence is that the picture of marriage that so dominated mid-century culture, with its defining insistence on constraint, on fate, on preordained roles, on natural law, on wifely obedience, on husbands' duties, on marital permanence, and on sexual fidelity, and its definition of the good life as in part, at least, dependent upon compliance with a law, a life, a role, a fate, and a partner, looks flatly anomalous. What could possibly be the point, it is now quite sensible to ask, of maintaining an institution so thoroughly tied to an understanding of value, virtue, and what it means to be human, that is now irretrievably lost to us?

When and Where We Enter: The Consequences of Uncertainty

The consequence of this radical uncertainty regarding the point of contemporary marriage, I suggest, is twofold. First, with both the meaning and the point of marriage so unclear, for any couple or individual now contemplating marrying, a very different question comes to the fore than the set of questions I rehearsed at the outset of this introduction. Rather than "Is he the one for me?" the question we now pose of ourselves, or pose for our children and friends as they contemplate tying the knot, is "why marry"? Not "why marry *him*?" but rather, "why marry at all?" "Are you sure you have good reasons?" "*Why* do you want to get married, not just to him, but in general?" Put more bluntly, "why bother?" It is just no longer quite so clear what the point of getting married might be. What is it that this couple can do inside marriage that they can't do outside of it? Again—what's the point? If they want to declare their undying love for each other, whether in private or in public, they can do so without marriage. Neither marriage nor the state is necessary to the idea of an oath, a covenant, or a commitment. We all know from childhood how to make personal promises; adult ones are no different. If a couple wants to forge a monogamous relationship, likewise, that's between the two of them. If they want powers of attorneys over each others' financial affairs, they can do that through contract. Yes, there are many legal benefits that accrue to the state of being married, but there is only a handful that will actually impact upon any particular couple's life. If the couple wants to raise children, it might be somewhat harder to do so outside of a committed and successful marriage than inside, but even if that's so, why not wait to marry until they choose to have them? And—even should they have children—if they are financially secure and committed to each other, it is no longer all *that* much harder to do so outside of marriage than in it. The child's birth certificate is not stamped "illegitimate." The community, oftentimes, will neither know nor care whether a child's parents are married. None of this is to deny what many of us feel, for ourselves and for our children both: it may well be true that a couple in their twenties or their thirties who love and respect each other and who want to stay together for life *should* marry, if they feel themselves ready, and if no one has any sensible objections. What is lacking is any obvious affirmative reason to do so. Pick it apart, and marriage starts looking like a useless appendix, without any apparent point.

And—the questioning doesn't end there. Once a couple decides—for what will likely be personal and individualistic reasons rather than socially preordained ones—to marry, they still may likely pose a series of questions to themselves (or, have them posed by marriage counselors) that were rarely asked, or much contemplated, fifty or sixty years ago. "What should *our* marriage be? What rules should we live by? What will we promise each other, and obligate ourselves to be and do?" Two individuals, these days, can make of their own marriage what they will, no less than they can rewrite their wedding vows. The stuff of their marriage—the expectations they bring to it, what they hope to get from it, what they will demand of each other, what they will not tolerate—will be, utterly, entirely, up to them. They choose the rules, the obligations, the rights, and the duties that define their union. Thus, a man can become a traditional domestic house husband of a high-income woman, if they so choose; or a woman can wed a domestic husband, if she can find one. She can put him through graduate school and then vice versa, she might stay home for six months after the birth of their first child, and he might stay home after the second. And so on.

Put all of this together, and at least this much is clear: a marriage, these days, is as much a moment of choice as a moment of commitment. There is a difference. What does this marriage mean to us? Should we sign a prenuptial agreement? What does it say about us, if we do? What should that agreement say? Should we clarify, now, what roles we wish to assume in this marriage? Should we make clear, now, what will be the conditions of our continued union? Should we clarify now who will do what household chores, which partner is responsible for earning the marital income, what sorts of sexual behavior and expectations we will bring to the marriage, whether or not we will pool our income, whether we will or won't give each other vows or promises of fidelity? Should we specify, now, our understanding of the appropriate penalty, in the event these promises are breached? Do I keep the house I brought to the marriage, should we divorce? Will we owe each other anything, should we split up five years down the road? Twenty years? Thirty years, or forty? Should we specify now what that amount of money might be?

Marrying partners have grown up, figuratively as well as literally. Start with the literal: Brides and grooms are older than they were at mid-century. Those who marry, now, have typically already rented that first apartment, finished school, started a job, and opened a bank account. They own things. They generate income. They become self-sufficient first—and then they contemplate marrying. A bride is no longer a child moving from one protective household to another. Now the figurative: these days, the bride and groom approach the marriage as consenting adults—and they act their age. They don't just do it because they are good children and they've been told they should. The content of the marriage is discretionary. The all-grown-up partners author it themselves—they produce the marriage. They know they can amend the marriage any way they so choose, and choose they do. The institution of marriage does not, any longer, produce "husbands" and "wives." Rather, husbands and wives produce marriages, and of a wide variety of forms. That is the first major consequence of our uncertainty.

There is, though, a second consequence of our current uncertainty regarding the meaning and point of marriage that is a little harder to characterize; the first chapter following is devoted to an attempt to do so. This question now presses, and in a way that is seemingly novel: Why should we, as a society, continue with this institution? This question—and it's a relatively new one—is today being posed by an extraordinary range of scholars, policy mavens, lawmakers, and activists, and a goodly number of even the married among them are now answering the question in the negative: we shouldn't. And, it is remarkably easy, at this point in our social history, to see what a society without this institution might look like, or to envision several possible social and legal configurations, without the institution of marriage. First of all, we could simply dissolve civil marriage entirely.[38] We could go through our statute books, state and federal, and erase all legal distinctions between married and unmarried. We could end the state's role in the licensing and recordation of marriages. We could leave "marriage" as a spiritual and religious matter to the church, the synagogue, or the mosque, and take the state out of the marriage business altogether. Individuals could and presumably would continue to marry within the meaning and context of their religious faith. Nonreligious people could have a private ceremony of their own making, or a very public party if they so choose, announce their union in their local paper, and write up an extensive contract—or if they prefer, a covenant—spelling out their roles, rights, and responsibilities. For both the religious and the nonreligious, though, the state would have no further involvement. All legal functions now served by "marriage" could, on this picture, be met by other social institutions, such as the church, could be abandoned altogether, or could be met through other, more malleable bodies of law, such as contract law. Thus, if couples wished to impose upon themselves binding obligations of an intimate, sexual, or economic nature, we could expand our law of contract to accommodate those desires; contract law has undergone similar expansions in the past.[39] If we felt the need to regulate, through law, the distribution of property when couples ended their private partnerships, rather than just letting them do it on their own, so to speak, we could certainly devise, from scratch, a "law of dissolution" that would directly address the relevant equities and needs—rather than through the cumbersome route of identifying "marital" roles and obligations, and then proceeding accordingly.[40] This would be a large task—comparable to the creation in the late nineteenth and early twentieth century of a modern body of "partnership law" for businesses, much of which concerns the distribution of assets when the partnership dissolves—but by no means undoable. A number of scholars, furthermore, have already jump-started the effort.[41] Current scholarship and past experience with our long and extremely varied histories of legal regimes regulating alimony, child support payments, community property, marital property, and so on, provide ample guidelines, and cautionary tales, with which to undertake the project.

Alternatively, we might, as citizens, decide that there should continue to be some state involvement in the public regulation of the private and intimate lives of adults, and that the best way to do so is to retain the institution of marriage as a means by which to mediate state involvement. We could retain the institution of "marriage," but define it so capaciously that traditional marriage "as we know it" would in fact, although not in form, be ended and replaced with various legal regimes that better serve whatever function we believe marriage today only imperfectly serves. Thus, if we decide that the recognition and regulation of "marriage" is good, in part, because it allows for some public regulation and public support of couples who have children, we might redefine the "marriage" that is subject to public recognition and regulation as all unions of two (or more) persons with children or the intent to raise children. If we think the good of marriage lies in the hedge against risk it provides its adult participants, we could seek ways to broaden the franchise—we could all use such hedges, not just the maritally lucky—and then seek ways to ensure, through law, that these hedges are well protected. Most broadly, if we think that the good of marriage lies in the "relational self" it encourages us to nurture, we might think of ways beyond and aside from marriage that might encourage, nurture, and bolster such selves. All of these possibilities regarding the future of marriage are now not just easily imagined, and easily described, but quite real possible courses of action. Each alternative briefly outlined above, as well as a good half dozen others, are now being actively imagined, argued, theorized and, to varying degrees, pursued by various legal and social reformers. Some version of any of these changes may well occur—likely piecemeal, and likely in only isolated jurisdictions—within the next decade.

Even the bare possibility, though, let alone the likelihood, that we might change our laws in some way and in the relatively near future as to radically change the dimensions of marriage, changes the tenor of the question, "What is the point, promise, or good of marriage?" The question "what good is marriage" is not just a descriptive question—whether abstract, rhetorical, utopian, dystopian, or hard-headedly pragmatic—about the content of our shared public values. It is also, today, what lawyers clumsily call a "policy question." We—meaning all of us—need to contemplate this question, not only because it is an interesting one, but also because lawmakers will likely take steps over the next half century to change the legal contours of marriage. We need to raise the question regarding the good of marriage not only to deepen understanding. If we can go some ways toward answering the question, it will help guide deliberation on whether, and if, and how, we change it.

This book will explore a range of answers to these questions—"what good is marriage?" or "what is marriage good for, if anything?" or, most simply, "why marriage?"—that have been raised and debated in contemporary marriage and marriage law scholarship. Each chapter will explore a different way of understanding marriage's promise—from the most critical, to the most traditional, to various reformist possibilities in between. Roughly, I've divided the arguments, and advocates, into three large clusters: "marriage defenders," "marriage enders," and "marriage benders" (or if you prefer, "marriage menders") and devoted a chapter to each. All the theorists, scholars, and activists we will meet, however—the defenders, the enders, and the benders alike—concur that we are at a real decisional crossroads. As a society, we can now decide what we should do with this institution, just as a potential husband and wife now typically decide what their own marriage should be. We can not sit by passively, and let it naturally "evolve." The time has come for action: for intelligent design of traditional social form.

I begin the book, in the first chapter following, with a quick look back at only our very recent history, to try to make more concrete (and more sustainable) my claim that today, not only the meaning but also the point of marriage, as an institution, has proven illusive. Chapter One's "look back" is by no means exhaustive; it is only meant to bolster the possibility that constructive redefinition, rather than either discovery or deconstruction, truly is the task at hand. Marriage today has no essence—although just a bit of historical awareness suggests that nor did it ever. The difference, though, and it is substantial, is that now more of us are acutely aware of that. We are not, in fact, bound by past practice, with respect to this institution, which is a very good thing indeed, and should be viewed as such by marriage's present-day defenders as well as its critics. We need to set ourselves the task of understanding what we want from this institution, and then define it accordingly, no less than we set our sons and daughters the task, when we watch them contemplate their own potential marriages, of articulating what their personal expectations for their union might be.

Chapter Two is given over to marriage's defenders, traditional and otherwise. The chapter begins with a brief look at the traditional understanding of marriage alluded to above: that marriage, configured as the union of one man and one woman toward the end of creating new life, is required by natural law. It then moves on to a relatively new and loosely utilitarian argument that has developed around marriage over the last twenty years. Marriage, so shows a large body of empirical scholarship, is very good for its participants, and for the children they create. Marriage makes both husbands and wives happy, healthy, wealthy, and financially secure. Children also benefit: children of intact marriages are better off on any number of metrics, than children of divorce or of single parents. Marriage is good, on this argument, not because it cleanses the sex that occurs within it of sin, and not because it engenders moral virtue in its participants, but rather, because it is utile: marriage is good, because it is good for its participants. That's reason enough to keep this institution intact. Third, we look at what might be called a communitarian ethical defense of marriage, offered by a number of scholars from varying political perspectives. Communitarian ethicists and scholars see in marriage the construction of an understanding of identity, of self, and of human nature, that is an appealing alternative to the overatomized, alienating conception of selfhood and humanity, that, in their view, is relentlessly pushed by our consumption-driven political life and market economy. Chapter Two concludes with a critical look at some of their arguments.

Chapter Three is given over to marriage's harshest critics. It begins with a fanciful argument to the effect that the entire institution, even if liberally reformed, is flatly unconstitutional: marriage in effect creates a separate and higher social caste that violates the spirit of the Fourteenth Amendment. Although fanciful—for both practical and legal reasons the argument has no chance of being adopted by any court—it reveals a tension between this traditional social institution and contemporary understandings of constitutional ideals that ought to give all citizens pause.

The chapter then turns to an examination of some feminist critiques of marriage. The point of marriage, so say its feminist critics, has been for too much of its history intimately bound up with the systematic subordination of women, both in the private and the public sphere. Although many of its most subordinating features have been removed or softened, nevertheless, continuing to either defend or reform this institution does little but distract from the pressing need to attend to the real needs of family, defined by reference to caregivers and dependents. Whatever commendable social policies the institution of marriage now serves can and should be better served through alternative legal structures.

The chapter next looks very briefly at a critique of marriage that has emerged from queer studies. The point of marriage, so say these critics, has for too much of its history been bound up with the marginalization and indeed the destruction of sexual minorities. It is an exclusionary club that does no discernible good for its members, and much harm to those it excludes. Furthermore, it reflects a mode of being and a way of life that gays and lesbians should eschew, not seek to emulate: an emotional and intimate life lacking in spontaneity, largely devoid of pleasure, and unduly passive. To lose gay life to married life would be a net loss, both for participants and indirectly, the rest of us as well.

Lastly, the chapter takes up an expressly progressive political critique of marriage. Marriage, so say a number of progressive theorists and activists, adversely impacts, through various ways, the well-being of poor people. As a practical matter, marriage is just not available—or not advisable—for many poor people as a viable life option: thus, for many, its wealth-enhancing potential goes unrealized.[42] But furthermore, the coupling of financial benefits to married people, with a moralistic insistence that "good" people get married, and "bad" people don't, leaves unmarried persons, and particularly unwed mothers, vulnerable to a punitive state and a community morally comfortable with its refusal to offer real financial help to people in distress. These people could, after all, marry, and if they don't or won't, well then, they shouldn't be having children in the first place. Rather than seek to help those who are attempting the Herculean task of raising children single-handedly, given our conviction that marriage is wealth enhancing, and that morally good people can and do marry, we can (and do) relax, sit back, and condemn: secure in the judgment that these women's stubborn refusal to marry is a moral flaw, and one, furthermore, that perfectly well might be visited upon the fates, the backs, and the well-being of their unfortunate children. In this rhetorical way, marriage exacerbates the poverty of unmarried persons, even as it enriches its participants.

Chapter Four examines marriage through the eyes of its benders or reformers: those who may be harshly critical of the existing institution, but who nevertheless wish to celebrate it, retain it, and extend it, albeit in what might be a radically altered form. The chapter looks at two recurrent reformist arguments. We begin with various arguments for marriage that have emerged from recent advocacy on behalf of the rights of gay and lesbian citizens to marry. Some of this advocacy relies on a supposedly "neutral," or "liberal," argument that for reasons stemming from our commitment to equality, gay and lesbian citizens must be accorded the right to participate in marriage, regardless of the institution's merits.[43] Others look to marriage as the appropriate response to recurrent pathologies in gay life,[44] while still others see gay and lesbian participation in marriage as potentially having a progressive and egalitarian influence on the "pathologies" of the institution.[45] All of these arguments share a reformist inclination: they seek to identify what is of value in the institution of marriage that we have inherited, cleanse it from what is unworthy, and then to extend it beyond its current parameters.

Lastly, the chapter concludes with arguments for retaining marriage, but in a form that makes it more simpatico with liberal ideals of justice and the state. State-based institutions must foster respect for certain liberal ideals, among them, a noncompromising insistence on the equal worth and dignity of every individual. Arguably, marriage, in its traditional form, violates this fundamental norm. Yet, marriage is of too much value for us to sacrifice. In the spirit of not tossing the baby with the bath water, these theorists can be read as saying, we need to mend but not end marriage, and we need to do so with the hope of reforming marriage, so as to make it a means to further, not undercut, our basic, and public, liberal ideals.[46] Marriage can, and should, these theorists urge, be a vehicle for, rather than an obstacle to, a heightened appreciation of the centrality of justice for all community members, tolerance for and of differences among us, and generosity of spirit toward those in need, in public and private life both. We end the book with a discussion of these optimistic, capacious—and quintessentially liberal—appeals.

CHAPTER ONE

A Look in the Rearview Mirror

*W*ith the help of contemporary historians' analysis and hindsight, we now know that the well-propagated metaphoric promise made by the institution of marriage at the mid-twentieth-century mark to individual participants embarking on adult life—its promise to deliver some measure of meaning, comfort, and financial security—was many times honored only in the breach.[1] Institutional marriage broke its promises to its participants more often than was acknowledged at the time, and more often than our current nostalgic embrace of the simplicity and traditionalism of that era cares to notice. In Professor Stephanie Coontz's provocative turn of phrase, this image of mid-century, traditional marriage, held as an ideal then, and held by some as an idealized counterpoint to today's uncertainties now, is nothing more than a rose-colored picture of "the way we never were." In her authoritative history of the era by that title, Coontz argues that for many married people of the post–world wars generation, marriage did not constitute a safe financial or emotional haven against hardship, or enrich the lives of those who participated in its strictures.[2] Marriage, at mid-century, Professor Coontz argues, was in fact a poor substitute for the communitarian safety net that to a considerable extent it displaced.[3] For poor people especially, as individuals came to rely on marriage, rather than community, to meet their needs, those individuals became poorer, and more isolated, and in many ways more vulnerable.[4] Marriage did not, Coontz argues, guard the impoverished individual against risk or poverty. Oftentimes it exacerbated it.

Likewise, married life in 1950, for many, was characterized not by harmonious accord, but by hierachic command on the one side and obedience on the other, sometimes enforced through unrecognized, unnamed, and unaddressed domestic violence, and in an atmosphere of considerable internal strife.[5] That violence, although plenty real within marriage, was almost entirely invisible to the larger society. By 1950, neither the neutral-sounding phrase "domestic violence" nor the more explicit label "wife abuse," had become a part of the working vocabulary of men and women in either law enforcement or prosecution.[6] Domestic violence was not a part of family law or marriage law courses taught in law schools. Nor was it taught, or for that matter *mentioned,* in criminal law classes.[7] By the early 1960s, physical violence between husbands and wives was becoming a part of the banter of situation comedies and late night comedic monologues on television, but the violence itself was nowhere on the public agenda, whether as a social, legal, or political problem.[8] The phrase "marital rape," and the possibility of forced and violent sex between a husband and a nonconsenting wife, was if anything even more invisible. It was, in fact, an oxymoron: neither a crime, nor a conceptual or logical possibility. "Rape" virtually everywhere, at the time, was defined as forced, nonconsensual intercourse with a woman *not one's wife.*[9] Thus, while men obviously could and many men did force their wives to have nonconsensual intercourse, that violence could not possibly have been understood by either party as a criminal act. As a consequence of all of this, many married women at mid-century lived in a very peculiar institution, in which rules and obligations were enforced not by moral duty or mutual understanding, but by an invisible, entirely privatized use of force that was neither identified as such, nor countered by any pacifying influence. For these women, 1950s marriage did not deliver on its promise of companionate intimacy. It was a surreal, lamppost-lighting twilight existence, inducing physical trauma and mental breakdown.

Nor did marriage of the post–World War II years come through on its promise of enriching the meaning of even its most privileged and safest participants' lives. In a story now often told, by the end of the 1950s, many of the overeducated and underemployed wives in the most financially secure marriages were experiencing a more general and yet to be named ennui—a lack of fulfillment and a frustration that would eventually bring forth a powerful rebirth of feminism. As described by Betty Friedan in her blockbuster exposé of married life, *The Feminine Mystique,*[10] the institution of middle- and upper-class marriage as it was then constructed infantilized women by truncating their intellectual and leadership capacities. A wife, Friedan argued, living in the middle of this mystique, lived in an altered, gauzy reality of boredom and inactivity, punctuated by the overriding imperative needs to tend to children, and to fulfill the wishes of a dominant spouse for domestic pleasures and sexual fulfillment—a spouse who could not possibly, by this unstated pact, view his wife as his equal.[11] She was, after all, by virtue of their marital roles, suited for, as well as limited to, domestic work that was repetitive, nonremunerative, dull, unchallenging, and uncelebrated. A person suited for such work, and rendered totally economically dependent by virtue of it, must be herself, dull, unchallenging, and uncelebrated, more like a house servant, or perhaps a child, than a partner. For women in traditional marriages who found the work of it neither worthy of respect nor earning it, marriage became an endless progression of daily deaths. For these women too, as well as their battered or impoverished sisters, only the idea of marriage—the marriage promise—was thriving. Their actual marriages were not.

The most interesting result of Stephanie Coontz's (and others') historical work on marriage, however, is that with her books as a guide, we can now see that there was nothing necessary or essential or timeless about the 1950's *ideal* of marriage—the "marriage promise"—either.[12] That shared understanding—the mid-century understanding of the meaning of the institution, the roles lived out within that institution, and the value those roles were to bestow on the individuals that took them up—that was so vividly a part of mid-century life, was *also* remarkably peculiar to its own time. The marriage promise in 1950 was different from what it had been at the turn of the century, just as it was different from what it was to become, twenty, thirty, and fifty years later. If anything, the mid-1950s understanding of marriage was further removed from earlier understandings of marriage, as it was to be from later ones.

It is useful, to drive this point home, to contrast the legal structure of the marriage promise of 1950 with that of a century earlier, as well as a quarter century later—the 1970s marriage—and then with that of the marriage promise of today. When we focus on the legal apparatus of marriage, what emerges is a picture of the 1950s marriage promise as a sort of historical pivot. Marriage, by 1950, had retained the sentimental content, but had shed some—by no means all—of the legal enforcement mechanisms that defined marriage in the Victorian era, and indeed into the beginning of the twentieth century. The 1950's marriage promise was "traditional," then, in two senses. As is widely understood, it promised that meaning, comfort, and security would come from "traditional" gender roles. But it was also traditional in a second sense: its norms were enforced, primarily, through tradition rather than law. By 1975, the marriage promise had undergone a second transformation, in law and culture both, at least as radical as the first: marriage retained the form of traditional marriage, but had shed much of the traditional content. The content of marriage—its meaning, roles, and norms—by the 1970s was largely a product of the individual will of participants, rather than defined by either law, as in the 1850s, or tradition. This was clearly reflected in the law and legal reform movements characteristic of that decade. I will call 1850s, Victorian marriage, "patriarchal." Following now-standard usage, I will call 1950s marriage "traditional." I propose that we call the marriage distinctive to the 1970s "contractual"—meaning, the content of the marital roles, as well as the meaning of marriage itself, were understood to be a product of individual will.

We'll begin with the earlier contrast—between the traditional marriage promise of the 1950s, and the patriarchal marriage promise of the 1850s. Then, we'll look at the contrast between traditional marriage of 1950, and the "contractual marriage" of the 1970s. In the last subsection, we'll contrast all of that with what is distinctive about the marriage promise of the first decade of this century.

Patriarchal Marriage of 1850 and Traditional
Marriage of 1950: A Contrast

The difference between the law of marriage in the 1850s and that of the 1950s was huge. The 1850s "marriage promise" consisted, in part, of three legal doctrines, each of which was absolutely central to the construction of marriage, marital roles, and the meaning of those roles in 1850, but all of which were either dead, or withering on the vine, a hundred years later. First, a man and a wife contemplating marriage in the "Victorian era" were contemplating entering an institution that, once invoked, entailed the literal—not figurative—erasure of the wife's civic, legal, and financial identity. Through the common-law doctrine of "coverture," the "individual" identity of the unmarried woman was transformed, by marriage, into the new marital identity of a wife. After she married she was no longer an "individual," for all legal purposes—she was, rather, a "wife." The greatest eighteenth-century legal authority of the English common law, in both England and the United States, Sir William Blackstone, succinctly summarized the doctrine of coverture in his encyclopedic treatment of Anglo law in this way: "By marriage, the husband and wife are one person in law: that is, the very being or legal existence of the woman is suspended during the marriage, or at least is incorporated and consolidated into that of the husband; under whose wing, protection and cover, she performs everything."[13]

This was not a peripheral feature of the marriage pact. Rather, and as recent legal histories of marriage and family law, such as Professor Dirk Hartog's history of United States Victorian marriage, *Man and Wife in America*,[14] and Nancy Cott's *Public Vows: A History of Marriage and the Nation*,[15] vividly show, coverture was the central, defining legal backbone of Victorian marriage.[16] "Coverture" was not just one simple rule; rather it was a complex body of common-law doctrines that, in toto, described the entirety of the legal relation between man and wife. At its heart, though, the doctrine of coverture denoted the "merger" (sometimes called "unity") of the wife's legal identity—and with it, the wife's financial assets—into that, and those, of her husband's.[17] The wife's identity, in Victorian marriage, was "covered" by that of her husband, for the duration of her marriage. Her own legal and financial identity was in effect held in suspension during marriage, and would only reemerge after her husband's death, or after a lawful divorce.

Coverture had a broad range of consequences, most of them financial. While married, for example, a wife could not buy, sell, or own property.[18] Her husband had full control over any real or personal property that nominally was conveyed to her during the course of the marriage. Any wages she earned, therefore, belonged to her husband, and he had the full power to dispose of them as he wished. She could neither sue for civic wrongs committed upon her, nor could she be sued by others for torts she might commit.[19] Her husband could be sued for her torts, and could sue for injuries she had sustained, but she could not. Nor could a wife form a legally binding contract, which meant, in part, that she could not form a binding contract of employment.[20] Children she bore during the marriage belonged to her husband. She would have no custodial rights to them, should the couple separate or divorce. When a woman became a wife, she became a part of the marital unity, and that unity, legally, was embodied in the person of her husband. Her husband had reciprocal—although unenforceable—duties that accompanied these rights. He had a moral duty to provide her with economic support. She had no such duty. The primary consequence, fully intended, of coverture was the wife's total economic dependence on her husband.

Second: the Victorian wife, unlike the traditional wife of the 1950s, was subject to the lawful "chastisement" of her husband.[21] In Victorian marriage, a husband had the legal right to inflict "reasonable" physical punishment upon a disobedient wife, should she disobey his orders, embarrass him in the community, expose him through her purchases on his credit to unreasonable levels of debt and liability, or in some other way dishonor his name or abuse his trust. This right (and obligation) to chastise disobedient wives with reasonable corporeal punishment could indeed be abused, and when it was, both law and moral sentiment would intervene and offer the battered wife some relief. So long as "reasonable," however—and the bounds of reasonableness could include bites, bruises, pinches, and whippings—the law would not intervene. Chastisement was a husband's prerogative. It was, to defenders of the regime, the heart, the essence, of what it meant to be a husband, just as obedience and submission to reasonable chastisement was central to the meaning of wife.

We don't know to what extent the power of chastisement was used; "chastisement" has not received nearly the degree of attention and study from modern historians as has coverture.[22] We do know, however, from the judicial opinions that touch on it, that the lawful power was defended, more often than not, by those who proclaimed themselves morally superior to those who might actually use the power. Thus, in an 1824 case from Mississippi, *Bradley v. State,* the judge opined:

> It is true, according to the old law, the husband may give his wife moderate correction, because he is answerable for her misbehaviour. Hence it was thought reasonable to entrust him with a power necessary to restrain the indiscretions of one for whose conduct he was to be made responsible. ... Sir William Blackstone says, during the reign of Charles the First, this power was much doubted. Notwithstanding, the lower orders of people still claimed and exercised it as an inherent privilege which could not be abandoned without entrenching upon their rightful authority, known and acknowledged from the earliest periods of the common law down to the present day. I believe it was in a case before Jr. Justice Raymond, when the same doctrine was recognized, with proper limitations and restrictions, well suited to the condition and feelings of those who might think proper to use a whip or rattan, no bigger than my thumb, in order to enforce the salutary restraints of domestic discipline. ...
>
> However abhorrent to the feelings of every member of the bench must be the exercise of this remnant of feudal authority, to inflict pain and suffering, when all the

finer feelings of the heart should be warmed into devotion, by our most affection-ate regards, yet every principle of public policy and expediency, in reference to the domestic relations, would seem to require the establishment of the rule we have laid down, in order to prevent the deplorable spectacle of the exhibition of similar cases in our courts of justice. Family broils and dissentions cannot be investigated before the tribunals of the country without casting a shade over the character of those who are unfortunately engaged in the controversy. To screen from public reproach those who may be thus unhappily situated, let the husband be permitted to exercise the right of moderate chastisement, in cases of great emergency, and the use of salutary restraints in every case of misbehavior, without being subjected to vexatious prosecu-tions, resulting in the mutual discredit and shame of all parties concerned.[23]

Chastisement, according to this court, was a right possessed from feudal times to the present by husbands, albeit only used by those husbands of the lower classes with little social clout.[24] Husbands possessed of the finer feelings of the heart should have no need for it. Nevertheless, the legal right, the judges held, was clear. A man could not be convicted for the battery of his wife, so long as the battery did not exceed the bounds of moderation.

As Yale Law Professor Reva Siegel has shown in a comprehensive historical review of the subject,[25] the purpose and justification of the law of chastisement gradually shifted through the course of the nineteenth century. The *Bradley* court itself alludes to this shift in understanding. In the eighteenth century and earlier, as the court notes, chastisement was understood to be, and openly acknowledged to be, a husbandly prerogative. Wives had an obligation to obey their husbands, and husbands had the right and obligation to rule. The family was a sovereign sphere, subordinate to the state, but nevertheless it was a sov-ereignty: the husband had a state-delegated right to rule—hence the need for the law of chastisement.

As the century progressed, however, the rationale for legalized private violence shifted. The explicitly patriarchal rationale for chastisement at the beginning of the nineteenth century gave way, by the middle of the century (and as the formal law of chastisement came increasingly under attack), to a line of reasoning less rooted in sovereignty and more rooted in the sentimental ideal of marital "harmony," and then eventually in the decidedly more modern-sounding concept of "privacy."[26] Privacy eventually proved to be the more enduring rationale. It is, after all, hard to justify marital violence on the basis of preserving marital "harmony." Privacy, though, looked less paradoxical, and considerably more sweeping. Furthermore, privacy had been "discovered," in the mid- to late nineteenth century, as an overrid-ing value central to the individual who feels himself battered by the industrial age: a prized possession of every common man and every nobleman both, with which either the high or low born could ward off the toxic and noxious ills of crowded, contemporary, modern, industrial life.[27] Privacy was the legal wall with which the individual could defend himself against the intrusions feared and occasioned by the growing information technologies—newspapers and photography—and the growing press of commercialism upon the private lives of all. The private home, this sentiment, as well as this newly developing legal theory, went, should be viewed as a sort of bulwark against all of that: separate, quiet, domestic, free from intrusion, and outsiders. All private persons—husbands and wives and children—had a stake in this privacy, not just the patriarch who could reside as sovereign in his castle.

By the end of the century, chastisement, for its dwindling band of defenders, had found a new rationale: it was the necessary residue of the limited reach of the police force of the state. Chastisement, on the modern rationale, was not lawfully delegated authority to the husband to rule his roost through force. Rather, it was simply the consequence of the nonenforcement or willful underenforcement of the criminal law within the privacy of the home. The purpose of that non- or underenforcement was not to reinforce patriarchal privilege within the home. It was to underscore familial privacy and marital harmony, desirable to and desired by all. In a handful of cases, Siegel shows, judges even explicitly *repudiated* the "old law" of "chastisement," while nevertheless refusing, for reasons of privacy and marital harmony, to find husbands who had concededly beaten their wives guilty of battery.[28] The law against battery, these judges reasoned, does indeed extend into the private home. However, they went on to say, the courts should nevertheless not convict these violent husbands for the battery of their wives. The law, according to the mid- and late nineteenth-century courts, should not cause the greater harm of threatening the sacred privacy of the marital home only to address the relatively lesser harm of trifling marital violence. Harmony and privacy require that the law, in its discretion, stay its hand.

Chastisement thus found a new *raison d'etre*. Chastisement, meaning the lawful use of physical force by husbands against wives, might not be a husbandly prerogative. Nevertheless, nonintervention into the home so as to deter or punish violent actions within it, was essential to the vital work of maintaining the privacy, the peace, and the security of home life. Thus reinterpreted, the law's refusal to intervene so as to deter or punish violent actions in the home need not rest on assumptions of the natural inclination of men to rule and women to submit—assumptions increasingly cast in doubt, in late nineteenth-century life, by emerging strands of first wave feminism. Rather, it could rest on the bland but pressing needs of all citizens, in a time of increasing intrusiveness, for marital harmony and domestic privacy: for a quiet reprieve, or repose, away from modern industrial life. Meddlesome criminal prosecutions for low-level violence would do nothing but threaten the "unity" and harmony of the household. It would be noxious to all concerned, and a grievous injury to the reputation of both husband and wife, to permit the criminal prosecution of husbands for chastising their wives. The essential privacy of the institution of marriage itself would be harmed by such a public airing.

The third legal difference: like all women, Victorian wives were disenfranchised from the vote, so wives had no real power to change any of this through organized, collective, political action.[29] The disenfranchisement of women, however, went further than the vote. It is more accurate to say that Victorian wives were disenfranchised from public life *in toto*. The Victorian wife, like all women, could not serve on juries[30] or serve as the executor of an estate.[31] By custom, by law, and by tradition, she was barred from entering learned professions, from joining trade guilds, and from engaging in much unskilled remunerative labor as well. If she had an education or job skills, she likely could not use them to generate wages. If she had views on political issues of the day, she could find no outlet. If she had leadership skills, she could not reasonably expect to exercise them. For wives, this disenfranchisement was doubly disempowering: while at home a wife was effectively subjected to the lawful command of her husband, who was, to her, a private sovereign, with the right to inflict reasonable physical punishment, confine her physically in the home, and exercise full power over the financial means of her survival. In public life, she had no vote, no voice, and no means of acquiring one. Perhaps unsurprisingly, the politically influential women of the times who did manage to overcome their disenfranchisement tended to be unmarried. Marriage was a peculiarly, and virulently, disenfranchising vocation.

The reason for the public disenfranchisement, for all women, whether or not married, was intimately entwined with the role of the wife. It did not rest solely on a blanket and false and "stereotypical" assumption that women were incapable of serving as jurors, bartenders, lawyers, or estate executors—the belief that it did so rest is likely a reading back into history of contemporary understandings of what motivates what we today refer to as "discrimination." Rather, it was the role of the wife, not the intellectual limitations of women, that precluded public life. A wife should not be a bartender, or a lawyer, or a bricklayer, or a juror, or a voter. Why? Not only because she would not be well suited to those tasks, given her femininity. More fundamentally, she should not undertake these tasks because to do so would be to undercut her availability—and perhaps her willingness—to take up the labors necessary to maintain hearth and home. The aggressiveness necessary for competent legal practice, for example, the Supreme Court of the United States opined in a late nineteenth-century case upholding the constitutionality of a state law barring women from practicing law, might spoil the female lawyer for the grace necessary for submissive domesticity.[32] As Justice Bradley wrote for the Court:

> The claim on the plaintiff, who is a married woman, to be admitted to practice as an attorney and counselor-at-law, is based upon the supposed right of every person, man or woman, to engage in any lawful employment for a livelihood.... It certainly cannot be affirmed, as an historical fact, that this has ever been established as one of the fundamental privileges and immunities of the sex. On the contrary, the civil law, as well as nature herself, has always recognized a wide difference in the respective spheres and destinies of man and woman. Man is, or should be, woman's protector and defender. The natural and proper timidity and delicacy which belongs to the female sex evidently unfits it for many of the occupations of civil life. The constitution of the family organization, which is founded in the divine ordinance, as well as in

the nature of things, indicates the domestic sphere as that which properly belongs to the domain and functions of womanhood. The harmony, not to say identity, of interest and views which belong, or should belong, to the family institution is repugnant to the idea of a woman adopting a distinct and independent career from that of her husband. So firmly fixed was this sentiment in the founders of the common law that it became a maxim of that system of jurisprudence that a woman had no legal existence separate from her husband, who was regarded as her head and representative in the social state; and, notwithstanding some recent modifications of this civil status, many of the special rules of law flowing from and dependent upon this cardinal principle still exist in full force in most states. One of these is, that a married woman is incapable, without her husband's consent, of making contracts which shall be binding on her or him. This very incapacity was one circumstance which the Supreme Court of Illinois deemed important in rendering a married woman incompetent fully to perform the duties and trusts that belong to the office of an attorney and counselor.

It is true that many women are unmarried and not affected by any of the duties, complications, and incapacities arising out of the married state, but these are exceptions to the general rule. The paramount destiny and mission of woman are to fulfill the noble and benign offices of wife and mother. This is the law of the Creator. And the rules of civil society must be adapted to the general constitution of things, and cannot be based upon exceptional cases. ...

[I]n my opinion, in view of the peculiar characteristics, destiny, and mission of woman, it is within the province of the legislature to ordain what offices, positions, and callings shall be filled and discharged by men, and shall receive the benefit of those energies and responsibilities and that decision and firmness which are presumed to predominate in the sterner sex.[33]

Thus, the picture of the domestic home and the role of the wife that a woman assumed once she entered marriage exerted a strong influence on the reach and justification of laws barring women from public life and from public responsibilities outside it. A wife could not be allowed to take on tasks that might conflict with her domestic labors, or with the character traits necessary to perform them—including a willingness to submit to authority. The vote, clearly, was reserved for civic equals. The wife's manifest inequality in the home—her subservience to her husband, her economic dependence upon him, her acquiescence in his rule—undercut both her need to vote, and the sensibility of permitting her to do so. Her needs would and should be represented by her husband's vote. Jury service likewise was incompatible with her role in the separate sphere. A wife's tranquility and sensitivity, her nurturing role in home life and in the upbringing of her children rendered her unfit for jury service, where she would have to bear the gruffness of lawyers and judges, and hear of the violence, crudity, and incivility of individuals caught up in criminal proceedings, either as defendants, witnesses to crime, or law enforcement officers. This exposure would threaten her abilities to perform her domestic duties at home, no less than her domestic role would limit her ability to mete out justice in the court room. For the same reason, a wife could not and should not be permitted to practice law, serve as the executor of an estate, and so on. A wife's capacities laid in an altogether different realm from the political: she served, she did not rule, she submitted, and nurtured, she did not fight, she tended to life, she did not engage in combat. She was neither the civic equal that democracy requires, nor the combatant that politics and the public professions demand.

And, whatever was or should have been true of wives, extended to all women, regardless of current marital status: all women were either wives, past wives, potential wives, or should aspire to being wives. Ergo—the exclusion of the gender *in toto,* not just the subset who were married, from public life.[34] The exclusion, though, at heart, was not based simply or even centrally on false or stereotypical views of women's intellectual or innate inferiority. It was based on the necessity of the labors intrinsic to the role of the wife, the necessity of certain qualities, including the ability to gracefully submit, to those labors, the necessity of those labors to marriage, and the necessity of marriage, in turn, to society itself. The natural law of the home thus shaped not only family law but also the collection of laws and customs mandating the exclusions of women from the workplace, the voting booth, and the jury box—what might be called the "law of disenfranchisement."

Taken collectively, the laws that jointly constructed coverture, the laws that permitted and justified chastisement, and the laws that excluded women from public and professional life, constituted the legal backbone of the Victorian promise of marriage. Marriage, so the promise went, would transform an unmarried girl or woman into a wife, create a unity of the wife's identity with that of her husband, and of her interests with his, would instill in her or bring out in her a propensity to gracefully subject herself to his rule, would speak to her suitability for home rather than public life, and would at the same time elicit his reciprocal although unenforceable obligation, duty, and responsibility to support her. In the 1850s, the positive law of the state was an explicit term of the promise: The law of coverture would guarantee her economic dependence; the law of chastisement would guarantee her physical subjection and her sexual availability; disenfranchisement would guarantee her service in the home.

Now, if we keep our focus—momentarily—only on the law, rather than the sentiment, the contrast with the marriage promise of the 1950s could not be more stark. By the 1950s, virtually *all* of the law behind the patriarchal marriage promise of the 1850s—coverture, chastisement, disenfranchisement—had crumbled. Start with coverture. By the 1950s, the doctrine of coverture (although not all of its implications) had largely disappeared from United States family law, as well as from the common-law countries with which the U.S. shares a common heritage. First, and as obliquely referenced in Justice Bradley's decision in *Bradwell,* by virtue of the Married Women's Property Acts of the mid-nineteenth century,[35] followed by a slow but steady erosion of various common-law rules that jointly constituted the doctrine of coverture, by 1950, married women everywhere could, for the most part, own, sell, and buy property in their own name. If a wife happened to earn wages while married, her wages belonged to her. If she brought property into the marriage, it remained hers, or became part of the couple's joint marital property, but in either event, it did so by virtue of state laws of marriage and property that treated her property identically with his. If she acquired property during the marriage, likewise, it was either hers or it belonged jointly to both partners, depending on the state's common law of marital property, but in either case, the law governing her ownership of property was no different than the law governing his. She was individually as well as jointly liable for whatever torts she committed, as was he. She was likewise liable for whatever debts she incurred. For most economic purposes, from the perspective of the law, a wife, by 1950, was no less capable, no less "agentic," and no less powerful than her husband: she had regained her individual legal identity. The role of "wife," by 1950, did not by definition preclude the role of the consuming, producing, or laboring individual. In 1950, a woman could be a wife and have an economic identity both. In 1850, she could not. The marriage promise of 1950, unlike that of 1850, did not contain a term ending the wife's legal and financial existence.

Likewise, by 1950, a wife was not presumed to be a subordinate in a political state, subject to her husband's lawful, delegated power to enforce his command through reasonable corporeal punishment. A wife in 1950 was not, that is, subject to the lawful if reasonable chastisement of her husband for her failure or refusal to obey his mandate. By 1950 no state any longer expressly granted a husband such a right. (*Bradley*, the Mississippi case quoted above, was formally overturned by the Mississippi Supreme Court in 1894.)[36] Rather, the physical punishment meted out to her for disobedience, that the law had earlier called "chastisement," was now understood to be criminal assault or battery, no matter the width of the whip, and no matter the outrageousness of the conduct that prompted it. Likewise, women could no longer be lawfully compelled by their husbands to remain in the home. Confinement in the home against the will of the wife would be kidnapping, not lawful restraint, and no less criminal than if they were strangers. The woman's body was, by law, her own. Her husband did not own it, and he had no rights over it. She was as entitled in the home, as they both were outside of it, to the state's protection of her right to physical integrity. If she was forced to endure her husband's violence, she did so as the victim of a crime, not as the subject of a lawful sovereign. She had every right, as his political equal, to expect the state's assistance in perfecting her coequal rights against private violence, domestic or otherwise. This is not to say that the laws of battery, assault, aggravated assault, or kidnapping were actually enforced within the home: as we'll see, there was no concerted effort to do anything about domestic violence on a broad scale until the so-called rebirth of feminism in the 1970s. But nevertheless, by 1950, the lack of enforcement of laws against assault and battery was not vigorously defended by judges or legislators as necessary to either a husband's right to rule, the harmony of the household, or the husband's right to privacy from meddlesome intruders. Neither the husband's natural "right" to chastise, nor the wife's natural duty to submit to reasonable physical correction when she breached her duty of obedience, were a part of the marriage promise of the 1950s.

Lastly, by 1950, women had not only won the franchise, but Rosie the Riveter and the wave of women for whom Rosie served as an icon, had already entered previously all-male workforces, even if only temporarily. Both events had a lasting impact on the marriage promise of the fifties: the public image of a wife as possessing interests identical to and fully protected by her husband's vote, and as physically and mentally incapacitated from wage labor, had been badly undercut. By 1950 some women had entered the professions as well, and some of those women were wives. The occasional woman, and the occasional wife, could be found in positions of leadership in law, medicine, the sciences, and politics, as well as in art, film, letters, academia, and so forth. A woman who maintained her household and practiced law at the same time knew that she could do it, and those who knew her or who knew of her likewise knew that it could be done.

The vote, won during the suffrage movement in the 1910s, drove the point home: Women's votes were cast and tallied as equal to men's—no three-fifths solution there. Women voted as political equals, presumably, because they were equal. This too had profound repercussions for private life, as suffragists had long hoped, and to a lesser degree, argued it would. If women voted as political equals, then clearly, they were no more naturally suited for submission, obedience, and acquiescence to authority than were men. Their votes were counted, and their votes mattered, presumably, because like men, women too were political animals—in the original, Aristotelian sense—through and through. They voted, and should vote, in order to translate their civic and political visions regarding the polity into power and influence over the shape of public life. The natural correlations that underwrote the separate spheres—a naturally submissive woman, well suited for domestic life and chores, and a naturally dominant man, equally suited for rule in the home and work in the commercial realm and political action in the public—was thoroughly belied by the suffrage movement, by suffragists, and eventually by the extension of the franchise. The inequality implied by the traditional understanding of home life, and the equality implied by the extension of the franchise, were clearly in tension, as both sides of the suffrage fight well understood. By constitutional amendment, however, women won the vote, and the traditional understanding of home life took a beating.

By 1950, in short, the legal underpinnings of marriage as a separate and sovereign world, in which the husband ruled the wife with state-delegated authority to enforce his command through reasonable force, if necessary, in which the wife rendered herself, through the decision to marry, an economic dependent of her husband, and from which her intrusive thrusts into public political and civic life would be easily recognized as not just impudent, but illogical, had largely—although as we shall see, not completely—disappeared. By 1950 all women, including wives, could vote, work, earn money, convey and acquire property, and expect to enjoy the protection of the state against private assault on her body, no matter where the assault took place. By 1950, the image, concept, understanding, and indeed the identity of a "woman" as a *citizen,* and an equal one at that, sparked by first wave feminism, and then culminating with suffrage, had begun to eclipse the image of woman as *wife,* with attendant and decidedly subordinate obligations and duties. By 1950, "coverture," "chastisement," and "disenfranchisement" really had hit the dustbin of history. Wives could work for wages and keep their earnings; to take those earnings from them against their will would be criminal larceny, again, no less so than if they were strangers. All women, including wives, could vote. Married women could inherit property even while married, and keep the inherited asset entirely within their own control if they so chose, to whatever degree a married man might. A married woman could sell and buy property. Wives, along with single women, divorcees, and widows, were on the path to equal citizenship. To get to that point required the abandonment of false ideas about women's capacities. But that change of consciousness was clearly not sufficient. It also required the dismantling of a legal regime. It required the dismantling, that is, of patriarchal marriage, and the role of the wife within it.

Patriarchal and Traditional Marriage: Continuities

So, coverture, chastisement, and disenfranchisement had disappeared by 1950, as had patriarchal marriage, if we define the latter by reference to those legal institutions. Nevertheless, marriage did not, by virtue of their disappearance, become an egalitarian institution, either in fact or ideal. Rather, even without coverture, chastisement, and disenfranchisement—even without state-sanctioned, legally enforced patriarchy—the cultural understanding of marriage at the mid-twentieth-century mark remained notably inegalitarian and role defined. Well into the 1950s and 1960s, a husband-to-be would embark upon his marriage with the expectation of supporting his wife, and becoming the head of household. Husbands throughout the fifties wielded exclusive authority to make major economic decisions on behalf of their families. Likewise, women would enter marriage expecting to be supported financially, and expecting to provide sexual, reproductive, and homemaking services in exchange for that support. Husbands were the breadwinners, wives were the homemakers, and were viewed as such. The legal doctrine of chastisement may have disappeared, but unpoliced, underprosecuted, and unpunished wife beating most assuredly had not, nor had the political hierarchy that accompanies it. Even without chastisement, a husband could reasonably expect his wife to obey his reasonable command—to be, in effect, his willing subordinate, voluntarily submissive to his rule. And, even without formal disenfranchisement, a middle-class or upper-class wife in the 1950s did not expect to exert a robust role in public life, whether through the vote, through employment, or through exercising duties of citizenship.

Even without the legal underpinnings that had at one time explicitly reinforced patriarchal marriage, the meaning of marriage, what it meant to be married, and even the perceived value of marriage, remained profoundly status driven as well as inegalitarian in the 1950s. The husband's role was still entirely different from the wife's, and the husband still had more authority and considerably more economic power. We can sum up the contrast, and the points of continuity, between the Victorian marriage promise and that of the 1950s in this way: in the earlier era, the roles of husband and wife were imposed by the state through an explicit delegation of authority to the husband, via the legal doctrines of coverture, chastisement, and disenfranchisement. In the 1950s, the roles of husband and wife retained much of the content and even more of the sentiment of patriarchal marriage, but the explicit, legal delegation of authority peculiar to patriarchal marriage had largely (by no means entirely) disappeared. The contrast between the marriage promise of 1850 and that of 1950 was in the amount of state-backed power, both economic and physical, that the husband could exert to enforce this bargain upon his wife, if she decided to contest it, or leave the marriage, or quit performing her domestic tasks. By 1950, husbands could no longer simply force the marital bargain upon their wives with the law's active endorsement. The legal supports of this under-standing of marriage as a separate political state, composed of a sovereign husband and subordinate wife, had fallen apart. Yet the sentimental and cultural content of the marriage promise that had once been so inextricably tied to exactly those mechanisms of enforcement, persisted. Women promised in their vows to obey their husbands. Husbands expected to be sole breadwinner for their families, and typically were, and wives expected to assume domestic and child-raising tasks, and to minimize their public and civic lives, and typically did. Why?

We can now account for the radical differences between the 1850s marriage promise and the 1950s promise by, in part, pointing to the rise of feminism, as a political movement. In a sentence: Mid-nineteenth-century feminism gave us the Married Women's Property Acts; late nineteenth-century feminism eventually yielded up suffrage. The economic, physical, and political authority of husbands over their wives was a central target of both feminist movements, although often times not explicitly stated as such, and never explicitly targeted. Both early and late nineteenth-century feminists believed, for strategic reasons, that the nature of married life, and the roles of husband and wife, must be conceded to be sacrosanct, rooted in nature, and immutable to change.[37] Nevertheless, the legal rules support-ing patriarchal marriage did change, and that fact alone presents a puzzle: How to account for the similarities between the promise of marriage in the two eras? Why was the 1950s marriage so status drenched, and so strikingly inegalitarian? Why didn't patriarchal marriage simply wither and die, as its legal underpinnings were tossed overboard?

Stephanie Coontz provides a compelling (albeit indirect) answer to this question by pointing, primarily, to economic factors: the Depression put a high premium on the availability of work, such that eventually, by the end of World War Two, work itself had come to be firmly identified with masculinity, entrenching the image of the male breadwinner and the homemaker wife.[38] Professor Nancy Cott, in seeking to explain the same phenomenon, also stresses the centrality of the Depression and the New Deal response to it: as she shows, New Deal progressives, no less than traditionalists, assumed, and then worked into the machinations of the law, such as most importantly the Social Secuity Laws, a model of marriage that rested explicitly on husbands as providers and wives as dependents.[39] These arguments are subtle and convincing, but they don't tell quite the entire story. Law—not only economics—surely also played a role in perpetuating not only the separate spheres, but the hierarchical nature of the traditional marriage and family. Chastisement, coverture, and disenfranchisement might have died, and with it, patriarchal marriage. Nevertheless, if we look beneath the surface, it is clear that the legal underpinnings of *inegalitarian* marriage (as opposed to patriarchal) by 1950, had not been entirely obliterated. Sometimes, old wine really is simply poured into new bottles, in law as elsewhere, complete with new and modern-sounding rationales. Reva Siegel calls this process "preservation through transformation."[40]

Most glaring, wives did not have full control over their bodies, within marriage, long after the demise of chastisement law, long after they acquired full control of their pocketbooks, and long after they'd won access to the voting booth. As Cott fully details, through the first three decades of the twentieth century, the lower courts and the Supreme Court quite explicitly confirmed husbands' ownership of their wives bodies. In three cases in particular, Cott shows, one involving tort immunity for intramarital violence, a second tort actions brought by a husband against a "correspondent" in his wife's adulterous affair, and one action involving congressional authority to forbid, through immigration laws, a man's bringing a lover or prostitute into the nation—the Court ruled in favor of husbands, or in the third case, in favor of congressional authority on the grounds that to do otherwise would interfere with men's possessory sexual rights to their wives' affections. Cott is certaintly correct that these cases are significant, but they are significant, in part, for the beliefs on which they rested, more than for what they held, and those beliefs persisted well into mid-century: a wife at mid-century, no less than in the 1920s and 1930s, lacked control of both her sexual and reproductive body. In the 1950s, no less than in the 1850s, a married woman could not be the victim of a "rape" by her husband, even if she had been subjected to forcible sex without her consent.[41] Rather, rape, in the 1950s, 1960s, and 1970s was *defined*, in all states, as the forced, nonconsensual sexual penetration of a woman not one's wife.[42] The "marital rape exemption" persisted as formal doctrine well into the 1980s, and there is still today a substantial lack of parity between the legal treatment of rape in marriage and rape outside of marriage. Likewise, in 1950 (as well as in the 1960s and 1970s, up until *Roe v. Wade*), a married woman impregnated as a result of forced marital sex—sex forced by violence or threats of violence, but not rape, by virtue of the marital rape exemptions—would not be able to obtain a legal abortion if she so desired, even when an unmarried woman, pregnant as a result of rape, might do so.[43] Since a married woman could not be "raped" by her husband, even a pre–*Roe v. Wade* "liberal" abortion statute that allowed for abortion in the event of "rape," by definition, did not extend to married women. Thus—a married woman could be lawfully forced to conceive and bear children against her will, even where an unmarried woman could not. Putting all of this together, a "wife," in the 1950s (and well beyond), was *by legal definition*—if we look at the definitions from the criminal law of rape and abortion—a woman who lacked full control over her sexual and reproductive body. Thus, almost a hundred years after she had gained control over her pocketbook, several decades after gaining the right to vote, and a full century after courts, commentators, and lawmakers quit referring to a husband's right to inflict corporal punishment on his wife as his husbandly "prerogative," wives continued to lack possessory rights over their sexual and reproductive bodies. Someone who lacks full possessory control of her body may well feel herself to be, and justifiably so, subordinate to whomever has authority to use her body—whether for sex, reproduction, or both, as he desires.

Equally important, although the demise of chastisement doctrine logically entailed the criminality of physical violence in the home, the state did not begin to seriously police against domestic violence in the home until well into the 1970s.[44] A thick shroud of privacy continued to surround the home, rendering "wife beating," in both the public and the prosecutorial mind, either a completely private matter, or at most a public health concern, rather than a crime, and therefore a matter for police. Likewise, courts and commentators both continued to cite the need to preserve both the privacy of the home and marital privacy as "public policy" reasons to limit the availability of civil remedies for such violence, through the construction or continuance of various "marital immunities" from civil suit.[45] Whatever their purposes, civil immunities from tort, as well as evidentiary rules limiting the duties of spouses to testify against each other, had the effect of preventing private suits against husbands for damages caused by their physical abuse of their wives.

Outside of law and legal rhetoric, various mental health professionals, as well as clergy, began to interpret family violence as a symptom of family dysfunction—caused, perhaps, by a wife's frigidity or more generally by her inattentiveness or insensitivity to her husband's needs and demands. If a wife was beaten by her husband, it evidenced her failures at the wifely arts of pleasing him. The proper response, then, of the community to domestic violence was to provide counseling and therapy, not police protection. Through counseling, administered by a pastor or priest, a woman might be given useful advice regarding how better to appease him. The possibility that the state might respond to physical violence in a private home by issuing a protective order, funding a domestic violence shelter, or providing legal assistance to victims, was nowhere in anyone's consciousness. Consequently, while there was a difference—even a profound difference—between the old legal regime that constructed physical violence of wives by husbands as a husband's political entitlement, and the new legal regime that constructed that violence as something brought on by a victim's domestic failure, that difference might not have been in practice quite so large as one would expect, either in terms of the availability of law enforcement dedicated toward policing against the violence, or in terms of the consciousness of husbands and wives regarding their rights and obligations. The woman trapped in a violent marriage still could not, in 1950, realistically invoke a greater power—the state—to assist her in warding off her husband's attacks. Unstoppable violence, whatever the rationale, brings submission, and obedience, in its wake.

Other legal structures as well persisted, that collectively preserved the effect, if not the rule, of coverture. In the 1950s a man could not lawfully confine his wife, through physical force, to the home. She could freely contract for employment, and had full right to whatever wages she might earn. On the other hand, no employer was required to hire her, no matter how well qualified she might be, and if he did hire her, he was not required to pay her wages or salary equal to that of male coworkers doing the same job. Explicitly gender-based discrimination in the labor market was not just occasional, and nor was it viewed as wrongful, perverse, or economically irrational. It was, rather, both pervasive and normal—it was a structural, not peripheral feature of the paid employment market. Labor market discrimination provided a powerful incentive to wives to eschew paid employment and stay home, long after husbands lost the right to keep their wives home by force.

That the consequence of irrational discrimination against women in the workplace would be that women might be all the more inclined to stay home and tend to domestic chores, likewise, provided employers, many of whom were themselves husbands, with an incentive, otherwise lacking, to discriminate. All else being equal, not hiring the best qualified person for a job, or not promoting or paying that person according to worth, will hurt a firm's pocketbook and hence be an economically irrational decision, particularly if competing firms are not behaving so irrationally. But here, all else was nowhere near equal: employers as a group had good reason—economically based—to encourage women to remain at home. Employers too, after all, were husbands. As a result, although not legally precluded from owning the fruits of their wages in earnings, there wasn't much fruit for the picking: employers were not legally required to hire, or to pay commensurately with ability, and they had good reason not to. The consequence was that an insidious and entrenched pattern of labor discrimination was firmly in place by the 1950s. Women were still, in 1950, effectively barred, either by formal trade rules or by informal joint practice, from many white-collar and blue-collar jobs and professions, from bartending, to bricklaying, to carpentry, to electrical work, to law, medicine, accounting, and so on. Schools did not have to admit women, unions did not have to accept them, and employers did not have to hire them. No law required them to, and no Supreme Court case interpreting the Constitution suggested that such practices, with state acquiescence, might violate fundamental constitutional norms. So—schools did not admit them, unions did not welcome them, and most important, employers, overwhelmingly, did not hire them, at least not into the job categories dominated by men.

Women's paid labor, as a consequence, became identified with the so-called pink-collar sector: secretarial work, nursing, and school teaching in the lower grades for middle-class women; hotel work, housecleaning, and childcare, for lower-class women. Employers advertised for workers in newspaper ads that were strictly separated by sex: "Help Wanted—Male" would be on the right-hand page of the paper and "Help Wanted—Female" on the left. Men worked to provide a living wage for their family; women worked for "pin money." Women's jobs were not expected to generate the income to sustain a family, and for the most part, because of fully lawful wage and hiring discrimination, they did not.[46]

And, although the wife could exit the home without her husband's permission, the marriage itself was not so easy to exit. A wife could divorce her husband if she could prove that he had committed adultery, or if she could prove him guilty of physical or mental cruelty, and if she succeeded in doing so, she might be rewarded with a substantial alimony award, as well as support for her children, should she assume custody of them. She could not divorce him, however, simply because he belittled her daily, or humiliated her, or degraded her intelligence in front of their children and friends, or issued commands in an imperial manner, or doled out spending money in a tightfisted way, or refused to grant her desire to continue her own education, or forced her to have sex when she did not wish to. She could not divorce him because he made financial judgments on her behalf and on behalf of her family with which she disagreed: that he insisted the family move to a far-flung state, uprooting her from her own community and family of origin, that he educate the children in a particular way, that he purchase this house rather than that one. She could not divorce him because he was indecent, or a scoundrel, or a compulsive gambler, or verbally abusive. Nor could she expect the state to assist her with any of this, if she wished to correct the behavior while keeping the marriage intact. The law would not end the marriage on these grounds, but nor would it reach into the marriage, and require of the participants a floor of other-regarding conduct. The marriage was both highly regulated, at the point of exit, but profoundly "private," while intact.

While the limited reach of the state into functioning marriages might have promoted marital privacy, it frustrated marital *justice*. Nothing in law, and certainly nothing in culture, imposed upon the husband, or the partnership, norms of justice. No one expected a marriage to persist only so long as it was *just*. No one thought the injustice of a marriage should be grounds for a divorce, or even public condemnation. No one thought that a husband should treat his wife well, or that a husband and wife should be regarded as equals, as a matter of justice. No one thought of marriage and justice in the same breath. Unjust marriages were, one suspects, as a result, fairly typical.[47]

The dismantling of disenfranchisement was likewise only partial: women eventually won the vote, as a result of the suffrage movement, but other exclusions from public life persisted. Women were routinely excluded from jury service through most of the twentieth century: this was not even challenged, much less ruled unconstitutional, until the 1970s.[48] Women could not serve as executors of estates, likewise.[49] Disenfranchisement was a dead letter, by law, in 1950, but nevertheless, a host of legal rules circumscribed women's role in public life. Women were excluded from the military draft, and female volunteers were not eligible for combat duty.[50] Women were not required to shoulder this fundamental duty of citizenship, thus undercutting a major cornerstone of the illusive civil and political equality that suffrage promised, but failed to fully deliver. The exclusion from military service also had material consequences: women did not directly benefit in any sizeable number from the vast outlays of public funds committed to returning war veterans, fueling their climb up the economic ladder into middle-class security.[51] Abortion laws put women who ventured outside of the institution of marriage for sexual pleasure to the Hobson's choice of risking serious injury or death in traumatizing and dangerous back alley abortions, raising an illegitimate child with little or no expectation of community assistance, or relinquishing that child for adoption. The only lawful alternative to all of that was a shotgun marriage. Private clubs, from the Boy Scouts, to the Kiwanis club, to private golf courses and little league teams in between, were allowed to bar women and girls from membership, and did so (and largely continue to do so), with a sort of mind-numbing monotony.[52] These exclusionary clubs, and the rules that constituted them, and still constitute them, had both concrete and rhetorical consequences: they kept women (and continue to keep women) from the webs of influence and connection that lend credibility and access to one's public life. They also communicated, and still communicate, a powerful lesson for girls and women everywhere: you are not suited for the tasks, values, skills, pleasures, and access to power that these private clubs facilitate.

Taken collectively, these legal rules, doctrines, and distinctions—what a later generation of activist feminist lawyers came to call the Jane Crow regime[53]—were a powerful, legal force, and they directly impacted both the institution of marriage, and the social understanding of the marriage promise, well through the decades of mid-twentieth century. Chastisement, disenfranchisement, and coverture, as a formal matter, were gone—but the law was by no means neutral on the question of women's role. Law played an active part, in the 1950s, in frustrating women's entry into well paying labor markets, from union crafts to white-collar management and professional work. Law played an active part in keeping women in abusive and violent marriages. Law played an active part in maintaining the "normalcy" of the unjust marriage—in part, through limiting access to divorce. Law played an active part in limiting or precluding women's active participation in civic life, from jury duty to military duty, and from reaping the rewards as well as shouldering the risks of those obligations. Law played an active part in keeping women's reproductive and sexual lives firmly within men's control. Taken collectively, the not so invisible hand of the law continued to play an active part in maintaining a Victorian ideal of status-drenched, inegalitarian marriage in the public imagination, long after its official endorsement of a husband's right to punish, confine, and control the assets of his wife had been officially decried.

So, law is a part of the story—a big part of the story—of the continuities, as well as the discontinuities, of the patriarchal marriage promise of the 1850s and the traditional marriage promise of the 1950s. But it is by no means the whole story. Beyond and around law lived *culture,* and the marriage promise in 1950, with its profound delineation of gender roles, was a cornerstone of it. To some degree, it was autonomous from law, and even impervious to politics. Just take a quick glimpse. Inegalitarian, role-defined, status-drenched, traditional marriage, a la 1950, was a mainstay of early childhood public, private, and familial education. Toddlers played with dolls or soldiers. They then went on to grade school where they learned to read using storybooks containing nothing but stories and pictures of working fathers and domestic, homebound mothers. They came home in the afternoon, and if allowed to, they watched television shows that depicted family life in literally no terms at all other than the strictly traditional. They moved on to junior and senior high schools that taught girls to cook and sew, and taught boys carpentry and auto shop. The athletically gifted among them participated either in male athletic squads that performed heroically, or in female cheerleading teams that led the applause. When they graduated high school, say in the early or mid-1960s, they would go on to college, perhaps, where the socially successful participated in fraternity and sorority life.

Outside of all of this education, the message was just as relentless: With or without a college education, teens and young men and women of the fifties and sixties would eventually encounter, as consumers, the mass marketing of a wedding industry still in its infancy, but with all the charms and innocence that infancy implies. Illegitimacy carried a stigma that a lifetime of good works would not erase, and girls who had sex and become pregnant outside of marriage justifiably in many cases thought their lives were ruined. Teenage girls earned money from babysitting while their boyfriends and brothers cut lawns for triple the wages. A huge consumer market developed at mid-century for goods made for the household, and the role of wife expanded to include the expert consumer: of the husband-wife duo, the wife should, could, and did develop the expertise to buy the best dishwasher, toothpaste, and loaf of bread for her family. Mothers taught their daughters the nobility, if not the necessity, of sacrificing self for family, and taught their sons the privileges, entitlements, and responsibilities that come with being head of a household. Both parents conveyed by example the behavior of leadership and submission necessary for a well-functioning, placid household. In concert, and in monotonous unison, toy manufacturers, movies, television, grade school, high school, colleges, the workplace, and the family all drove home the message, filling an ambiguous space left by the changing legal regime. Wives, that message went, could not be forced against their will by brutish husbands to stay home, be economically dependent, individually impoverished, and clean house and bear children. A *good* wife, however, would do all of that and more, and do so voluntarily and happily, for a loving, decent, and well-chosen husband. A wife could not be forced into any of this. But a virtuous wife could, and should, submit to it, so long as she chose her husband wisely.

Lastly—under law and culture both, laid religion. Brides vowed obedience to their husbands, and were taught the virtue of following his command. In Catholicism and mainstream Protestantism, the husband obeys Christ as the wife obeys the husband, and what this turns out to mean in practice is that the wife in effect models the virtue of wifely obedience for her children, as the husband models obedience to Christ for his wife.[54] Christianity taught the virtues of submission, of sacrifice, and of altruism, and associated all of it with femininity in marriage. To look outside of marriage for fulfilling sexual pleasure was a sin, but likewise, it was just as sinful to refuse to submit to one's husband's sexual demands. Battered women were routinely counseled by spiritual guides to learn the subtle feminine and wifely art of anticipating and fulfilling their husbands' needs before his temper became uncontrollable. Husband and wife were both children of God, but although equals to God, that did not render them civic equals in the godly household. The wife had a role to play, as did the husband. The wife's role was to be a good mother, but also a good wife, and a good wife graciously submitted to her husband's rule.

So, through the interplay of economics, law, religion, and culture, the Victorian ideal of inequalitarian marriage, with rigid role definition, dependent wives who serve and productive husbands who rule, remained surprisingly intact, although the enforcement mechanism had changed dramatically. Marriage in 1950 was understood as a union of man and woman, for the creation of children through lawful and blessed sexual intimacy. It contemplated a family structure in which the husband would produce income for the family, and the wife would maintain the household and raise children—not because she had to, and not because if she tried not to the husband could force the issue, but rather, because that was what a good wife did. She would be economically dependent upon him—again, not because he could force the issue if that was his whim, but because the role expected it of her, and she wished to comply. She would sacrifice self for family—not because if she did not that sacrifice could be coerced (it more or less could not be) but because sacrifice of self for family was her highest expectation of her self. Sacrifice was, for her, not sacrifice at all. It was self-actualization.

Traditional Marriage and Contractual Marriage: A Contrast

Now, compare this 1950s marriage promise—call it the traditional promise—with the marriage promise of the last quarter of the twentieth century. For reasons I'll explore in a moment, it makes sense to call the marriage promise of the 1970s, 1980s, and 1990s "contractual." Again, there are continuities as well as discontinuities. In some ways, it's important to stress, the landscape did not change all that much from 1950 or so to 1975. Marriage rates did drop, and divorce rates rose, between 1950 and 1980, and perhaps most important, the age of participants in first marriages went up substantially.[55] But the drop in marriage rates and the rise in divorce rates was not quite the calamitous, precipitous change—certainly not the death of marriage and the end of civilization—that traditionalists had feared, and bemoaned. In the 1970s, young men and women continued to marry, albeit at an older age than did their World War II–generation parents of the forties and fifties. Divorced and widowed older adults likewise continued to remarry, although at somewhat lower rates than had divorced and widowed older adults of a quarter century earlier. But nevertheless, the numbers here don't tell anywhere near the whole story. Apart from the changing demographic profile, there was clearly a seismic shift in our understanding of the institution—in terms of what marriage is, what it means to be married, and what the good of marriage might be, to married people themselves, to those who do not marry, and to society as a whole. In Coontz's provocative phrasing: "It took more than 150 years to establish the love-based, male breadwinner marriage as the dominant model in North America and Western Europe. It took less than 25 years to dismantle it."[56]

What was the difference? Obviously, not for all of us, but nevertheless for many of us in the various post–World War II generations—the baby boomers, the generation X'ers, generation Y'ers, and so on; those of us who came of age in the 1960s, 1970s, and 1980s—the marriage promise of the last quarter of the century was completely different than its counterpart of the 1950s. Marriage, a la 1970, 1980, and 1990, meant a man and a woman presumptively wed for life, barring serious unhappiness, whose union would be recognized by law, by community, and if relevant, by various mainstream faiths. Within a marriage, a potential husband and a potential wife could expect to cooperate with household tasks, either split equitably, or randomly, or along the lines of a benign and chosen allocation of labor along traditional lines. Husband and wife could expect to enjoy sexual intimacy and sexual fidelity from each other, and to bear and raise children together, should they mutually decide they wish to do so. If they chose to, they could expect to enjoy the company and support of their partner in old age, in sickness, and throughout whatever traumas this vale of tears might throw one's way. In the community, they could expect some moderate degree of recognition and approval for their decision to marry—but only that, a moderate degree. Should the couple decide not to marry, and live life singly or cohabitate, they would not encounter significant disapproval or legal disadvantage, even should they have children. As married partners, they would see themselves, and others would see them, as participants in an historical and enduring tradition. But here again, should they decide against marriage, they would find plenty of acceptance for other less traditional ways of organizing and living out their adult, intimate lives. They could each view themselves and each other as a "head of household" if they wished, and they would often act and be expected to act as a representative of the interests of their family. They would each jointly and severally, as is said in law, be fully responsible for the well-being of their dependents—meaning, for the most part, their children—and each other. They would each be, because of that, representative of something larger than oneself. They would not, however, by virtue of their marriage, cease to be a "self," an individual, or an autonomous, choosing agent. Self-sovereignty, within the marriage of 1970, remained fully, gloriously intact.

The greatest difference between the marriage promise of the 1970s to 1990s, and that of the 1950s, was the *optionality* of marriage in the 1970s, and the optionality of the roles of the partners within it: that is why I propose to call its promise "contractual." What the institution of marriage promised to its participants, in the 1970s–1990s, that distinguished it so cleanly from what it had promised in the past, was *choice*. Marriage, so the new promise read, is a menu of options. Inegalitarian, gendered, "traditional" marriage was most assuredly *one* of the options and a popular one at that—but, nevertheless, traditionalism, a la 1970, was a choice, not a way of life, to turn a popular bumper sticker on its head, and the difference is huge. Inegalitarian and gendered marriage, for vast swaths of the marrying population, was no longer mandatory—making it something less (or more?) than a "tradition." It no longer had pride of place in our cultural imagination, in our legal system, or in our mainstream religions, as it undeniably did, in the 1950s. The marriages themselves, perhaps as a consequence, became far more individualistic: the expectations each party brought to the marriage was understood to be a matter of that individual's, or couple's, stated preferences, desires, and expectations. Prescripted, gendered, marital roles, accordingly, began to deteriorate. Parents of the seventies and eighties could, but they did not have to teach their children to read out of primers that glamorized gendered and inegalitarian family life, and many did not, and insisted that their children's' public school teachers not do so as well. As parents they could, and many did, seek out ungendered or cross-gendered toys, and where the children resisted, they tolerated with ironic whimsy their toddlers' traditional preferences for GI Joe and Barbie. Cheerleading made a comeback in the 1990s after fading from the scene, but it made a comeback as a demanding sport, not a halftime diversion to the athleticism on the field. Title IX, mandating equal expenditures of funds for women and men by colleges and universities receiving federal money, both in academic and athletic programs, became a way of life on college campuses.[57] Sex-segregated shop and home economics classes disappeared, of if retained, they were integrated and became a bit of a goof. After completing high school or college, men and women cohabitated, lived in small groups, or lived singly, and encountered little or no societal resistance for doing so. Pregnancy and motherhood outside of marriage were not universally frowned on across the board, and illegitimacy lost its sting. By the end of the decade illegitimacy was no longer a legal impediment to virtually anything.

The marriage promise of the 1970s, in popular understanding, was not only more optional, it was also more egalitarian than that of the 1950s. Women did not expect, upon marrying, to thereby become subordinate to their husband, relatively impoverished within the marriage, economically dependent, or unemployable. Marriage, by the mid-1970s, was for the benefit of the adult, marrying, individual participants. It was not necessarily, any longer, an institution, the *raison d'etre* of which was either the submission of wives or the well-being of children. The marriage promise, so to speak, was silent on both the necessity of wifely obedience and even the presence of children, much less the subject of their care. Marriage was pretty much, by the 1970s, a union between a presumptively equal man and woman, on terms agreed upon by the two of them, period.

Finally, marriage of the 1970s was far less coercive. Women did not expect, when they married in the 1970s, to be entering a relationship within which their consent or lack of consent to the sexual demands of their husband would be regarded by both of them as of no consequence. Nor did they expect to become, by virtue of marriage, under the thumb of their husbands—that by marrying, they thereby expressed their consent to his rule, would expect to obey his commands, and would have no complaint to moderate physical punishment, should they refuse. Women and men both expected sex within marriage to be pleasurable for both parties, not a matter of duty, obligation, or coercion for either. Marital rape was still not a crime, at the beginning of the decade, but by the end of it that had changed: the major, albeit unheralded, reform movement of the 1970s was the wholesale reversal of at least the most egregious aspects of the marital rape exclusion from virtually every state's criminal law.[58] Likewise, acquaintance rape and date rape were being recognized as crimes of violence: increasingly, and in retrospect seemingly inexorably, we were moving toward the commonsensical assumption that rape is rape, assault is assault, and battery is battery. Women, by the 1970s, did not expect physical "punishment" to be the appropriate response to their "misbehavior" in marriage. More broadly, women did not expect marriage to be a site of coercion, lawful or otherwise. Brides began to strike the vow of obedience from their wedding ceremonies.

So, marriage, by 1970, promised choice, not tradition, a rough equality, rather than an explicit subordination, and sexual pleasure and domestic cooperation, rather than coercion or duty. It promised equal distribution of household chores, if the parties chose equality, or a traditional distribution, if they chose tradition. But either way, it was up to the parties. The marriage promise of the 1970s and forward to today, for many, contained not a word about domesticity, separate spheres, breadwinners, women's role, the virtues of wifely obedience, or the feminine mystique. Marriage of the 1970s promised, in effect, a regime of contract, not a regime of traditional status. How, and why, did this happen? How can we possibly account for such a profound shift—largely accomplished in twenty-five years—in our understanding of marriage? How did marriage become a matter of choice?

There were no doubt any number of contributing factors, but our cultural historians generally point to four major ruptures in national life, between 1950 and 1975, that may have played a role: one cultural, one technological, one political, and one legal.[59] Let me just summarize the first three and then focus more pointedly on the last. First, the cultural. On the heels of Berkeley's free speech movement in the early 1960s, came San Francisco's free love movement of the late 1960s, with ripple effects that lasted at least throughout the next decade. Somehow, at some time in the mid-to late 1960s, a liberatory ethos came to the fore, loosely identified with the cultural rebelliousness of the era, that espoused an open hostility to traditional marriage and to all of its attendant values—lifelong monogamy, sexual fidelity, gender roles, and child-raising . To many baby boomers that came of age in the 1960s, marriage came to look like a way of life that could and should be resisted, not only for oneself, but across the board, as stifling, or insufficiently expressive. Fidelity, structure, internal order, sacrifice, self-denial, and consistency over time—all collectively marital values, or virtues—came to be viewed as flatly inconsistent with a very different set of desires: a desire for spontaneity, an openness to the meanings and feelings of the moment, a frank embrace of physical pleasure, and a will to love many rather than one. Sexual attraction, so went the new ethos, is to be acted upon, as well as its lack: if you can't be with the one you love, then love the one you're with, unless and until you find one day that you don't want to or you can't, and then, well, leave. All of this freedom to love, to enjoy sex, to Be Here Now and to exit—to forge momentary connections without commitment; connections meant to last decidedly short of a lifetime—was facilitated, we might surmise, by social and geographical mobility, by a booming economy, easy-to-come-by jobs, low-rent apartments, disdain for materialism and consumerism, and above all else, by birth control. It was further bolstered, it is fair to surmise, by the Playboy ethic that preceded it, and that likewise proclaimed itself hostile to marriage, albeit on the very different grounds that marriage was a prison any self-respecting male libido should resist. But whatever its causes, the message regarding not just traditional marriage, but all marriage, conveyed by a social movement committed to the freeing of love as well as the freeing of political prisoners, opposed to oppressive social institutions as well as economic ones, was clear and condemnatory: marriage stifles love; and love should be free.

Second, politics: during roughly the same time—the late sixties and early seventies—a women's movement was reborn, that focused, this time around, quite explicitly on the unmet needs and squelched human potential of wives in traditional marriages. The sentimentality, the quietude, and the complacency of the domestic sphere—a sphere within which women were ideally expected to live out their adult lives caring for their children, husband, and home, with no involvement in either the civic affairs of community and democracy, or in remunerative labor—came under withering critique from within. A significant segment of an entire generation of bored, stifled, infantilized, and overeducated housewives found they were more than willing to place political labels—oppression, inequality, subordination—on what Betty Friedan called, in her classic treatment, the "unnamed malaise." The role assigned, by traditional marriage, to wives was stifling. It squelched human potential. The work was monotonous and dull. It could not sustain an adulthood; it couldn't even come close. It was infantilizing and worse, to be dependent upon one's husband for money, companionship, and entrée into the outside world. If women were choosing this life, they'd been duped: duped by culture, by the glamour of their own weddings, by *Cosmopolitan Magazine*, by men, and by their own mothers. The traditional wife was no way to live. Marriage slighted the human potential of half the race. It was an unsustainable, unstable regime. Furthermore, unlike in decades and centuries past, women had *chosen* marriage—no one had forced it on them. If they chose it, they could unchoose it. They should force the reform of their marriages. If that proved impossible, they should leave them.

Third: technology. Entirely aside from the free love movement and political feminism, came a revolution in birth control technologies—a revolution hatched in laboratories, but that fueled the politics of the era. With birth control, the connection between marriage and children was irrevocably severed: a married couple could choose to have children or not have them, just as a parent could choose to marry, or not. Marriage was no longer the choice that paved the way for the fated conception of children—rather, the decision to stop taking the pill, remove the diaphragm, or quit using the condom, and in some cases, to commence fertility treatment, was. On the heels of the invention of safe, effective birth control came, in pretty rapid succession, the Supreme Court's decision in *Griswold v. Connecticut*,[60] that guaranteed married people that their power to control their own fertility within marriage could not be taken away from them by a moralistic state. From there, it was a short step, legally, to the extension of such a right to the unmarried individual—a step the Court took in *Eisenstadt v. Baird*,[61] just a couple of years later. The combined effect of *Griswold* and *Eisenstadt* was not simply that they paved the way for *Roe v. Wade*[62]—although they did that. The combined effect of *Eisenstadt* and *Griswold* is that they tore asunder the natural connection between marriage, lawful and blessed heterosexual intercourse, and the conception of children. Without that connection, whether or not to parent became a matter of choice, for married and unmarried alike. It was no longer in God's hands, once the individuals had taken the step of marriage, whether the marriage would be blessed with children. It was within the individual's control. Without that connection, marriage, in its traditional mode, suddenly lost its point.

But finally, there was law—so much changing law that it's fair to call it a legal revolution. Both the law of marriage and the law outside of marriage underwent a profound transformation. Marriage law, by the 1970s had finally, belatedly, become a part of what lawyers commonly call the vast two-century-long migration of private law "from status to contract." The private law governing business, and markets, and corporations, and sales, had long ago made that transition: relations between innkeepers and boarders, landowners and tenants, employers and employees, buyers and sellers, and so on, were governed by the contract between them, rather than by their status in their community. This shift, from status to contract, was largely complete, in most areas of private law, by the middle of the nineteenth century. Marriage law, it was widely believed by family law scholars of the 1970s and 1980s, had taken much longer to make that migration, but somehow, somewhere between 1950 and 1975, it clearly did. No-fault laws made marriage terminable at will. Pre- and postnuptial agreements, separation agreements, and surrogacy agreements were drafted and increasingly enforced. Couples contemplating marriage agonized over and then wrote and uttered their own vows. Marital roles came to be, in law as well as in popular imagination, what the parties agreed to, rather than that to which the parties submitted. Marriage law, by the mid-1970s, looked more like contract law and less like status law, and an individual marriage, in 1970, looked much more like a contract—individualized, subject to change, a product of two people's wills—than a tradition. Whether this change in our law was anomalous and puzzling, or inevitable and overdue, is largely a matter of "framing." If we look at marriage law as a part of "family law" and if we think of family law, in turn, as a part of our "public law"—meaning, those areas of law that concern the relation of individuals, and associations of individual, with the state—then the migration of marriage law from status to contract does indeed require explanation: Why should the state's interest in this institution in effect entirely disappear, leaving marriage to nothing but individual whim and preference? Why should *this* body of law, this body of law that recognizes and regulates the relation of the state to this primary social institution, be demoted, leaving the social relations it once governed to the domain of private choice? Since when, and why, and how, did marriage become a matter of choice? If, though, we think of marriage as the law governing relations between citizens rather than the law governing the relation between the state and the individual—then the shift from "status to contract" was long overdue, and the question is not why it happened at all, but why it took so long. Either way, though, whether anomaly or inevitability, a part of the answer lies outside the realm of marriage law and its dynamic, but nevertheless within the realm of law.

Most important, outside of marriage, "equal employment" became a widely disseminated and largely well-understood legal entitlement. Discrimination in the workplace, by the mid-1970s, was flatly illegal, and most people knew it.[63] The sex integration of all male workplaces was proceeding apace—albeit not across the board. Female "firsts" in the workplace were widely celebrated—astronaut, Supreme Court justice, CEO, college president. Women voted in large numbers and wives did not always vote as their husbands voted. And of course, the Supreme Court ruled first in *Griswold* and then in *Eisenstadt* that states could not criminalize birth control in or outside of marriage, respectively, and then in *Roe v. Wade*,[64] in 1973, that states cannot criminalize first- and second-term abortions. The abortion procedure became available, safe, and relatively cheap for most women, birth control even moreso.

The impact of *Roe v. Wade*[65] on traditional marriage hardly needs belaboring: for several decades since, the conflict the case brought to the surface, between an entirely individualistic understanding of reproduction, and a traditional conception of not only women's nature and marital role, but of human nature, has dominated our politics. What's largely forgotten is that Title VII, and its prohibition against "discrimination based on sex" in the workplace,[66] Title IX, and its prohibition against sex discrimination in schools,[67] and the dozen or so Supreme Court decisions striking statutes that discriminated against women in various ways in public life,[68] had at least as great an impact on our understanding of marriage as they did on our understanding of workplace and schoolhouse fairness. Laws that mandated nondiscrimination on the basis of sex in the workplace and in schools went a long way toward eradicating the sensibility of gender differentiation in the home—a gender differentiation that still remained long after the demise of coverture.

How does it do so? Well, Title VII covers "women," but of course, many women are also wives. So, a "wife," post–Title VII, not only has the right to keep whatever wages she earns, but an employer cannot refuse to hire or pay her fairly solely on account of her sex. "Pin money" is gone—it is flat out illegal. After a series of cases, followed by the Pregnancy Discrimination Act, it is just as illegal to discriminate against women on the basis of pregnancy as well—and with this legal development, the long time-honored practice of firing women, whether married or not, who began to "show," met its demise.[69] With nondiscrimination against women, wives, pregnant women, and women with children in the workplace all established as a firm right, rooted in norms of fairness and legal mandate both, comes a full, frontal challenge to the logic of domesticity, similar to, but in many ways broader than, that suggested by suffrage of three-quarters of a century earlier. Suffrage, after all, could be—and often was—defended on the grounds that the domestic sphere of womanhood needed representation in the public sphere, that women's softer side would be a good influence on politics, or that women's special needs and vulnerabilities sometimes needed tending. Suffrage, then, stood in an ambiguous relation to separate spheres ideology: it undercut the notion that women are not equal citizens, but at the same time it could live side by side, if uncomfortably, with the notion that women were peculiarly suited for domestic life and ill-suited for the public sphere. The consequences of equal employment, though, were not so ambiguous. If as a matter of fact, some women, like some men, can perform as firefighters, carpenters, and lawyers, and if women as a matter of law must be presumed capable of so performing, unless it is shown that particular individuals cannot, then there is no longer any sense whatsoever in insisting that women are peculiarly suited for the home, solely by virtue of their sex. A woman firefighter, police officer, managing partner, or judge hardly seems more submissive, more altruistic, less competitive, or more maternal, than her male partner. If women are no less than men suited for the workplace, for advanced academic achievement, for politics, and for civic responsibilities, as Title VII, Title IX, and the Supreme Court cases that followed in their wake all insisted, then they cannot also be suited for subservience. Equal employment, by 1975, was established as a right, and even more than equal voting rights, it seemingly implied equal distribution of work and responsibilities at home as well as in the workplace. In the face of the logic of equal employment law, to say nothing of the logic of the paychecks to which it led, the role differentiation at the heart of traditional marriage came to look increasingly anachronistic.

These changes, and to a lesser extent the no-fault divorce revolution that preceded it, did not happen willy-nilly; they were fueled by a wave of liberal feminist lawyering, theorizing, conferencing, teaching, studying, advocacy, and ingenuity. By the mid-1970s, a wave of feminist legal reform, led by (now) Supreme Court Justice Ruth Bader Ginsburg, Law Professor Wendy Williams, Dean Herma Hill Kay, and Law Professor Susan Deller Ross, was well under way, and by the end of the next decade was largely complete.[70] Make no mistake about it: this was one of the most, and perhaps the most, successful legal reform movements undertaken in the twentieth century. The 1970s feminist legal reform movement was not focused on family or marriage, or on the triad of coverture, chastisement, and disenfranchisement. It was focused on a different triad: the triad of discrimination in the workplace, exclusions from the public sphere of civic responsibility, and on reproductive freedom. There was, though, a deep continuity between the two movements, which recent scholarship on the two eras is only now beginning to unearth. The underlying target of both reform movements—the early one, surreptitiously, but the latter one, quite explicitly—was the continuing social and cultural commitment to separate spheres, the domesticity of women, and the traditional form of marriage that supports it.

For all of these reasons—political, cultural, legal, technological—and I'm sure for a host of others, resistance to the traditional marriage promise of the 1950s was widespread by the three-quarter mark of the twentieth century. Marriage itself, though, did not die. Rather, the cultural resistance to traditional marriage as stifling of emotional, pleasureable, and hedonistic freedoms, the women's movement's resistance to marriage as a site of inequality and oppression, the technological severance of the connection of marriage with the conception of children, and the changes in law rendering birth control, abortion, and nondiscrimination in public life and the workplace all a matter of right—all of this, taken collectively, did not doom civil marriage itself. It did, though, transform it. With birth control pills firmly in hand, and, in many cases, with egalitarian ideals and legal rights and entitlements firmly in mind, men and women in the 1970s and 1980s did continue to marry each other. They did so, however, later in life than they had in earlier decades—they chose marriage as adults, rather than being funneled into marriage as the gateway to adulthood, or coerced into it as the least bad of dreary alternatives. And they did so with individualized marriage vows and individualized marital expectations for each other, rather than with the expectation of stepping into a preestablished role. Lastly, they did so with a set of egalitarian expectations for the marriage utterly foreign to the marriages of their parents. The individualized, egalitarian, and chosen marriages of the 1970s were in all of these ways, utterly unlike the traditional marriage of the 1950s. Marriage, in the 1970s, meant a man and woman, united for life or until they mutually decide to split, and in order to provide companionship, affection, and material support for each other, on whatever terms they mutually agree to, under the sway of vows they write themselves, and for the benefit of themselves and whatever children they might later decide to have.

From Contract to Politics

And finally—what is the marriage promise of the early twenty first century? What the institution of marriage promises, uniquely, in the first decade of this century, is open political deliberation over its nature. That deliberation might, or might not, have the effect of expanding private choices within it. Our deliberations might lead to the construction of an institution we call "civil marriage" that is more open, and more individualist, than what we witnessed in the seventies: we could, for example, define marriage as the union of any number of adults of any sex, with the intent of providing mutual care to themselves and their dependents. Or, our deliberations might lead to the construction of an institution called "civil marriage" that is less open: we might define marriage as the union of a man and woman for life, with very restrictive exit options, and without access to birth control. Either way, what will distinguish the institution will be the degree to which it will be a product of collective politics, rather than a product of individual choice. Marriage, by the end of the era we've not embarked upon, will no longer be whatever is produced by the individual choices of brides and grooms, husbands and wives. Nor will it be a product of the hidden causal tentacles of "tradition" or of patriarchy. Again—marriage will be a product of our politics.

Before explaining in greater detail what that means, and why in my view it is so important, it's useful first to look at the road not taken. From the contractual marriage promise of the 1970s, it is easy enough to imagine that marriage could have withered and died. If individuals can choose to marry, or not, choose to have children, or not, choose traditional gender roles, or not, choose to stay in the marriage, or not, why not conclude that there is really nothing to marriage but individual choice, and hence, nothing to marriage, period? Individuals can do with contract law, coupled with private promise, or vows, or covenants, anything that the law of marriage facilitates, if by "law of marriage," we mean something like the contractual ideal we were approaching in the seventies and eighties. From marriages of choice, we could have proceeded to dissolve civil marriage entirely. Property law, contract law, and tax law could have filled the lacunae left by the disappearance of the quaint-sounding "law of marriage." If you promise to sell me wheat, but renege on the promise, I can sue you for breaching that contract; likewise, if you promise to live with me, share the rent, have a sexually monogamous relationship, and help me raise our children, and you renege on that promise, I should be able to sue you for breaching that promise. Whether you are a business partner or an intimate partner, the same rules of fair dealing—the same contract law—should apply. If you promise me something, and you don't deliver, you've wronged me, and I should be entitled to relief. It just shouldn't matter, on this Kantian, or Holmesian, or utilitarian, understanding of promise-keeping, injury, and compensation, what the content of the promise is. The law doesn't care one bit about the content of the promise—whether it concerns barley or hay, computers or firewood—nor does it care if the contract you've breached is fair or unfair, foolish or wise. If you've promised me something, and breached, and injured me because of it, you owe me damages. That's pretty much the sum total of our law of contract. Likewise, why should it care whether the promise concerns the sale of wheat or the raising of children? A broken promise is a broken promise. The consequences should be treated comparably.

When we dissolve our relationship, should we choose to do so, likewise, in a world without civil marriage, we could distribute whatever assets we might have jointly acquired by reference to whatever preexisting contract we might have written, just as might a business partnership. Or, if we were foolish enough not to have written up such a contract, we might ask a court to assist us in arriving at a fair distribution, and to do so by reference to rules that might be drawn from the law of property, or business associations, or, if none of these seem to be appropriate, then, if need be, by reference to amorphous and loosely defined "rules of equity"—rules that have, since antiquity, been used by courts and chancellors when common-law rules seem inadequate. Nowhere, though, would recourse to a peculiar and particular "law of marriage" be required. Contract law, property law, and an evolving law of personal association, if need be, could more than do the trick. We could have made this transition, furthermore, with remarkably little difficulty: marriage law, certainly by 1980, had already shown plenty of signs of moving in this direction. Prenuptial agreements were upheld more and more frequently by 1980; now they are upheld as a matter of course. To the greatest extent possible, parties are urged to agree to privately negotiated settlement and custody agreements, upon divorce. Contracts between unmarried cohabitants, by the 1980s, were occasionally upheld, now they are much more so. Parties divorce at will, and marry at will, with fewer and fewer restrictions on their power to bring their contractual intentions to fruition. Why not just finish the job? Eliminating civil marriage altogether, if we continue with this projectory, would not have been a terribly radical step. Parties could continue to, and no doubt would, enter into holy matrimony, as defined by their religion. As far as the state goes, though, the only state concern should be with assuring that the parties' contractual intentions are fulfilled, so long as no third parties are injured in the process. This seems liberal, and liberating. It also, by 1980 or so, seemed sheer nigh inevitable. A goodly number of family law and contract law scholars at the time assumed that we would do precisely that.[71] Marriage law would simply become a branch of contract law, and would then eventually be subsumed within it altogether. The end result is that marriage law, and with it, civil marriage, would just disappear, and basically with little or no fanfare.

That is not what happened. Marriage, and marriage law, did not wither on the vine of contract. Nor has marriage simply reverted back to its traditional or patriarchal promises, the efforts of some marriage traditionalists notwithstanding. A couple of states, but only a couple of states, now offer "covenant marriage" as an option—intending, no paradox meant, to give parties the option of limiting their future options—by covenanting at the point of marriage that they will not later on rely on their rights to no-fault or unilateral divorce. Not too many marrying couples have taken the bait. There is some, but not much, enthusiasm for reverting back to fault divorce as a matter of law. A promarriage and profatherhood movement has come to the fore, but it has not made as much progress as one might have guessed it would, in fundamentally moving the culture back to a traditional understanding of marriage. Weddings are becoming more lavish than they were in the 1970s, and privileged young adults have far less ambivalence about their value. But marriage itself is not noticeably becoming more "traditional"—women's workplace participation rates have stayed relatively stable or declined during this time, as has men's participation in child-raising and domestic labor. Indeed, marriage's great popularity, compared with the 1970s, might be precisely because it has so irretrievably lost its traditionalist trappings.

Rather, what distinguishes marriage in the 2000s from that of the 1970s, the 1950s, and the 1850s, is the degree to which its definition has become a political, public question. The "choice" that marriage now poses is not only to potential participants: to marry or not, to adopt traditional gender roles or not, to have children or not, to divorce or not, and so on. The choice marriage now poses is addressed to citizens. We have to ask and answer the question "what is marriage?" not as a personal matter—as in, what is marriage to me, what do I wish to make of my marriage—and not as an academic question—what has marriage been in the past, how has it evolved, what social ends does it serve, and so on. We now must face the question "what is marriage" in our role as citizens, and voters—who will construct, through the mechanisms of democracy, and to no small degree, some of the rules we all live by. What should marriage be, not only to me, my sons and my daughters, but to my society? Should it be a "union of a man and woman," or could we sensibly extend it to a union of two men or a union of two women? What possible reasons would we have for not doing so? If the purpose is to provide a shelter in the storm, should we also extend it to nonsexual but companionate unions, between any two people who so constitute themselves? Two siblings, perhaps, or two neighbors, or two cousins, or two very close friends? If we do that, couldn't we extend it to include more than two? What if three or four adults decide to pool resources, nurture each other, and be there for each other in times of crisis? Should we sanctify all such polyamorous unions, whether they are sexual or not?

The public dimension of the marriage promise of the aughts is qualitatively different from the individual choice dimension of the marriage promise of the 1970s. When we vote in a referendum on the definition of marriage, we decide what this set of rules should be, not only for ourselves, but for each other. We decide not "is marriage the right thing, in my life, now, for me" or, should I opt for a traditional marriage, or a "covenant marriage," or a nontraditional marriage, but rather, which of these forms of marriage would be a good thing for my community? If we think marriage is a good thing, and we think it is such because of the sense of commitment it fosters, then we could expand marriage broadly so as to include every possible set of adult commitments aiming at mutual comfort and reassurance. Or, if we think marriage is a good thing, because it fosters a healthy environment within which to raise children, then we could define marriage as all adult commitments that contemplate the raising of children. We could also, it bears emphasizing, restrict choice within and around marriage: we could repeal no-fault divorce, as a number of traditionalist scholars and activists are now urging, or introduce "covenant marriage" so that we might consensually bind ourselves to a civil marriage that disallows no-fault. Or, as many states now have, we can define it as a union between man and woman, and define our state constitution such that it can never be changed. We could restrict access to birth control, even within marriage, assuming a Supreme Court willing to overturn *Griswold* as well as *Roe*. But however we choose to define it, it is now clear, as it was not, in 1970, or 1950, or 1850, that we are indeed choosing to define it. We are not inheriting it. Whether we like it or not, we are faced with the choice, as citizens, of how to construct this institution and not simply with the choice, as individuals, of whether we wish to live out our individual lives within it.

And, the public choice is pressing upon us. Our political representatives are debating and deliberating and voting on the nature of marriage, with or without our input. Marriage will be redefined, in some fashion, in many and perhaps most states, over the course of the next decade. To do this definitional project thoughtfully—to decide reflectively, and not reflexively, what marriage should be—we need to deliberate over the value, or the goodness, we hope to garner from it. Marriage is a house we build, not a state of nature. If we reflect on what we hope to gain from marriage, or on what good we think it might bring us, we might better understand how we ought to build it.

∽

∼ CHAPTER TWO ∽

In Defense of Marriage
("When I'm Sixty-Four")

*D*oes marriage need defending? If so, against what? Should the institution of marriage, no less than our individual marriages, be celebrated, as a great, enduring success story? And if so, why? A surprising number of political activists, policy analysts, community leaders, legal scholars, philosophers, theologians, social scientists, and moralists of all stripes see a great deal to celebrate in the institution of marriage, and likewise, see all sorts of threats against which it needs defending. Precisely what the celebrants of marriage are celebrating, however, and what threats they see when they defend it are very different, depending on what they understand the institution of marriage to be. In fact, what promarriage activists and scholars see, defend, and celebrate, when they look at marriage, is so different, they are often arguing at cross purposes with each other, no less than with their joint antagonists.

Promarriage advocates, to oversimplify, see the institution of marriage that they defend and celebrate through at least three very different lenses. One group, self-labeled "neonatural lawyers," see marriage as necessarily "traditionalist," and worthy of celebration for just that reason, but also subject to all sorts of modern threats, by virtue of the traditional understanding of "husband" and "wife" that it encapsulates.[1] A second group, whom I will call "social utilitarian," understands "marriage" as a civil and legal, rather than traditional, institution, and worthy of defense and celebration on basically utilitarian grounds: the institution of marriage, as it is now constituted and defined by law, makes its participants healthy, wealthy, and happy.[2] The institution should be celebrated on those utilitarian grounds alone. Marriage so understood is threatened, to the degree it is, mostly by contemporary skepticism about and misunderstanding of its social value. A third group—that I will call "virtue theorists" or "communitarians"—see marriage as essentially expressive of a particularly virtuous way of life, characterized by a heightened sense of responsibility for and commitment to intimate others.[3] For the virtue theorists, marriage is threatened above all by the hyperindividualist, consumerist, basically selfish, and present-focused understanding of what it means to be a person and what it means to thrive, that prevails in contemporary social and economic life. All three groups celebrate marriage, and defend it against perceived critics and threats. But the answers they give to the more specific questions spelt out above—does marriage need defending, and against what, and should marriage be celebrated, and why—even for those who are united in their bottom line promarriage stance, are vastly different. The differences rest at root on very different understandings of what marriage is and what about it is of value.

The Neonatural Law Defense of Traditional Marriage

So, let me start with the celebrants of traditional marriage. What is "traditional marriage" and does it need defending? Surely if, by "marriage," one means a union of a man and a woman, for life, sanctioned by church, state, and community, and open to the possibility of creating life, then yes, marriage needs defending: it needs defending against contemporary law, against our modern social practices, and against its many critics. No-fault and unilateral divorce have made exit too simple; the law, then, has thus undermined part of the basic point. Cohabitation, single parenthood, sex outside of marriage, and the social acceptability of all of that have made marriage too optional, and the use of contraception inside marriage has made the creation of new life tangential to its experienced meaning. Feminist and queer critics have undermined its privileged status, basically by highlighting the harms that this institution and its promoters have wittingly or unwittingly caused. All of this—the availability of legal alternatives to marriage, the social acceptability of sex outside marriage, the availability of contraception within marriage, and the ease with which marriages can be ended—is reflected in high divorce rates, low birth rates, and low marriage rates. If traditional marriage is defined as above, it is no longer the norm, statistically, and perhaps no longer "normative" as well. It is no longer a widely embraced and well understood guide for conduct.

Only seemingly paradoxically, however, the greatest threat to traditional marriage, in recent times, at least in the eyes of its most adamant proponents, has come neither from social practice nor from critics, but rather, from another group of promarriage advocates: those who value "marriage"—albeit not "traditional" marriage—so highly they would like to extend the franchise. According to these "promarriage" activists, marriage is indeed a good thing, but not because it unites a man and a woman in a relationship that is at heart characterized by its openness to the conception of new life. Rather, marriage is a good thing, these advocates urge, because it encourages very long-term, and for the most part unconditional, personal commitments: the essence of marriage, for these promarriage reformers, is not union of man and woman, but rather, the commitment of two persons to the interests and well-being of each other and to their joint dependents. Those commitments, in turn, are a good thing, not because of any spiritual or biological union of "man" and "woman" that they realize, but rather, because they deepen individual responsibility, enrich the personal experience of each individual to the marriage, give adult life a holistic shape and point, create an environment conducive to the nurturance and rearing of children, generate wealth through the pooling of resources, and protect participants against physical catastrophe, economic misfortune, and emotional isolation.

Now, if marriage "as commitment" is such a very good thing for these and a host of related reasons, then, these promarriage reformers ask, quite logically, why not extend its reach? Why not allow persons previously excluded from this privilege into marriage's embrace? Why not extend marital privileges to same-sex couples? The idea of an enduring and personal "commitment" obviously need not be limited to "one man" and "one woman." A man can make such a commitment to another man; a woman can do so to a woman. Why not go further and extend the privilege to polygamous groups, or to polyamorous groups? Why not extend the marital franchise to any group, or any couple, that so desire to make this sort of commitment—whether they are defined by sexual behavior, or not? Indeed, given our societal commitment to the equal treatment of our co-citizens, how can we possibly justify *not* so extending it? It seems irrational in the extreme.

The very naturalness of this question, given the legalization and the increasing normalization of same-sex sexual relationships, combined with the common-sense appeal of a definition of marriage that centers on the "commitment" that is at its heart, has brought to the foreground, in scholarship that addresses the "marriage wars," an heretofore relatively marginalized and Catholic understanding of marriage, defined by almost exclusive reference to the unity of man and woman that traditional marriage fosters, as both reflected in and constituted by sexual acts that are open to the possibility of conceiving new life. This natural law, or as its defenders refer to it, "neonatural law" definition of marriage, and argument for traditional marriage that it supports, has its roots in the writings of St. Augustine, ancient biblical authorities, and contemporary papal writings[4]—but it is no longer limited to those sources. Rather, according to its proponents, the neonatural law argument for marriage as definitively joining one man, and one woman, is no longer an argument that, at least by its own terms, depends on the ascription to any particular religious faith. Rather, according to the neonatural lawyers that propound the view today, the rightness and goodness of marriage, conceived as a two-in-one-flesh communion of a man and a woman, that is both actualized and consummated in reproductive acts of marital intercourse, is apparent to all, Christians and non-Christians, through the exercise of reason, in contemplation of, and toward the understanding of, human nature. Thus, the goodness of marriage as expressive of the unity of husband and wife can be, but need not be, learned through the study of scripture and authoritative interpretation of that scripture. Like all the tenets, prescriptions, and mandates of "natural law," this one too can also be learned through the study of our nature, informed by experience, and honed by observation and logic.

So, what is the neonatural case for marriage? As put forward most vigorously in the past decade by Robert George, Professor of Philosophy at Princeton, and Gerard Bradley, Professor of Law at the University of Notre Dame,[5] the natural law argument for traditional marriage—and against same-sex unions—has two major prongs. The first is definitional. Marriage, according to George and Bradley, at least when "considered not as a mere legal convention," is, by definition, a "two-in-one-flesh communion of persons that is consummated and actualized by sexual acts of the reproductive type."[6] As such, marriage, so defined, is an "intrinsic," or "basic," or noninstrumental, good.[7] Because it is a basic, intrinsic good, it provides a fully sufficient and noninstrumental reason for marital spouses to perform marital, sexual acts "of the reproductive type."[8] It provides a reason for marital spouses to do so, furthermore, whether or not they are capable or incapable of producing children, and whether or not they receive pleasure from them.[9] The significant fact about marital reproductive sex acts, Bradley and George argue, is not that such acts can or will lead to the conception of new life, or that such acts are conducive to (instrumental to) pleasure, but rather, that such acts are of the form necessary to the biological species for the reproduction of life. Therefore, engaging in these coital reproductive acts, within marriage, expresses as well as constitutes a fully integrative conception of the human being—physically, spiritually, and mentally.[10] Marriage itself is thus the basic good that justifies heterosexual, genital, coital intercourse within the marriage, and marriage is also, by definition, that which is "actualized," not just consummated, by those "sexual acts of the reproductive type." It is a very tight, closed circle (and unapologetically so): marriage is what justifies heterosexual, coital sex, when it is justified, and those sex acts are in turn part of the definition of marriage. Sex, then, so long as it is of the reproductive type, is justified and can only be justified by reference to an ongoing marriage of which it is a part: the sex actualizes the two-in-one-flesh communion. When engaged in the single act of reproduction, the couple acts as a unity: only the union of the two of them can perform this single act. This single act brings the two together as one flesh. Thus, the two-in-one-flesh defines the marriage, and justifies the sex within it.[11]

It is also the *only* robust moral justification for human sexuality, or for engaging in sexual acts. Sex engaged in for any instrumental reason—whether for the production of pleasure or even in the hopes of conceiving a child—is not morally justified.[12] Only sex acts of the reproductive type (genital, coital intercourse) are actualizations of the two-in-one-flesh that is marriage, and only such acts are morally good. All instrumental sex, but particularly sex engaged in solely for pleasure, is immoral. Sex to produce warm feelings of companionship, sex to make love, sex for friendship, contracepted sex within marriage for the purpose of producing pleasure, even sex for the eminently desirable end of conceiving a child—is all no different, at heart, from sex for money. Sex is intrinsically good, when it is good, and it is intrinsically good only when engaged in because it is of the reproductive type—meaning the type of sex conducive to the reproduction of the species (rather than, good for the purpose of actually reproducing). Instrumental sex uses either one's own body or the body of another as an instrument toward the end of some other purpose. For that reason it is "disintegrative," and a threat to bodily integrity.

Therefore, Bradly and George conclude,

> In choosing to perform nonmarital orgasmic acts, including sodomitical acts—irrespective of whether the persons performing such acts are of the same or opposite sexes (and even if those persons are validly married to each other)—persons necessarily treat their bodies and those of their sexual partners.... as means or instruments in ways that damage their personal (and interpersonal) integrity, thus, regard for the basic human good of integrity provides a conclusive moral reason not to engage in sodomitical and other nonmarital sex acts.[13]

From this second claim—that nonmarital sex acts not only lack the prima facie moral justification of reproductive-type sex, but also are damaging to personal and interpersonal integrity, Professors Bradley and George (and John Finnis and a number of others) go on to build a series of arguments against both homosexual conduct, same-sex civil unions, and same-sex civil marriage—claims we will examine in a later chapter. Here, though, it is worth looking with some care at their understanding of marriage and the morally good sex that in their view occurs within it. Again, the heart of their claim is that marital sex acts are uniquely (unlike nonmarital sex acts, as well as sodomitical sex acts between married partners) noninstrumental, and it is by virtue of that fact that they both justify and constitute the marriage within which they occur. Marital, reproductive-type sex actualizes the marriage, understood as a two-in-one-flesh communion of persons. That is not its *purpose,* rather, that is what such sex *is.* As the marriage it actualizes is an intrinsic good, the sex that actualizes that marriage serves no further instrumental purpose—pleasure, intimacy, love, or reproduction. Nonreproductive-type sex acts, by contrast, pursued for instrumental reasons, "damage the basic human good of integrity." Reproductive-type sex acts, by contrast, "alone among sexual acts can be truly unitive, and thus marital; and marital acts, thus understood, have their intelligibility and value intrinsically, and not merely by virtue of their capacity to facilitate the realization of other goods." Such acts alone actualize the two-in-one-flesh communion that is marriage. They are, then, of great moral significance indeed.

And why is it, that reproductive-type marital sex acts have this great moral significance? As the law regarding the necessity of consummating marriage once reflected, Bradley and George suggest, marital reproductive sex acts reveal marriage to be a bodily, as well as spiritual and emotional union, and it is that unity of body, emotion, and spirit that is at the heart of reproductive-type marital sex. The bodily union is absolutely necessary to the moral justification of this action. Marriage, thus, is not merely "metaphorically" the coming together of two persons, with deep psychological attachments and mutual responsibilities. Rather, marital sex acts (that actualize the marriage) unite the couple biologically, rendering the pair a "single reproductive principle," performed by the mated pair "as an organic unit." Bradly and George then quote Grisez:

> Though a male and a female are complete individuals with respect to other func-
> tions—for example, nutrition, sensation, and locomotion—with respect to reproduc-
> tion they are only potential parts of a mated pair, which is the complete organism
> capable of reproducing sexually. Even if the mated pair is sterile, intercourse, provided
> it is the reproductive behavior characteristic of the species, makes the copulating
> male and female one organism.[14]

Thus, the biologically unitive nature of mammalian reproduction is what puts sexual intercourse at the center of marriage, as both necessary for its consumma-tion, and as necessary to the moral justification for its occurrence. The reproductive act characteristic of the species is what defines marital intercourse, and marital intercourse defines marriage. Marriage must, then, be defined as the union of man and woman. Anything else—and you're calling chairs, tables, and tables, chairs. Same-sex marriage, Bradley and George conclude, is a moral impossibility.

If this is right—if marriage is a coming-together-in-one-flesh, through re-productive-type marital acts, and if marriage is of intrinsic, basic value because of that, then marriage is indeed threatened on all sides. It is threatened with the social acceptability, not just of same-sex unions, but also of all instrumental sex, and that covers a very wide swath of human sexual behavior: not only sex for money, but also sex for pleasure, sex for companionship, sex for procreation, sex for security, sex for good feelings, sex for intimacy, sex for love, and broadly, sex as a means of expression. But is it right? Does marriage have intrinsic value because of the moral significance of the reproductive-type marital acts that occur within it? Bradley and George candidly acknowledge that it is not the kind of assertion that is susceptible to ordinary forms of proof. Rather, they assert,

> One either understands that spousal genital intercourse has a special significance as
> instantiating a basic, noninstrumental value, or something blocks that understand-
> ing and one does not perceive correctly. [O]ur liberal friends ... honestly do not see
> any special point or value in such intercourse.... By contrast, many other people
> perceive quite easily the special value and significance of the genital intercourse of
> spouses."[15]

The question is focused, Bradley and George argue, by examining the moral signifi-cance of marital sex engaged in by elderly couples who have no chance of conceiving new life, and no expectation of receiving pleasure from the sex. Should they nevertheless engage in sex? Does the sex have a positive moral valence, should they do so?

> [Focus on the] ... case of an elderly married couple who simply no longer experience pleasure in their acts of genital intercourse. They are however still physiologically capably of performing such acts and can do so without emotional repugnance. Is there any point to their continuing to perform them? ... We say yes.... Our answer is valid if marriage, and the genital acts that actualize it, are intrinsically good, and, thus, have an intelligible point even apart from their capacity to produce pleasure.[16]

Such acts are intrinsically good, Bradley and George conclude, because they involve the body and mind acting in a unified way, and toward the unified, unitary end of mating, where mating is understood as behavior specific to the species, and not as behavior that might further the couple's instrumental desire to conceive a baby:

> Mating is mating ... because it is the reproductive behavior characteristic of the species, or in Finnis's words, the behavior which, as behavior, is suitable for generation. Mating is ... an irreducibly unitive activity.... And, inasmuch as the interpersonal unity achieved in the mating—the reproductive type acts—of spouses is intrinsically good, spouses have a reason to mate quite irrespective of whether their mating will, or even can, be procreative.[17]

By contrast, all nonmarital sex

> suffers from at least one grave moral defect: Sex that is not for the intrinsic good of marriage itself—sex, that is to say, which is wholly instrumentalized to pleasure or some other goal—damages personal and interpersonal integrity by reducing persons' bodies to the status of means to extrinsic ends.... To treat one's own body ... as a pleasure inducing machine, for example, or as a mere instrument of procreation, is to alienate one part of the self, namely, one's consciously experiencing and desiring self, from another, namely, one's bodily self. But these parts are, in truth, metaphysically inseparable parts of the person as whole. Their existential separation in acts that instrumentalize the body for the sake of extrinsic goals, such as producing experiences desired purely for the satisfaction of the conscious self, disintegrates the acting person as such.[18]

Bradley and George's liberal critics have focused largely on the second, exclusionary prong of this argument: their claim that nonmarital sex, as they define it, is immoral. Thus, Professor Stephen Macedo, whose essay prompted the Bradley and George argument summarized above,[19] faults the neonatural lawyers, not so much for their view of the noninstrumental nature of marital sex and the intrinsic goodness of marriage, as for their failure to comprehend the possibility that other forms of sex might ground equally meaningful, basic goods, and equally good, meaningful relationships.[20] For example, pleasurable, affectionate, giving, and passionate sex, enjoyed within a committed, same-sex relationship, might constitute and actualize the intrinsic good of intense, interpersonal commitment, even if the sex is not of the "reproductive type," and even if the relationship is not one within which sex acts conducive to the reproduction of the species—mating—occur. If this is right, then even if Bradley and George are right about the nature of marital sex, Macedo suggests, and even if they are right to view marriage as they understand it as of intrinsic value, they are wrong to conclude that marriage is the only inter-personal relation of value, and the only interpersonal relation that might be partly constituted and actualized by sex, even of the nonreproductive sort, as of intrinsic value.[21] Their failure, in other words, is not in their conceptualization of sex and marriage; their failure is in their inability to imagine worthy alternatives to it.

But is marriage, as understood by George and Bradley, worth defending? Macedo largely concedes the point, asking instead whether George, Bradley, and other neonatural lawyers have failed to make the imaginative leap from their understanding of the goodness of heterosexual marriage, to the goodness of other forms of intimate association, including intimate associations of same-sex couples. It's also worth asking, however, albeit briefly, whether the marital sex that George and Bradley view as constitutive of marriage is truly the intrinsic good they claim. Are reproductive-type sexual acts, within marriage, of such moral significance, by virtue of their "actualization" of a two-in-one-flesh communion? It's hard to see what the argument for this assertion would be. Bradley and George clearly see the problem. The failure to see the special moral significance of these acts, Bradley and George assert, is likely caused by some sort of "cultural or environmental blockage" of correct understanding:

> Intrinsic value cannot, strictly speaking, be demonstrated. Qua basic, the value of intrinsic goods cannot be derived through a middle term. Hence, if the intrinsic value of marriage ... is to be affirmed, it must be grasped in noninferential acts of understanding. Such acts require imaginative reflection on data provided by incli-nation and experience, as well as knowledge of empirical patterns.... The practical insight that marriage ... has its own intelligible point, and that marriage as a one-flesh communion of persons is consummated and actualized in the reproductive-type acts of spouses, cannot be attained by someone who has no idea of what these terms mean; nor can it be attained, except with strenuous efforts of imagination by people who, due to personal or cultural circumstances, have little acquaintance with actual marriages thus understood. For this reason, we believe that whatever undermines the sound understanding and practice of marriage in a culture—including ideologies that are hostile to that understanding and practice—makes it difficult for people to grasp the intrinsic value of marriage and marital intercourse.[22]

They offer their hypothetical scenario, of the elderly couple spry enough to engage in coital reproductive-type sex acts, but no longer fertile and not having any pleasure from them, as an example that they hope will clarify the issues, if not prod that elusive understanding of the "intrinsic value" of "marital intercourse." So, let's look at it a little more closely. Is it really clear that this couple, who have no hope of conceiving a child and no expectation that the sex will be pleasurable, has a good reason to engage in sex? Is this sex *good,* solely by virtue of the fact that it is marital and of the type of activity conducive to the reproduction of the species?

I want to suggest that the example might inadvertently highlight the problems, and limits, of their view of the intrinsic moral significance of marital sex, at least as much as it highlights the opposite. And, whether or not that's so, it at least highlights an asymmetry. The reproductive-type sex act that George and Bradley view as having such heightened moral significance is the penetration of the wife's vagina by the husband's erect penis, followed, if physiologically possible, by his ejaculation. That is the reproductive-type act necessary for the reproduction of the species; that is what they mean by "mating." Note: the significant act is not the sexual penetration that *in fact* leads to the conception of a child, nor is it sexual penetration experienced as pleasurable—it is, solely, the sexual act that is of the type necessary to the reproduction of the species. Presumably, although Bradley and George do not mention it, and although it has not always been legally required, the act must be consensual on both sides, in order to have this moral significance. Thus, even if the act is marital and of the reproductive type, presumably if it is also rape, it is not morally justified, by George and Bradley's lights. We should then imply a third condition: sex, for George and Bradley, to be intrinsically morally good (and therefore justified) must be marital, meaning it must be between married partners, must be the penetration-ejaculation act necessary for the reproduction of the species, and must be consensual on both sides.

Even if the act is consensual, however, there nevertheless remains an asymmetry: the sex act Bradley and George valorize, taken alone, is far more likely to be pleasurable to the husband, than to the wife, by virtue of familiar facts of female and male anatomy. Women are less likely than men to take pleasure in the unadorned physical penetration of their vagina by a man's penis. Their proposed condition that the hypothetical couple of their imagining finds the sex mutually unpleasurable notwithstanding, the reproductive-type sex act, as described by Bradley and George, and even if consensual on both sides, is more conducive to male pleasure than it is to female. And, the pleasure that the husband might anticipate and welcome that accompanies the reproductive-type sex act (vaginal-penile penetration and ejaculation) is assuredly, Bradley and George tell us, morally acceptable.[23] That the male, but not the female, might experience pleasure as an experiential aspect of the unadorned penile-vaginal penetration, doesn't apparently vitiate the intrinsic good of the intercourse that constitutes marriage. Thus, the marital, reproductive sex act that the neonatural lawyers view as of such heightened moral significance, and that actualizes and constitutes the intrinsic good of marriage itself—is the subset of all sexual activity that is demonstrably and physiologically unpleasurable to women, in the main, but pleasurable, or at least satisfying, in the main, to men.

Does this asymmetry matter? Not, presumably, for George and Bradley, who neither mention nor discuss this as a problem. On their view, again, the pleasurable or unpleasurable nature of the sex, so long as it is marital, is of no consequence. Neither pleasure nor the satisfaction of desire is a good reason for engaging in sex. Pleasure or sexual satisfaction might at most be an innocent by-product, but it ought not be the desired end result. The lack of pleasure or desire is also not a sufficient reason to *not* engage in the intrinsically good act of marital sex, which is an intrinsic good. If the lack of desire or pleasure of both partners is not a sufficient reason to not engage in this intrinsically good act, presumably the lack of desire or pleasure of one partner, but not the other, is likewise not a sufficient reason. The conclusion, then, implied by their premises (also not expressed by them in this way) is that sex that is pleasurable, desired, satisfying, and wanted by the man, but unpleasurable, undesired, and unsatisfying by the woman, so long as it is a reproductive-type sex act, within marriage, and I suppose so long as it is consensual, and in their words "not repugnant" to either party, is morally good. Couples have a reason to engage in it.

Is *this* right? Again, neither Bradley nor George consider it a problem that the sex they regard as an intrinsic good will be, many times, for one but not the other of its participants, unpleasant. It ought to be a problem, though, for the rest of us, and thus it is somewhat surprising that Macedo, as far as I can find, has not noted it. Feminists, however, have. In thoughtful responses to Bradley and George, law professors (and feminist gay rights activists) Mary Becker[24] and Chai Feldblum[25] have both argued that the marital sex that Bradley and George valorize is likely to be far more conducive to male than female pleasure, and that this renders the sex they view as constitutive of marriage morally problematic. In my view, they are right, but the problem is deeper than they argue, precisely because the sex in question is marital sex. Decades, and perhaps centuries, of feminist advocacy and scholarship have tried to show that sex within marriage, performed without regard to a wife's pleasures or positive desires, can be positively injurious to women, both physically, psychically, and perhaps politically as well. Thus, by virtue of groundbreaking contemporary legal-social histories, we now know that nineteenth-century feminists fully realized that, in addition to obtaining the vote and control over their property, women could not possibly be equal until they also gained control, within marriage, of their bodies—and they used various euphemisms to describe the problem, to an audience not comfortable or familiar with explicit sexual discussion.[26] In the twentieth century, the tolerance of unwanted sex in the workplace and the marital rape exemption in marriage both became feminist targets in the 1970s.[27] Neither movement directly targeted unpleasurable, duty-driven marital sex, but nevertheless, both do by indirection: marital rape targets a particularly violent form of unwanted sex at home—nonconsensual, forced marital sex—and sex harassment targets a form of unwanted, and unpleasurable, albeit often nonviolent sex and sexual expression that occurs at work. Feminists in the 1960s, 1970s, and 1980s that were engaged in various women's health projects argued in a variety of ways that women, by all means including wives, should demand that the sex they engage in be pleasurable to them—not only for the sake of their pleasure, although that is no small matter, but also as a matter of entitlement and self-sovereignty.[28] In the seventies and eighties, radical feminists, most notably Andrea Dworkin, argued passionately that heterosexual intercourse, particularly marital intercourse, that was pleasurable to men but not women, was both paradigmatic of and constitutive of women's political subordination to men.[29] All of these arguments, so vastly different in tone, context, and historical setting, have a common thread: the sufferance of unpleasureable sex, particularly in the marital home, and even when it is consensual, evidences a very basic lack of self-sovereignty over one's body—a lack of self-sovereignty, furthermore, that might be particularly distinctive of women.

It should not be that hard for either liberals or conservatives to "imagine" that willingly engaging in unpleasureable and duty-driven sex, particularly over the course of a married lifetime, can contribute to a woman's sense of herself as unworthy, and if uninterrupted, can contribute to a very real form of subordination. (To borrow a page from both Bradley and George and their liberal interlocutors, perhaps the failure to see this is due to cultural or personal factors that "block understanding" and leads to a failure of perception.) A woman who engages in unpleasurable sex, and who feels or is powerless to withhold consent on the basis of her own lack of desire, not only engages in an action that evidences her lack of agency, she may well also be engaging in an action that, over time, actually robs her of agency. Physical boundaries are important indicia of self-sovereignty in virtually every other context imaginable.[30] We don't allow those boundaries to be crossed—in fact, we have elaborate bodies of constitutional law that sometimes prohibit the state from crossing them, without the consent of the sovereign, embodied individual.[31] Yet, women's bodies, in pregnancy and intercourse, are routinely physically penetrated and occupied. Both experiences, of course, may be joyous and beautiful and profoundly pleasurable, when consensual and when wanted, which they very often intensely are. But when they are only tolerated—not wanted—they are quite literally a physical invasion of the self. It is not irrational to assume that it is a form of invasion and occupation, furthermore that can induce feelings, and even the reality, of interpersonal submission to the person (or fetus) who occupies.

Thus, while we are right to worry, with Macedo, that the natural lawyer's defense of marriage carries with it an excessively punitive stance toward all nonmarital and nonreproductive-type sex, within as well as outside marriage, and an overly harsh stance toward pleasure generally,[32] we should also pause to worry over the quality of the marital sex that is so central to this defense of traditional marriage. That sex bears at least an unappealing family resemblance to the sex that feminists, for the last hundred and fifty years have tried, in various ways, using various forms of verbal indirection, to question, problematize, or minimize. Sex that is asymmetrically unpleasant for wives, but not husbands, and nevertheless performed, may be a part, even a substantial part, of an underlying subordinating dynamic. Women may consent to undesired and unpleasurable sex, in marriage, for all sorts of reasons: to maintain a peaceable household, out of friendship, out of love, or, as Bradley and George would have it, out of a moral sense of marital duty. If consensual, none of this sex is rape. But that doesn't make it morally good, much less, an intrinsic, basic human good. Indeed, it might make more sense to think of it as a basic human harm, and ironically for the same sort of reason that George and Bradley identify, but then attribute to gay sex rather than marital sex. George and Bradley worry that instrumental sex, particularly when instrumentalized to pleasure, dangers the self by "disintegrating" the desirous self that wishes and wills the sex, from the body that experiences the sex. The result is damage to personal (and interpersonal) "integrity."[33] They may, though, be right to worry about disintegration, but wrong to identify the distinct reality of the "desiring self" and the "experiencing self," of the person engaging in sex for pleasure, as exemplary of disintegration, and as thereby damaging integrity. This seems backward. Let me just raise as a possibility that the decision to willfully engage in unpleasurable sex, whether to secure the instrumental end of domestic peace, or to fulfill a sense of religious or marital duty, and to do so without regard for one's own pleasure or desire, far more than the decision to engage in sex-for-pleasure, can cause a "disintegration" of conscious mind and body, and damage personal integrity.[34] The choosing, preferring, willing self dissociates from the hedonic experiences of pain and pleasure that ideally, when a self is integrated, unite sensation, self-understanding, preference, and willed choice.

Where does this leave us? Bradley and George do cleanly articulate one understanding of the intrinsic value of marriage, and one description of the sexuality that marriage produces and legitimates. It is an understanding of the point of marriage, however, with dwindling appeal. It is not only up against a wall of hedonists, interested only in the pleasure to be had from instrumental sex, and legitimate challenges by feminists suspicious of asymmetrically unpleasurable sex within marriage. Most broadly, the neonatural lawyers' understanding of marriage and marital sex as expressive of an intrinsic good is undercut by a widely shared sense that marriage itself, to say nothing of the sex within it, *ought* to be of instrumental value: it ought to serve decent human ends, and ought to serve ends beyond the species' specific union of man and woman, actualized through penile-vaginal intercourse, valorized for no other reason than that that is the type of act by which the species reproduces. That marriage so understood might serve the teleological end of the species—mating—is just not sufficient to justify marriage institutionally, or any particular marriage individually, if the institution (or the particular marriage) turns out to be harmful or unjust on other grounds. Marriage, whatever the case for sex, needs to be useful, if it is to survive and be worthy of celebration. It must bring tangible benefits to the participants and to the larger society. It must do less harm than good, on average, for both participants and larger social interests, if we're going to continue with it.

Bradley and George's account of marriage does logically justify limiting marriage to one man-one woman: if they are right, then mating behavior is at the heart of marriage, and of all forms of justified human sexuality. It is only intercourse between one man and one woman that predictably leads to the reproduction of the species. But this does not sound like a compelling argument for marriage—at most, it sounds like a circular argument for defining marriage as a union of man and woman. On its own terms, it rests only on the bare claim that any particular marriage is an intrinsic good, when defined as they define it, and that the sex within it actualizes this intrinsic good and can and should serve no further human purpose. This is an explicitly and even aggressively purposeless view of both marriage and the sex that constitutes it. The sexuality that marriage ought to produce is disconnected from the production of pleasure, children, or intimacy. Children may be a gift of such unions, but they are not the point of them; pleasure might be produced, but must not be sought instrumentally, that marital partners might love and protect each other across time, likewise, might be a desirable and desired consequence of marital sex, but it cannot be the point. But it is this very "purposelessness"—a purposelessness that in their view is central to the moral significance of the sex within marriage—that renders the argument less than compelling to those of us who simply don't intuitively see the moral distinctiveness of purposeless, unpleasurable, nonreproductive marital sex of a reproductive form. As they state, if we identify the value of marriage, and the point of marriage, with the sex acts of reproductive form that constitute it, then same-sex marriage is indeed a "moral impossibility," and the institution of marriage itself is gravely threatened by irresponsible social change that contemplates just such an impossibility. Yet, if we identify the value and point of marriage with reproductive-type sex acts, marriage thus defined just does not seem all that valuable, intrinsically or otherwise. Surely, much more can and should be said on behalf of this institution, and its place in our lives, than that it actualizes the sort of sexual acts—penile-vaginal intercourse—that is generally necessary for the reproduction of the species.

Non–Neonatural Law Arguments Defending Traditional Marriage

Marriage need not be either defined or defended as the natural lawyers define it, and for most contemporary marriage defenders, it isn't. There are at least two non-natural law understandings of marriage that have appeared in the scholarly and advocacy literature that are more plausible, and that enjoy considerable currency in our contemporary debates. First, the value, or point of marriage, both personally and institutionally, might be that it leads to good lives—lives that are more financially secure, emotionally enriched, sexually satisfying, and companionate. Marriage, in short, has great utility. Second, the value of marriage might be that it creates a mode of living that is in some important sense relational, rather than individualistic, and grounded in responsibility and commitment, rather than in rights, entitlements, or consumption. It may generate a way of being that has some value, quite apart from its utility, but also quite apart from its natural "unitive" potential. The married individual is, essentially, committed to others, and commitment to others constitutes a good, and virtuous, way to live. If either utility or virtue (or both) is at the heart of marriage, then it might well be worthy of celebration, but not for the reasons identified by the neonatural lawyers; rather, marriage might be worthy of celebration because of the happiness it brings its participants and the virtue of the lives it structures. And, if this is the nature of marriage, and its point, the institution might well be threatened, but the nature of the threat is very different. It is not threatened by the prospect of "same-sex marriage," or even by the mere social acceptability of alternative life styles. Rather, it is threatened by inadequate appreciation of the added value marriage brings to life, thus diminishing the felt desirability of the institution. If utility (understood broadly) is the value and point of marriage, then it is threatened by the prevalence of conditions that render marriage an unavailable or unattractive choice, for many, but particularly for poor women. If commitment and responsibility are central to the point, definition, and promise of marriage, then marriage is threatened, above all, by a consumption and production-driven economy, that encourages a way of being that valorizes, above all else, individual gain, individual achievement, and individual wealth.

These arguments, of course, overlap: the reason marriage has great utility, according to its utilitarian defenders, is partly because of the commitment that is at its heart, and the reason that commitment is characteristic of a virtuous way of life, is in part, that it leads to a life that is good, and—no small matter—happier, than otherwise. Nevertheless, the arguments are very different, and at various points might point in different directions. I'll take them up sequentially below.

The Utilitarian Defense of Civil Marriage

The instrumental or utilitarian case for civil marriage is straightforward and robust. Marriage is very good for participants, and for the children they produce. According to a vast and growing body of scientific research, much of it pioneered by Professor Linda Waite and journalist Mary Gallagher, married people are simply better off than their otherwise comparably situated co-citizens, and on virtually every standard traditional measure of utility: wealth, health, and happiness.[35] Marriage improves our enjoyment of life, our security against risk, and significantly increases our net worth. Children likewise fare far better in marriage than outside of it.[36] We would be foolish indeed to blithely toss it overboard, either individually or societally.

Start with happiness. Married women and men both are more satisfied with their personal lives than are single, widowed, or divorced women and men.[37] Married individuals of both sexes report higher rates of satisfaction with their sex lives, and also report having more sex, and by substantial margins.[38] Marital happiness also seems to be something that improves as we age: participants in second marriages are happier than those who divorce and remain single[39] but more significantly, unhappy marriages, if they are not physically abusive, tend to improve over time, bearing out the adage regarding the seven-year itch.[40] Stick it out, endure the rough spots, and happier years to come will be yours. Couples and married individuals reporting low satisfaction with their marriages in the early years, if they stick with it, tend to report higher rates of satisfaction as they age.

On wealth, the evidence is if anything even stronger: marriage increases both accumulated wealth and earned income. Married women earn more than single women, although mothering brings the income of both groups down, compared with married or single women (respectively) who are not mothers.[41] (Thus, the real "wage gap" is between mothers and nonmothers of both sexes, not so much between women and men. Another way to put the same point is that *mothering*—not gender alone and not parenting alone—accounts for the difference between women and men's wages, as reflected in the often-cited statistic that women earn 69 cents for every dollar earned by men. If we compare only nonmothering women [whether married or not] with all men [whether or not they are fathers] much of the wage gap disappears.) Married men earn substantially higher incomes than unmarried men; this is by now such a widely recognized phenomenon as to have earned a moniker: the "marriage premium."[42] Married individuals likewise have accumulated more wealth than single people.[43] Married couples buy homes, invest a significant part of their income, and manage their assets routinely and competently; single people, unmarried mothers, and cohabiting individuals with or without children do all of this only sporadically. Mothering and not marrying in conjunction has particularly severe effects on wealth: single mothers are the poorest cohort of adults, both in terms of income and in terms of accumulated wealth.[44] Divorce also depletes the wealth of mothers, and much more so than it does that of fathers.[45] Finally, married individuals are far better protected against economic downtowns or personal economic debacles than single individuals. All of this now leads some researchers to refer to marriage as the "best insurance plan around."[46] Whether or not that's true metaphorically, it's clear that married individuals are far more likely to be literally insured than unmarried individuals, for the simple reason that employers' health plans routinely cover the nonworking spouses and other dependents of employees. For this and a host of other reasons, married couples weather economic storms, so to speak, far better than their unmarried counterparts.

Likewise, on health. Married couples do better than unmarried or divorced individuals, cohabitants, or single parents, on all standard measures of health.[47] Married persons live longer, suffer from fewer long-term debilitating illnesses, and have healthier life styles.[48] Married persons are less prone to obesity, less likely to smoke and drink to excess, less likely to have and transmit sexually transmitted diseases. They are more likely to make use of preventive health care: they make and keep regular medical and dental appointments for themselves and their children. They are far more likely to have health insurance. Men experience the greater "health premium" from marriage, benefiting from their wives' health-conscious attention to diet and doctors both,[49] but women likewise enjoy a significant, if not as substantial a boost in their overall health.[50] Lastly, married women are now less likely to suffer from domestic violence, or violence from intimates, than cohabitants.[51] Both married men and women are less likely to be victimized by violence inflicted by strangers or acquaintances as well. Married women are less likely than unmarried women to be victims of rapes by strangers or acquaintances.[52] The research on all of these findings—that marriage makes individual participants healthy, wealthy, and relatively happy—is vast, and for the most part undisputed.[53]

A comparably solid body of research has examined the impact of marriage on the well-being of children, and with if anything even clearer results.[54] Children who live out their childhood in intact families, with both marital partners in the same home, fare far better than children of single parents or divorced parents. They are less prone to suffer the consequences of poverty. They are less sickly, and more inclined to be insured against illness and disease. They get better medical care. They have better educational prospects. They are less at risk of dropping out of school, and more likely to attend postsecondary schooling. They have better diets and healthier lifestyles. They are more likely as adults to secure meaningful employment. They are themselves more likely to marry, as adults, and to do so successfully, thus passing (and magnifying) the marriage premiums on to their own offspring, likewise.

Why does *marriage* have these somewhat startlingly utile effects? There are, of course, a few caveats, quibbles, and qualifications more than worth noting. Most important, perhaps, some of the positive benefits of marriage are a consequence of the favorable treatment married partners receive from law and the private sector both. That married partners are better insured, for example, is a function of the fact that insurance plans held by employers for their employees typically cover spouses, and only sometimes cover partners. Unemployed spouses are thus more likely to be insured than unemployed single people or unemployed non-marital partners, but this is because of the structure of insurance, not the superior capacity of marriage as a family form to induce responsible behavior. Likewise, married women suffer less domestic violence than unmarried women, but that is in part because married women and women in marital-type relationships are the beneficiaries of state-sponsored programs targeting domestic violence between married spouses, including provisions for heightened penalties against abusers, the availability of civil restraining orders, and better access to police and judicial intervention.[55] These state- or employer-sponsored benefits bestowed on married people might well provide an individual with a pragmatic reason to marry. But they clearly don't suggest a reason to societally value marriage: if we're rewarding people who marry, it ought to be for some reason pertaining to the institution of marriage, and not simply because they are doing well by virtue of the benefits of the rewards they receive upon marrying. As Law Professor Anita Bernstein cogently argues in her thorough critique of Waite and Gallagher's thesis,[56] it is not an argument for the institution of marriage to show that married people do better than unmarried people, if the reason they do better is because we treat them better.

Nevertheless, the research (as well as common sense) shows substantial rewards of marriage that go well beyond the legal entitlements married partners receive.[57] The commitment of a marriage seems to be truly good for people who make it, financially, emotionally, physically, and even sexually. Married people, so the research shows, tend to plan better, regard each other more highly, pool their skills and talents and wealth more efficiently and productively, and take each other into account in their decisionmaking, with more regularity and more focused attention, and higher payoffs, than either cohabitators, single persons, or romantically or emotionally entangled unmarried people. If we leave aside the additional wealth that is a function of legal entitlements, there is still a "marriage premium." It is important to try to understand why.

The major researchers and theorists in this subfield have provided a range of answers, but there are some commonalities. We might synthesize from their speculations and their analyses a two-part answer. The first sort of reason, suggested by Linda Waite's research, has to do with the nature of commitment: commitment alone brings significant benefits.[58] Waite identifies four: 1) a long-term contract allows partners to make choices that carry immediate costs but eventually bring benefits, 2) commitment permits a sharing of economic and social resources in a form of coinsurance against life's uncertainties, 3) commitment allows for economies of scale and specialization of labor, and 4) commitment connects each partner to the connections of the other (such as in-laws) that are themselves a source of benefit and value. There are no doubt other benefits that flow from commitment as well. For one thing, a lifelong commitment to another person gives us an additional incentive to plan so as to further our own welfare-based future, as well as a resource on which to draw, when either planning for or experiencing future downturns. Commitment both gives us a good reason to plan for our future security, and it makes it easier to do so. It gives us a partner to whom we are obligated to do what we can to ensure our own future security and health, as well as a partner whose job it is, so to speak, to "drop everything and be there," when we ourselves encounter a crisis in life. It gives us an awareness of future risks as an object of our concern, both for our partner and for ourselves, because of our responsibility to our partner. This is an other-regarding and future-regarding orientation toward life, and even toward time, that is more conducive to happiness than relentless "presentism" and, simply, narcissism. Second, a solid, no-holds-barred, unqualified commitment to another also gives us peace of mind, or a resting place, with respect to the central romance in our lives: we know who we love, and who loves us, so we are not in a perpetual state of emotional exploration, uncertainty, or agitation. Third, commitment and the security it gives us make our daily routines easier, particularly when children enter the picture. It is easier—far less stressful—to share life's hassles.

These sorts of reasons alone, however, do not explain the utility of civil marriage, per se, over and above that of cohabitation, at least when the latter is combined with a serious private commitment to a lifelong union. Marriage, as the song goes and as is endlessly repeated in the scholarship, is physically no more than a piece of paper: Why should it matter? What does the public marriage add to the private commitment? Here, researchers have increasingly turned to explanations drawn from a growing body of social science scholarship regarding the impact of "social norms" on our overall well-being.[59] Contrary to pop songology, according to the "social norms" scholars, "marriage" is far more than the piece of paper on which the license is issued. "Marriage" is a set of norms of conduct, social expectations, and rules of behavior. Marriage-as-norm tells us how to behave. Such guidance—such norms—might be restrictive of our precious individual liberty, but nevertheless, the guidance that norms provide, even in adult life, makes life easier. The "marriage norm" is particularly potent. It tells us what to expect of ourselves and our spouse when we marry, and it tells us that if we fall short, we can expect social opprobrium in the bargain. It tells us to take care of our spouse, and to take care of ourselves so that we might better do so, and to take care of our children, and to plan for the future, and so on. Most important, perhaps, it tells us that this is indeed a good way to live; it confers what some authors call "impersonal value" on a mode of being.[60] By so doing, it limits choice and endless speculation over the question "how should I live?" just as the choice of a marital partner limits choice and sexual experimentation on the question "with whom shall I be intimate?" That limitation can reduce a barrage of sensation, doubt, and unanswerable questions with which we'd otherwise be plagued. If we accept the norm, the norm alone makes our choice to live within marriage a prima facie good one. It is sort of a presumptive judgment: the state, community, society, and tradition sanction marriage, because marriage is a good way to live—therefore, marriage is a good way to live. Marriage makes us feel good, in part, because the state and our community tell us we are good, by virtue of participating.

Of course, if we look a little closer at some of these findings, the picture is not quite so rosy. Married, cohabiting, and dating women, collectively, suffer from violence committed by intimates, more than single women suffer from the violence of strangers, collectively.[61] This does not speak well of the nature of intimacy, marital or otherwise. Women's overall economic well-being improves with marriage, but the incomes of both married and single women drop precipitously when mothering enters the picture. The same is flatly not true of fathering. This suggests something is very wrong with our understanding of the relation between work, career, and productivity, on the one hand, and mothering, on the other, or alternatively that something is amiss with our understanding of the relation between fathering and mothering.[62] Third, while marriage overall is a good bargain for both sexes, bad marriages are very bad for the mental health and happiness of both, and worse, apparently, for women than for men.[63] Fourth, women continue to be hurt, financially, by divorce, making the bad marriage, for some women, mandatory.[64] And finally, women's utility gains in marriage overall are not as great as men's: marriage makes women and men wealthier, but men more so than women, a difference that turns out to matter a lot at divorce. Marriage improves the health and longevity of men and women, but the health benefit is greater for men than women, and general happiness likewise, a difference that turns out to be quite substantial in unhappy marriages.[65] None of this implies that marriage is not overall a good bargain for women. It does mean that it is not as good a bargain for women as it is for men and that it is a greater risk for women than men: even good marriages don't give women as sizeable a premium, and bad marriages are worse for women than for men. It also means that mothering, but not fathering, is not a good deal for those who undertake it, in turn suggesting that there is something fundamentally unfair with the structure of family and work life, viewed as an institution that structures caregiving—rather than as an institution that simply structures intimacy.

Entirely aside from the contested magnitude of the greater utility to men and women of both good and bad marriages, that there is a difference at all is consequential, on both utilitarian and nonutilitarian grounds. As a number of feminist political philosophers, including Susan Okin in the 1980s,[66] and more recently Law Professor Linda McClain,[67] have argued, families are the arena in which children acquire the values they will carry into adulthood and citizenship. If the family is fundamentally unjust, this does not bode well for the sense of justice of adults so nurtured. Children who are raised in a violent household are obviously scarred in well-documented ways. But the greater number of children raised in homes in which traditional mothers are not battered, but are routinely put down, or humiliated, or treated with contempt by their husbands, are also internalizing the normalcy of inequality and the acceptability of injustice. If a mother and wife has acquiesced in all of this—if she thinks of the disregard, lack of compensation, and lack of respect that she encounters daily as just one face of her altruism, or of her mothering obligations, or of her religious duty—then the children, and particularly the girls, so raised will learn as well some deep lessons about the connections between lack of power and self-debasement. Minimally, they will all—boys and girls—learn that caregiving labor, while in some obvious sense absolutely necessary for the survival of the species, is not valued. It should not be surprising if, as citizens, their public choices reflect that lesson.

Nevertheless, the utilitarian case for marriage is a robust one, if one is looking at the health, wealth, and happiness of participants. People are better off married, on average. Individual welfare improves, once married, for women as well as men. Marriage, in brief, is good for you. If this is right, it is an important finding, and not only for utilitarians. Physical and mental health, wealth, happiness, longevity, sexual satisfaction—these do sound, to many of us, like "intrinsic goods," more so, perhaps, than the intrinsic good of the "two-in-one-flesh" identified by Bradley and George as the definitional moral good of marriage. And, if the empirical claims hold, then Waite, Gallagher, and their colleagues present a fully coherent and eminently reasonable response to the question: "Why marriage?" Or, "What is its point?" The moral good of civil marriage, if their research holds, is the good, improved lives that are led within them, or the greater probability that good lives will indeed be led within them. The moral good of marriage is the greater utility, defined capaciously, to which it leads. The point of the institution is that it gives us a way to organize our lives in such a way as to increase significantly our chance at a happy and long life.

More precisely, civil marriage, as compared with private commitment ceremonies, unadulterated personal promises, nontraditional family forms, informal cohabitation, or single life, gives us an impersonal structure, validated by historical and current social norms, within which to mold our own expectations and aspirations for our own and our partner's intimate lives. It gives us confidence that the form we've adapted to—a committed intimate relationship—is a good one. It gives us answers to questions that would otherwise overwhelm us—How should I organize my intimate life? Should I be intimate with one, or a multitude? Should I hope for a monogamous relationship that endures, or will serial monogamy best suit my nature? Is this relationship as good for me today as it was yesterday? Should I stick with it? Psychological and emotional ease, or resolution, on those questions gives us some peace and no small degree of security. The result, apparently, is increased wealth, improved health, and a dollop of happiness and sexual satisfaction to boot. That's nothing to dismiss lightly.

Some Reservations Regarding the Utilitarian Case for Marriage

On the other hand, is the utility of civil marriage really all that we need to know, in order to fully answer doubts about marriage's goodness? There are at least three problems with this strong utilitarian argument for the institution of marriage. The first is simply that the utilitarian defense of marriage (or accounting of marriage) is overwhelmingly concerned with the utility of the institution of marriage *to its participants*—husbands, wives, and children—and virtually ignores the harms done *by* marriage to nonparticipants and the overall social order. That marriage is extremely beneficial to participants doesn't mean it is a generally good institution, even on strictly utilitarian terms. Both the institution of marriage and the promarriage rhetoric that its defenders generate might harm nonparticipants, and if the harm is great enough, it may outweigh whatever gains in health and wealth accrue to participants. Second, the institution of marriage may be unjust, even if utile, and if so, it is morally problematic, even for the individuals it well serves. And third, the utilitarian defense of marriage may not be as strong as it first appears, even on its own terms. I'll take these problems up in that order.

Harms to Nonparticipants

There are two distinct ways the institution of marriage, particularly in our current political climate, may be harming nonparticipants. The first might be called harms "of exclusion," and the second, harms "of legitimation." By harms of exclusion, I mean not only that the goods of marriage will not be available to those individuals or couples who are excluded, by definition, from its reach. The problem is greater than that. The institution of marriage, and particularly its moralistic rhetoric, might do affirmative harm to those it excludes. We will take these exclusionary harms up in detail in the next two chapters, as they are central to the arguments made both by critics, for ending marriage altogether, and by reformers, for retaining it but in substantially modified form. Here, just consider briefly the possibility, and only by way of example, that the institution of marriage, as currently constructed, might damage, rather than enhance, the lives of those lesbians and gay citizens who wish to parent, and who wish to do so within a marriage, but cannot, because of the definitional restrictions of marriage to opposite-sex couples. The institution of marriage, if viewed as the optimal or only acceptable family structure within which to parent, but from which gay and lesbian parents are excluded, puts those partners to the choice of having children outside of marriage, with the various penalties that imposes, or not having children at all. Those who decide not to parent will sacrifice the considerable joys of parenthood (and the children they may have otherwise bore or adopted will be deprived of the "family premium" that benefits children of intact marriages). Those who parent anyway will not only be deprived of the various "marriage premiums" relating to parenthood accorded to married, heterosexual parents. They will also encounter considerable friction by virtue of their desire to parent outside of traditional marriage. The partner of a biological parent may or may not be able to adopt the child, depending upon the state's law, and the couple, should they choose to adopt a child not biologically related to either of them, may find it virtually impossible to do so, and will in any event find it considerably more difficult than a married couple.[68] The nonadoptive and nonbiological parent will not have the legal entitlements of a legal parent, ranging from insurance coverage typically extended to spouses of employees, to visiting room privileges, should the child fall ill.[69] The couple will face considerable uncertainty, with respect to custody and all related legal issues, should they separate.[70] They will often face hostile or uncertain school officials. And depending on where they live, they will face some degree of social disapproval. Their children will, to some degree, suffer from these consequences as well. These parents might be better off in a world in which the institution of marriage did not exist, than in a world in which marriage exists, but from which they are excluded.

The second type of harm to nonparticipants, which I call "legitimation," is less obvious but may be more consequential. The wealth, happiness, and health enhancing effects of marriage might legitimate our societal inclination to underserve the needs of the least well off among us, and might as a consequence actually worsen the prospects of those who cannot partake of marriage's largesse. If marriage is a "way out of poverty," for example, as many utilitarian marriage proponents now claim, and even more so, if it is the "*best* way out of poverty," then there is that much less of a need for social programs that target poverty, from Social Security, to publicly provided health care, to childcare, to minimum wage guarantees, and so forth. The solution to one's poverty, if we take this argument seriously (as we should) is to marry. If one chooses not to marry, well then, one has "chosen" poverty. If poverty is a chosen lifestyle, then it is of no moral concern to the community. The wealth-enhancing qualities of marriage, in short, combined with a firm belief that those who wish to marry surely can do so, and that those who choose not to marry have earned their fate, thus "legitimate," in the minds of those who might otherwise be inclined to act, a passive nonresponsiveness to poverty, and particularly to the impoverished conditions of single mothers. This is what I'm calling the "legitimation harm" of marriage.

This is not simply an abstract or fanciful worry. Let me describe in some detail one way in which the profoundly moralistic and intensely legitimating rhetoric that swirls around the institution of marriage may today be doing real harm to poor people in general, but more specifically to poor women who mother, and who for various reasons are not married, and to their children. First, go back about ten years. Recall that in 1996, a Republican Congress, spurred on by President Bill Clinton, passed the Personal Responsibility and Work Opportunity Reconciliation Act (PRWORA),[71] the main purpose of which, in Clinton's memorable phrase, was to "end welfare as we know it"—meaning, end the federal guarantee of income assistance to poor and unmarried mothers.[72] As its name was meant to suggest, the underlying philosophy behind the Personal Responsibility and Work Opportunity Reconciliation Act was, in part, to shift responsibility for the well-being of poor children off of government, and off of society, and off of the community, and off of the "village," where, as a result of the misguided welfare policies of the past it had come to roost, and back on to the shoulders of the families, parents, and mothers of the children themselves, where it more properly belongs. The way this shift of responsibility was to occur, primarily, was by ending the "welfare entitlement" of poor mothers to federal assistance. Instead, states were to condition governmental assistance to poor mothers on the mothers' willingness to work. Furthermore, the period of time she would be entitled to this conditional help would be limited, rather than open-ended, as it was under the old "Aid to Families With Dependent Children" regime. Toward these ends, the act required states that were to receive "block grants" from federal coffers for "Temporary Aid to Needy Families" (so named to underscore the temporary nature of the assistance) to limit the period of time a needy mother may receive aid for her family;[73] it permitted states to cap the number of children she can have for whom she will be able to seek aid,[74] and it required states to impose work or job training requirements as a condition of aid.[75] Thus, today, because of the 1996 law (and its various reauthorizations), a poor mother can receive aid, but only for a limited number of children, and only for a set period of time, and only if she can demonstrate that she is employed or receiving job training. She cannot expect aid for all of her children, she cannot expect the aid to continue until they reach the age of maturity, and she cannot expect to receive any aid at all if she is not working or in training. All of this was a substantial departure from "welfare as we knew it" as it had existed from the time of its origins, in the early decades of the twentieth century, through 1996. Mothers, by the Clinton-era reform, were admonished to take "personal responsibility" for the well-being of their children. They were to do so through availing themselves of "work opportunities." Welfare, understood as an entitlement to aid simply by virtue of one's parenting in poverty, was dead.

This much is familiar history. What is not so well understood is that the 1996 act was not then, and most assuredly is not today, simply a "back to work" statute requiring that poor mothers work as a condition of receiving state aid. For many of its authors (although, likely, not for Clinton himself), the law aimed to encourage not just work, and perhaps not primarily work, but rather, *marriage* as the alternative to old-style welfare dependency. Again, although this is not widely understood, the original law itself clearly reflected both goals. Thus, under PRWORA, states were rewarded with "bonuses" for bringing down the rate of out-of-wedlock births,[76] as well as for investing resources in obtaining child support payments from fathers, the proceeds of which reimburse the state for the welfare grant itself.

In the subsequent reauthorizations of PRWORA during the Bush years, however, this "marriage promotion" aspect of the law has come, increasingly, to occupy center stage.[77] As a result of Bush-era reforms, states are now encouraged, through bonuses administered through PRWORA, to use some of their block money to establish and run "marriage training" sessions, the purpose of which is to advise and educate poor men and women, both married and unmarried, in the relational skills required to maintain a healthy marriage. States are encouraged to use portions of their block money to mount effective public relations campaigns explaining to the public the economic and emotional benefits of marriage. Under the proposed 2006 amendments to PRWORA, currently being debated in Congress as this book goes to press, the work requirements (if they pass) will be stiffened, the current rules permitting high school and college training to "count" as "work" will be eliminated or cut back, and the resources devoted to all of the marriage promotion efforts will be substantially increased.[78] Marriage promotion efforts, overall, will be enhanced. "Welfare reform" today means, increasingly, not promotion of the work ethic, but rather, promotion of marriage.

What was the "point," then, given this recent history, of the welfare reform act of 1996, of the 2002 reauthorization, and of the current proposed amendments? There is no simple answer to that question. Clearly, the work ethic rhetoric and the title of the act notwithstanding, the point even in 1996 was never to simply encourage all mothers to join the workforce, to take personal responsibility for their families by assuming the responsibilities, rights, and paychecks of meaningful employment, and to thereby economically empower them in a contemporary work-oriented society. Clinton might well have wished it—his recent musings on the tenth anniversary of the passage of the act indicate as much[79]—but—reality check!—the minimum wage jobs the vast majority of these young mothers were and are taking up, as they transfer from welfare to work, don't empower anybody.[80] Nor was the aim of the reform to improve the parenting of these poor children. As all parties were acutely aware, requiring very poor young women and girls with babies and small toddlers at home to work or go to school, puts severe strains on their parenting and on the resources and time they can devote to parenting.[81] The effect of PRWORA, a number of researchers now worry, might be to *weaken* the bond between poor mothers and their children. Nor was the goal simply to lift these families out of poverty by transferring them from welfare to paying jobs. Early on, it seemed as though it might have had that affect (regardless of whether it was the goal): the original welfare reform bill of 1996, coupled with a hike in the minimum wage, generous assistance with childcare and transportation vouchers, and an earned income tax credit for low-income workers, and perhaps most important, coincident with a growing economy, lifted some welfare-to-work families from poverty. Since 2000, though, as the economy has soured, and without subsequent increases in the minimum wage, the gains in poverty reduction among poor mothers and their children have been reversed, and if anything the poverty rate of single mothers is now worsening.[82]

It is important to remember, given this mixed record on the goal of empowerment-through-work, that according to the drafters *themselves,* a major goal of the act was not to send people to paid employment, but rather, to end the "problem" of "out-of-wedlock" births. For many, this was the act's primary goal, as was made vividly clear by the "Legislative Findings"[83] that can be found in the act's very first chapter. Just the first five of these findings are worth quoting:

(1) Marriage is the foundation of a successful society.

(2) Marriage is an essential institution of a successful society which promotes the interests of children.

(3) Promotion of responsible fatherhood and motherhood is integral to successful child rearing and the well-being of children.

(4) In 1992, only 54 percent of single-parent families with children had a child support order established and, of that 54 percent, only about one-half received the full amount due. Of the cases enforced through the public child support enforcement system, only 18 percent of the caseload has a collection.

(5) The number of individuals receiving aid to families with dependent children (in this section referred to as 'AFDC') has more than tripled since 1965. More than two-thirds of these recipients are children. Eighty-nine percent of children receiving AFDC benefits now live in homes in which no father is present.

At the tail end of twenty-five such Findings, the section concludes: "Therefore, in light of this demonstration of the crisis in our Nation, it is the sense of the Congress that prevention of out-of-wedlock pregnancy and reduction in out-of-wedlock birth are very important Government interests and the policy contained in part A of title IV of the Social Security Act (as amended by section 103(a) of this Act) is intended to address the crisis."

These "legislative findings," the promarriage rhetoric that surrounded its initial passage, the Bush administration's "marriage initiative" that accompanied the act's reauthorization in 2002, and the prominence of the promarriage movement in the current legislative battle to amend it, all jointly suggest that PRWORA was originally and even more so is today intended to drive home the message that parenting outside of marriage is irresponsible, and to drive home that message, in part, by making that parenting difficult—more difficult than under the discredited regime of "welfare."[84] Now of course, the bottom line legal imperative of the act—the sovereign's command, so to speak—was and still is to transform poor mothers into workers, by conditioning their TANF payments on demonstrated employment. But the social norm the act conveys, if we take seriously, as we should, the marriage promotion measures as well as the work requirement, and if we attend, as we should, to the act's own proclaimed findings and goals, is *not* that poor mothers *should* be workers. The message, rather, is that poor mothers should be *wives*, and wouldn't be so poor (and such a burden to the taxpayer) if they were wives. The "problem" identified by the findings in the act, is not poverty, and is not unemployed parents, but rather, out-of-wedlock births, and the solution to the problem, the act suggests, is not full employment of poor women at decent family wages, to say nothing of the community-based childcare that would facilitate it, but rather, marriage. Work, in short, is the stick that the act uses to push women toward different, and more responsible, choices. Work, and the responsibility, enhanced standard of living, and engagement with the outside world it represents, is *not* the carrot.

The conclusion a poor mother or a poor woman contemplating motherhood should reach, the legislation can be read to imply, is that if she wishes to mother she would be better off with a husband than with either a welfare entitlement or a paycheck, or, she would be better off not having children at all. Ideally, she should turn to a husband, not the state or an employer, to support her when she is herself rendered dependent by virtue of her mothering. Critics of welfare reform, particularly feminists, have often criticized the welfare reform movement of the nineties as well as the aughts for its apparent hypocrisy: forcing poor women into the workplace is seemingly at odds with the "family values" orientation of the conservative wing of the Republican Party, that more typically espouses the value of at-home mothering.[85] But there is no inconsistency, if we take very seriously, as we should, the act's own expressed understanding of the problem. If we keep front and center the promotion of marriage, rather than the reduction of poverty, as the goal of this welfare reform law, we can easily spell the argument out in a way that removes any inconsistency. Old-fashioned welfare is not a good way to live, the law's authors can be read as saying, but neither is out-of-wedlock work and mothering. With or without state assistance, work is not compatible with mothering small children in impoverished conditions—the lack of transportation, high-quality childcare, meaningful jobs with health insurance, and a family wage all render both responsible work life and responsible parenting illusory—and the act does very little to rectify any of this. The "social norm" the act embodies is *not* that women with children should work, and that if they do so, the state will guarantee them dignified work, a living wage, decent benefits, health care, and the possibility to engage in responsible parenting. Rather, the point is that poor women who want to mother ought to *marry*. They should be dependent upon a breadwinner, rather than work for low wages that are eaten up by childcare in any event. This, after all, is the natural, or prelegal reality: mothers can't be wage earners without either spousal or community support. So, mothers in need of a wage should be married, and dependent upon their husbands, at least while children are young. The "personal responsibility" to which the act makes reference in the title, then, is not the personal responsibility of holding down a job. More pervasively, it is the responsible decision to either have children only if and when married, or to forego having children. If one desires children, the responsible, moral thing to do is marry a breadwinner.

What have been the consequences of welfare reform? First look at what it has not done. It did not bring poor women and their children out of poverty. Poverty rates of poor mothers and children fell between 1996 and 2000 as the economy grew, and then rose again from 2000 to 2004, but in neither case did either the work requirements of welfare reform, or the promotion of marriage, lead to such substantial increases in the income of poor women as to make them not poor.[86] In some cases, the reform actually exacerbated poverty, and its ill effects on families. Some unclear percentage of women (10–20 percent is what is often reported, but the researchers all note that this is an unreliable figure) who leave the welfare rolls cannot find or sustain work, and wind up having no income whatsoever.[87] Other families suffer by virtue of the "family cap"[88]—the refusal of some states to give aid to families over a certain size. For these families, welfare reform, and the marriage rhetoric that fuels it, has been disastrous. One researcher explains:

> The outstanding negative feature of welfare reform was the family cap.... By reducing welfare benefits relative to family size, the family cap made it very difficult for parents to provide the basic necessities of life for their children (e.g., food, clothing, diapers, housing, and transportation to the doctor). The family cap presented parents with additional challenges in providing material, cultural and educational opportunities for their children. By limiting parents' purchasing power, low grant levels also contributed to difficulties protecting children from harm (e.g., by forcing families to live in dangerous neighborhoods).... Thus the family cap's effects are an example of how severe poverty conditions can render effective care and protection of children a virtual impossibility.
>
> On the whole, parents in this study experienced poverty-related conditions as chronic stressors.... But depth of poverty also mattered.... [S]evere poverty

conditions can overwhelm some parents' psychological and material coping skills, and render them incapable of effectively caring for and protecting their children in spite of the love they may feel for them. Welfare reforms such as the family cap, which facilitate severe poverty conditions, will also impinge upon and potentially disable the caregiving capacities of some parents—with serious consequences for children.[89]

Nor has the act succeeded in its stated aim of bringing down the incidence of out-of-wedlock births, thereby increasing—through attrition, so to speak—the number of married, two-parent households among the working poor.[90] There has been a slight uptick in the number of two-adult *households*, but apparently virtually the entire increase is a function of an increase in the number of women choosing to live with men who are not the biological fathers of their children.[91] The act has not raised marriage rates, or measurably deterred women from having children outside of marriage.[92]

Why not? Why hasn't the act had the effect its designers intended? One explanation proffered by some researchers is that the act was premised on a false assumption. The welfare reformers sought to bring down the incidence of out-of-wedlock births, primarily by changing the incentives of women who choose to mother outside of marriage, and all on the assumption that their "decision" not to marry, albeit irrational, was fully voluntary, and hence reversible. If poor women and girls who mother do so outside of marriage because of a willful stubbornness, or a foolish or immoral resistance to the idea of marriage, they can be encouraged to change their minds: remove the support for such bad decisions. The assumption, however, on which the conclusion was based, might well have been false, and might well be false. The reason that poor mothers don't marry before they mother may not be because they willfully choose not to out of loose morals or otherwise.

In an excellent summary and discussion of research on the point, Kathryn Edin and Maria Kefalas, in an influential book-length treatment of the subject entitled *Promises I Can Keep,* have shown that women on welfare are if anything *more* inclined to value marriage and marital ways of life than their more affluent peers.[93] Rather, poor women who mother don't marry, when they don't, Edin and Kefalas argue, generally because, *for them,* whatever may be the overall or average utility of marriage, marrying the fathers of their children would in fact jeopardize their own wealth and health, as well as that of their dependents, not improve it. The fathers of the "out-of-wedlock babies" born to poor women are often neither employed nor employable, or alternatively, they are employed at such low paying jobs that they would have little to offer economically. They lack skills, and the market lacks the jobs for their unskilled labor. According to Edin and Kefalas, the mothers view the fathers of their children as yet another dependent, and quite reasonably seek to minimize, not maximize, the negative effect of their dependency by not marrying them. They don't marry, in short, for pretty much the same reasons that the act presupposes they ought: they don't marry because they fear that if they did so, it would decrease their own wealth and that of their children. Their fears are not unreasonable. The act did nothing to change any of this. It did not target the job market for poor young men as a reason—perhaps the major reason—for the low marriage rates among poor people. It did not seriously address the lack of job skills of many of these childrens' fathers. It did nothing to actually make marriage possible for those women who want to mother, but for whom marriage is not a viable option. Under the 2002 reauthorization, some states now conduct "marriage skills" courses, the point of which is to help young couples navigate the emotional terrain of joint living and parenting. There's nothing wrong with such courses, and although yet untested they may well have a positive effect on the relational skills of poor people, no less than similar counseling has helped middle-class couples who pay for it. Such courses, however, do nothing toward making the marriage itself more likely than not to occur.

What has the act accomplished? To its credit, the act has indeed moved substantial numbers of women from being nonworking welfare recipients, under the old law, to either working and receiving TANF, or leaving welfare altogether for work. Many women have benefited both psychically and psychologically from being wage earners, who would not have so benefited, but for the act. For these women and their children, the net effect of the welfare reform act—meaning primarily the work and school requirement—has been positive. But there have been negative repercussions as well. One consequence of the 1996 Personal Responsibility and Work Opportunity Reconciliation Act is that poor women who are now wage earners as well as mothers spend less time with their children.[94] The act requires a certain number of hours spent at work or in job training, and those hours will, perforce, be hours spent apart from dependents.[95] For some mothers and for some children, this is not a welcome development. And, as noted, welfare reform in its entirely has clearly worsened the situation of many mothers and their children— primarily, the women and children whose assistance is terminated by virtue of the family cap and the five-year limit—who cannot find or sustain employment, and whose measurable income drops to zero. Whatever may be the case for taxpayers and the public purse, the effect on these women of the welfare reform movement has been negative, and for their children, profoundly so.

But last, and what I want to focus on here are the "legitimation harms" of this reform, and these harms affect the well-being of even the "success" stories of welfare reform no less than those left behind. The rhetoric, symbols, and stated goals of PRWORA may have further legitimated the conditions of poverty in which these now-working families live out their lives. So long as these women are "working," we are told, perhaps not their problems, but at least our problems with them, are solved. They may still be in poverty, but we are no longer supporting them; they have assumed "personal responsibility" for their lives and their families. And—if they would only marry, even their poverty would end! By marrying, we believe, they will at last have taken full "responsibility" for their families. They will no longer be poor! It's their choice. We no longer need care.

Now of course, even assuming that welfare reform has had these bad affects— that it has worsened the situation of some poor women and their children who are mothering outside of marriage, that it has compromised the parenting of those women who continue to receive TANF but must work in order to receive it, and that it has further depleted our already shallow reservoir of goodwill toward both the working and nonworking poor and our sense of responsibility for their well-being—the institution of marriage itself did not directly *cause* any of this. Rather, it has been the excesses of the law—onerous work requirements, the family cap, the five-year limit—coupled with a dangerous and ferocious ideology that denies communal responsibility of any sort for the impoverished conditions of the worst off, and then followed by the shameless trumpeting of welfare reform as a success, where success is measured solely by the reduction in welfare rolls (and hence, the reduction in the tax burden) that caused it. Surely, it is unduly harsh to lay responsibility for these legislative failures at the feet of those social utilitarians who make the case for marriage. At least some of the social utilitarians, furthermore (notably Linda Waite),[96] have gone out of their way, both before and after passage of PRWORA, to make clear that in their view, the strong utilitarian case for marriage does not imply that the refusal or failure to marry should be penalized, economically or socially. Rather, what we should infer from the utilitarian case for marriage, in the minds of at least some of the utilitarian promarriage scholars, is that society may well have an interest in promoting the conditions that will encourage good, safe, economically productive, and emotionally rewarding marriages, not that we have an interest in promoting (or requiring) even bad marriages over single motherhood.

Nevertheless, promarriage rhetoric, and more broadly the "marriage initiative," was decidedly part of the political story behind the passage of this act, as well as its justification and goal.[97] Even more so, today, the "marriage promotion movement" is front and center in welfare reform.[98] That rhetoric, and those arguments, have quite directly—explicitly and intentionally—legitimated the diminution in public support for poor women and their children. Jason DeParle, a prominent research journalist on all aspects of the welfare reform movement of the 1990s and aughts, observed in his authoritative book on the history of welfare reform:

> Funding for the Personal Responsibility Act expired in 2002, setting up a long-awaited reauthorization debate. There were all sorts of fights that George W. Bush could have led as a "compassionate conservative," especially with the welfare surpluses gone and state budgets reeling. He could have brought health insurance to needy workers, increased on the job training, or extended a hand to inner city men. He could have offered federal money for more after school programs. (He tried to cut them.) If he was serious about helping the working poor be could have created

subsidies for states to create tax credits like Wisconsin's. Instead, the debate that unfolded was both rancorous and obscure. ...

The one proposal to gain broad attention was the "marriage initiative," a plan to redirect $300 million a year of welfare money into marriage promotion efforts, ranging from advertising campaigns to courses on budgeting and conflict resolution. Much of the Left responded with derision, and the obvious criticisms were true: it was totally untested, the decision to marry is deeply personal, some communities lack marriageable men. But similar things could have been said about teenage pregnancy, which government and civic campaigns in the 1990s helped cut by 30 percent. Rather than dismiss it, why not see it and raise it one—with an equally large "fatherhood initiative" to help inner city men find jobs and reconnect with their kids.[99]

The legitimating impact of marriage and marriage rhetoric, I conclude, should count as a cost in the overall utilitarian assessment of the institution, at least if we include in that tally the cultural effects of the norm on which the institution rests. The institution of marriage, in addition to all else it does, sends the message, more loudly now than in past decades, that parenting should only be done within marriage, and that if and when it is not, the resulting poverty is properly borne by the mother and her children themselves, and not by the larger community. Marrying may be very good for participants, at least in terms of health and wealth. The institution of marriage, however, combined with its moralistic history and the current norms it generates, can be very bad for those who can't or won't participate, but who wish to mother (or, in the much less frequent circumstance, to father). It puts poor girls and women to the Hobson's choice of foregoing motherhood, or choosing abortion, or making what Edin and Kefalas, quoting their subjects, call "promises we can't keep": a promise to be faithful in a bad marriage, even though that marriage may well be profoundly harmful to one's own and one's children's health and overall well-being.[100] It gives the rest of us a powerful excuse for washing our hands of any responsibility for their struggle.

Utility, Justice, and Happiness

There are at least two further problems with the social utilitarian case for marriage. Both problems are acutely presented by the social science literature on the relatively greater utilitarian benefits of traditional over egalitarian marriage,[101] but they also render problematic, although perhaps to a lesser degree, the utilitarian defense of civil marriage quite generally. First, as is often the case, that which is utile is not necessarily fair, and sometimes, unfairness might be reason enough to discount at least some of that value-added utility. As the research itself seemingly shows, happy but inegalitarian marriages, in which the woman does virtually all the housework and the husband earns virtually all the income, rest on some deep-seated inequities, and can lead to some profound economic vulnerabilities, particularly at divorce or widowhood, for the nonincome-earning wife.[102] But the conflict between the utility and the fairness of marriage is by no means limited to such radically inegalitarian marriages that end in divorce. Rather, and as research has shown now for over twenty years, women in functional, ongoing, contemporary dual-earner couples continue to do vastly more housecleaning, and considerably more childcare, than do their husbands.[103] If we look only at hours worked (rather than earned income), this inequality in dual-earner couples constitutes if anything a deeper inequity than occurs in traditional marriage.

What feminists now call, following economics Professor Arlie Hochschild who coined the phrase, the "second shift phenomenon," is present in all income classes, and regardless of who is the higher wage earner.[104] Husbands in dual-income households do considerably more childcare than husbands did at mid-century, but far less than their wives, and continue to do next to no housecleaning. Thus, the second shift phenomenon: wives work two jobs, the income-earning one and the nonremunerative housekeeping one, to their husbands' one job. This is not an insignificant disparity. It means less leisure time for women than men, and more physical labor. It adversely impacts upon women's wages in the paid labor market. And, whether or not the result is a net increase in the happiness of the couple, it is an unfair distribution of labor. Even in happy marriages, the unfairness alone is, or ought to be, cause for concern.

The second problem is causally related to the first. The very unfairness of the second shift phenomenon, coupled with the mental and physical exhaustion it can cause, might contribute to a wife's sense of her own relative lack of importance—the triviality of her grievance, the unbearable "lightness of her being"—and of her own lack of entitlement to just treatment. The easiest way to resolve the cognitive dissonance of one's sense that the world must be a fair place, particularly when the world consists of those who love us, and one's own unfair treatment by those very hands, is either to conclude that the treatment is deserved, and hence not unfair at all, or that the unfairness is trivial, and of no consequence. Either one's self-importance, or one's sense of oneself as someone who enjoys an entitlement to be treated justly, suffers.[105] And, if one's sense of self is diminished, one's sense of oneself and one's marriage as "happy" might be, to that degree, skewed. A wife in an inegalitarian or second shift marriage might report herself "happy," in other words, for the same reason a worker in an exploitative labor agreement might report himself satisfied with his wage package: the alternative—divorce, in the first case, unemployment, in the second—is worse. The wife can separate, in which case she still will be responsible for the second shift, and will also lose the support of her husband, quite possibly leaving her worse off. Or, she can neglect the second shift, and endure a filthy house, unwashed laundry, takeout meals, and mildly neglected children. This too may be intolerable. Or, she can try to force a change in her husband's behavior, which can be tantamount to banging one's head against a wall. Given bad options, she may choose the least bad: continue to do the work herself. No differently than in an exploitative labor contract in conditions that favor employers, the wife might well report that her marriage is satisfactory—it beats the alternatives. And—the marriage might well be a happy one, if by that is meant that it produces more health and wealth (etc.) than would be produced by the two partners individually. But if this is anything close to an accurate depiction of the choices against which the wife proclaims the marriage to be a happy one, we should take the professions of happiness with the proverbial grain of salt. What those professions may reveal is paltry choices.

Is this cause for concern? And if so, how much concern? Should we make, as skeptics are wont to say, a federal case over who's doing the dishes? We should be cautious before dismissing these worries as trivial. The seeming "triviality" of the issue, no less than the wife's profession of her own happiness, might reflect nothing but one result of the unfairness itself: the issue might seem trivial because the victims of the practice—housewives, working mothers, "stay-at-home moms," "soccer moms," and "security moms"—are still, so often, trivialized, minimized, and infantilized in our mainstream media. Simply, there is no clear, non-question-begging answer to the question, "How much should this matter?" and this is true even for the people most directly involved. Some quite recent research suggests that the women involved in these marriages in which women work a double shift, or marriages that are in other ways the more traditional, are in some ways happier than women in egalitarian unions.[106] In fact, according to Steven Nock, who has authored or coauthored a number of these studies, the unhappiest marriages in dual-wage-earning couples seem to be those in which women work a double shift, are aware of the inequity, resent it, but can't change it. Where no one is "keeping the books," however, Nock argues, both partners are satisfied, in spite of, and perhaps because of, the inequity—even where both partners work. Nock himself concludes from this that the optimal solution to the pseudo-problem of the double shift is self-evident: "don't keep the books." Or, mixing metaphors, do the second shift, but don't punch the time clock. If knowledge of unfairness leads to dissonance, rather than address the unfairness, simply willfully blind yourself to the knowledge. For perhaps obvious reasons, this hardly seems a satisfying solution, on either the macro or micro level.

Let me summarize. The problems with the utilitarian argument for marriage, even aside from the general failure of their proponents to address the impact of the institution on nonparticipants, are two-fold: first, it is unclear how one resolves the conflict between utility and equity, and second, it is also not at all self-evident how to weigh all of this self-reporting. Married spouses may indeed report themselves satisfied even with highly inequitable domestic arrangements. Yet, and as the feminist and liberal philosopher John. S. Mill argued long ago, there really is a difference between "satisfaction" and "happiness": the goodness, depth, and genuineness of felt happiness is very much a function of the breadth of one's experience, the quality of one's education, the range of choices facing one, the degree of self-regard one possesses, the sense of oneself as worthy, and so on.[107] We might be happy with things as they are, relative to a slew of bad choices, and although it surely matters that we are and feel ourselves to be happy, it by no means follows from that feeling of satisfaction that we should be content with the status quo. We might feel ourselves to be "happy" when we are at most making the best of an unnecessarily limited set of bad options. Likewise, and perhaps more to the point, with regard to the reported satisfaction of women in unequal marriages, our self-reporting of our own happiness, our happiness itself, and our sense of satisfaction with our lot in life is very much a function of our sense of ourselves as deserving, as equals, as sovereign, as mattering, and as significant, as well as our sense of the world as just or unjust, malleable or given, contingent or necessary. We might be inclined to be happy even though we know we are being treated unjustly, if the injustice is truly trivial, or if the goodness of our lives apart from the injustice is great. Alternatively, though, we may be inclined to be happy, in spite of injustice, because we regard ourselves as inconsequential, and we regard the causes of the injustice from which we suffer as irreversible. All of these factors will influence our happiness and our experience of it, and all of these factors might be present, and mightily, in an unequal but placid marriage. One need not hold to a strictly Marxist view of material determinism or false consciousness to see that the self-reported happiness of women in unequal and unjust marriages might rest on pretty thin ice.

Now, a reservation about these reservations. All three of these problems with the social utilitarian argument for marriage, in my view, are basically limitations on its breadth. They don't undercut the argument itself. We should not infer from the overall utility of marriage for participants that the institution is generally of great utility for the entire society. We must take the costs of marriage on nonparticipants into account, particularly the costs of the institution and its rhetoric on the poor and on gay men and lesbians. Likewise, we should not infer from the utility of marriage to participants that we therefore need not be concerned about the fairness of the institution, or the fairness of particular marriages, for participants themselves. And third, we should not assume from reports of satisfaction that the participants are as well off as they could possibly be—that the institution is therefore beyond critique. Obviously this is not the case. Even given all of these limits, however, the utilitarian case for marriage is still very strong. The happiness, health, and wealth that marriage generates, for a very large percentage of the population, is considerable. We should be more than a little hesitant to blithely turn our back on it, in our private lives, or to propose its overthrow, in our public lives.

Communitarian Defenses of Marriage: Marriage as Commitment

The third defense of marriage that has emerged in the last decade regards marriage as commendable primarily because of its anti-individualistic core.[108] Marriage both presupposes and requires participants that will regard their "identity" as constituted in significant part by their relationality, and ideally, marriage generates an "identity" so constituted as well.[109] Relationality, or commitment, does not require the participants to regard themselves as submerged, or obliterated, by the larger oneness of the marriage. It does though expect of participants that each partner regards the interests of the marriage, and the interest, well-being, and health and happiness of the other, equally as his or her own. It does require the participants to view themselves as fully responsible to the well-being of the other, and as identi-fied with that responsibility: the responsibility I bear to my spouse is part of what makes me who I am, in other words, not simply a burden I somewhat willingly or unwillingly bear. The essence of marriage, in this view, is the commitment it asks of its participants. The value of marriage is that of all determinants, institu-tions, constituent parts, and influences upon modern life, particularly in capitalist democracies, marriage stands virtually alone in the way it constructs personhood: as at its fullest, at its best, at its most actualized, in relation to others, rather than in splendid isolation. The value of marriage, or the good of marriage, lies in this relational identity—not in the utility it brings to each partner individually, and not in the one-flesh union of man and woman. The value of marriage is that it both expresses and constructs our relational selves.

There are two separate strands of the communitarian defense of marriage as commitment, although they broadly overlap. The first strand is most concerned with the effect of marriage on the individual's construction of self understanding, and the second, with the effect of marriage on the married individual's responsi-bility for dependents, as well as his or her dependence on others by virtue of that responsibility. I will refer to the first subargument as centered on the construction of individual identity, and the second, as centered on the construction, and protec-tion, of relations of care. Let me begin with the identitarian strand.

One pervasive feature of modern life in Western culture, according to a num-ber of gently left-wing social critics, is the atomistic self that navigates it. The self we inhabit today is one that is almost entirely constructed by, and valued for, the choices he or she makes. We confront choices in the marketplace, and we con-struct those markets through our choices. We confront choices in our intimate partners: we now choose who we love and marry whom we choose; we are not cast into our marital roles by well-meaning but inevitably self-interested family members who decide for us what extended family we shall enter. We confront choices in the workplace: upon hitting the magical age we decide whether to fin-ish high school, to proceed to college, or go directly to an entry-level job, skilled or unskilled. We decide where we want to live, and what "lifestyle" to adapt. If we go on to college we confront choices in school the way we confront choices on a menu: we have many options from which to choose. And, we assume that the value of each option is entirely a function of the cumulative affect of our choices. So, if enough of us choose Colgate toothpaste, that gives that toothpaste its value; if enough of us with the option to do so choose to go to Harvard, that fact alone gives Harvard its value; if we choose to work as an accountant rather than do construction or to pay our accountants more than our general contractors, that renders the former of greater value. Value is a function of our fulfilled preferences, revealed through our choices between options. We construct value as we choose that which furnishes our lives. We don't live lives of "objective" value. We create value through our subjective choices. Individuals, making individual choices, are the font of social value.

What, if anything, is wrong with this understanding of the self, and its relation to value? It sounds innocuous enough. According to our communitarian and virtue philosophers, however, this is, in short, no way to live. There are several problems. First, it misdescribes the nature of *value*. We all, or most of us, want to live lives of moral value, but moral value simply is not a commodity, or a product of commodities—we don't create moral value by choosing it. Moral value (whatever may be the case for the value of toothpaste or automobiles or Harvard) must be "objective" if it is anything at all—we choose something of moral value because it is valuable, we don't create its value by choosing it. To think otherwise, as the cliché goes, is to know the price of everything and the value of nothing. We don't "choose" to be generous rather than selfish, and hence confer moral value on generosity. We aspire to be generous, or compassionate, or courageous, or kind, or principled, because these are good ways to live, and we either fail or succeed in living up to our aspirations. Virtues have "objective moral value." Their value is not a function of how much we'll give up to possess them (or, their price).

Relatedly, when we think our lives have value, it is generally not because of the thousands of daily choices we individually and autonomously make, and the value we thereby create. Our understanding of our own value is simply not so "atomized." We view our lives as of value, largely because of, and the extent to which, we feel ourselves to be rooted in forms of life that transcend both our daily lives, and the daily choices we make. Thus, we value our roots in a family tree that we most decidedly did not choose, we value our ties to our communities that we may sustain but did not create, we value our interlocking webs of friendships, we value our own and our colleagues' joint, collaborative work we do in recrafting the world for our children's development, or for our parents' comfort in their old age. We view ourselves, when we are comfortable with ourselves, as having contributed to the world's goodness by participating in that goodness, not by creating it through the exercise of our will. We hope to achieve some integrity over time, between our various selves as expressed and asserted in the world at different times. We also hope to achieve some continuity between ourselves and our larger world, by our contributions. As a committed, relational self, we seek not to fragment the world and ourselves in it through the continual reassertion of a consuming and producing chooser. We seek to unify the world, and ourselves in it, through remaining true to ourselves and to those to whom we have expressed our commitments.

Third, the picture of self as essentially a chooser, according to the communitarian critique, misdescribes the nature of choice itself, and of the individual making it. Our choices do not spring from our desires, unmediated by social forces, manifesting themselves in a happy congruence of preference and felt satisfaction. Rather, our choices, our preferences, and perhaps even our desires are largely a function of the cultures in which we are immersed. But of even greater moment, we create ourselves not only by the choices we make. We also create ourselves, and the moral meanings of our lives, by the care we give to those who are dependent upon us, by the love we generate with those with whom we are intimate, and the nurturance we have enjoyed in our own periods of dependency. It is the care, the love, and the nurturance that in turn creates the moral meaning, and value in our lives—not our freely willed choices to engage those activities. Indeed, when we are on the receiving end of that nurturance—when we are in our own periods of dependency at the beginning and end stages of life—choice plays no role in the matter whatsoever. We are loved and cared for, if we are lucky, and our choice has nothing to do with it. But as caregivers, likewise, we only choose these roles, or activities, in a limited sense. For many, caregiving and loving and nurturing is work that is thrust upon us. But even when not, we understand that the value of those roles, and the value of the work we do when we occupy them, is as great as it is not in spite of, but in part because of the unchosen nature of the work done within that role, (whether or not we chose the role)—the sense that we do relational work because we are human, because we must, because it is the right thing to do, because it is obligatory, and not because we're getting a lot for it in a good bargain. When we parent, for example, we understand that there is, in the words of one legal scholar, "no exit" from this work, by choice or otherwise, and nor should there be.[110] We do the relational work in our lives because of our connection to the object of our care, nurturance, and affection. We don't do it for the surplus value we'll enjoy as we choose to do it or not do it, as measured by the difference between what we'll pay and would have paid. We don't do it in order to create quantifiable monetary social value. We do it because it is demanded of us, not by a sovereign, but by our moral sense.[111]

Marriage understood as a serious (whether or not lifelong) commitment both expresses and to some degree constructs this relational self. When married, we may know that we can divorce at will, but nevertheless, for most of us, a large part of what it means to be married is that we don't, on a day-to-day basis, regard leaving the relationship as a real option—that is simply what it means to be committed. We are in it for the long haul, and consequently, we quite willfully limit, rather than expand, our choice. Unlike the idealized array of choices in the marketplace, the very idea of marriage is intended to limit, and to even erase, choice as a determinant of daily life, in the intimate realm. We build the relationship over time, from who we are and who we understand the other to be. We don't build the relationship as a series of atomistic choices to stay or go, to contribute or not contribute money to the household, to do or not do the chores requisite to keep the household running, to bargain and rebargain out a sensible and mutually beneficial deal. As a consequence, we build an identity for ourselves, for our marriage, and for our partner that endures over time; it is not one that is subject to constant change through constant choice. Our self gains permanence, and integrity, through the course of the marriage, as it sheds choice.

Marriage is one of the few social institutions that not only respects our relational lives, but structures and validates them, and does so quite publicly. We are rewarded, by social acclamation, in marriage, for *not* being individually and egoistically consumptive—we're supposed to share the bread, not take it all for ourselves—as well as for not being particularly productive. We're expected to spend our leisure time at home with our family. At home, we are praised for *not* being the value-creating, profit-maximizing market participants we're otherwise urged to become. We are rewarded, by social acclamation, for limiting our individualized selves, and for asserting instead, within marriage, a relational self. As markets reward and structure and socially validate our choosing self, so marriage rewards, structures, and expresses social validation of our relational, committed, enduring self. We are rewarded and commended for staying in the marriage across time—for foregoing better options as they present themselves—but also for fidelity, for staying sexually faithful to our partner while in the marriage. We forego the choice to leave, and we forego the choice to be sexually active with multiple partners. We are rewarded and commended for putting the interests of our partner on a par with or over our own interests, in deciding where to live, when to move, what jobs to take, or when and how to relocate. We are rewarded and commended for taking often severe cuts in our income in order to parent. We are rewarded and commended for foregoing pleasures, diversions, and consumption to accommodate the differing tastes and preferences of our partner, and to do so as a matter of habit, rather than a matter of conscious calculation. We learn, and model for others, in marriage a way to live that is not exhibited on the stage our markets set: a world of sacrifice, of nonconsumptive pleasures, of endurance over time, of foregone rather than exploited choice, and of responsibility and commitment to others as at the core of one's being, rather than a chosen addendum. The market presents us with a deficient way to live, and a false and normatively unattractive conception of our own individual identity. The institution of marriage presents a better one. That is its value. That is the good that marriage is and does.

The second strand of the communitarian, relational defense of marriage as commitment concerns not so much our self understanding, as our caregiving labor, and our relations of dependency that result from it.[112] Marriage, in brief, no matter what its flaws and manifest injustice, promotes, acknowledges, and valorizes our relational self by structuring, and then supporting, both the caregiving work we do, and our relations of dependency that are its consequence. We have all been the beneficiaries of this labor. We are not born choosers, ready to construct social value by consuming and producing in market economies. We are born into a protracted period of dependency: a few years of total and profound dependency on the caregiving of others at the onset of life, another decade or so of economic and social dependency, an interlude of relative independence, and then a decade or more of dependency on younger caregivers. During our period of independence, furthermore, those of us who are giving care to dependents will be, by virtue of that role, yet again dependent upon others for the economic support of ourselves, and of those to whom we are giving care. The full-time, round-the-clock care of infants and toddlers, as well as the eighteen-hour-a-day care for children and adolescents, and then again, the round-the-clock needs of elderly family members, renders whomever is giving all that care relatively incapacitated from wage labor. For some of those periods, the incapacity will be total, for other parts of it not so much so, but nevertheless very much a part of the experience. During those periods, the caregiver is herself "relationally" or "secondarily" dependent—dependent on others for her own economic needs to whatever degree that the infant, toddler, child, or aging adult is dependent on her for sustenance and care.

Marriage is the way—imperfect and unjust, as presently constructed, but nevertheless—that we have structured the provision of all of this caregiving labor, without unduly burdening the larger society with the endless needs of countless dependents. A well-functioning marriage permits one partner to provide care, and do little or nothing else, during a child's infancy and toddlerhood, and during an aging parent's decline, while the other provides economic support. Alternatively, it permits the partners to spot each other in the giving of this care, while each is employed in part-time work. When children are older or grown, it permits the partners to continue to specialize their labor—allowing one to tend to relational and domestic tasks while the other earns an income for the two of them, if such a division seems desirable. But the true, great contribution of marriage to overall societal well-being is in the recognition and support it indirectly provides caregivers of children. Married partners enjoy the economic benefits of scale. But further, married partners enjoy an array of legal benefits, including favorable tax treatments, inheritance rights, automatic joint ownership of assets, coverage on each others' employers' health insurance policies, enhanced Social Security protection, and numerous discounts, both governmental in origin and stemming from the private sphere. All of these benefits, taken collectively, rest on as well as express a societal recognition that this work is highly valuable. The superior treatment of—accommodation of—married couples, in our laws of tax, inheritance, and work benefits, is, then, partly, an indirect financial payment to caregivers. It makes easier the provision of this care, by easing the financial burden of the couples that jointly provide it.

The Libertarian Threat to Relational Marriage

Of course, there are problems with this relational understanding of the good that marriage does, as the relational feminists, communitarians, and virtue theorists who have urged it either readily concede, or—more often—insist. If marriage and marriage law is supposed to facilitate the giving of care to dependents, it does a remarkably poor job of it. First, marriage and marriage law is, notably, the cause of the serious impoverishment of many women and their dependents both, not the cure of it. This is not as paradoxical as it seems. Only when her marriage is well functioning do women enjoy the economic benefits outlined above. When it is not, women are simply exploited: they are working for no pay at caregiving jobs that have little to commend them by way of intellectual or sensory stimulation. Given the lack of direct state support for caregiving outside of marriage, they have few realistic and palatable options. They are accordingly trapped not only in their bad marriages, but also in the unpaid job of mothering, and this holds true, even given equal employment opportunity, nondiscrimination policies, and liberal divorce laws.

Nevertheless, if we would only recognize, as we currently do not, that the facilitation of relational caregiving *is* the central good of civil marriage, these theorists quite sensibly argue, we could pursue or advocate for changes in our marriage laws that would both strengthen that understanding, and also cure its current injustices. We could, for example, as a number of relational feminists (including me) have argued, urge the creation, or recognition, of a quasi-constitutional or at least political "right" to give care—a right comparable to a free speech right or a right to equal employment—defined, roughly, as a right to care for dependents without risking severe economic impoverishment, political disenfranchisement, or social isolation.[113] We could then seek the passage of laws that would make that right meaningful. Most idealistically, and perhaps not too naively, we might be more inclined to recognize the existence of nonmarital caregiving relations worthy of protection, if we would acknowledge that protecting caregiving is the reason we protect marriage. By centralizing this understanding of marriage, and then centralizing, rather than marginalizing, marriage, we could conceivably identify the care that is its *raison d'etre* as a public, and not just a private, virtue.

Most important, a societal understanding of the idea of marriage as commitment might trigger an understanding of the public value, virtue, and good of caregiving labor, and from that understanding, in turn, a number of reforms might follow, all of which might render marriage a more just institution, both internally for participants, and externally for nonparticipants who also give care. If we reduce marriage to contract, and to individual will, we will have lost the social opportunity that a public examination of marriage provides: to enrich our appreciation of this public good and reform our institutions accordingly. Thus, the argument concludes, the institution of marriage is necessary to the recognition of the public value of caregiving, and that public recognition, in turn, is necessary to the reforms needed to render marriage, and the caregiving labor that takes place within it, more just. Mary Shanley describes the sorts of reforms:

> A number of reforms would move society toward greater justice in marriage. One such reform would be to ensure that people can find jobs that pay a living wage. There must be equal pay for equal work.... Benefits must be extended to all workers, not just those who meet the ideal worker model (and basic health benefits should not be tied to employment status). Work must also be restructured in such a way that it accommodates caregiving, through a shorter workweek and more flexible scheduling, for example. If caregivers are not to be marginalized, high-quality, affordable child care must be part of any comprehensive family policy, as must the kind of child allowance common in European countries. Paid parental leave for both men and women would create an incentive for men to participate in child care.... In the event of divorce the wages of both a primary wage earner and a primary caregiver should

be treated as joint property, reflecting the commonality of marriage, particularly if there are children or other dependents.[114]

Now, what of these arguments? Why are they so central to our debates about marriage now, and what is their target? It is important to stress that the communitarian defense of marriage as commitment is often (not always) propounded by activists, theorists, and scholars of the family, who clearly support a reform agenda regarding marriage, including expanding marriage so as to include same-sex couples, and encouraging legal reforms that might render marriage more internally just. For the most part, communitarian and virtue theorists want to see marriage become a commitment between two people, not necessarily a man and a woman, and a commitment of equals grounded in mutual intimacy and shared purpose, not a relation of sovereign and subject, or empowered and subordinate. Thus, the communitarian proponents of marriage typically support a "transformative" version of marriage, not a traditionalist one: marriage, they argue, is at heart a commitment, and a committed way to live is a good way to live. If they are right about that (and I think they are), then surely marriage should be expanded, so as to include those presently excluded, and reformed, such that the "commitment" does not become a masquerade for a damaging dependency.

Nevertheless, the focus of the communitarian understanding of marriage that is the subject of this chapter, is not so much reform, as it is defense. The communitarians (for all their differences) see a common threat to traditional marriage that prompts them to defend what they concede is a flawed institution. The worry they share is that precisely because of a recognition of the injustice and inequities of civil marriage, a broad coalition of community activists concerned with marriage policy—including progressives worried about its inequalities and exclusions, and libertarians worried about its undue restrictions on individual freedom and will—will urge its abandonment, rather than its reform (to end it, rather than mend it), and precisely because those injustices, exclusions, inequities, and infringements on liberty are quite real, those arguments just might, eventually, succeed. Marriage, the communitarians worry, would, through the force of these arguments, come to be replaced by a purely individualized, contract regime: any inequality done by law, rather than private will, would thereby be ended. There would be no state-based exclusions of anyone based on sexual orientation or anything else, there would be no infringement on the rights and responsibilities of individuals to set their own terms of their intimate affairs. Marriage, as an independent, objective norm, prescribing a committed and relational way of life, would end. This, the communitarians urge, would be a pity. For all its injustice, ending marriage entirely would be a clear instance of throwing out the proverbial baby with the bath water.

Is this a realistic worry? Is civil marriage really so endangered? From our current vantage point, the fear looks exaggerated: the force of contemporary politics, at least, appears to be almost entirely in the direction of preserving marriage, not bringing us closer to its demise. Appearances, though, can be deceiving, and the communitarians might be right to think that this is one such instance. The efforts of traditionalists, promarriage movement advocates, and moral-value neonatural conservatives notwithstanding, there may be something to the worry that at the end of the day marriage could indeed die a thousand deaths through a barrage of libertarian reforms and criticisms. Marriage, after all, as communitarians and traditionalists and reformers all point out, is already a deeply anomalous institution, if we look at it in the context of private law more broadly understood. As we saw in Chapter 1, even in the modern era, civil marriage still confers benefits on the basis of a "status"—a chosen status, certainly, but nevertheless a status—the status of being married. As such, marriage and the law promoting and protecting it is unlike the rest of our private law (meaning, the law governing relations between private parties, rather than between individuals and the state) in virtually all respects: procedural, substantive, jurisprudential. Outside of marriage law, our private law is overwhelmingly contract based, and becoming more so with every passing year. Abolishing marriage law entirely, and putting a contract regime governing intimate relations in its place, would, for many contract law devotees, be a logical, and seemingly inevitable, historical development.

Let me draw the contrast, and then the progress of marriage law in light of that contrast, a little more starkly. For the most part, in the rest of our private law that deals with the relations between persons who make promises to each other (the law, say, of contracts or property), the law seeks to define and understand their legal obligations to each other by reference to those promises—their "contractual understanding"—rather than by reference to any legally created status. Did this individual breach a duty to that individual, and as a consequence does he owe him compensation? In answering this question, at least with respect to parties in any sort of contractual agreement, it is now common to say that one's "status"—whether one is a property owner, or an innkeeper, or a tenant, or a servant, or a master, or a tradesperson, or a buyer, or a seller, or an employer, or a capitalist, or an employee, or a worker, or a consumer, or a corporation, or an individual, etc., etc., etc.—rarely enters the picture, if at all. This irrelevance—the irrelevance of what we *are*, in determining what we *owe* to whom—is what is meant by the oft-repeated phrase that the movement of nineteenth- and twentieth-century private law has been a movement "from status to contract." The consequence of the breach of your privately assumed contractual obligation is measured by the same rules, whether you are IBM or an individual buyer, whether you are Enron or an employee or individual stockholder, whether you are a university or a research assistant. We no longer have, and certainly no longer pledge allegiance to, rules of private life that determine rights and obligations by who and what we are: tradesmen, corporations, workers, employers, capitalists, landowners, and so on.

Against this powerful oceanic movement from status to contract, marriage law in its entirety still stands as a major exception. Although the initial decision to marry is presumably a voluntary one, and bears a marked resemblance to a "contract," nevertheless, from the commencement of the marriage onward, a vast array of rights, obligations, and entitlements are a function of one's status, and not a function of any willed decision. Marriage law really is absolutely unique in this way: although it begins with a promise that looks to all the world like a contractual one, the conflicts to which the promises arise are not resolved by reference to the promises themselves, or by contract law, or even by contract principles, but rather, by a body of status rules that have a decidedly old-school cast. Because of that, when viewed against the jurisprudential assumptions of other bodies of private law—contract law, corporate law, the law of agency, employment law, and so on—marriage law sticks out like a sore thumb. It is, of all Victorian things, *status* driven. And—as both marriage proponents and critics note—there's something very unstable indeed about a body of law so deeply at odds with the major juris-prudential assumptions of the era. There is little doubt that marriage law—even given the inroads made by contractual innovations, such as prenuptial agreements and separation agreements—is an historical anomaly. It won't be all that surprising if it goes the way of the horse and buggy.

That, though, is precisely the danger. The peculiar value of marriage as com-mitment (according to communitarians) strongly suggests that this anomalous state of affairs should continue. Marriage law reinforces commitment, and does so to a degree well beyond what we might expect of contract law, precisely by virtue of the status it defines, confers, and validates. Husbands and wives have duties to each other by virtue of being husbands and wives, and those duties transcend any obligation the law of contract might impose, by virtue of a promise made by a man to a woman. Were we to lose marriage law, and rely solely on contract, we would lose the essence of marriage—*because* marriage law is still status driven. The problem is not—only—that contract law, currently constructed, explicitly excludes many—perhaps most—of the promises made by domestic partners in intimate contexts from its sphere of binding obligation. That is, in fact, changing: increasingly, these private contracts made by domestic partners (both married and unmarried) are enforceable. But the inadequacy of contract law, as a means of governing the relations of married partners, goes far beyond its scope.

Let's look at just one of the more obvious contrasts, and then reconsider what would be lost to us, were marriage law to be subsumed by contract. When we make a contractual promise, we might breach it with no moral approbation, so long as we are willing to pay our "promisee" (the person to whom the promise was made) the value of our breached promise. By contrast, when we marry, we are obligated unconditionally, and the moral approbation that would be our due, should we breach that promise, is very much central to its meaning. When we make and breach a contractual promise, we are required to pay a financial penalty measured by the value of the breached promise. When we break a marital com-mitment, we may or may not owe a duty of support, but neither the extent of our financial obligation nor the meaning of the moral censure we thereby deserve are a function of the monetary value to our spouse of that breached commitment. We don't think that way when we marry—what is the value, to me, of this promise I'm receiving, what is the value, to him, of the promise I'm making, the value of which I know I'll owe, should I decide to breach—nor should we. When we contractually promise, we are allowed to and even expected to (to some degree) continually reevaluate, by reference to our own utility, costs, and benefits, the value, to us, of sticking to the promise, the cost of our potential liability, should we breach, the damages we might sustain and might be obligated to pay should the contract be the object of litigation. Should the contract at some point no longer be "worth it"—should the cost of our performance, for example, turn out to quite unexpectedly exceed what we expect to "get" from the contract, even factoring in the cost of paying damages for our own breach—it is widely assumed, at least by lawyers, that we will and should breach, and that the law should permit us to do so. This is sometimes called, by courts and contract law specialists, the "theory of efficient breach": the law should impose no moral or punitive sanction on the breacher, so long as he is willing to pay the promisee the value of his breached promise, should the cost of completing a contract turn out to be in excess of the value of the contract. To hold otherwise, would simply be economically wasteful. The law, it has been agreed for over a hundred years, should be rigorously morally neutral with regard to these "efficient breaches"—breaches of contracts that are so beneficial to the breacher, that it is in everyone's interest that they occur, so long as the nonbreaching party is paid off. Efficient breaches are wealth maximizing, and hence socially desirable. Judges have now so opined, students have so learned, and lawyers have so reiterated, for well over a hundred years.

Quite the contrary, though, with respect to marriage, so long as we view marriage as commitment. We are not presumed to be held to these promises only so long as it is efficient that we do so. There is just no such thing, in marriage law and practice, as an "efficient breach" of a marriage vow. The point of the marriage promise, in fact, is precisely to ward off the kind of "efficiency" thinking that contract law aims to encourage—or at least not discourage. The vow, in other words, creates a "status," not an economic expectancy, and therefore is not a contract, and it does so intentionally, and meaningfully. A promise to marry is not a contractual promise, and a marriage is not a contract—it is a commitment, and the two are not the same thing. Being "married" then, really *is* a status, and not a contract. This is not an historical anomaly. Marriage is a way of being, not a promise to pay money should a promise be breached. If we lose completely this understanding of both marriage, and marriage law, as status based, communitarians worry, we will have lost the distinctive value of marriage itself. Folding marriage law into contract law carries precisely that risk.

Accordingly, the great threat to marriage, from the perspective of this communitarian understanding of its value, is certainly not same-sex marriage (which, for the most part, the communitarians generally support) and it is not a lack of understanding of the social and individual utility of marriage. It is, rather, the ubiquity of contract, and contract law, and the attraction of contract, and the commodificationist, individualist, and exchange-based theories of value that contract and contract law embody, that the communitarians see as potentially putting marriage at risk. The risk that marriage will be submerged within contract, furthermore, is observable at the individual, social, legal, and intellectual, or philosophical, level. Individually, one of the reasons, perhaps one of the major reasons, individuals opt for cohabitation over marriage is the outsized commitment that marriage entails. Societally, marriage is losing its appeal as individualism gains: when we emulate Huck and "light out for the territories," we typically do so as singles, not as rooted, married couples wedded to each other and our communities. Legally, marriage as status is slowly losing ground to marriage-as-contract: prenuptial contracts are increasingly upheld, surrogacy contracts are replacing legally defined parental obligations, contract, not law, rules the day at the point of divorce. And lastly, marriage as status is losing ground to marriage-as-contract on the playing field of ideas. While some marriage reformers, including advocates of same-sex marriage and some feminist critics of the family, continue to press the case for a status-based understanding of marriage, others are joining forces with libertarian- and economics-minded reformers, and urging the dissolution of marriage in toto, opting for a world of intimate relations in which contracts, individually negotiated, rather than any form of marriage law, would govern.[115]

What would we lose, were we to go this route? We would lose the idea of marriage as an objective good, and of married life as an objectively good way to live. Marriage, in a pure contract regime, would be another option on the menu. But we would also lose the potentiality of marriage, marriage law, and marriage policy, as an object of political and public debate, discussion, and consensus. We would lose the public face of marriage. The state would declare no interest, the community would have no say. Marriage would no longer be a subject of democracy, once it became solely a subject of individual contract. There might be much to be said for that outcome; we'll look in the next chapter at some arguments why it might be an improvement over the status quo. But it clearly carries risk. One of them is simply political: we would lose the opportunity, as citizens, to articulate and express a public understanding of what are, and ought to be, the responsibilities and rights of individuals in committed relationships intended to endure for a lifetime, to each other, to themselves, and to and from the state.

Some Reservations about the Communitarian Defense of Marriage

Let me hold off on a full discussion of the implications of the end of marriage for the next two chapters. I will close off this chapter, instead, with a quick look at some of the problems with the communitarian understanding of marriage as commitment. Let me begin with the argument from self identity, integrity, and authenticity. Again, the claim, in brief, is that marriage, the institution of marriage, and the societal valorization of marriage laudably recognize and support the construction of a relational, rather than excessively individualized identity, and that this relational identity is central to individual integrity and authenticity in the face of a commodificationist society that otherwise vigorously atomizes life. Even assuming, however, that a relational rather than overly individualistic self is a good thing—assuming, that is, the rough accuracy of this softly neo-Marxist critique of our I-Podized private lives—is it so clear that *marriage* is the route to get there? Perhaps not. First, it surely isn't the case that marriage is *necessary* for the creation of an integrated, committed, relational identity—we all know plenty of unmarried persons who are profoundly relational, anticommodificationist, deeply committed persons in their private and public lives. But nor is it the case that it is *sufficient*. Indeed, marriage might often be counterproductive—meaning, marriage might at least sometimes be productive of a radically alienated, rather than connected or relational self. Sometimes, marriage becomes a truly hellish commitment, and at that point, exit, individuation, and self reconstruction look much better, in terms of authenticity and self integrity both, and oftentimes are much better than whatever "integrity" may be had from remaining in a relationship that one experiences as oppressive. Sometimes, the constancy and permanence of a marital commitment, albeit not "hellish," is spiritually or emotionally deadening. Sometimes, perhaps often, the connection, and the relationality, and the "holism" of the marriage that is "bigger than the sum of its parts" can only be achieved by blotting out the self—self-annihilation—rather than by a mutually enriching moral commitment. At such a point, personal integrity might well be better served by the early exit and clean break that are so decried by communitarian advocates of marriage.

It is not all that clear, however, even of relatively satisfying marriages, that such marriages, and the social institution, structure, and rhetoric that accompanies them, well promote the sorts of values of authenticity, integrity, and relationality that communitarians seek from them. Obviously, those values, and that sense of self, can be achieved outside of marriage. We can construct a committed, integrated, relational identity by binding ourselves in webs of obligation to our communities, our workplaces, our local government, our families of origin, our close friends, or even, god help us, our careers. We can join civic and bowling leagues; we don't have to bowl alone. We can make more friends, and stick by them, through hell and high water, better than we currently do. We can become Big Brothers and Big Sisters to those in need. We can surely create lasting ties that bind, and binding ties that last, without marriage.

Now none of this is flatly inconsistent with the valorization of marriage that the communitarians promote. Communitarians as a group understand there are bad marriages as well as good, and none of them wish to see the end of divorce altogether—although some of them do wish to see higher barriers to divorce, and greater continuing obligations of each spouse to the other, after its termination. Many of the communitarians are also critics of traditional marriage, as it is currently constituted (although some are not), and most deplore the extreme form of dependent relationality, with its concomitant duties of wifely obedience that characterized nineteenth-century marriage explicitly, and mid-twentieth-century marriage implicitly. Nevertheless, taken cumulatively, it seems to me that a more realistic portrayal of the internal quality of many marriages, combined with some empirical sense of how marriage impacts upon our communitarian and relational instincts outside of marriage, might spark some measure of healthy skepticism, among communitarians, that marriage is the best bet for deepening community ties, combating atomism and consumerism, or countering the forces of capitalist hyperindividualism, and so on.

Why? Simply, at least for some of us fully sympathetic to the larger political goals of most virtue ethicists and communitarians, their focus on marriage seems just a bit counterintuitive. Marriage, at least for many of us, in our personal lives, and perhaps for all of us in our current political world, may well be more of an obstacle than a vehicle for the relational commitments the communitarians so rightly value. On a personal level, our very personal and individualized inclinations to marry, and our moral conviction that we should stay married, and our habitual tendency to live out our couch potato days within that thickly spun cocoon of our married lives, might well sap our initiative to develop our relational selves in other, and more communitarian, directions. Even relatively happy marriages are insular and isolating experiences for many people. Such a marriage may indeed commit the individual to the marriage, and the marriage partner, but precisely by virtue of so doing, it may limit rather than invite further commitments to larger communities—larger communities of need, of mutual obligation, of political or civic purpose, or even of friendship and pleasure. The contentedness of our married lives, in other words, might be one of the reasons we "bowl alone," when we bowl.[116] Whether the flame of marriage, both personally and societally, is worth the candle it consumes—the time, energy, and moral drive that we might otherwise place in our relations of commitment to others in our communities—is just not at all clear. But whether or not it is so worthy is not answerable by noting what is surely true: that marriage, both individually and societally, does indeed reflect, express, valorize, and construct our "relational selves."

And what of marriage as a vehicle for the delivery of care? It may well be that this is central to the moral good of marriage; I believe it is. And, it is also true, I believe, that caregiving is a fundamentally devalued primary good. But it surely doesn't follow that we should therefore valorize, protect, or even retain marriage. That marriage is the way we structure, valorize, and to some degree compensate caregiving in this society means, partly, that those who try to give care outside of marriage will suffer accordingly. They do not receive the benefits of marriage—either those provided by an approving government or by a loving spouse. It also means, of course, that those who do the caregiving within marriage—overwhelmingly still women—are to some degree (and whether happily or unhappily) trapped in those marriages: the solicitude, support, partial compensation, and valorization will indeed not be forthcoming when the marital tie is broken. Marriage may be a vehicle for the delivery of care to children and aging parents—but it may also be a very poor vehicle. And, it may be a very poor vehicle even if it presents a better deal than a slew of worse alternatives. This should not be surprising. If we look at caregiving a little more crassly, as the job that it is, but with very meager compensation, then, like most very poorly paid jobs, particularly of the unskilled variety, doing the job for even very meager compensation is better than doing the job for no compensation at all.

Nor has marriage, even when understood as an institution that exists, largely, as a vehicle for the delivery of caregiving labor, triggered a widespread appreciation of the value of that labor, and a political and social movement to support, and pay, the caregivers that perform it, whether married or not. Marriage as an institution has not, so far, prompted us to consider what "other" forms of caregiving relations ought to be protected and promoted; quite the contrary. Single mothers do not bask in the reflected glow, or glory, of more traditionally domestic wives who mother. Nor are they assumed to be more deserving of societal protection, and assistance, by virtue of not participating in the largesse of marriage. Marriage has not sensitized us to the need to societally support all caregiving labor and all caregiving relations in this culture. Rather, and precisely because marriage is so widely regarded as the best way to structure the giving of care to dependents, those who become caregivers outside of it are often deemed less deserving, and less worthy of societal assistance; they are, rather, too often deemed deserving of punishment. Marriage has not been the spur to conscience that makes us able to see the degree to which we societally neglect the needs of the dependents among us—both those "primarily dependent" due to infancy, or sickness, or declining health, or those secondarily dependent, due to their caregiving obligations. It has, rather, legitimated, and mightily, our refusal to admit those who provide care to dependent others within our own field of vision, and our circle of reciprocity. Their failure, or refusal, to marry becomes their moral flaw, rather than our failure to care for them as they struggle to care for others, being our own moral flaw.

⋐ CHAPTER THREE ⋑

Marriage and Its Critics
("Let's Call the Whole Thing Off")

$\mathcal{S}$hould we end civil marriage? Why would anyone suggest such a thing? On what grounds? What would our world look like, were we to do so? One reason we might do so—and one that well frames the major arguments that have been pressed toward this end, and that I will examine in this chapter—is that civil marriage, even liberally reformed so as to include same-sex couples in its purview, is unconstitutional. It is fundamentally at odds with some of our most basic constitutional ideals.

Let me quickly add by clarification that this claim has never been pressed in a court of law and I'd venture to guess never will be. I'm quite certain it would never prevail, not within the lifetime of anyone reading this. In fact, and as I will discuss in some detail below, the Supreme Court has held, repeatedly, that the "right to marry" is a "fundamental interest," and a "civil right," that cannot be unduly burdened by law in the absence of a compelling state interest to do so. A state may not, for example, deny a marriage license to a man that wants one because he has failed to pay child support to children of previous marriages[1] nor may it burden the right to marry or choose one's marriage partners with miscegenation laws,[2] or allow a challenge to the paternity of a husband of a child born within the marriage,[3] or interfere with marital rights or privileges in any number of other ways.[4] Far from making marriage an object of constitutional scrutiny or criticism, the Supreme Court, and a number of state supreme courts as well (most recently, Massachusetts), over the last century, have gone a long way toward making the right to civil marriage a part of our fundamental law, beyond even democratic, political change, much less any more fundamental constitutional transformation.

It does not follow, however, from the very low chance that the Court would ever so hold, that the practice of marriage, or the laws that construct it, are constitutionally unproblematic. Courts can be and have been wrong about the meaning of the Constitution, and over very long spans of time.[5] They could well be wrong about the constitutionally protected status of marriage. It would not be the first time that a social practice, once constitutionally protected, came to be viewed eventually, and by the Court itself, as constitutionally suspect, and then eventually as unconstitutional.

Even beyond the possibility of judicial mistake, however, the Constitution, as a public declaration of legal ideals, means considerably more than what the Supreme Court says it means, and for at least two distinct reasons.[6] First, and as a growing body of scholarship makes clear, there may well be constitutional norms, ideals, or aspirations that can neither be fully articulated or enforced by way of judicial processes, simply by virtue of the practical limits on judicial powers. For example, while the Court can readily strike an errant state law as unconstitutional, it cannot construct laws that might be constitutionally required. It is not a lawmaking institution. It doesn't follow however that the Constitution is silent with respect to necessary laws. There may well be such laws, mandated by constitutional norms that the Court simply cannot enforce. If that is right, then it is more than just possible—it is quite likely—that those constitutional norms, as well as their implications, have been obscured by our two-century-long reliance on the Supreme Court as not only the ultimate, but increasingly the only, oracle of constitutional meaning. This may be true, furthermore, in the case of the institution of marriage. A court could never undertake the massive legislative task of recrafting family law (and a host of related doctrinal fields) so as to render the institution of civil marriage consonant with constitutional obligations. It doesn't follow, however, that the Constitution is silent with respect to this pervasive feature of our current law of intimate and private relations.

But second, not only the Constitution itself, but also constitutional *argument*, understood as a type of critical political and moral reasoning, or critical thinking about social practices, exists, and should exist, independent of what courts might do or say. The Constitution may be a source of law, but it may also be something else: a source of political inspiration, perhaps, or simply a guide for good governance. Understood as such, the Constitution, and the ideals of good governance it articulates, clearly belong to us all, and bind us all. We all have an interest in understanding and at times using the critical tools of analysis and appraisal the Constitution facilitates. Understood as one form (among others) of social criticism, furthermore, constitutional argument has distinctive virtues: most notably, it rests on claims about the content, and implications, of secular political ideals that purport to unite us as Americans. At times in our history, those claimed political ideals have been ignoble, and when that has been true, constitutional argument (both on and off the Court) has been not only a moral failure but a moral disaster; think of the impact of popular constitutional rhetoric regarding the property rights of slaveholders on the prebellum southern intelligentsia, or the rhetoric of "states rights" federalism during the Jim Crow era and its aftermath. There have also, however, been noteworthy successes—instances where constitutional criticism of extant social and legal practices have brought us, as a nation, closer to articulated and decent and just moral ideals.[7] If there's any plausibility at all to the claim that marriage, even generously construed, might be unconstitutional, it's important to understand why. Is secular marriage itself in tension with our constitutional ideals? Or is it a part of them? Whatever courts might or might not do with a constitutional argument that civil marriage, even liberally construed, is unconstitutional, it is helpful to understand the initial plausibility of such a claim.

The first section following is an only somewhat fanciful argument to that affect. In the following sections, I review additional arguments that have been presented for ending marriage, and the final section is given over to some reservations about the project.

The Dubious Constitutionality of Civil Marriage

So—is civil marriage itself unconstitutional? Let me just suggest the outline of one argument to the effect that marriage is in tension with ideals expressed in the Fourteenth Amendment of the Constitution (one of the three Reconstruction Amendments), and more specifically, with that amendment's so-called "Equal Protection Clause."[8] The Equal Protection Clause, in part, guarantees that "No State shall deny Equal protection of the laws."[9] What does "equal protection of the law" mean? Over the last 100 years, but particularly in the last half century,[10] the Supreme Court and commentators have agreed that at least part of what it means is that laws that rest on distinctions between groups, and then differentially treat one group better than another, might violate this so-called equality provision of the Fourteenth Amendment, particularly if they rest on irrational or malignant feelings of bias or hatred against the ill-treated group. Clearly, both marriage and the law that defines it, no matter how liberally interpreted, effectuate a substantial differentiation between people who are "married" and people who are not, with the latter treated more harshly, in ways that impact upon basic and cherished lifelong pursuits. Married people in our society are treated very differently and far better than unmarried people, solely by virtue of their legal status. The constitutional question, then, is whether that differentiation, and then the differential treatment, violates our fundamental, constitutional commitment to "equal protection of the laws."

Let's look at just a few of the more obvious ways in which married people are favored over unmarried, and then at the various tests the courts and commentators have used, in deciding whether the differential treatment, by law, of various groups of people does or doesn't raise constitutional issues. First, married persons receive substantial benefits upon the deaths of their spouses, by way of inheritance law, pension rights, and Social Security law, that are un-available to unmarried persons upon the deaths of their loved ones, to whom they may have been similarly attached, and with whom they may be similarly economically interdependent.[11] Likewise, married persons can rest assured, as they reach the end of life, that their surviving spouses will be assisted by these programs, while unmarried persons cannot "rest in peace," at the end of life, with respect to their intimates they leave behind. These laws historically rested on the gendered assumption that wives were economically dependent upon their husbands, and were thus more needy at the death of their spouse than were either single people—presumably more independent—who survived their loved ones, or husbands who became widowers. The gendered distinctions in these benefits packages have now been ruled unconstitutional—with the result being that husbands and wives are now regarded as equally *inter*dependent upon each other (rather than wives more dependent than husbands) so that wives and husbands, and widows and widowers, are treated equally with each other. No such ruling was forthcoming, however, challenging the distinction, pervasive in our laws governing Social Security, pensions, and military benefits, between mar-ried spouses, and unmarried, but equally interdependent, couples. Today, then, it's fair to say that the extremely preferential treatment given married persons over unmarried persons, by Social Security laws and pension plans, rests on the assumption that married people are by definition "interdependent" with each other (and are therefore relatively needier at times of death or incapacitation of their spouses), while unmarried people have no such attachments. Obviously, in many cases that assumption is simply false.

Second, married people are the beneficiaries of a number of presumptions and entitlements regarding parenting that are unavailable to unmarried people, including unmarried couples who are parenting. For example, married persons receive extreme forms of deference and preferential treatment when adjudicating custody rights over children born to the married partners during the duration of the marriage, at the points of separation and divorce—deference and preferential treatment not available to unmarried parents.[12] Married persons have traditionally been preferred as foster parents to unmarried persons[13] (although this practice has as of late been changing). Both the preferences and the presumptions are based on the sanctity of the traditional assumption that children are and should be born to and raised by marital partners. This assumption as well, though, will oftentimes be untrue. While it is clearly the case that children fare well in two-parent households, and that children raised in single-parent households are at risk on a wide range of indicators of well-being, there is considerably less evidence that children do not fare as well in households headed by committed same-sex couples as hetero couples, or in households headed by nonconjugal (not sexually intimate) but nevertheless committed partners. It is also not clear the extent to which the better outcomes for children in marital households are a result not of the superiority of that form of family, but rather, a result of its preferred status in law.

Third, married persons are given rights to visit their spouses in hospitals, and have an automatic entitlement to act as their spouses' guardian, in their spouses' names, should their loved ones become incapacitated and not able to voice their own desires.[14] These rights are unavailable to unmarried persons who may likewise have a need for such a designated "friend" to visit, serve as guardian, or speak in one's name. In the private sphere, married persons are generally covered by health insurance policies provided by their spouse's employer. Unmarried persons in equally committed relationships are not so covered, and unmarried persons who are not part of a "couple" likewise have no such opportunity to be covered on a friend's insurance policy. This list could be vastly expanded. By one relatively authoritative count produced by the General Accounting Office in 2004, at the request of ex-Senator Frist's office pursuant to debate over the possibility of a Defense of Marriage Constitutional Amendment, married persons enjoy legal and private benefits not shared by unmarried persons that number in the *thousands*.[15] Civil marriage, when viewed as a system of preferential treatment of one group over another solely by virtue of status, begins to look a good bit like the Jim and Jane Crow regimes so carefully and painstakingly dismantled by the courts during the mid-twentieth century. It looks like a straightforward case of the state providing unequal protection of law, and doing so solely on the basis of status.

Now, not every differentiation in the law, not even every differentiation that severely affects one group but not another of similarly situated persons, is *therefore* unconstitutional—if that were the case, we would have no law. Virtually all laws draw lines, and all laws affect some group better than others. (Persons over 16 can get a driver's license, persons under 16 cannot; persons over 65 are entitled to Social Security, persons under 65 are not; persons who earn $30,000 a year pay x amount in taxes, persons who earn $20,000 a year pay less, and so on.) Some of these rules, and categorizations, are surely less wise than others; that fact alone does not make them unconstitutional. Furthermore, the lines drawn by even very rational and thoroughly desirable laws treat some individuals unfairly, simply by virtue of the nature of rules. (Some 15-year-olds are more mature and potentially better drivers than some 17-year-olds, some persons under 65 are more needful and more deserving of Social Security than some persons over 65, some persons who earn $30,000 a year might have greater needs and be in fact less capable of paying a higher tax rate than some who earn $20,000, and so on.) And, perhaps more to the point here, if laws differentiate between persons, but in a way that permits the affected individuals to choose whether or not to be in the burdened category, that will militate hugely against the presumed unconstitutionality. If you do the crime, you'll do the time, which will certainly make you less well treated than those who don't have to do time, but you ought to and can choose to avoid this ill treatment by not doing the crime. So—not every unfair law, or every unfair application of a facially fair law, gives rise to an equal protection problem. All laws differentiate. All laws discriminate between groups. The constitutional question is not whether a law discriminates or differentiates. Laws do so by virtue of being laws. The question, basically, is whether a law does so unfairly.

Over the last half century, courts and constitutional lawyers have developed a series of questions, or equal protection "tests" in determining whether a law that delineates and then differentially treats various groups, does so *so* unfairly as to render the law unconstitutional. If a law "flunks" the "equal protection test," it violates our constitutional norm of equality. That series of questions, or tests, taken collectively, is the argumentative core of what we might call, borrowing a felicitous phrase from Professor William Eskridge, our "equality practice," by which I mean the practice, engaged in by constitutional commentators, lawyers, and citizens, as well as judges, of holding the fairness and rationality of laws up to the light of the demands of equality and equal treatment.[16] The tests of equality under the Constitution, as developed in our equality practice, embrace some of our most widely shared principles of political morality. The Constitution, and the equality practice it inspires, at least raise some of the right questions, with respect not only to laws that have been tested in court, or might be, but also with respect to laws and social practices alike that may not be.

The "test" for whether a law or set of laws violates the Equal Protection Clause of the Fourteenth Amendment by virtue of the adverse impact it has on a delineated group, is now conventionally understood to involve (at least) four steps, or questions. The first question has to do with the nature of the adversely affected group, and it has several subparts. First, is the group that is adversely affected by the law in question, one that is defined by characteristics over which the individual has no control.[17] Is the group that is first delineated and then adversely affected by the law one that is also characterized by what the Court sometimes describes as an "immutable" characteristic (such as skin color, or biological sex, or ethnicity)? Second, is the group both "discrete" and "insular," and because of those features, peculiarly disabled from influencing the ordinary political process? Is this a group that, because of its nature, will be more likely than not to lose in the political process, and for unjustifiable reasons? If so, then it might be in need of some protection against standard majoritarian democratic machinations. Finally, is the group one that has historically suffered from societal and legal maltreatment? If the group affected is of this sort, both courts and commentators have come to call the group a "suspect class"—suspect, because the Court should be "suspicious" of the state's purported rationale for the adverse treatment.[18] It may be likely, or even probable, that the legislature, in crafting a law that adversely affects such a group, was not even intending to legislate in the public interest, but rather, was intending primarily to harm that group, and to do so out of animus toward it. If the class affected is "suspect" in this way (as was the "group" of African American citizens adversely affected by the regime of intentional racial discrimination that the courts dismantled during the 1950s and 1960s), then the law in question might well be unconstitutional, depending on the resolution of the second part of the equal protection "test."

So, here's part two. If the answer to the first set of questions is yes, then the adversely affected group is "suspect," and constitutional lawyers proceed to ask a second set of questions regarding the state's purported goal, and they do so under a test that has come to be called "strict scrutiny." The idea here is simply that the Court will "strictly scrutinize" the goal that the state claims to be pursuing, wherever a law adversely impacts a group defined by an immutable characteristic that has historically suffered from social and legal maltreatment.[19] In such cases, the Court now reasons, the only chance such a law can possibly be constitutional is if the end served by the legislature, through the law, is one that is "compelling."[20] As a matter of history (not logic), over the last half century that the Court has been applying this test, where the group that is adversely affected meets the criteria spelt out above—the group is one that is defined by characteristics (such as race) over which the individual has no control, and the group is one that has been the target of social and legal maltreatment (again, such as race)—the state's purported ends have been found *not* sufficiently compelling to sustain constitutional scrutiny in almost every case where the question has been cleanly posed. Beginning with the Court's unanimous decision in *Brown v. Board of Education*[21] in 1954, finding segregated public schooling unconstitutional, the Supreme Court, and the lower federal courts, have used this logic to strike down state and federal laws that discriminate against citizens on the basis of race, as well as on the basis of a number of other "suspect" characteristics as well, such as alienage, illegitimacy, ethnicity, and religion. Race, though, continues to be the paradigmatic "immutable characteristic" that defines a suspect class, giving rise, in turn, to strict scrutiny, and the need for a compelling justification for any law that separates citizens on the basis of it. With the major exception of affirmative action regimes (that are not presumptively the product of ill will or animus, and are accordingly "scrutinized" under a less demanding standard), such laws are now noncontroversially unconstitutional, and have been understood to be such since 1954.

What if the answer to the first question is "no"—meaning there is no "suspect class" involved? We move on to step three, sometimes called "fundamental interest analysis." Even if there is no suspect class involved, the law might still be unconstitutional. If the lines drawn by a law are drawn in such a way that a "fundamental interest" is severely impacted, that also might trigger "strict scrutiny" under the Equal Protection Clause, and hence the need for a compelling justification to uphold the statute. The Court found as much in a handful of cases in the 1960s and 1970s—most importantly, cases involving laws burdening the access to courts, to voting, to marriage itself, and to travel, of poor people. State laws that burden the exercise of these "fundamental interests," the Court held, could be for that reason constitutionally problematic, whether or not a suspect class is involved.[22] The modern Court—both the Rehnquist and the Roberts Court—has not done much with this line of authority since, leading some to the reasonable conclusion that this body of equal protection law (the "fundamental interest" prong) has atrophied. Nor has this body of law developed in such a way as to constitute a basis for constitutionally challenging the broad array of laws that adversely affect the interests of the poor.[23] Nevertheless the "fundamental interest" line of cases from the 1960s and 1970s Warren and Burger Court era have never been overturned. Their reasoning, furthermore, may be relevant here: as I will briefly discuss below, although the Court has never so held, *parenting* young children may be a "fundamental interest," and some of these marriage laws might render parenting by unmarried poor people unduly burdensome. If so, the law that has this affect, no less than a law that burdens a suspect class, under the logic of the "fundamental interest" prong of equal protection analysis, should be subjected to "strict scrutiny."

Finally—step four—what if there is no fundamental interest, and no suspect class involved, but the law nevertheless adversely affects some interest—albeit not fundamental—of a disadvantaged class? The law still may be unconstitutional, but it is far less likely. A law that neither touches on a fundamental interest nor adversely affects a nonsuspect class, the Court has reasoned, is presumptively constitutional, so long as the state can meet the undemanding test that the goal that the state is pursuing is "reasonable," or, put differently, so long as the classifications the law creates are rationally related to some legitimate state end.[24] This is an easier "test" than the "compelling state interest" test—the law doesn't have to be wise, or desirable, or sensible, just minimally reasonable—but it still has some content: the idea behind it is that laws drawn by state and federal legislators that adversely affect even nonsuspect classes must be reasonably drawn to further legitimate legislative ends. Where the groups adversely affected by a law are not "suspect," however, the Courts have been extremely deferential, for concerns of comity, or respect for the lawmaking, democratic function of the legislative branch. The Court cannot, and should not, become a supralegislature, pontificating upon and then upholding or striking state or federal laws, on the basis of its own sense of what is and is not reasonable. Thus, legislation that adversely impacts upon and expressly discriminates against particular sectors of the economy (such as people making over $100,000 a year) or particular economic interests (such as medical doctors, or the automobile industry) are clearly not "suspect classes," and such legislation—the bread and butter, so to speak, of legislative activity—is routinely upheld (and rarely challenged).[25]

Sometimes, it's not clear whether a group adversely affected by a law should be understood as a "suspect class" (triggering "strict scrutiny"). Where groups are in the middle (such as, the Court has somewhat notoriously reasoned in the past, women, and likewise mentally retarded citizens, because they might have an immutable characteristic, but they are not a group with an unambiguous history of social animosity and outright hostility that has been experienced by racial animosities), the Court has cut the difference and employed a test somewhere in the middle: the state's goal must be more than simply "rational," but need not rise to the level of "compelling." This mid-level review is sometimes called "rational scrutiny with a bite."

Thus, equal protection law can be summed up as contemplating three distinct "levels of review." A law that burdens a suspect class or adversely impacts upon the exercise of a "fundamental interest" will be subjected to "strict scrutiny" and only upheld if the state's interest is compelling. A law that does neither, will only be struck if it is patently irrational: if there is no discernible rational relation between the purported state goal and the lines drawn to achieve it. Laws that burden groups that are not "suspect," but that are nevertheless to some degree disadvantaged, will be subjected to a mid-level of review: more rigorous than the rational basis test, less rigorous than the compelling interest test. Under this structure, over the last fifty to one hundred years, we can sum up the results in this way: "Economic and social welfare regulation" is generally given near-total deference. These laws will not be held unconstitutional barring extraordinary circumstances. Racially discriminatory laws, by contrast, as well as laws that burden other religious or ethnic groups, are routinely struck, under the heightened level of review called "strict scrutiny" (or were routinely struck, post-*Brown*, when they were still ubiquitous), as are laws that unduly burden some fundamental interests of poor citizens, such as rights to vote, to use the courts, or to travel. Laws affecting gender have been in the middle category. They have for the most part been struck under a "mid-level scrutiny" test if the goal strikes the judges as not sufficiently important to justify the gender-based classification.[26] They have also, however, been occasionally upheld.[27]

So, keeping these questions in mind, return to marriage laws. What are we to make of marriage laws, meaning, both the laws that define and create marriage, and the laws that allocate benefits and burdens on the basis of marital status? The marriage laws of all states differentiate between married persons and unmarried persons, and under the marriage laws of virtually all states, unmarried persons are treated worse than married persons. The constitutionality of all of this adverse treatment of a legislatively defined group, then, should depend on whether such differentiation is an unequal protection of the law. That question, in turn, should depend first upon where the differentiations effected by civil marriage fall, on this spectrum: is the differentiation between married and unmarried one that adversely affects a "suspect class," which can therefore only be upheld if the reason the state does so is "compelling"? Or, do the laws adversely impact upon a fundamental interest? If a suspect class or fundamental interest is involved, are the state's ends compelling? If not, is the differentiation sufficiently "rational" to meet the less demanding test of "minimal scrutiny"? Or, does it fall in the middle category? Again, if the class of unmarried persons is a "suspect class" or if a fundamental interest is adversely impacted, then the differentiation of unmarried and married persons should only be upheld if the state's interest in the law in question is compelling. If it is not a suspect class and if there is no fundamental interest involved, then the laws would be upheld so long as their reasons for doing so is at least rational, which has turned out to mean, in practice, not patently absurd.

In a moment, I will outline an argument that even a liberally defined civil marriage law that permits same-sex as well as opposite-sex couples to marry, might be unconstitutional, and under any of these so-called tests. But first note, if only to set aside for now, that if "civil marriage" is limited to heterosexual man-woman couples, then there is a very strong case that the exclusionary aspect of the law is indeed unconstitutional under both federal and state constitutional guarantees of equal protection—as the Massachusetts Supreme Court famously found in *Goodridge v. State of Massachusetts*,[28] and as Justice Marshall quite eloquently argued in her majority opinion in that case.[29] We'll look at same sex-marriage more broadly in the next chapter, but note here just that the argument for the unconstitutionality of the exclusion of same-sex couples is remarkably straightforward. The persons that the law adversely impacts—gay and lesbian citizens—might well constitute a "suspect class." Evidence is mounting that homosexuality is indeed an "immutable characteristic" over which the individual has little or no control, and homosexuals, as a group, have certainly been subjected to both societal and legal maltreatment. And, the right to marry, the Court has repeatedly found, is indeed fundamental, of absolutely central importance to both the society that marriage stabilizes, and to the individuals on whom it bestows such enormous tangible and intangible benefits.[30] With respect to this excluded group, the question that must be answered with respect to the constitutionality of a civil marriage law that precludes their participation is simple: Is the state's purported justification for the differentiation at the heart of their marriage laws a "compelling" one?

And what is that justification? What is the point of defining marriage in such a way as to limit it to opposite-sex couples? The only rationale that the State of Massachusetts asserted, in *Goodridge*, in defending their statutory exclusion of gay and lesbian citizens, is the state's interest in protecting the well-being of children. The state has an inarguable interest in the well-being of children, the state argued, and traditional marriage best protects that interest.[31] But if that's the rationale for excluding gay and lesbian citizens, the law is in trouble, if we assume that gay and lesbian citizens constitute a suspect class, such that strict scrutiny is in order. There is very little evidence to support the proposition that gay and lesbian couples are not just as capable as heterosexual couples of raising, nurturing, protecting, and educating children.[32] Indeed, there is a growing body of evidence that there is virtually no difference in the "outcomes" of children raised by gay or straight couples. Justice Marshall reviewed the evidence, basically found as much, and concluded that the law could not even meet the relatively undemanding "minimal scrutiny" or rational basis test. She accordingly found the law unconstitutional.[33] Gay and lesbian couples must be allowed to marry; to do otherwise violates their right to equal protection of the law. Ergo—gay and lesbian citizens now may marry in Massachusetts. They are accorded, that is, the equal protection of the laws governing marriage.

This is a powerful argument—in part, because it is so simple. Although built on the equal protection and due process clauses of the Massachusetts State

Constitution, furthermore, the same arguments could be made with equal force under the comparable clause of the federal Constitution, as well as under most other states' equal protection clauses. It is a safe bet that the decision will endure. It has also, of course, sparked a ferocious backlash. It has prompted a round of proposed federal and state constitutional amendments (including in Massachusetts itself), as well as literally countless state and local referenda, all of which seek to limit the effect of this decision to Massachusetts, and prevent the spread of this constitutional reasoning to other parts of the country.[34] Politics aside, however, the bare constitutional logic of the *Goodridge* decision is unassailable. It's not rash to predict that eventually, meaning over decades, Justice Marshall's decision in *Goodridge* will be recognized as not only an expression of wisdom, compassion, and moral righteousness, but also as a constitutional bellwether. There's no clearer statement, anywhere, of the basic unfairness, and therefore the unconstitutionality, of not allowing gay and lesbian citizens the right to marry.

We'll look at *Goodridge* (and arguments against it) in more detail in the next chapter. Here, I want to ask a different question, and that is whether the power of the *Goodridge* decision has inadvertently obscured a deeper societal unfairness, and perhaps a deeper breach of basic constitutional guarantees, than the same-sex bar, and that is the unfairness of even the liberal nonhomophobic marriage law that the *Goodridge* case itself brought into the world. Marriage laws that include gay and lesbian couples within the universe of people who might wed nevertheless continue to differentiate between persons who are and aren't married. What are we to make of *that* differentiation—the differentiation, that is, between all married persons (including married same-sex couples in Massachusetts), and all unmarried persons (including both unmarried persons in "couples" that still cannot qualify for "marriage," and single, uncoupled persons)? Many people who are not married, even in Massachusetts, are nevertheless parts of families. A mother coparenting small children with her own mother; a sister living over decades with her brother, who ultimately expend considerable joint resources caring for their aging parents; two neighbors or friends who live and raise their children together, and pool their resources in order to do so—what of those? These are families too, and might well be characterized by the same interdependencies, mutual affection, and joint capacity for the work and responsibilities of caregiving that we believe presumptively true of marital partners. Yet, we bestow benefits only upon those families headed by married, and sexually joined, couples. Is that a difference that withstands the light that the Constitution, our equal protection tests, and our equality practice might cast? What might the practice of equality, constitutionally guided, have to say regarding the fairness of this basic social institution?

Let us run the civil institution of marriage itself, rather than the gay and lesbian exclusion, through the various tests of constitutional equality, as outlined above. Again, that structure asks four basic questions: is the impacted group a "suspect class?" The suspect class question, in turn, has two major components: is the class hurt by the law that is defined by reference to an immutable characteristic (such that one does not have the freedom to opt in and out of the group), and second, is it a group that has borne the ill effects of a history of societal and/or legal maltreatment? How does the class of "unmarried persons" fare under this test? Alternatively, do marriage laws adversely impact upon a fundamental interest of a disadvantaged group? And if the answer to either question is yes, is the state's purpose, or goal, in promoting marriage a compelling one? If the answer is no, is the state's legislative scheme at least minimally rational?

So, take it from the top. On first blush it may appear as though unmarried persons are unmarried by choice, and that therefore the class cannot possibly be "immutable"—in which case (assuming no fundamental interest) there is no suspect class, no "strict scrutiny," and no need to find a compelling justification for whatever state interest the state may have in civil marriage. But this "first blush" may be because we have become overly accustomed to thinking of the conjugal, sexual "coupling" that marriage requires as natural, inevitable, desirable, and certainly open to all—with the only challenging question being whether or not gay and lesbian couples fit the category. The status of "marriage," however, is not so easily attained for many people, not because the *couple* of which they are a member is irrationally excluded, but rather, because they are not part of a conjugal, sexually defined couple at all, and have no prospects of becoming one. While it is clear that some conjugal couples might opt for cohabitation over marriage—thus rendering fully "voluntary" their "choice" not to marry—it is equally clear that some unmarried persons who may nevertheless be very much a part of a "family" cannot marry at all, because they cannot find a marriageable partner. Many poor women, for example, cannot find a suitable life partner, for the straightforward reason that there are no potential spouses in their community that would be anything but a major drain on their already stretched resources—not due to willfulness on their part, but rather, due to the unavailability of decent jobs for unskilled or low-skilled workers.[35] These women, according to one recent study and review of the literature, "put motherhood before marriage" not because they disdain marriage, and certainly not because they willfully opt out of it, but because marriage is not an economically viable choice.[36] Many of them are nevertheless undeniably parts of families: they raise children, they form partnerships with other adults, they pool resources, they share risks, they form and live within a web of interdependent adult relationships, and so on.

It is not only poor mothers, however, who often find themselves outside the magical ring of married persons. Others of us, regardless of economic class, can't find a marriageable partner because we simply have not found someone mutually appealing. Others of us don't marry, perhaps, because we simply lack the inclination to pair up; general tendency of the species notwithstanding, it just doesn't hold true for us. Yet, many of these persons as well are members of "families." Some of the unmarried may be fiercely independent rugged individualists or confirmed old bachelors who prefer to remain as such, but clearly not all: some unmarried persons are just as fully integrated into functional, committed, loving, but nonmarital and nonconjugally coupled families as are their married neighbors. Surely by now—when the traditional marriage is no longer even the norm, much less the overwhelming choice—we realize that a "family," understood as a group of interdependent, mutually affectionate, intergenerational caregivers and dependents, is not contingent upon the existence of a "married" couple at its head.

So, let's ask this question: is this "class"—the class of unmarried persons who are nevertheless members of families, and who, both as individuals and as family members, are disfavored because of that status—a "suspect class"? Is the class of unmarried adults defined by an "immutable characteristic"? Is it a class that has been the object of approbation, bias, prejudice, or hatred? Is it one that is so "insular" that it is peculiarly disadvantaged from participating in the ordinary political processes of lawmaking? Is it a demarcation that should trigger suspicion, with respect to a legislature's motives when passing laws that adversely affect it? None of the characteristics—poverty, lack of an appealing potential partner, or simple idiosyncratic excessive individualism—seems "immutable," at least in the same way the Supreme Court clearly meant when they coined the phrase "immutable characteristic."[37] Being single is obviously not like being African American, or female, or of a particular ethnic background, or mentally retarded, or illegitimate—all characteristics the Court has deemed to some degree immutable. But none of them seem particularly "chosen" either. We don't choose to live in a community or neighborhood where there are few jobs, fewer still with decent wages or benefits, and because of all of that few viable potential marriage partners. We don't choose to fail to find a life partner. We don't choose to be idiosyncratically averse to doing so either. Yet many of us find ourselves in these predicaments, and thus in the "class" of persons for whom marriage is not a realistic option. For many people, the state of being unmarried is indeed caused by an "immutable characteristic"—if by immutable, we simply mean that it is caused by some set of circumstances that is not within our power to control.

Likewise, it is not hard to find evidence that this group has been subjected to a campaign of approbation and ill will by the larger society—from the blanket of moral stigma cast on unwed motherhood and "illegitimacy" of the 1950s, to the "welfare queen" of the 1980s, and the orchestrated attempts of the current Bush administration, and the Clinton administration before it, to cast single parenthood as irresponsible, and an unwarranted drain on the public purse. The history of these campaigns alone should be enough to trigger a suspicion that there is a real tension between our celebration of marriage, our insistence that only families headed by marital partners are deserving of respect, and our castigation of unmarried families as irresponsible and nothing but a societal burden, on the one hand, and our constitutional aspiration of a society that insists upon an equal protection of laws, for all, on the other. It doesn't follow, from a tentative conclusion that this group might be a "suspect class," that marriage laws are therefore unconstitutional. What might follow, though, is that we should view them rigorously, or "strictly."

Marriage laws might also sensibly trigger "strict scrutiny" under the "fundamental interest" prong of equal protection analysis. Marriage laws might burden the ability of unmarried persons to *parent*, in ways we will explore below, and it doesn't seem unreasonable to suggest—indeed the Court has itself suggested, and on a number of occasions—that parenting (no less than voting, interstate mobility, education, or marriage itself) is a "fundamental interest." For many people, parenting is the central adventure of an adult lifetime, and for almost all parents, it is a primary source of love, satisfaction, and happiness in their adult lives.[38] In fact, much of what the courts have said about why the "right to marry" should be understood as fundamental, applies with equal force to an interest, or right, to parent. Judge Marshall, in *Goodridge*, summarized the law and the reasoning of these marriage cases in these now justly famous passages:

> Civil marriage enhances the "welfare of the community." It is a "social institution of the highest importance." Civil marriage anchors an ordered society by encouraging stable relationships over transient ones. It is central to the way the Commonwealth identifies individuals, provides for the orderly distribution of property, ensures that children and adults are cared for and supported whenever possible from private rather than public funds, and tracks important epidemiological and demographic data.
>
> Marriage also bestows enormous private and social advantages on those who choose to marry. Civil marriage is at once a deeply personal commitment to another human being and a highly public celebration of the ideals of mutuality, companionship, intimacy, fidelity, and family.... Because it fulfills yearnings for security, safe haven, and connection that express our common humanity, civil marriage is an esteemed institution, and the decision whether and whom to marry is among life's momentous acts of self-definition. ...
>
> It is undoubtedly for these concrete reasons, as well as for its intimately personal significance, that civil marriage has long been termed a "civil right." The United States Supreme Court has described the right to marry as "of fundamental importance for all individuals" and as "part of the fundamental right of privacy" implicit in the Fourteenth Amendment's Due Process Clause.[39]

Okay, but isn't all of this also true—maybe, more true—of parenting? Parenting, surely, enhances the "welfare of the community"; in fact, it is absolutely essential both to the welfare of the community and the global village. Parenting, surely as much or more than marriage, anchors an ordered society, and creates stable relations between caregivers and dependents. Parenting, no less than marrying, and likely more so, is "a deeply personal commitment to another human being" that both rests on and fulfills ideals of "mutuality, companionship, intimacy, fidelity, and family." Parenting undoubtedly "fulfills yearnings for ... connection that express our common humanity." Parenting is or ought to be an "esteemed institution." The decision whether to parent ought to be among life's momentous acts of self-definition; in fact, in its own contraception and procreation cases, the Supreme Court itself has repeatedly said as much.[40] The lifelong act of caring for dependents—our own children as well as our own elderly parents—in which so many of us at one time or another engage, is surely of fundamental interest to us. We ought to recognize it as such, in our constitutional jurisprudence. It is of "fundamental" importance, furthermore, to all individuals. Perhaps parenting—more broadly, caregiving—should be recognized as a fundamental civil right.

Unmarried parents who are truly, profoundly "single"—parents without partners, family members, or friends that are equally committed to their dependents' well-being—will indeed have a much harder time nurturing and raising children than their married peers.[41] Unmarried and particularly "unfamilied" parents—by which I mean unmarried parents who do not have committed, dependable assistance in their parenting—will have fewer economic resources to draw upon, and they will have less time to devote to parenting. They will not be as able to shield their children from the impact of severe economic, physical, emotional, or psychic downturns their family—of themselves and their dependents—may sustain. They will not enjoy "economies of scale," or have the pooled resources with which to guard against risk. All unmarried parents, however, both the truly single, and those in committed, but unmarried relationships, will find their parenting burdened by marriage laws, and by the scores of financial benefits withheld them by virtue of that status. Unmarried poor parents will not have a deceased marital partner's Social Security or military pension on which to draw—and nor will she have the possibility of drawing on that of a deceased companion, coparent, or intimate. She will not have the benefit of favorable tax treatment, or private health insurance provided to spouses, that are routinely accorded married persons. She will not have a partner with a virtual "power of attorney" to make decisions on her behalf or that of her children, should she become incapacitated. Either directly or indirectly, the law is deeply implicated in a regime that has an adverse impact upon a class of people trying to engage in a basic, fundamental life activity—bearing, nurturing, and raising children—and trying to do so outside the protective perimeters of marriage.

The state's marriage laws burden caregiving in another way as well, less obvious but perhaps more significant. The civil institution of marriage has the effect of channeling societal resources that perhaps ought to be devoted to assisting poor people in particular, but all of us more generally, with the basic financial burdens of caregiving, toward families organized around marriage, rather than toward families organized around caregiving. This is a sensible allocation of scarce resources only if we assume both that caregiving occurs quintessentially within marriage, that one or both of the marital partners is rendered relatively dependent because of it, and that this is the way it ought to be—only if we assume, that is, that marriage is a functional social unit that consists of a dependent caregiving partner and an incomer earner. If all of that is true, then there's at least some rhyme or reason to those thousands of benefits bestowed upon married, but not upon unmarried, caregivers: rather than support caregiving, we rather valorize and support that form of family within which caregiving quintessentially and optimally occurs, and then support it, indirectly, but substantially, through Social Security presumptions, tax treatment, and the like. This implicit "preference" for the caregiving that occurs with marriages, however, coupled with financial benefits that underscore it, is doubly problematic. First, it burdens the caregiving that occurs outside of it, by simple neglect. Those attempting to parent, or give care, outside the socially preferred form do not receive the indirect financial assistance from the state conferred by virtue of marriage laws. But second, that neglect is then compounded by the moral approbation we attach to the unmarried status. We do not have, and have never had, in this country, either an ethic of societal responsibility toward the poor, or much of a social welfare net to meet their needs. And, we do not have such an ethic, or such a welfare net, in part, and perhaps in large part, because of our valorization of marriage. Civil marriage, we believe, is the way our fundamental interest in not only parenting, but in caregiving more generally, should be structured. Those who are needy, and outside the strictures of married life, are accordingly deemed less worthy of assistance. Need alone, given our understanding of the limited role of government in the duty to assist poor people, has never been sufficient to trigger substantial support.

Is this a cause for concern? Or, is it simply the predictable consequence of a reasonable state and community decision to encourage people who want to parent, to first marry, and to *discourage* those who don't wish to marry, from parenting? Is it morally or constitutionally acceptable, in other words, for the state to discourage adults who wish to do so, from parenting children on the basis of their failure to marry? Or, does the state's marriage law, particularly when viewed in conjunction with our contemporary welfare law and policies, which clearly do just that, un-constitutionally burden a "fundamental interest" by virtue of the burden they place on parenting outside of marriage? The answer: it depends. It depends, largely, on whether we view parenting as a "fundamental interest," or a "fundamental right," that we should accord to all adult citizens, and regardless of their ability to marry. If we do so view it, then marriage laws that comparatively disadvantage parenting outside of marriage, even on the not unreasonable assumption that parenting is best pursued within marriage, may well unduly burden the fundamental interest, or right, of unmarried persons to parent. Is there such a fundamental interest, or fundamental right?

There is no clear answer to such a question, but it is worth noting that the Court has held, repeatedly, that at least married persons have a fundamental right to procreate, and raise their children, in the privacy of their home, and that single persons have a fundamental right to make the decision whether or not to have children without being burdened by state law criminalizing birth control. Obviously, there is a huge distance from the logic of such cases to the conclusion that our fundamental interest in parenting cannot be burdened by a civil institution such as marriage, that burdens it in part simply by legitimating a social lack of interest in providing financial assistance to those who need it. Nevertheless, it is hard to see why parenting should not be deemed fundamental. Many of us do it, all of us have needed it, none of us would be alive without it. Without parental care, we die when we are infants, and without parental care, we fail to thrive when we are children. Without parental care, as young adults, we become asocial, or antisocial, and dysfunctional. There is little else we do, or in which we all have an "interest," that is as universal, meaningful, and essential to human life. Many of us want very much to become parents, and even more of us, whether or not we wish it, do become parents, and wish to do it well rather than poorly. All of us who parent do so at enormous sacrifice. I don't know that it follows that we have a fundamental right to state assistance when we seek to parent outside the protective parameters of the preferred marital form. As noted at the outset of this discussion, no court has ever so found, the Court has held repeatedly that there is no "constitutional right to welfare." Nevertheless, I would suggest at least this limited, aspirational, and decidedly nonadjudicative constitutional inference: if we have a fundamental interest in parenting, then perhaps we also have, as citizens, a fundamental duty to set up our social and legal institutions in such a way that parenting does not impoverish us—and does not impoverish us, whether or not we marry.

Last: even if unmarried persons are not a suspect class, and even if there is no fundamental right adversely affected by marriage laws, nevertheless, marriage laws might be unconstitutional, if the distinctions they draw between married and unmarried persons are simply irrational. Now, very few laws—particularly laws pertaining to economic and social distributions of benefits—have ever flunked this prong of the equal protection test, but nevertheless, let me return briefly to our starting point—laws that financially benefit married persons solely by virtue of marital status—to suggest that these laws ought to. Recall that married persons, by virtue of their status, receive a wide array of benefits that unmarried persons do not, in large part on the assumption that married persons are "interdependent" with each other, and therefore, at various points in their lives, needier, should their partner die or become incapacitated. As we noted, this generalization clearly suffers from over- and undergeneralization: not all married persons are so interdependent, and many unmarried persons are interdependent. What is worth stressing, though, is that the problem with these benefit schemes is significantly deeper than just their over- and underbreadth. Rather, the benefits that accrue to the status of being married, if we follow contemporary law and fashion and deny the stereotypical assumption that wives are economically dependent on their husbands, seem patently, and fatally, irrational.

Let me just take one example: the Social Security benefits that accrue to married persons, upon the death of their spouses. Retired married partners whose spouses die—widows and widowers alike—are entitled to either their own Social Security payments *or their spouses'*—whichever is higher. This "marital bump" in Social Security payments during widowhood is one of the major economic benefits of marriage over cohabitation, at least with respect to federal law. But why should a married worker who has paid into the Social Security system over his or her married life, receive a "marital bump" not available to the unmarried worker working the same job for the same number of years? We can, of course, easily explain the origin and history of this difference. The drafters of the Social Security Laws, in the Depression and post-Depression era, assumed quite explicitly that a "wife," *by virtue of her marital status,* was needier than an unmarried woman—the wife, after all, presumptively, had engaged in lifelong unpaid marital labor that she would not have engaged in had she remained single.[42] Given that assumption, it made sense, or so they thought, to give the wife a "bump," at the death of her husband on whom she was dependent. The marital bump, in other words, was originally specifically for *wives,* presumed to be dependent and therefore needy by virtue of their marriage, not for "spouses" presumed to be "interdependent." But whether for good or ill, this "stereotypical" thinking about dependent wives and providing husbands has been struck as unconstitutional, in Social Security law and elsewhere. Consequently, the "marital bump" in Social Security payments is now available to *all* married Social Security beneficiaries, husbands and wives alike, and obviously, whether or not they have been rendered needy by virtue of their marriage. The married wife, or husband, is entitled, on the death of her spouse, to either her own or to his Social Security payment, whichever is larger. The single worker, and Social Security recipient, gets no such bump.

So—what is the bare logic of that? Frankly, none comes to mind. When we wipe out from the law the assumption of wifely dependency that motivated the "marital bump" in the first place, we seemingly wipe out the rationality of providing married partners higher Social Security. Put differently, the rationality of providing married partners higher Social Security payments on the deaths of their spouses than single payees rests on the assumption that the married beneficiary is more needy than the unmarried, precisely because of the status of being married. That was the assumption behind the initial decision in the 1930s to treat wives more generously than either married men or unmarried women and men. But if we no longer assume that—if we assume that marriage is just two partners, equally interdependent on each other, and then give the bump to both, now premised not on a disabling dependency, but rather, the more benign "interdependency" of marriage—then not only is the marriage bump irrational, it seems flatly backward. The marriage partners may indeed be "interdependent" upon each other. But what we now know is that precisely by virtue of that inter-dependence, they are therefore more likely to be *better* off—not worse off—than their unmarried co-citizens; this is the meaning of the "marriage premium" so heralded by marriage's utilitarian defenders.[43] Married partners, in other words, are better off, and less needy, by virtue of their interdependence on each other—they are interdependent on each other, but are therefore *less* needy, and presumably *less* dependent on the state. The unmarried, not the married, should get the "bump," if the justification for a bump rests on a disparity in relative need pertaining to marital status.

Now, let me summarize where this hypothetical and fanciful argument has taken us so far. Arguably, marriage laws create a disfavored class of persons—un-married people—that may be so "suspect" as to trigger the need for "heightened scrutiny" of the state's purpose. Alternatively, marriage laws may so burden the fundamental interest that unmarried people have in parenting, or caring for disabled or elderly persons, as to likewise trigger heightened scrutiny. Finally, the lines drawn between married and unmarried with respect to benefits, and even assuming no suspect class and no fundamental interest, may be simply irrational. They may be so under- or over-inclusive as to bear no rational relation to any conceivable state goal. If any of this convinces, the case is not quite made, but the burden of constitutional argumentation shifts quite substantially to the state. For the state's marriage laws to be constitutional, the state's interest in maintaining those laws—the state's interest, in other words, in the practice of sanctioning some relations over others, and then favoring those within those relations—must be upheld only if found to be "compelling." This question, like the first, also has two subparts. First, what was, or is, the motivation behind the state's action? And second, is the end in question truly necessary to meet legitimate state goals? Is there a less burdensome way those goals could be met?

This, finally, gets us to the nub of the inquiry, in constitutional terms, as well as the point at which the content of this hypothetical constitutional argument becomes indistinguishable from moral and political argument made by marriage's contemporary critics. What *is*, exactly, the nature of the state's interest in the marital state of its citizens? The interest the State of Massachusetts asserted in *Goodridge*,[44] is that the state's interest in marriage lies primarily in the well-being of children that are oftentimes the product of marriages.[45] More broadly, the state has an interest in marriage, and in promoting marriage, because it has an interest in "privatizing" essential caregiving duties, so as to ease the strain on the taxpayer-funded "safety net." The state is largely charged with the moral and political duty of promoting the well-being of dependents, and particularly of poor dependents—this has been the common ground of various theoretical justifications for the authority of state actors to intervene in persons' private affairs, familial and otherwise, for hundreds of years. Obviously, the state cannot do so directly. It cannot birth, nurture, and raise dependent children to adulthood, or care for the elderly until death. A state might rationally conclude that it is far better for families to take on the task, the burden, the responsibility, and the rights that attend to child-raising, than that states do so in taxpayer-funded communal homes. States do have an interest, then, in protecting, to some degree insulating, and in general supporting the institution—the family—that provides this labor and assumes these responsibilities. If so, then it is surely constitutionally permissible for states to support families in their attempts to provide care for dependents, insulate them from excessive public scrutiny in their attempts to do so well, and to some degree subsidize them—through tax credits or deductions, publicly funded education, family leave provisions, survivor benefits to Social Security entitlements, intestacy law, and the like. There is nothing irrational about the state's attempts to promote the well-being of families that in turn provide the bulk of the caregiving to dependents on a daily basis. That is a plausible set of state objectives; these are entirely commendable goals. They may well be "compelling," and if so, laws that further these interests are constitutional.

The problem, however, lies in the second subpart of the test: even if this fairly states the nature of the state's goals in regulating *families*, the categories the law draws through its marriage laws—between "married" and "unmarried"—are over- and underinclusive both, with respect to those ends, and trigger a not unreasonable suspicion that something else is afoot. Marriage law does not concern itself, directly, with the well-being of children, or the capacity of the adults that decide to have a family, to provide care. Marriage law concerns itself, rather, with the nature of the sexual relationship between the adults, the number of partners to the relationship, and whether or not there is a sexual relationship—the nature of the sexual relationship defines marriage, and that there be one, is a condition of the existence of marriage. But this just seems odd, even ridiculous, if the reason for the state's interest in marriage is the well-being of children (or more broadly, the well-being of dependents). The existence or nonexistence, as well as the type, nature, or content, of a sexual relationship between two adults is seemingly irrelevant to the quality of care those adult individuals may or may not bestow upon their dependents—whether children, aging parents, or others—and each other. What has sex got to do with it? If the state's goal in regulating and defining marriage is to promote the caregiving labor that is often, but not always, at the center of such marriages, then doing so by defining and regulating marriage in the way that it does is just flatly irrational.

To put this in the doctrinal terminology of the Court, the lines the state draws through its marriage laws are underinclusive and overinclusive with respect to the state's purported goal. Begin with the latter. Many marriages—defined as a state sanctified conjugal relationship—do not involve caregiving labor in the slightest. Two consenting adults marry, decide not to have children, have well-paying jobs, and divorce ten years later—well before either they or even their adult parents require any care from the other. Why should they be the recipients of the states' promarriage policies, if caregiving for dependents is the reason for the state's interest, and they've done none of it? They are hardly easing the state's burden of seeing to the well-being of dependents. There seems no reason to privilege this couple over homosexual couples, cohabiting couples, or nonconjugal couples—but more to the point, there seems no reason to privilege this couple, period.

The underinclusiveness is even more serious. Many unmarried people give care to dependents, but are not the beneficiaries of the state's promarriage largesse. While overinclusiveness suggests a certain degree of excessive, or fastidious, or puritanical, or perhaps voyeuristic interest in the nature of sexual relationships between consenting adults, the underinclusiveness suggests a callousness with respect to the very persons the state purports to be concerned about, when regulating marriage, and that is adults giving time and resources so as to provide for dependents. If the point of civil marriage, and hence the nature of the state's interest in the institution, is to promote, protect, and support the provision of caregiving to dependents, then the state's solicitude should extend to those individuals or groups of individuals who actually do that labor, and thus fulfill that state goal. Some married partners do so, as do some same-sex couples. But likewise, so do many teams of adults comprised of mothers and grandmothers, sisters, brothers, or friends. Sometimes, two sisters, or a brother and sister, might unite in the shared, joint enterprise of raising a child, or caring for an elderly parent. A collective of adults might do so—a biological mother and her closest friends or neighbors. Extended family members might well do so—an aunt, grandmother, or grandfather, might unite so as to raise a child of an incapacitated biological mother or father. An unmarried cohabitating partner might take on the parenting of a "step" son or daughter. And clearly, many many people might undertake the work of providing care and nurturance to children, unassisted by any particular other adult or set of adults. These "single" parents too do the work that purportedly justifies the state's interest in marriage. Why shouldn't each of them be declared a "marriage"? Less metaphorically, why shouldn't each receive the benefit of the state's solicitude for married persons, if it's the case (not unreasonable to assume) that the state's interest in this institution in fact rests upon the state's interest in insuring the well-being of dependents, and doing so through the support of the families that provide it?

Under and overinclusiveness often prompt courts, when facing a law that adversely affects a suspect class, or impacts upon a fundamental interest, or simply seems irrational, to look more deeply—more suspiciously—into the state's asserted interest. What happens if we follow through on that logic here? What else might be the state's actual interest in promoting a marital way of life?

One possibility, argued with great force by law Professor Martha Fineman in a series of books and articles on civil marriage, is that the state's promotion of marriage rests on a policy of maintaining the deeply gendered and the uncompensated structure of caregiving labor.[46] States promote, protect, and encourage marriage, so that the work of caregiving—overwhelmingly done by women—will continue to be uncompensated and undervalued, but will nevertheless continue to be done. The uncompensated nature of caregiving labor works to the state's interest—it keeps the need for public revenue for this work low—but its gendered nature offers an even more direct benefit to men—the work, from which they benefit, gets done, and is kept largely out of their hands. Once a woman marries and does a fair amount of caregiving, in a world that thoroughly privatizes caregiving labor, and compensates only noncaregiving labor, she will find herself in a quite profound cycle of dependency. She will not have developed the skills to take her into the wage-paying labor market. She will not have accumulated wealth. She will have become completely dependent upon her husband—a dependency that is exacerbated, not alleviated, by his viable threat of no-fault divorce.[47] She will have no or few realistic alternatives to remaining with him, and so remain with him she will, and live out her life more or less at his whim. Women's disproportionate caregiving thus both gets the caregiving labor done, without significant contribution from men, *and* maintains women's dependency on their husbands. Men's domestic needs are met, they get cared-for children (and oftentimes cared-for mothers as well, who are cared for by their daughters-in-law, more than by their married sons) and dependent wives. That the state subsidizes this arrangement through a series of benefits to married partners, in turn through tax dollars that come largely from his paycheck, is a small price for him to pay.

Now, why—or how—does this happen? No state literally requires women to perform a disproportionate amount of caregiving (or household) labor, and to do it for free. Fineman's explanation is subtle. Historically, she argues, wives were indeed forced to do this work (as well as provide sexual services) within civil marriage, with the enforcement authority in the hands of the husband. Through the laws of coverture, the husband was in effect delegated authority by the state to employ force to ensure compliance. Consequently, marriage was quite literally the social institution within which women's labor was directly exploited—confiscated is not too harsh a word—all facilitated by the state's refusal, on grounds of patriarchal privilege, to intervene. The wife was legally obligated to endure her husband's mistreatment, possible violence, and ill support, with no recourse from law and virtually no viable exit. She did not have the legal power to resist his sexual advances, or the pregnancies that resulted. She would not be entitled to keep any earnings that she might obtain by taking employment outside the household, and she could not legally bind herself to a contract of employment even if she could find someone willing to employ her. So—she bore and cared for his children, made herself sexually available, and submitted to his commands. The legal structure of marriage both reflected and constructed all three of these basic duties.[48] Today, Fineman argues, the legal skeleton of this overtly patriarchal form of marriage has (for the most part) disappeared.[49] A woman can exit a marriage at will (as can her husband); a wife can work in paid employment and employers are legally obliged to pay her comparably to what they would pay a man for the same work; and violence within a marriage is as illegal and criminal as violence outside of it. Yet women continue to disproportionately perform uncompensated caregiving labor, both inside and outside of marriage, and continue to be relatively impoverished by it, as a result. Why?

It is the continuing existence of the institution of civil marriage, Fineman argues, that continues to impoverish women through their caregiving.[50] It no longer does so through the doctrine of coverture: the delegation to the husband of patriarchal sovereign authority within the home, along the lines of the nineteenth-century model. Rather, Fineman argues, marriage itself, the state's valorization of it, and the intense rhetoric that surrounds it, first privatizes and then "masks" the caregiving labor women do.[51] Within marriage, the disproportionate caregiving labor remains invisible, hidden, private—and uncompensated—and keeps the women who do it tied to the men upon whom they become economically dependent. The state rhetorically assigns caregiving labor to the family, but then defines "family" not by reference to the relationship to which care is central—mother-child, or caregiver-dependent—but rather, by reference to the relationship between the presumptively equal adults, to whom not caregiving in any guise, but rather, sex, is central. The relationship at the center of the family is the marital relationship, although the labor at the center of family is caregiving. The labor of caregiving, accordingly, fades from view. It is important, but definitionally incidental. The result is one mighty distraction. The state regulates not the caregiving that is in fact the vital work at the heart of family, but rather, it regulates the sex at the definitional heart of marriage. Thus, civil marriage, with its obsessive and definitional focus on the irrelevant morality and sexuality of the adult pair (Are they heterosexual? Are they adulterous? Are they bigamists? Are they sodomists? Are they monogamous? Are they in it for life? Have they divorced? and so on), keeps the state's attention and regulatory apparatus squarely on the adult couple, rather than on the mother-child pair, and their needs.

By defining family by reference to the heterosexual marriage, and then assigning the work of caregiving to the family so defined, we in effect render that work invisible. It is the horizontal "marriage" that makes a family, to which children may or may not be appended. Today, if anything, the presumptive equality of women has arguably exacerbated the invisibility of caregiving labor. Thus, today, when caregiving labor is performed within the marriage, it is presumptively performed by equal partners who have fairly negotiated its terms to their mutual satisfaction. There is all the *less* reason, then, that the labor should not be entirely "privatized." There is no need for direct state support of the caregiving within the marriage, or the woman who provides it—although there is a need for state support of the marriage itself. The state, then, doesn't support the caregiving, but rather, supports the marriage within which the caregiving occurs. And the state does all of this, nor for the old-fashioned reason that doing so is a way of deferring to a sovereign patriarch, but rather, for the newfangled reason that the state always defers, and always should defer, to the private, consensual arrangement of free and equal adults.[52] To do otherwise would be unduly paternalistic.

And as between the two of them, what will happen? The woman will continue to do the bulk of the unpaid care—and continue to do so to her detriment. She will do so, in part, because she still will earn considerably less than her husband in the wage market, so if one of them should stay home and do unpaid labor it should be her, if the couple is thinking this through rationally. She will do so because she considers it part of what it means to be a mother; he will feel no comparable need because staying home to diaper and feed babies is clearly not considered part of what it means to be a father. She will do so because post partum she will be physically and emotionally more inclined than her husband to take a maternity leave in order to remain home with a newborn. With respect to the housework, she will do more than he, perhaps, because if she doesn't do it, it won't get done, and she can't bring herself to live in filth. She will do it because he has few incentives to do it himself, and in her view, the work must be performed.

Why will she stay in this unfair arrangement? Well, she loves him, perhaps. But aside from love, she will stay because the alternatives are too bleak—they will leave her more impoverished than will her unequal marriage. The state support for marriage, even on the assumption that the support is justified by reference to the caregiving labor that occurs within it, is nevertheless state support *for marriage*—not for caregiving. The result is that caregiving both inside and outside of marriage is unsupported: inside marriage, because it is made invisible by the consensuality of the institution itself, and outside marriage, because although it is painfully visible—it is just not preferred. The harsh treatment given caregivers outside marriage is thus symbiotically connected to the blind eye given caregivers within marriage, as well as the preferential treatment given marriage itself. Caregivers, then, both in and out of marriage, are hurt by the state's refusal to meaningfully protect, promote, and facilitate caregiving labor outside of marriage. The penalty exacted on unmarried mothers renders even a bad marriage a more appealing alternative—and gives caregivers an incentive to seek them out and stay in them, even at substantial cost.

I will evaluate (and express some reservations regarding) this argument in a moment, but first it is worth noting that other "marriage critics" have posited somewhat different understandings of the state's interest in marriage. First, some radical feminist activists and theorists have argued that state-sanctioned civil marriage basically bolsters men's interest, not only by facilitating the exploitation of women's caregiving labor, but rather (and perhaps more centrally) by facilitating the exploitation, or the appropriation, of women's sexual pleasure and sexual labor. There is little question but that marriage, prior to twentieth-century reforms, facilitated that appropriation—whether or not it did so by design. Sexual intercourse was as mandatory for wives within marriage, as it was forbidden to women and girls outside of it. At common law, dating back at least five centuries, wives by definition could not be "raped" by their husbands—rape was defined as the nonconsensual intercourse of a woman, not one's wife, by a man.[53] Marital sex, then, could be consensual or nonconsensual, mutually desired or not, mutually pleasurable or not—with no consequences and certainly no penalty attached either way. Cultural and religious byways of sexual information reinforced the legal bottom line: a wife's duty was to submit to her husband's sexual advances. Refusing to do so was not her right; it was, rather, a breach of duty.[54]

As with women's caregiving labor, however, it is clear that the appropriation of women's sexuality is no longer accomplished, within marriage, through the blunt instrument of patriarchal privilege. Husbands do not and cannot expropriate their wives' sexuality through the lawful use of force. In what sense, then, if any, can this be characterized as nevertheless still the underlying point of civil marriage? Today, even the harshest critics of traditional and historical marriage more often argue that it is not. Thus, in her authoritative history of Western marriage, Stephanie Coontz argues that just over the last one hundred and fifty years we have witnessed a massive transformation of this social institution, from one premised on the glue of wifely "obedience" to the glue of love—of sentimental attachment.[55] Surely this is right, regarding our ideals, and it is likely also true, albeit only to some extent, regarding our practices. It may be fair to assume, today (at least, more fair to assume than it was a hundred or fifty years ago), that when a husband and wife have sex, it is because they both mutually desire it, or at least consent to it, and not because the wife submits, with or without pleasure, to her husbands' sexual demands. (And, it's worth noting, as Coontz does, that if this means that the "point" of civil marriage has shifted from obedience to love, there is absolutely no reason to limit it to man-woman configurations of lovers.)[56] On the other hand, it may also be the case that to some immeasurable degree, the legal reform has predated and prefigured the social reform that would make sense of it. It may still be true, in other words, for many married partners within our larger national life, that the purpose of marriage is indeed to organize, discipline, and largely appropriate women's sexuality. For some, perhaps, sex within marriage may result not from love, fellow feeling, mutual pleasure, desire, or consent, but rather, from harassment, subtle threat, or a feeling of sheer inevitability. It is hard to know. Nevertheless, it does seem to be the case that the state has a dwindling interest in facilitating the appropriation of women's sexuality, through marriage. If, or to the extent that such appropriation was ever, the point of civil marriage, it seems to be no longer.

A third possible understanding of the state's interest in marriage has been recently proposed by a group of queer theorists. Perhaps the point of civil marriage—the "real" state interest in the institution—is to police, marginalize, sanction, and thereby contain nonmarital sex of all sorts—straight sex outside of marriage, queer sex, teenage sex, sex for pay, bathhouse sex, sodomitic sex, group sex, sadomasochistic sex, polygamous sex, polyamorous sex, noncoital sex, and so on. This is not implausible and certainly not a new idea (as queer theorists themselves point out)—a version of this thesis was famously put forward over a century ago by Sigmund Freud,[57] and popularized by devotees of "free love" in the first couple of decades of the twentieth century.

Today, a prominent architect of queer theory, Professor Michael Warner, in an influential work titled *The Problem with Normal,* has revitalized the claim, arguing with great verve that the primary function, and the primary result, of marriage is to delineate the normal and the abnormal, privileging the former and subjecting the latter to penalty, shame, and moral condemnation.[58] The point of all of that condemnation, Warner urges, is not so much to minimize the sheer amount of nonmarital sex, but rather, to underscore its non-normalcy. The result is the otherwise bewildering and contradictory cultural array we now witness. For the normal to exist, there must be an abnormal. So, the abnormal is not wiped out—it's just rendered repeatedly abnormal. We have, then, at the same time, MTV and *Sex and the City* and *Melrose Place* and *There's Something About Mary,* and at the same time, very public hand-wringing and condemnation of all of that. This is not just markets at work. The "normal" highlights the "abnormal" precisely so as to maintain its position on the hierarchy. The result, for those on the bottom rungs of the ladder, is considerable oppression and misery: state toleration of abuse and violence against gay men and women; lack of police enforcement of violence against prostitutes; homophobic and sex-panicked moralistic campaigns against sexual minorities. The result is also, Warner makes clear, a considerable degree of frisson, sexual pleasure, and stimulation—the abnormal to some degree thrive on the shame produced by their societal condemnation. What we don't need tossed into this mix, Warner argues with no small degree of passion, is "gay marriage."[59] The impact of the gay marriage movement, were it to be successful, would be further valorization of the normal and further oppression of the abnormal.

The less direct, but equally damaging, consequence of the "same-sex marriage movement" is the threat it poses to the sexual underground—the existence of sexual markets and transactions unbound by convention, unashamed of shame itself, undeterred by threat, and turned on rather than off by the prospect of at least contained sexual danger. The realm of the abnormal, Warner urges, should not just solicit our concern as a potential target of unjust discrimination or abuse. It is also of intrinsic merit, whether recognized or not. The world of sexual abnormality is a domain in which conventional values are inverted, and all toward the celebration of pleasure and power—with the risk of danger fully accepted in the bargain. Normal, with its finger-tutting, its obscenity trials, its hierarchic organization of human sexual pleasures, its prurient and voyeuristic obsession with the deviant, its tendency toward self-denial and self-oppression, and its fear of the marginalized other seemingly threatens, but actually facilitates, the abnormal: the existence of the abnormal is as much dependent upon normalcy as normalcy requires the deviant. What the abnormal is threatened by is co-optation—depletion of the troops if nothing else. Marriage, then, as it exists, is containable, tolerable, normalcy—a good enough counterpoint to the existence, perversity, and thrill of the abnormal. Gay marriage, though, is a serious threat. With its intrusions into gay life, the same-sex marriage equality movement and the normal it so perfectly represents really does threaten to obliterate abnormality. And that would be a tragedy—not only in terms of the human lives that would be twisted, yet again, in a futile attempt to conform to a corset that just doesn't fit, but an overall loss as well—if we lose, through co-optation, the sexual underground; we will have lost a domain of expression, creativity, human camaraderie, pleasure, power, and community, of substantial and independent social value.[60]

Let me summarize where this has taken us so far. I've tried to sketch the contours of one fanciful-yet-serious argument for the unconstitutionality of even a liberally reformed institution of marriage, and the thousands of laws that constitute, support, and define it. Civil marriage, so this argument goes, is unconstitutional, because the laws that support and define it constitute a denial of the equal protection of the laws. It draws distinctions between persons that are patently irrational, and as a result of those distinctions, it adversely impacts upon a discrete minority—unmarried adults. Further, it impacts upon them in a way that directly hinders a fundamental interest—their interest in giving care to dependents, both children and aging adults. The purported justification for civil marriage—that the distinctions drawn by our laws of marriage all aim to support and protect the caregiving work that takes place within families, so as to lighten the burdens of government—is a bad fit with the institution supposedly justified: many married people engage in no caregiving work, and many unmarried people do. That fact alone raises a justifiable suspicion that the stated goal is not the only goal, or not the true goal. And indeed, a look beneath the surface reveals a murkier history, and arguably, an ambiguous current reality.

It is not implausible to suggest that the reason for the state's interest in civil marriage is not simply to support caregiving labor, but rather, to maintain its highly gendered, and largely uncompensated structure, and to do so, furthermore, not so much to ease the burden on "the taxpayer," but rather, so as to provide a quite real, tangible, financial benefit to men. The "marriage premium" heralded by the social utilitarians is higher for men than for women; women do more uncompensated childcare and household chores than do men; women's income suffers a substantial hit when they decide to mother, even within marriage, while men's fathering imposes no strain on their income potential. Men gain from marriage more than women, and what they gain is intimately related to these facts: they gain the household labor for which they do not pay, and nurtured, cared-for children in the bargain. Clearly, the various clerks of county courts do not harbor a desire to discriminate against women when handing out marriage certificates. But the institution of civil marriage is constructed by law, and as constructed, it has an obvious, thoroughly transparent, and much commented on, tendency to perpetuate gendered labor. So long as that labor remains uncompensated, and gendered, it works to the benefit of men much more than women. It remains uncompensated, finally, for reasons that go to the heart of the justification of marriage itself: marriage is the way we organize and privatize caregiving labor, without unduly imposing upon the public purse. Privatized, familial caregiving, within marriage and family, is uncompensated by design, not happenstance. It is very much the point of the institution to keep it that way, according to its celebrants and critics alike.

Nor is it implausible to suggest that the reason for the state's interest in civil marriage has, at least historically, had much to do with the appropriation of women's sexuality for men's use, and perhaps to some degree marriage might still serve that end. And lastly, the state's interest in civil marriage might have something to do with demarcating the normal and the abnormal—so as to retain, but marginalize, and to some degree to vilify the latter. If all of this is right—if the institution of marriage impacts harshly upon a quasi-suspect class engaging in a fundamental life activity, and if its purpose is not the benign one of supporting caregiving, but the considerably less compelling ones of exploiting women's reproductive labor and sexuality, and marginalizing sexual abnormality—it's an easy inference that this institution, created entirely by state action, is unconstitutional.

Should We Call the Whole Thing Off? Utilitarian Arguments against Marriage

The hypothetical constitutional argument outlined above for dismantling marriage incorporates the major arguments that have been made in contemporary scholarship for ending marriage, most notably, those put forward by law Professor Martha Fineman. Professor Fineman concludes from her arguments not that the institution is unconstitutional (she doesn't apparently have any interest in that question, one way or the other), but rather, that it is fundamentally unjust. Marriage is just unfair: to women, to children, to unmarried persons, and to sexual minorities. If we care for justice, we should simply end this legal institution, and we should do so regardless of how much "good" it does.

Fineman has also, though, made some utilitarian arguments for ending marriage. Civil marriage, she urges, does real harm. Ending it would immediately accomplish three laudable ends. Let me quickly review these claims, and then I will conclude with some reservations about the "ending marriage" project in its entirety.

First, ending marriage, Fineman suggests, would definitively end—rather than piecemeal and by dribs and drabs—the state's deferential and conflicted stance toward the violence, and particularly the sexual violence, that still occurs within marriage and quasi-marital relationships, and toward which the state is still something less than fully committed to policing, prosecuting, deterring, and punishing.[61] If we were to simply end the legal institution of marriage, then assault and battery within intimate relations would be plain old assault and battery, whether it occurred between spouses, cohabitators, dates, or strangers. Intimate violence might require rules, procedures, protective orders, and policies that would differentiate it from nonintimate, or stranger, violence, but the marital relationship of the perpetrator and the victim would not be a relevant factor. Likewise, she suggests, sexual harassment would be sexual harassment, intentional infliction of emotional distress would be just that, and rape would be rape. We have an array of legal norms criminalizing or sanctioning assault, battery, harassment, infliction of emotional distress, and rape, and the application of those norms are all compromised, to varying degrees, by marriage. Rape within marriage is still punished differently than rape outside of marriage in about half of all states;[62] intentional infliction of emotional distress, although a common enough tort, is literally never pressed by one spouse against another; assault and battery are crimes within marriage but nevertheless often not as rigorously pursued, prosecuted, or punished.[63] Sexual harassment is a well-recognized civil rights violation when it occurs at work or school, but it has not even been theoretically extended to the domain of the home. If the quite basic norm and legal prohibition against sexual harassment were applied to intimate relations, spouses or cohabitators might be slightly more inclined to accord each other at least the respect and civility they grant strangers. If civil marriage were to end tomorrow, it doesn't follow as a matter of logic that the rape, battery, harassment, or infliction of emotional distress that currently goes unaddressed would suddenly be part of the public agenda. But the anomaly of not responding to these civil and criminal wrongs with the same urgency as when the conduct occurs in nonmarital-like settings would at least be highlighted.[64]

Second, Fineman argues, ending marriage would take the state completely out of the business of moralistically sanctioning or penalizing sexual behavior between consenting adults.[65] If there was no institution of marriage, there would be no reason to either praise or blame consenting adults on the basis of their sexual lives. The state would simply have no interest, just as it has no interest in the nature, the content, or the point of friendships adults might or might not form. Sexual intimacy might or might not lead to the conception of children, but in either case, and even assuming the state's legitimate interest in the well-being of children, the state would have and profess to have no interest in the nature of the intimacy that might have led to the conception of those children, or in its form. Criminal law, then, could be limited to its noncontroversial and liberally defined ends: sanctioning, deterring, and punishing nonconsensual behavior of competent and responsible adults that causes harm to others. "Family law" could be reconfigured so as to focus solely on the caregiving relations between dependents and those who care for them, rather than the nature of the sexual relation between adults. The laws governing entry and exit into marriage could be dissolved. "Sexual orientation," if we were to end civil marriage, would be of no interest to the state. Campaigns to encourage, promote, or require marriage as a prerequisite to state assistance with caregiving—with their clear implication that heterosexuality itself is a prerequisite to such assistance, and therefore, a prerequisite of good mothering—would end. Responsible parenting might require the presence of more than one adult in a child's life, and a state might legitimately encourage citizens to team up, before taking on that work. But responsible parenting does not require the presence of adults with any particular sexual orientation. Ending marriage "as we know it" would end the many subtle and unsubtle forms of state-sponsored discrimination against same-sex parenting.

Third, Fineman argues, it would remove the wall of privatization around caregiving and the impoverishment that caregiving can cause.[66] Caregiving, she argues, were we to dismantle marriage, would come to be viewed as what it is: a human activity that inures to the benefit of the larger society, in which that society has a substantial stake. The community might, then, assume some of the responsibility for insuring that those who provide it are themselves cared for. The single, sexually active, and economically struggling teenage mother would be highly regarded for and supported in her caregiving work—her sexuality would simply be beside the point. Whether it occurs within religiously defined "marriage," within the context of some other configuration of cooperating adults, or between no one but a mother and infant, caregiving labor would be valued, credited, and supported. Until the institution of marriage is dismantled, Fineman argues, that quite major shift in perspective cannot possibly occur.

I would add one more to Fineman's catalog of the potential gains to be had from ending marriage. Although Fineman never quite puts it this way, ending civil marriage would arguably dismantle a constituent marker, and creator, of *caste*—by which I mean a rigidified, social and economical stratification of a society into groups with radically different entitlements, privileges, and qualities of life. Marriage, given the economic conditions of vast swaths of our population, is, for many people, an unattainable status—rendering the "status" of being unmarried all the more unchosen. This makes marriage a "status" institution, but in a sense vastly different from and less defensible than that which has captured the imagination and sympathies of Professor Regan and others: it is status based not in the sense of privileging community over individual will, but rather, it is "status based" in the malignant sense that it renders the "status" of being unmarried unworthy, undignified, and unentitled, and all a function of factors beyond the individual's control. There is, after all, a limit to the degree to which individuals can attain this idealized state of being, that brings in its wake such real spiritual, emotional, and material benefits. As we expand those benefits, in order to encourage marriage as the optimal relationship within which to have children, it might become, and sooner rather than later, well nigh impossible to nurture and raise children on one's own, if one is poor. Child-raising, at that point, will have become a privilege of married people, as marriage becomes a privilege of the relatively well off—not of economic elites, certainly, but of the nonpoor. Being a parent, or a mother, or a caregiver, or a responsible caregiver, and a successful caregiver, at that point, will not be a matter of will, heart, and imagination. Rather, it will be a matter of whether one was born into circumstances that well position you in later life for the marriage market. At that point, marriage will have become not just the mark of a laudable—and chosen—"status" that implies a profound commitment to another adult human being that transcends contract. Rather, it will have become "status" based in a different sense altogether. It will have become the marker of a morally repugnant caste.

Now, to repeat, neither Fineman, nor any critic of civil marriage of whom I am aware, has cast their argument in constitutional terms. They are prudent to be hesitant. There is more to social life—and more to law—than is dreamt of in our "equality practice," either as envisioned by the framers of the Equal Protection Clause of the Constitution or as articulated by modern egalitarians. Not only egalitarian and libertarian norms, but tradition too runs deep in our law and legal institutions. A "traditionalist" could as readily conclude from this argument that it proves nothing but the limits of egalitarian understandings of constitutional guarantees, as guides to public and private life both. Sometimes, "tradition" gives way to "equality practice"—witness the Jim Crow regimes of segregation, and the Jane Crow laws of gender differentiation, both of which were also rooted in traditionalist ways of life, and of traditionalist understandings of life's meaning. Sometimes, though, equality gives way to tradition, accommodating it, working within it, or working around it, but not uprooting it. After all, much else about modern life likewise fails the equal protection test. Inheritance laws, free markets, preferences in college admissions for children of alumni, internet dating, the salaries of athletes in major sports franchises—all of these could be shown without too much difficulty to adversely impact various suspect classes, and all are wildly over- or underinclusive with respect to their purported goals. So might be the case with marriage. We might tolerate marriage, in spite of its inegalitarian consequences—some of us might revere marriage in part because of them. Marriage creates ties that connect us with particular others, to whom we become resolutely and deeply unequally committed. Blinded by love, we marry and create children upon whom we bestow the most inegalitarian, unequal proportion of our resources imaginable. Family life, and the irrationality of marriage that is still at its core, might be a necessary or at least appreciated counter, in our private life, to the egalitarian regard we must hold out for others, in our public life. There has always been, in our "equality jurisprudence" as developed by courts, a balancing between preservation of tradition and movements toward equality. There is little reason to think that this generation of courts would strike that balance in such a way as to call into question the existence of marriage.

On the other hand, our "equality practice," including those aspects of equality practice that are not reflected in judicial decisionmaking, is a very real force in public life, including our increasingly public debates over the status of marriage. Sometimes arguments that have constitutional resonance do so not because they will succeed in court, but rather, because they reveal tensions between our felt political ambitions, or aspirations, as a people, and the state of our current politics, and current political choices. Radically inegalitarian conditions, or traditions, or patterns of social life, might be so widespread, and so pervasive, and so deeply entrenched in ways of life, that it is simply impossible to imagine any court finding that that condition, tradition, or pattern of social life raises a constitutional and judicial question.[67] There would be consequences of such a finding—the need to fashion an appropriately sweeping remedy—that no Court could handle, and that no Court should. Sometimes, tensions between constitutional ideals and current practices should be resolved through small-bore political debate, community activism, and local legislative work, not through grand judicial pronouncement. The dubious constitutionality of our marriage laws, in my view, is one such instance. Equality practice and constitutionalism, I conclude, cast a critical light over the institution of marriage. That light ought to inform our political deliberations about the future of this particular legal construction.

In Baltimore City, where I live, pursuant to a federal, state, and city campaign to promote marriage among low-income residents, the City has now put billboards in a number of poor neighborhoods. Some of those billboards picture a young African American couple cradling a baby, and others picture a young African American woman looking resplendent on her wedding day. All of these billboards are plastered with the slogan "MARRIAGE WORKS." It's enough to make you want to cry. The pictures are sentimental and sweet. And—marriage *does* work. The social utilitarians are right. It is indeed *so* much easier to successfully raise children with a helpful and income-earning spouse in hand; we hardly need a mountain of evidence to support this proposition. Children do thrive when raised by two committed adults. Every sensible person passing those billboards will share the hope that every troubled, financially insecure, overstressed, doubly employed young, single mother in Baltimore—who lives in a dicey neighborhood, who sends her children to underfunded, unsafe, unsanitary, and extremely unpleasant schools, who rarely sees her children because of her now-mandatory work schedule, who rides a bus with double transfers to get to jobs in different parts of the city from where she lives, who relies on her own mother or grandmother or neighbors for childcare, who struggles to pay rent and utilities on top of weekly groceries, and who prays that her children will make it safely through one more day—will find and marry a nice young man like the one on the poster. If she would only marry, the hope goes, she might find decent housing and put her baby in a good school. She might find a 9-to-5 job that would give her and her husband an additional wage, while leaving time for her to cook meals and play with her younger children and help her older children with their homework. We assume that the nice young man in the poster, if only she could find him, would help her raise sweet and successful children, and still have time left over to enjoy all those pleasures that life has to offer, besides. If she could just find such a man, marriage might work for her. Just having this loving partner would do so much. Mary Gallagher, Linda Waite, the marriage movement, and the Baltimore City poster are all quite correct. Marriage works.

Yet, marriage does other work, as well. Marriage works to marginalize non-heterosexual couples who wish to enjoy the security, commitment, and public recognition of heterosexual marriage. Marriage works to demarcate some lives as normal and others as abnormal. Marriage works to hide the uncompensated caregiving labor that occurs within them. Marriage works to label as unfit and undeserving the unmarried mother seeking help raising children outside of marriage. Marriage works to limit the pool of persons entitled to community support in their caregiving. Marriage and promarriage rhetoric has worked quite directly over the last decade to limit the pool of poor persons raising children who are entitled to federal aid, the amount of money they will receive, and the number of children they will receive it for. Marriage works to weaken the safety net for poor and working-class people—both married and unmarried—in financial difficulty. Marriage works in these ways as well, and when it does, it doesn't look so much like a social institution that simply offers rewards and recognition to those who take on the pleasures and responsibilities of intense interpersonal commitment. It looks much more like a social institution that defines caste: a stratification of our society into economic, social, and intersocial pyramids, with different qualities of life depending on where one happens to fall.

When "marriage works" in these ways, it seems to me that marriage violates core constitutional values. As Professor Cass Sunstein of Chicago Law School has long argued, at the heart of the Constitution's overall scheme of government, and particularly our Equal Protection Law, is a very simple ethical principle: we are not a caste society. Sunstein calls this the "anti-caste principle."[68] There is, of course, a gap—and a substantial one—between constitutional aspiration and economic reality. Against the ballast of constitutional principle, there is little doubt that we are now drifting toward a class-defined caste social order, with an ever-widening gap between our social and economic reality and our constitutional aspirations. Consider class: middle-class life is becoming both fragile at the bottom and at the same time harder to penetrate from below. It's become a one-way slide. Public education continues to ill serve poor children in K–12, and higher education is so prohibitively costly as not to be any sort of option at all for many of our high school graduates. Basic health insurance is completely out of reach for large segments of the population, and life insurance is just an unthinkable luxury. Skilled and unskilled blue-collar jobs no longer offer the lifelong employment security they once did. The unionized sector of the work economy continues to shrink. Risk itself is privatized—the risks that were once covered by governmental programs and realistic expectations of lifelong employment are now borne by the individual. Home ownership is threatened by overextended consumer credit. Now consider gender. Women still earn substantially less than men at comparable jobs; women still do substantially more of the uncompensated caregiving and domestic labor in the household; and women's income is still reduced by their parenting, while men's income is not. Consider race: gaps in income, health, longevity, infant mortality rates, educational achievement, educational opportunity, and home ownership persist between black and white citizens, advances since the civil rights movements of the 1950s, 1960s, and 1970s notwithstanding. Finally, consider sexual orientation: straight people can and do marry, and enjoy the consequent benefits. Gay men and lesbians cannot. The hardening of these differences should trouble us, particularly if we care about constitutional values.

Constitutional scholar Bill Eskridge opines, in the conclusion of his book *Civil Unions and the Future of Gay Rights*: "A community that does not treat a group of productive citizens the same as other citizens has some explaining to do. When a state discriminates against a social group for no good reason, it disrespects the dignity owed to members of the group as human beings and as citizens."[69] Eskridge is speaking in this passage about the differential treatment of gay and lesbians couples wishing to marry. But the point should be broadened. This community, and our state, has some explaining to do, and not just to its gay and lesbian citizens.

Does marriage exacerbate or ameliorate these trends? Where does marriage fit in with this? First, marriage itself threatens to become yet another demarcation delineating yet another caste: unmarried people are not treated the same as married people by our community, so it seems we have some explaining to do. But marriage also threatens to worsen every "drift" toward caste briefly delineated above: the difference between the treatment of rich and poor, black and white, men and women, gay and straight. The poverty of poor people is worsened by being unmarried, while the community's moral responsibility to come to their assistance is muted by marriage rhetoric: what these people should do is marry, and then they wouldn't *be* poor. The gap between black and white citizens is likewise exacerbated: unmarried black men and women are the most often pathologized, they are the most often blamed for their plight, and they bear a disproportionate amount of the continuing overt and covert white racism that persists in post–affirmative action social life. The gap between women and men, and between wives and husbands, likewise is exacerbated, not addressed, by marriage: marriage may be overall good for all, but it is better for men than women, and while married women fare better than unmarried women, this may show little other than that marriage is the lesser of known evils. That marriage exacerbates the differences between the treatment of gay men and lesbians on the one hand and straight men and women on the other, hardly needs elaboration. Marriage offends constitutional principles, and does so whether or not a Court would ever so hold. The case for ending it is strong.

Some Reservations . . . Perhaps We Shouldn't Call the Whole Thing Off

It doesn't follow, though, that we should call the whole thing off. Let me conclude this chapter with my own reservations about Martha Fineman's powerful argument for ending marriage, whether it is cast (as I believe it should be) in hypothesized constitutional form, or (as it is more typically cast), in its moral and political form.

First, ending marriage today might not be wise, even if it were possible, and even if it is unjust and unconstitutional in its current form. First, consider the short-term consequences. As Fineman's critics have tirelessly, a bit tediously, but probably correctly pointed out, the result of ending marriage tomorrow would be a huge increase in the numbers of impoverished women and children.[70] There's plenty of evidence for this. Unmarried nonresidential fathers, both one-time cohabitators and noncohabitators, are less committed to the support of their children than married and divorced nonresident fathers. That fact alone is pretty damning of this reform project, if we conceive of it as a straight policy proposal: erase marriage, and marital distinctions, from our statute books. Second, although marriage may rhetorically exacerbate some of the "caste features" of modern life, it is not so clear that the institution of marriage invariably, or unambiguously, exacerbates inequality. As Waite and Gallagher argue, marriage does effectively lift some people out of poverty. It does so whether or not it also legitimates our collective failure to construct minimally decent social welfare institutions. [71]

More importantly, though, even if marriage on balance exacerbates rather than alleviates caste, it simply doesn't follow that what we should do is end it. Look at an analogous institution. Higher education has many of the same qualities as the institution of marriage. College too improves the financial future of participants while the lives of nonattendees are left in shambles; college too has high economic entrance requirements; college too constitutes a moralistic marker between those who are presumed to have "character," and therefore succeed in adult life, and those who lack it; and so forth. Yet, we should not and do not conclude from all of this that we ought to therefore abolish higher education, from local community colleges on through to the elites. Rather, if we are concerned about the caste-promoting features of higher education, as we should be, we should rather conclude that we need to begin the hard work of democratizing and reforming it. Perhaps we should think similarly of marriage.

What of gender? Here as well, ending marriage might expose the problem of uncompensated care work, but it is not at all clear it would end it, rather than exacerbate it. Many women who mother without partners do *all* the caregiving, and all the income earning, and suffer hugely because of it. Ending marriage as a way to address this could backfire, not only for the obvious reason that the numbers of women doing so would skyrocket, but for less obvious reasons as well: it might simply legitimate nonsupport. Indirectly, but possibly as consequentially, and as communitarians warn, it could accelerate, rather than address, the seemingly inexorable trends toward excessive, irresponsible, commodificationist, capitalist, hedonistic individualism—in which markets are the arbiters of value, and satiated choice the beginning and end of all questions of worth. This could not possibly help either married women trapped in income-draining relationships, or single mothers trying with no small degree of desperation to navigate a hostile terrain for themselves and their children. We need more responsibility, both societal and individual, both communal and paternal, toward our youngest and most vulnerable children. What the critics of marriage have exactly right is that poor women trying to raise children outside of marriage need help rather than moralistic censure. Ending marriage might—might—reinforce that message. But there's no guarantee. It could just as well send the message that responsibility for others, whether related or not, is entirely a matter of either personal whim, or individual contract. It is hard to see how this could truly ameliorate, rather than exacerbate, the dilemmas posed by single parenthood.

For those of us critical of marriage, but not ready to join the ranks of those urging that we should end it, the obvious alternative is reform. If marriage can be reformed internally, the differences between men and women in caregiving and domestic labor, for example, might actually be ameliorated rather than exacerbated by marriage. There is precedent for this: reforms of marriage, and of marriage law, have made contemporary marriage a *more* safe, not a less safe, way of life for women, at least with respect to domestic violence. Married men are less, rather than more, prone to abuse or rape their wives than unmarried men and their cohabitators or girlfriends. In a similar way, it might be possible to reform the institution of marriage, to address disparities in childcare and domestic chores: marriage at least gives states an institutional point of entry to the problem. (Who does more housework

MARRIAGE AND ITS CRITICS ("LET'S CALL THE WHOLE THING OFF")

and childcare: husbands or male cohabitators?) Opening marriage to same-sex couples could go some distance toward reducing the differences in treatment of gay and straight citizens across the board. Improving the job prospects and educational opportunities of poor citizens might improve their marriage rates, with a cyclical effect overall: better jobs and education make for more marriages, which in turn make for better jobs and better education for parents and children alike.

Toward what end should our "equality practice" be put? Should we aim to democratize and equalize civil marriage? Can we imagine a good and decent law of civil marriage that serves all: participants and nonparticipants alike? Or, should we aim to end it? Marriage is a deeply traditional institution with a profoundly inegalitarian and antidemocratic past. Unsurprisingly, then, many of its defenders are quite firmly committed to that inegalitarian and antidemocratic past. It is not unduly radical to suggest that the best way to deal with the inequities marriage creates is by direct critique, with an eye toward dismantling the institution itself. On the other hand, marriage has already been democratized and reformed to such an extent it would be virtually unrecognizable to anyone from just a hundred years ago, and there's no reason that trend can't continue. The question that presses upon us is whether marriage can be reformed in such a way as to bring the institution in line with our democratic and egalitarian aspirations, without sacrificing the particular values, and value, that marriage brings to our lives.

It is important to stress, I believe, that whether we press our equality practice toward the end of ending marriage, or reforming it, change will be incremental. Marriage will not be suddenly transformed into a democratic and egalitarian civil institution open to all, exploitative of none. The state's relation to it will not magically switch gears, becoming heretofore concerned only to bolster, protect, and facilitate the committed care of dependents, uninterested in participants' sexual behavior and fully respectful of nonparticipants. Nor will marriage suddenly disappear from our cultural and legal landscape, found unconstitutional, one day, by an authoritative judge in Massachusetts or elsewhere. Rather, as inegalitarian and nondemocratic marriage meets our "equality practice" we can envision two alchemical processes, should equality practice prevail: marriage could slowly evolve, or it could slowly dissolve.

Sometimes, furthermore, it will be hard to tell the difference between the two. We could reform marriage toward the end of justice, and find, willy-nilly, that we have reformed it out of existence. We might, for example, aim to overturn every legal distinction—either legislatively or judicially—until there are simply none remaining. Civil marriage really is, as Justice Marshall insisted in *Goodridge*, a legal construct, and if we dissolve or reverse every legal rule that constructs it, we will have dissolved marriage. Civil marriage could lose first its legal significance, and then its legal existence, and when it does, one can safely surmise, it would lose some of its social significance as well. In some ways, or for some purposes, it doesn't really matter toward which end our equality practice is poised. Gays and lesbians would be equally well served, in terms of equality, by a formally equal marriage law as by no marriage law at all. In Fineman's utopia, where other bodies of law directly protect caregiving, women caregivers—mothers—may be equally well served by a reformed marriage law that lends the state's authority to the cause of "just marriage" as by no marriage law at all. Women fully protected against domestic violence are just as protected within a marriage defined in such a way that the violence within it is equally criminal as that outside of it, as they are protected against intimate violence outside of marriage.

Nevertheless, it seems to me that this clearly isn't true across the board—which is just another way of saying that in the final analysis it does matter to what end our "equality practice" is put. As we advocate and litigate for gay marriage, there is no question but that we further valorize marriage—and thereby risk further marginalizing unmarried gay and straight citizens alike. As we push for "just marriage" in which husbands have incentives to labor equally as women within marriage, we might worsen, rather than improve, the actual living conditions of unmarried mothers—if only by misdirecting aide and political energy away from their more pressing, and dire, circumstances. Seeking reform here, as well as elsewhere, risks what I've called above (and what critical legal scholars have long called) "legitimation costs": for every victory we legitimate by masking the larger injustices remaining, as we celebrate our vanquishing of the smaller ones. At the same time, though, there are risks the other way as well. If we aim to end civil marriage, we risk more than just the near certainty of a short-term loss in exchange for the promise of a longer-term gain (although it does have some of that). We also risk throwing out the baby with the bath—we might lose something of tremendous value if we toss this particular unjust institution overboard.

Think again of the poster: *Marriage works*. Marriage *does* work; it bears repeating. As I have tried to explain in this chapter, civil marriage might "work" in ways that violate some of our deepest constitutional and political aspirations. But marriage also works in ways we ought to—and do—applaud. In my informal polling of my friends' views on marriage, conducted while preparing to write this book—a group that is disproportionately feminist and liberal—I find a recurrent comment: "I'm sort of ashamed to be a part of this exclusionary and sexist club, but I've gotta say, marriage works for me." "I think marriage promotes sexist and homophobic stereotypes, but hey, it works for me." "If Maryland (or Ohio, or Washington D.C., or Virginia) legalized gay marriage, all my objections to that fruit of the poisoned tree notwithstanding, I'd get married in a heartbeat." And so on. I feel pretty much the same way. For most of my respondents—I didn't find too many skeptics—and for me, marriage works, and we all mean by that something other than that it works as an insurance policy. Marriage works for me financially, certainly, but in other ways as well; it works psychically, emotionally, sexually. Marriage critics should tread lightly. We need to think very carefully about why it is that marriage seemingly works for so many people before we urge its demise. W also might want to think about some midway positions. The next chapter looks in some detail at two proposed reforms.

CHAPTER FOUR

Just Marriage
("We Can Work It Out")

*I*magine two possible reforms of civil marriage, both offered toward the end of rendering marriage a more just institution. First, imagine a civil marriage law that is open to couples of the same as well as opposite sex. Second, imagine a civil marriage law that, to the greatest extent possible, encourages an equal division of childcare and household labor between the parties. These two simple proposals for reforming marriage have generated immense interest among marriage advocates, critics, and devotees. The first has already resulted in one major state supreme court decision, declaring the exclusion of gay couples from civil marriage unconstitutional,[1] as well as unjust and unwise, and a major backlash, resulting in a growing number of state and local constitutional ballot initiatives, statutory laws, and referenda declaring a traditional definition of marriage to be a part of the state's foundational law;[2] a federal law—the Defense of Marriage Act—that aims to limit the effect of any state decisions extending marriage to include same-sex marriage to the confines of those states;[3] a New York State Court of Appeals decision finding no state or federal constitutional right to marry that would extend marriage equality to same-sex couples;[4] and a proposed federal constitutional amendment that would explicitly limit marriage to opposite-sex couples.[5] Are these two simple reforms that have so transformed our politics truly necessary? Perhaps as important, are they sufficient? Would they leave marriage a more just institution? Do they respond to the criticisms that have been leveled against marriage, and do they retain the value that marriage defenders claim for it?

Same-Sex Marriage

Imagine a same-sex couple in their mid-thirties that have lived together for about ten years. They are fully committed to each other emotionally, they are sexually monogamous, and they intend to spend the rest of their lives together. They enjoy the support and goodwill of their respective families, friends, and neighbors. They have recently jointly purchased a home, with the deed in both of their names. They both work at steady jobs with good incomes. They both have health insurance through their employers. They are settled into their careers. Now, they would like to have children. They are considering various options for doing so, including adoption as well as assisted conception, such as in vitro fertilization, or IVF, with either known or anonymous sperm donors. They have spoken with potential sperm donors, sperm banks, and adoption agencies.

Civil marriage would undoubtedly make this couple's lives easier in a number of ways; or put negatively, the inability to lawfully marry will make the couple's lives more difficult than they would be otherwise. Adoption through a state-run agency will be difficult in some states, and impossible in a few, both because of their unmarried status and their sexual orientation.[6] Their marital status and sexual orientation will also play a role, however, if they conceive the child themselves. If they succeed in conceiving and birthing a child through assisted conception, the partner who carries the baby to term will likely feel the need to cut back on her employment for a short time after the birth in order to recover physically and to bond with and possibly breastfeed the newborn. One or the other or both partners might likewise feel the need and desire to cut back for a longer period, in order to have as much time as possible with the infant, and toddler. Toward these ends—physical recovery of the biological mother, bonding with and breastfeeding the newborn and infant, and raising and nurturing the toddler—they might jointly decide that one partner should work part time, or perhaps take six months or a year off from work altogether. After that year or half year passes, they might decide (as do many heterosexual married new parents) that the parent who remained home should continue to do so, perhaps until the child begins school.

Should that partner seek to do this by shifting to part-time status at work, or by quitting her job, however, she will lose her employer-sponsored health insurance.[7] At this point, the couple is likely to become acutely aware of the difference marriage can make, if they have not already. Were the couple married, the nonemployed or less employed partner would almost invariably be covered on her spouse's employer-provided health insurance policy. Unmarried, the couple will face a substantial cost, unless the working partner happens to be employed by a Fortune 500 company or a local or state government that provides such coverage to domestic partners. If not, the couple will lose not only income but also health insurance at precisely the point when both are sorely needed. Were they married, of course, they would also lose income. They would most likely not, however, lose health insurance.

In many other ways as well, some of them not apparent unless or until one of the partners dies, becomes disabled, is imprisoned, or seeks to end the partnership, this couple's lives will be made more difficult by virtue of their inability to legally marry. For example, when one of the partners dies, the surviving unmarried partner of this duo will not be entitled to a part of her partner's Social Security payments, as she would be, were they married.[8] Particularly if the surviving partner has spent a good bit of her life raising the couple's children and keeping house, rather than earning her own income, she will be severely disadvantaged, compared to comparably treated housewives in traditional marriages (who themselves are not particularly well treated either). Nor will she be entitled to any part of her partner's pension upon her partner's death, in most cases, or to a part of her partner's veterans' benefits, or discounts based on her partner's armed forces status, as she would be were they married.[9] She will not be entitled to the tax-free inheritance of her deceased partner's retirement savings, should her partner die.[10] If the couple separates, the nonbiological parent of their children in some states will not have presumptive custody or visitation rights with the child or children.[11] She will have to bargain for those rights separately, and hope the court will uphold her contractual entitlement; the law will not give her any assistance. Likewise, should the couple separate, the parent who has done the bulk of the child-raising and housekeeping, and who accordingly has not participated in the wage market, will not be entitled to her fair share of the marital property the couple has acquired, alimony payments, or child support, as would her divorcing neighbor in similar financial circumstances.[12] A court of law might—but then again very well might not—enforce a separation agreement that spells out a distribution of wealth in the event of separation, but again, there will be no premade body of law protecting her interest in the absence of such a contract, or should a court find it unenforceable.[13]

Even while together under the best of times, this couple's lives will be complicated by their unmarried status. The nonbiological parent, for example, will not typically have access to their children's school records. The employed partner will not be entitled to sick leave guaranteed under the Federal Family and Medical Leave Act, should her child or partner become ill and require care.[14] Nor will she be entitled to unemployment benefits after leaving that job, should she be required to relocate, because of her partner's required job-related move.[15] The couple will not be entitled to live in neighborhoods that are deemed "families only" and litigation challenging the constitutionality of such designations will not likely succeed.[16] Neither partner will have next-of-kin status for emergency medical decisions and hospital visitation status,[17] and neither party will be able to invoke various spousal privileges in a court of law.[18] Neither party will have access to reduced rate memberships at private health clubs, social clubs, or various private organizations that routinely provide reduced rates for spouses, and there is virtually no chance that a court would find these widespread private policies illegal, discriminatory, or unconstitutional.[19] Neither party will have prison visitation rights,[20] access to life insurance provided by employers' policies for spouse-beneficiaries,[21] or access to survivor benefits in wrongful death claims.[22] Neither partner will be entitled to a share of her partners' court-ordered recovery as a crime victim, should there be such a recovery, as would a spouse.[23] Neither will have the ability to file a wrongful death action, in the event her partner is accidentally and torturously killed.[24] The couple will not have the option or ability to file joint home and auto insurance policies.[25] They cannot file joint tax returns or file jointly for bankruptcy.[26] They cannot transfer property from one partner to another without incurring transfer tax consequences.[27] And so on: this list could be expanded ten-fold. The General Accounting Office has identified, and listed, over *one thousand* federal benefits, responsibilities, and rights that accrue to individuals, solely by virtue of marital status.[28]

State marital benefits are likewise extensive. In *Goodridge*, the Massachusetts Supreme Court, in the course of finding the ban on same-sex marriage unconstitutional, summarized the state benefits as follows:

> Tangible … benefits flow from marriage. The marriage license grants valuable property rights to those who meet the entry requirements, and who agree to what might otherwise be a burdensome degree of government regulation of their activities.… The Legislature has conferred on each party in a civil marriage substantial rights concerning the assets of the other which unmarried cohabitants do not have. [The court then cites case law refusing to extend marital rules regarding distribution of property at divorce, rules regarding rights to recover for loss of consortium, and rights to separate support or alimony, to cohabiting parties].… The benefits accessible only by way of a marriage license are enormous, touching nearly every aspect of life and death. The department states that hundreds of statutes are related to marriage and to marital benefits. With no attempt to be comprehensive, we note that some of the statutory benefits conferred by the Legislature on those who enter into civil marriage include, as to property: joint Massachusetts income tax filing; tenancy by the entirety, (a form of ownership that provides certain protections against creditors and allows for the automatic descent of property to the surviving spouse without probate).… extension of the benefit of the homestead protection (securing up to $300,000.00 in equity from creditors) to one's spouse and children; automatic rights to inherit the property of a deceased spouse who does not leave a will; the rights of elective share and of dower (which allow surviving spouses certain property rights where the decedent spouse has not made adequate provision for the survivor in a will); entitlement to wages owed to a deceased employee; eligibility to continue certain businesses of a deceased spouse; the right to share the medical policy of one's spouse; thirty-nine-week continuation of health coverage for the spouse of a person who is laid off or dies; preferential benefits in the Commonwealth's medical program; access to veterans' spousal benefits and preferences; financial protections for spouses of certain Commonwealth employees killed in the performance of duty; the equitable division of marital property on divorce; temporary and permanent alimony rights; the right to separate support on separation of the parties that does not result in divorce; and the right to bring claims for wrongful death and loss of consortium; and for funeral and burial expenses and punitive damages resulting

from tort actions.… Exclusive marital benefits that are not directly tied to property rights include the presumptions of legitimacy and parentage of children born to a married couple, and evidentiary rights, such as the prohibition against spouses testifying against one another about their private conversations, applicable in both civil and criminal cases … qualification for bereavement of medical leave to care for individuals related by blood or marriage; an automatic family member preference to make medical decisions for an incompetent or disabled spouse who does not have a contrary health care proxy; the application of predictable rules of child custody, visitation, support, and removal out-of-State when married parents divorce; priority rights to administer the estate of a deceased spouse who dies without a will, and the requirement that a surviving spouse must consent to the appointment of any other person as administrator … (citations to authorities, primarily the Massachusetts civil code, are omitted).[29]

Many of these benefits and privileges, of course, will never be required by most couples, whether same sex, opposite sex, married, or cohabitating. Most of us go through most of life not needing survivors' benefits, prison visitation rights, joint bankruptcy proceedings, and court-ordered crime victim recovery payments. But some of these benefits will be needed at some point in life by almost everybody, and more then a few of them will be needed at moments of great need—the birth of a child, the death of a partner, divorce, one's own or one's partner's disability from employment, one's own or one's partner's imprisonment, accidental injury, chronic and disabling sickness, or bankruptcy. Planning for such unlikely but calamitous contingencies is a part of what it means to responsibly parent, as well as to responsibly care for oneself and one's partner or intimate loved ones. It is wise, responsible, and caring to make sure that one's dependents will be provided for in the event of an early death, that children will be cared for postdivorce, that property will be sensibly distributed in either event, that income will not be disastrously interrupted in the event of sickness or accidental disability. That the state, *through over a thousand laws,* makes it somewhat easier for married partners, but not for unmarried partners, to plan responsibly for risk, is a major difference in the treatment of couples who share with their straight and traditionally married friends and neighbors a common desire to engage in responsible caregiving.

There are also nontangible benefits and privileges of civil marriage, however, as well as these hedges against risk, that accrue to married partners on almost a daily basis, and the absence of those nontangible benefits, particularly from the lives of those trying to parent while unmarried, will be felt frequently—even routinely—by unmarried but equally committed same-sex couples. The most important of the nontangible benefits conferred by civil marriage, by far, is the legal and social legitimacy to the union that civil marriage confers. The state sanction of a married couple's union sends a powerful message to the couple's community, of the legitimacy, orderliness, and well-being, of their private lives, and the absence of that message can be sorely felt. How does this happen? Think again of the parenting same-sex couple. Schools, both public and private, summer camps, private clubs, and athletic recreation leagues generate endless forms and permission slips, all of which typically require names and phone numbers and email addresses and cell phone numbers—"contact information"—of a "father" and a "mother." Parents—meaning "fathers" and "mothers"—are summoned to visit or to volunteer at their children's schools frequently (some of us think, constantly); neighborhood friends are well aware of children's household arrangements; pediatricians and their nurses and receptionists will seek comparable information; Girl Scouts and Boy Scouts might loom large, with information needs and endless requests for parental participation, and their well-known heightened sensitivity to same-sex couples. Either by passive observation or through overt requests, the couple parenting a child is known to the child's teachers, to neighborhood vendors, to the parents of the child's friends, to camp counselors, to scout leaders, to athletic coaches, and so on. The identity, and hence the marital status, and certainly the gender, of a child's parents are no secret and not at all regarded as "private": this information is routinely either asked for or casually observed. This very public awareness of this very public status conferred on an otherwise private life is not just a side product of marriage; it is in many ways its essence. It is an essence that is nicely represented by—even encapsulated in, but is by no means limited to—the publication in a local newspaper of the wedding "announcement," or the pronouncement in a wedding ceremony of very public vows. Rather, public awareness of one's marital status is a gift the community bestows continually, throughout the duration of the marriage. Just to emphasize: it is bestowed not just by intimates and friends, but also by strangers and acquaintances that matter in some concrete way to the couple and their dependents: their health care providers, coaches, teachers, neighborhood vendors, their children's friends, the parents of those friends, civic organizers, school principals, and so on.

Does this public recognition matter? Certainly. As conservative proponents of marriage vigorously argue, one of the great benefits of civil marriage is that the state's validation and approval of a couple's legal status translates into community validation, and approval, of that couple's social status, heightens their standing in the community, and most important, solidifies and normalizes the community's understanding of their relation to their child or children.[30] When we marry, the state, the law, and the community will all approve; and as we all might recall from our own childhoods, approval matters to all of us, a lot. And, that approval is continually bestowed. State, legal, and social validation is cemented in every one of the transactions noted above—with counselors, coaches, teachers, principals, doctors, nurses, pharmacists, receptionists, and so on—on a daily basis, over and over, individually and collectively. When a couple is known by the community to be joined in civil marriage, the expectation is formed, and then deepened, that they will stay that way. Civil marriage is the institutional vehicle by which this vital identity, and the expectation of permanence that goes with it, is conveyed to the community: "we are married, we should be seen as married, we mean by that to proclaim our intention to remain together."

Marriage proponents across the political spectrum are clear that this approval has a very high value. As a community's awareness and expectation of the married couple as a "couple," rather than as two individuals who happen to share an address, grows, so grows the couple's own sense of the marriage to which they belong, as something that exists independently of each of them, and that is bigger than each of them individually.[31] The marriage becomes something worth preserving, and something for which to make sacrifices, and something with standing in its own right. The individuals become that much more inclined to stick with it, through thick and thin, good times and bad, and not to recalibrate, recalculate, rethink its utility or the "benefit of the bargain" from day to day. That quintessential sense of the marriage and the family as "bigger than each individual," and as worth preserving regardless of individual calibration of utility, is central to the marriage's durability, and that durability, in turn, is at the heart of the various "marriage premiums" celebrated by marriage proponents: the durability of the marriage makes possible the financial economies of scale and specializations of labor identified by economists as central to the improved financial well-being of married people, as well as the improved health and happiness measured by social scientists more generally. That sense of the marriage as something that does, ought to, and will endure, however, does not spring up magically from the moment it is declared as such. It is something that is created, and then developed, nurtured, and deepened, by the community, and with each small act of public recognition, across time.

Marriage laws make this development possible for opposite-sex couples, but not possible for same-sex couples, and that is a significant difference in the way that same-sex and opposite-sex couples are treated by the state, with very real consequences in the lives of the citizens that treatment affects. Same-sex couples can have meaningful religious commitments, lavish celebrations, anniversary parties, and so on, for the benefit of themselves, friends, families, and intimates, but they can not have the imprimatur of state approval of their union, and the automatic community acceptance and understanding that imprimatur confers. That community acceptance and understanding is of value in its own right. More important, though, community recognition and acceptance also contributes, and mightily, to the couple's self-understanding: to be treated as married is to view oneself as married. How we view ourselves is largely a function of how we are viewed by others, and the same is true of whether or not we view ourselves as married—whether we understand ourselves as a part of something larger than our self. That self-imaging, in turn, is precisely what creates the stability, and the longevity, of the relationship, and it is the stability and longevity of the relationship, overwhelmingly, that generate the various marriage premiums emphasized by the social utilitarians: the increased income, the better management of risk, the emotional security as one approaches old age that one will not be abandoned, and so on.

Of course, some of this community acceptance, the self-imagining, the stability and longevity of the union, and the marriage premiums that attach to all of that can be generated, or replicated, without the involvement of the state. A same-sex couple no less than an opposite-sex couple can communicate their intentions, their joy, their commitment, and their convictions to their community of friends, neighbors, and loved ones without a marriage license in hand. But just as clearly, that massive self-generative communicative effort is not going to be a complete substitute for what the state confers. It is the secular, civic state—not a loose confederation of intimates and friends—that is, for the vast majority of citizens, the representative of the nexus of political power and community life. The state and only the state can confer legitimacy on a couple from that complex—and unique—point of intersection. The state is unique. It is not the neighborhood association, or the church, or family intimates, or a circle of friends. There's nothing that matches it. The only possible conclusion from all of this is that the state's refusal to validate these loving unions is implicated, and perhaps to a considerable degree, in the diminution in the quality of life that results from the lack of community recognition that marital status, in turn, bestows.

The apparent unfairness of this, lived out in the lives of many people but easily understood, and even easily imagined, by virtually everybody, has given rise to a multifaceted political movement, the purpose of which is to broaden marriage so as to include same-sex couples. That movement, however, is philosophically (and legally) complex. At least three quite different arguments have been put forward for same-sex marriage from those seeking to change the law so as to include these couples in its reach: one based on constitutional and legal norms of justice and equality, one based on moral claims regarding the content of a "good life," and the third premised on the salience of public arguments that rest on social utility. The first is sometimes identified, or regarded, as a "liberal" argument, the second as a "communitarian" or values-based approach, and the third as a utilitarian argument. Very roughly, the liberal (or as it is sometimes called, "formal equality") argument is most frequently pressed in courts of law; the communitarian argument may have the most resonance politically; and the utilitarian argument, thus far, is largely confined to academic scholarship.

On the other side of the "marriage wars" debate there are now at least three salient objections to the simple proposition that marriage is a fundamental right that should be extended to same-sex couples. The first argument, voiced by social conservatives, is based on the claimed moral and social superiority of heterosexual marriage as a form of family, and the immorality of homosexuality. The second, put forward by some feminist and progressive activists and scholars, is grounded in a concern regarding the impact of both the valorization of traditional marriage and the same-sex marriage movement on poor, single mothers, and more generally, on nontraditional family forms. The third, most often voiced by queer theorists, is grounded in an aversion to the form of life that marriage and marriage rhetoric seeks to valorize, whether that valorization emanates from gay or straight marriage devotees. I'll look at these six arguments regarding same-sex marriage—three for, three against—in that order.

Formal Equality

First, the apparent similarity between the gay couple who wishes to publicly declare their intention to commit to each other for the rest of their lives and to responsibly care for each other and their dependents and the straight couple wishing to do so, and the very different treatment the law accords the two groups, gives rise to what is called in law a "formal equality" argument for ending the ban on same-sex marriage. Before detailing the argument, let me explain what is meant by that. "Formal equality," as lawyers use the phrase, is the only apparently simple demand of justice (that dates from antiquity) that "likes be treated alike." What formal equality requires is that the state must treat individuals and groups who are "alike" in relevant respects, similarly, and treat groups and individuals that are differently situated, differently. Like individuals, for example, must be treated alike by courts of law: this mandate of formal equality is behind our "rule of precedent," or as it is sometimes called, our rule of "stare decisis," that requires that a rule laid down in a case decided yesterday be applied today to individual cases that raise similar or identical issues. A related moral ideal stands behind our constitutional norm of "due process"—individuals cannot be subjected to rules that change over time; or put differently, an individual has a constitutional right, in effect, to be subjected only to those rules of conduct that are applied to others similarly situated. So, if one individual receives a ten-year sentence for the possession of crack cocaine, then another individual charged with the same crime should receive the same sentence. Similarly, just as judges must treat like individuals alike, legislators must likewise treat like groups alike, or at least our dominant interpretation of the Fourteenth Amendment's Equal Protection Clause now so requires. State and federal laws invariably draw distinctions between groups, but to the greatest degree possible, they too must do so in a way that respects this norm of formal equality. So, if white citizens may use a public swimming pool, then black citizens must be entitled to use the pool as well; these citizens are "alike" in their needs for recreation, and so they must be treated alike in their entitlement to it. If men can serve as jurors, then likewise must women be so entitled; women and men are alike in their abilities to do this work, and so must be similarly treated with respect to their entitlement—and responsibility—for it. And so on. Hundreds, and at the state level, thousands of cases have elaborated this fundamental point, and value, on both the individual and group level. Underlying both the individual and group-based interpretations of this phrase is the sense that to treat individuals or groups of individuals differently from each other, when they are in all relevant respects similar, is both unwise and unjust: it places the citizen or group treated differently outside the community of coequals.

Why? What is the wrong, or the injustice, of formal inequality? If there is no difference between groups but a radical difference between the state's treatment of them, the courts now reason, then it is fair to be suspicious of the motive underlying the different treatment. If black and white citizens are in fact similarly situated, but black citizens are treated differently and more harshly, it is fair to infer that the legislature is acting on the basis of malicious motivations, rather than their perception of the public interest. Something like this inference has underlined our major judicial advances in formal equality over the last century: there seems to be no difference between black and white school children seeking an education, or black and white citizens seeking a drink at a water fountain, or a swim in a public pool or the use of public libraries. Black and white citizens alike share the same need for an education, water, recreation, and so on. Thus, there is no rational reason to treat these groups of citizens so differently—hence, the suspicion that racism, and nothing more lofty (such a God's design or social utility) underlies the hundreds of legal distinctions drawn between them that were characteristic of the Jim Crow regimes that blanketed social life up until the middle of the century just concluded.[32] Likewise, if there is truly no difference in the capacity of some women and some men to perform as firefighters, jurors, lawyers, judges, graduate students, carpenters, voters, etc., then there is a good reason to suspect that it is rank sexism, and nothing loftier (such as the superiority of men for the public and women for the domestic sphere) that motivates the many distinctions drawn by the state in the Jane Crow regimes during roughly the same time period.[33] Over the last half century, the United States Supreme Court, various state supreme courts, Congress, and some state legislatures as well came to accept this reasoning, and jointly, over several decades, the legal apparatus of Jim Crow regimes, and then later Jane Crow regimes, were systematically dismantled. In both cases, the rationale for the dismantling of the hundreds of laws that jointly treated blacks and whites, as well as men and women, so differently, was basically some version of this appeal to formal equality: where there are no differences between groups, then there is no justification for differential treatment between them. Where the group so injured is one that has historically been the object of hatred, approbation, censure, social discrimination, or oppression, the inference is well founded that the reason for the differential treatment is some overhang of that history of hatred, contempt, or censure. That is not a legitimate reason for different treatment—hence the unconstitutionality, and the injustice, of laws and rules that do so.

Does the same reasoning apply here? Does the state's refusal to allow gay and lesbian citizens the right to marry constitute a violation of formal equality, comparable to the apartheid regimes of Jim Crow in the Southern states at midcentury? Is this too a failure to treat like groups similarly? Clearly the argument hinges crucially on whether the group—same-sex couples wishing to marry—is "like" or "different" from the favored group—opposite-sex couples who are accorded the right to do so. If same-sex couples wishing to marry are like opposite couples wishing to do so, the refusal to allow them to do so looks like a denial of formal equality, and hence of equal protection of the law. If the two groups are for all relevant purposes similarly situated, it is not at all unfair to suppose that it is homophobia, and not any rational discernment of difference, behind the continuing refusal to grant the privileges, rights, and responsibilities of marriage to same-sex couples.

In a moment I will review one argument—basically the argument found persuasive by the Massachusetts Supreme Court in the *Goodridge*[34] decision—to the effect that the state's refusal to permit same-sex marriage constitutes just such a violation of formal equality, and is accordingly unconstitutional.[35] Before doing so, though, two points are worth noting. First, it is important to note at the outset that throughout our constitutional history, the question at the heart of the formal equality inquiry is only an easy one, when it is easy, in hindsight. Racial segregation was defended by segregationists on the grounds that whites and blacks were different, and that, accordingly, separation was part of God's design, that it reflected the natural superiority of the white race, and that social utility as well as divine will demanded it: that integration would do nothing but lead to unrest. Gender segregation and gender exclusions from public life likewise were defended on the grounds that women and men are different—not that either group is an appropriate target of opprobrium, hatred, or contempt. Only after some societal consensus was reached on the empirical and ethical wrongness of these claims did we all come to view them, and call them, racism, or sexism. "Segregation now, segregation tomorrow, segregation forever" is now viewed as a shameful rallying cry of white racism; likewise the "cult of domesticity" is now viewed as a gilded cage that does women considerably more harm than honor. These views are now widely seen both as wrong and immoral. We should not, though, infer from our current consensus on those regimes that only starkly inaccurate false stereotypes—and the consensus that they are indeed starkly inaccurate—can ground constitutional calamities. These beliefs were not so viewed at the time the constitutionality, justice, fairness, and sensibility of the laws that built on them, and reinforced them, were being debated—or decided. There's no reason to expect such unanimity here. The question behind the constitutional inquiry is whether such differences exist. The question is not whether there is societal consensus that they either do or do not. There clearly is no societal consensus. That doesn't mean that the ban on gay marriage is therefore constitutional.

The second point worth noting is perhaps more crucial, and more often overlooked: the question whether such differences exist is a contextual one, not an absolute one. The issue is whether differences exist with respect to characteristics of the groups that should matter to the state—not whether there are any differences at all. Indeed, there are always differences between any two individuals, any two groups, or any two of anything at all that can be named and distinguished. Thus, there were certainly differences, for example, and very important ones, between white and black citizens in 1954, when *Brown v. Board of Education*[36] was decided, as there still are in 2007: black citizens were more likely than white citizens to be descended from slaves, although the correlation was by no means perfect. As a result, their histories differed. Black citizens had been differently subjected to slavery, reconstruction, postreconstruction, the era of lynching, and Jim Crow, all radically differently than the experiences, both individual and collective, of whites. By virtue of their different histories, black citizens also had vastly different experiences of religiosity, of education, of family, of marriage, and of community, than whites. The question confronting the Court in 1954 was not whether there were, in fact, or in nature, or "in reality," differences, either individually or collectively, between black and white citizens; the question was whether there were differences that relevantly pertained to the segregatory regime in question. Likewise, there were certainly differences between women and men in the 1960s and 1970s, during the dismantling of Jane Crow, and there are still salient and familiar differences between the two sexes today. Women and men have different roles in biological reproduction, as well as a host of other differences, irrespective of their cause: women earn less money and have less control over wealth, women work longer, women do more childcare, women are, today, somewhat more likely to hold high school and college diplomas, women have longer life spans, women don't as a group have as much combat experience, etc. The question, for purposes of formal equality, is not whether there are differences between two groups that are differently treated by law. Of course there are differences—if nothing else does, the differing legal treatment itself will in turn bring about differences. The question is whether there are differences between the groups that are relevant to a legitimate state objective, and that justify the state's different treatment of them, in pursuance of that objective.

So, what might some differences be between the same-sex couple wishing to marry, and perhaps eventually to parent as well, and the opposite-sex couple with the same ambitions, and are any of these differences of the sort that would justify their radically different treatment by the state? Let's begin by simply listing some differences. One difference concerns the nature, quality, and perhaps the point of the sexual relations between the two couples: same-sex sexuality is not going to be focused on either reproduction, or "sex acts of the reproductive form," to use Bradley and George's awkward phrase.[37] Sex between a same-sex couple will not be engaged in toward the end of reproduction, or toward the end of conjoining in a sex act of the reproductive form, and will therefore be more likely to be exclusively focused on other goals: on physical pleasure, on the creation of intimacy, or on the shared joy of what I'd call affective physicality—the expression of affection through physical gestures. The pleasure, intimacy, affection, and expression of all of that, to be had from sexuality, is more likely to be viewed by the partners in a committed same-sex couple as central to the point of the sex, and it is (somewhat) more likely to be seen as such in a same-sex rather than an opposite-sex union. Recall that for Bradley and George, sex motivated by a desire for pleasure is flatly immoral: disintegrative of the unitive nature of mind, body, and soul.[38] Pleasure as a side effect of sex, motivated by the desire to participate in the reproductive sex act characteristic of the species, is morally acceptable, and perhaps even desirable and legitimately desired. But it cannot be the point of the activity. Sex between persons of the same-sex, who cannot engage in such acts toward the end of either reproducing or engaging in reproductive-type sex acts, is far more likely to be engaged in toward the end of pleasure, intimacy, or both. Pleasure or intimacy is the point of the marital sex, for same-sex couples, whereas it might or might not be for opposite-sex couples.

Second: same-sex couples that parent will have children that, on average, will not be as genetically connected to both parents as the children of opposite-sex couples. Opposite-sex couples might adopt, employ a surrogate, a sperm bank, or IVF, and might accordingly parent children who likewise are not genetically connected to both parents. But same-sex couples virtually by definition, at least until some technological-biological breakthrough, will have children that are at most genetically connected to one of the parenting partners, while opposite-sex couples most likely will have biological children connected to both of them. The genetic connection between parent and child will therefore be different, as between opposite- and same-sex couples.

Third: children of same-sex couples will be raised in an environment that is more tolerant of sexual difference and possibly more open to gender variance than opposite-sex couples.[39] Again, this will not be a firm correlation: the children of opposite-sex couples likewise might be raised in an environment that is tolerant of sexual difference and gender variation. Nevertheless, it is not insensible to suppose, and research bears out the supposition, that children of same-sex couples are not being raised in an environment where traditional gender roles are reinforced: one in which a wife/mother is in charge of domestic chores and child-raising, while a husband/father generates income in the wage market.

Do any of these differences render the two groups of couples so unlike as to justify their radically different treatment by the law? Take them in the order listed above. What of the first difference—that same-sex couples are more likely to be, in Bill Eskridge's phrase,[40] sex-pleasure positive? Is this a difference that justifies the law's differential treatment? It depends on the point and definition of marriage. If marriage is defined as the natural lawyers suggest—the union of a man and woman as expressed by sexual acts of a reproductive sort (or sexual acts engaged in for reproductive purposes)—then the exclusion of gay and lesbian couples is transparently justified: such couples might be for life but they cannot be "unitive" in the sense meant by marriage. Remember that for natural lawyers such as Professors Bradley, Finnis, and George, sex for pleasure is flatly immoral: it destroys the unity of body and mind to use the body as an instrumental tool of physical pleasure. For all three, only sex for reproduction, or (more broadly) sex acts that are "of the reproductive sort"—meaning marital vaginal-penile penetration—is morally permissible, and for all three such sex is morally definitive of marriage. That same-sex couples cannot physically engage in sex that is either for reproduction or that are of the reproductive sort is precisely what makes same-sex marriage a "moral impossibility," to use George's phrase, or more directly, an oxymoron. Same-sex marriage is inconceivable, for natural lawyers, because of the nature of the sex that occurs within it. Such a marriage lacks the positive moral good definitive of marriage, and encourages the sex that is disintegrative of identity.

Do any of these differences justify the state's differential treatment? Not likely. First, the natural lawyer's definition of marriage, as the unity of woman and man as expressed in sexual acts of the reproductive type, does not well capture either the state's understanding of the definition of marriage, or its interest in it. Whatever might have been the case in the past, it is clear today that all states regard couples as equally married regardless of the motivation of their sexual conduct and regardless of whether or not they engage in reproductive or noncoital or contracepted intercourse. Indeed—states today typically regard couples as married regardless of whether or not they engage in any sex at all, of any sort, ever. If the state's interest in marriage did track the natural lawyers', then the rational distinction for the state to make would be between those couples who engage in the right kind of sexual conduct, and for the right reason, and those who do not. The state clearly draws no such distinction. Whatever might be its status in natural law thinking, the line between opposite- and same-sex marriage cannot be justified in law on the basis of the difference between proper and improper motivations for sexual conduct. States do not have any interest, nor should they have any interest, in whether or not private sexual conduct between married partners is engaged in for pleasure, reproduction, or for some other reason. As long as no harm is done by it, they have no such interest, furthermore, regardless of whether pleasurable sexual conduct is or isn't morally defensible.

Likewise, the state has no interest in the degree of genetic connection that might exist between parents and children. Once an adoption is completed, there are virtually no legal distinctions between an adopted child and a genetically connected one. Permitting marriage here would actually lessen the administrative burden on the state, which otherwise must devote some resources to facilitating adoptions of children genetically connected to one but not both parents. A state interested in ensuring that children in need of adoption are well placed in familial homes will seek to maximize, not minimize, the number of families that might potentially seek to adopt children, and the way to do that is through permitting, not barring, same-sex marriage.

Finally, there do not seem to be any provable differences in the abilities of gay and lesbian couples on the one hand, and straight couples on the other, to parent, save the one noted above: children raised in gay households are more likely to have and express tolerant attitudes toward homosexuality in general and to hold more flexible views regarding gender roles than children raised in straight households.[41] Such children are not, however, prone to greater criminality, they are not more inclined to drop out of school, they are not more likely to have trouble getting or holding a job in early adulthood, and they are no less likely to be straight or to marry. They are just as educated, healthy, and law abiding as their peers. They are not more prone to gender confusion, although they may be more likely to disavow sex-based divisions of labor. According to some researchers, girls raised by lesbian couples may be somewhat more assertive than otherwise, and boys raised by gay couples may be somewhat more nurturant.[42] Even these findings—which hardly damn either egalitarian or gay and lesbian parenting—are sketchy at best.

What other possible differences might justify the differential treatment of gay and lesbian couples wishing to marry? There aren't many—or any. The absence of any such verifiable difference prompts the reasonable inference that the different treatment of gay and lesbian couples wishing to marry—or at least the continuing refusal to do so—is based on nothing but irrational dislike, or bigotry. There is a substantial history of antigay animus to sustain this conclusion. Gay and lesbian citizens are badly hurt by this differential treatment, and they are so hurt on the basis of a criterion—sexual orientation—over which they have little or no choice. There is no compelling rationale for the different treatment. The conclusion ought to be that the different treatment is a deprivation of "formal equality" that violates the Equal Protection Clause of the Constitution. This is just what the Massachusetts Supreme Court argued, and ultimately what they found, although they did so on the basis of the Massachusetts, rather than the United States, Constitution.[43] Differential treatment for no good reason of a group historically subject to irrational social opprobrium is unconstitutional. Differential treatment of gays and lesbians wishing to marry is based on nothing but societal dislike. It is irrational, hurtful, discriminatory, and unconstitutional.

This is a powerful argument, constitutional, legal, and otherwise. In just a few artfully crafted pages, Chief Justice Marshall, of the Massachusetts Supreme Court, brought the struggle for gay marriage in line with a particular narrative about American constitutional and political history both: about Americans' struggles with outsider groups, about our difficulties with difference, and about our moral victories. Here too, she suggested, as we did with our history of racial apartheid, as we did with our ideology of separate spheres, we can use our constitutional commitments to equality and liberty to overcome our xenophobic qualms; we can use law to allow moral principle to triumph. At the same time, the opinion does not trumpet the priority of law over a community's morality, history, or tradition; quite the contrary. The strength of the decision, I believe, lies in the fact that while it appeals and makes recourse continually to the virtues of legalism, of formal equality, and of constitutionalism, it *also* appeals (as do all great constitutional decisions) to more universal and more humanistic longings—in this case the longings we all know and feel for intimacy, for sexual pleasure, to love and raise our children, and for the ties of family. Marshall does indeed assert the primacy of law, and principle, and constitutionalism, and formal equality over particularism, and bigotry, and narrowmindedness. But she also celebrates the commonality of all of us—as Americans, as biological beings, as familial mammals, as human beings—with respect to longings we all share. She wrote her opinion in her own voice indeed, and a complex and textured voice it is: it is the voice of a justice, a wife, a mother, a citizen, and a neighbor. She wrote in a voice that transparently reveals that she knows the importance of these familial matters. Her decision rests on vivid assumptions about hope, community, and moral progress that are tremendously appealing: by refining our institutions, over time, she is telling us, we can articulate their basic fairness, and render them in accord with our fundamental, constitutive commitments to equality, and our fundamental promise to respect each other and treat each other with dignity. We can create a more just and more inclusive communal life. This decision inspires us to *overcome,* just as we did, or like to think we did, with respect to racial apartheid, and assures us that we can do so without doing violence to those we hold dear, including our institutions and our traditions as well as our own families. It really does appeal to our better angelic natures. It also has the ring of truth. Which part of this woman's opinion would you care to deny?

Yet, there is no question that Justice Marshall's decision in *Goodridge* has inspired a ferocious backlash. We now have over thirty-five states with some sort of ordinance, law, or constitutional amendment on the books, all aiming to ban forever the possibility of gay marriage, and a federal constitutional amendment offered that would do the same at a national level. Because of the backlash, we have working-class voters in the (few) solidly red states of the nation voting against their pocketbook interest for a party that promises to do little but restate, every two or four years, its opposition to all things homosexual, but most centrally, gay marriage. As I write this, pragmatists and strategists from the Democratic Party at all levels of political engagement wince at the possibility that a "red state strategy" centered on hostility to gay marriage could realign—yet again—party loyalty over the next half century, just as the "Southern strategy" centered on hostility to civil rights did likewise over the last half century, cementing in place a socially conservative governing party, or worse, while strategists from the Republican Party embrace just that opportunity.

Nevertheless, it is important to affirm—and with full acknowledgment of the tremendous capacity for unintended harms, now realized and still threatened, that this one decision can and has brought down upon us—that this decision, by this Massachusetts Supreme Court justice, is a decision for the ages. By affirming equal dignity, by extending equal respect, and by reasserting basic communal values of inclusion, she opened up, again, the possibility that this country can find its moral compass. It's a bright spot in an otherwise terribly bleak political and constitutional decade, and we should be loathe to turn out backs on it.

Communitarian Values

Formal equality defenses of gay marriage are, according to some of their friendly critics, more than just a bit too, well, formal. They tend to miss the forest for the trees. That "a" is like "b," and that "b" should therefore be entitled to whatever "a" is entitled to, might be true and important, and perhaps obvious to those who view "a" as like "b," but it won't be at all convincing to those who view "a" and "b" differently. Those who do so need to be convinced that the similarities between "a" and "b" are more salient than the differences, and those who view "a," but not "b," as entitled to something need to be shown why the entitlement should also flow to "b." In the context of gay marriage, a number of advocates and scholars from within as well as outside of the gay rights community, and who agree with *Goodridge*'s bottom line, have nevertheless faulted the "formal equality" argument on which it rests, and for more or less this reason.

Those who view gays and straights differently, and find the idea of gay marriage oxymoronic, tend to do so most often on explicitly moral grounds, and on the explicitly moral grounds that formal equality arguments quite intentionally elide. Opposition to gay marriage is typically premised on a moral belief that gay sex is immoral, and that the state has a legitimate interest in promoting "morals" among its citizens. The moral difference just is the difference between gay and straight couples that in turn justifies their differential treatment by the state: the former engage in immoral conduct that the state should not condone, much less sanctify. The argument from formal equality fails to address this difference, and accordingly fails to address what lies at the heart of the continuing opposition—still prohibitively substantial, at least in this country—to expansion of marriage rights to same-sex couples.

Why does this happen? There's nothing about the "formal equality" argument itself that suggests it should. Devotees of formal equality no less than their critics are well aware that the salient difference between gay and straight citizens, on which defenders of traditional marriage rest their case, is the differing societal perception of the morality of the sexuality in which the two classes of couples engage. The logic of formal equality does not alone imply the elision of the need to demonstrate the likeness of classes, before asserting the necessity of their like treatment. Rather, the reason the formal equality argument—as made in *Goodridge* and elsewhere—tends to minimize the need to address the "moral difference" between gay and straight sex, and therefore between gay and straight couples, is because formal equality is itself embedded in a larger constitutional view of the state, which is itself indebted to contemporary liberal theory. Within contemporary liberalism, at least from about the mid-1960s to the present, it is simply viewed as axiomatic that the state can have no legitimate interest in the purely moral quality of the conduct of its citizens, so long as that conduct does not do demonstrable harm to nonconsenting third parties, on the grounds that the state should be "neutral" with respect to competing conceptions of "the good life," both moralistic and otherwise. A state should no more support one understanding of the good life because it purports to be a moral way of living than it should support another because it purports to be more spiritual. Therefore, liberals typically conclude, the state has no legitimate reason to prefer straight to gay marriage on the minimalist reason that gay sex is immoral, and that the state ought to encourage moral—hence straight—behavior.

The liberal insistence on state neutrality with respect to the nature of the moral good, the good life, and the inculcation of virtue, was without question at the heart of the formal equality argument in *Goodridge*, although Justice Marshall did not dwell on it at any length. More significantly, and more explicitly, it was also central to the U.S. Supreme Court's most important and most recent equal protection decision, *Lawrence v Texas*.[44] In *Lawrence*, the Supreme Court struck down a Texas statutory ban on homosexual sodomy as an unconstitutional infringement of individuals' rights to equal protection of the law. The state law banned homosexual, but not heterosexual, sodomy, and the Court found no rational way to distinguish between the two. Moral disapproval of the former, but not the latter, the Court held, was just not sufficient:

> This case raises [the] issue ... whether, under the Equal Protection Clause, moral disapproval is a legitimate state interest to justify by itself a statute that bans homosexual sodomy, but not heterosexual sodomy. *It is not. Moral disapproval of this group, like a bare desire to harm the group, is an interest that is insufficient to satisfy rational basis review under the Equal Protection Clause.... Moral disapproval of a group cannot be a legitimate governmental interest under the Equal Protection Clause because legal classifications must not be "drawn for the purpose of disadvantaging the group burdened by the law."* ... Texas' invocation of moral disapproval as a legitimate state interest proves nothing more than Texas' desire to criminalize homosexual sodomy.... And because Texas so rarely enforces its sodomy law as applied to private, consensual acts, the law serves more as a statement of dislike and disapproval against homosexuals than as a tool to stop criminal behavior. The Texas sodomy law raises the inevitable inference that the disadvantage imposed is born of animosity toward the class of persons affected.[45] (Italics added.)

The case is noteworthy not only for its holding, but also for its reasoning, which was starkly and classically liberal. It was also a departure from the earlier "privacy" cases it cited as authority, all of which, including *Griswold*,[46] *Eisenstadt*,[47] *Roe*,[48] and *Casey*,[49] had rested not so much on the imperative of state neutrality with respect to the nature of the good life, or on the inability of states to legislate on matters relating to public morals, but rather, on the need to delegate decision-making with regard to family size, family planning, and family constitution, to family members (and abortion decisions to the women concerned and their doctors). Virtually none of these decisions—including *Roe* and *Casey*—had starkly declared the state to have no legitimate interest in the morals of citizens, or in the task of inculcating virtues conducive to a good life. Rather, what the Court held, in these earlier decisions, was that the good life the state very much has an interest in promoting, in the context of family life, requires parents, married persons, or individuals themselves be given the autonomy or the right to decide these questions, rather than states. Morality, in other words, is very much the state's business, but morality, in the context of family and reproductive life, is best served by respecting individual, marital, or familial privacy. This is quite different from unambiguously deciding the state has no interest in promoting the morals of the citizenry.

In *Lawrence,* the Court was far more explicitly "liberal" in its reasoning. Perhaps homosexual sodomy is "moral," perhaps it is "immoral," but, the Court argued, if it is consensual behavior and does no demonstrable harm to the individuals, to bystanders, or to the larger community, the state has no legitimate reason to criminalize it, at least so long as it fails to criminalize heterosexual sodomy.[50] The state must be neutral on these moral questions about fundamental ways to live. It cannot and should not endorse "lifestyles," and it cannot and should not endorse one understanding of moral ways of living over others.[51] Consensual sexual behavior between adults cannot possibly cause cognizable harm to either participants or to the community. The state has no legitimate interest in regulating it.[52] Neutrality on questions of morality, no less than the felt need to treat gay and lesbian citizens with equal respect, and accord them equal dignity, was therefore at the center of the Court's decision in *Lawrence.*

In the context of the gay marriage debate, and particularly given the Court's decision in *Lawrence,* this liberal stance has great force. If it is true that a state cannot promote a particular way of life on the straightforward grounds that it is a moral one, and if it is also true that a state cannot criminalize homosexual sodomy on just those grounds, then it surely follows that a state simply cannot promote, encourage, and reward traditional marriage on the grounds that hetero-sexuality is a more moral form of sex than same-sex sex. To do so violates basic, defining premises of the liberal state, as well as the constitutional corollaries of those arguments: privacy, liberty, and state neutrality. This makes for a very tight and very powerful argument: if the morality of their conduct is off the table, then there are no defensible differences between gay and straight couples. Any other possible reason a state might have to promote marriage fails to distinguish gay from straight couples.

It also makes, however, for an argument that dramatically fails to join issue with those who disagree—a group that, on this issue, constitutes about half of all voters nationwide, and possibly a majority of all legislators in state and fed-eral congresses. Opponents of same-sex marriage typically feel no allegiance to the quintessentially Millian and liberal claim, relied upon in *Lawrence,* that the state simply must not promote or deter conduct on the basis of its moral or im-moral nature. Rather, social conservative opposition to gay marriage is grounded squarely in the joint beliefs that the state, through the institution of marriage, quite properly regulates and recognizes the morality of marital, heterosexual, coital sex, and that homosexuality is immoral, both as conduct and as lifestyle. Liber-als take issue with social conservatives' views regarding whether or not the state can "legislate morality." But perhaps out of an excess of confidence regarding the power of their claims regarding the necessity of state neutrality, they then leave untouched the middle premise of the social conservative argument, to say nothing of the substance of many citizens' beliefs: that homosexuality is immoral. With that premise intact, the moral argument for restricting marriage to heterosexual couples is straightforward, whether or not it is constitutionally valid: the relevant difference between the equally committed, monogamous, parenting straight couple, and the similarly situated gay couple, is that the gay couple is engaging in immoral behavior. The straight couple is not. The state not only may, but very likely must, take cognizance of that difference, and legislate accordingly. The liberal response to all of this takes a dangerously high ground: regardless of the morality of the conduct, liberals argue—meaning, in effect, *even if you are right*—that is not a legitimate basis on which states may act.

There are a number of problems with the liberal rejoinder. First, although I'll mention this only to set it aside, there is a difference between criminal bans on gay conduct, on the one hand, and the state facilitation of gay marriage, on the other, and there is therefore a difference between *Lawrence* and *Goodridge*. *Goodridge* does not follow from *Lawrence*. What was at stake in *Goodridge* and other cases like it is a social institution, with attendant rights and responsibilities provided by the state to individuals; what was at stake in *Lawrence* was the state's authority to intervene in private life and private homes toward the end of hauling people off to prison for engaging in consensual conduct that demonstrably harms no one. *Lawrence* can arguably be decided by reference to not much more than the liberal premise that the state should not "criminalize" or legislate against immorality, where it is consensual and does no harm to third parties; *Goodridge*, however, cannot be. *Goodridge* ultimately requires the state to act so as to facilitate gay union and marriage, and not just refrain from acting in a way that impermissibly criminalizes conduct that is at worst immoral rather than affirmatively harmful. The mandate of state neutrality toward the good might justify the outcome in *Lawrence*. It is not so clear that it is sufficient to mandate same-sex marriage.

A more basic problem with the liberal's "neutrality" response in this context, however, is that the classical liberal—both on the Court and off—should not be so confident regarding the state's role in the promotion of a morality. A good bit of state legislative action is premised on precisely the claim that some such action is necessary to promote, on behalf of citizens, a morally good life: think not only of prohibitions against certain kinds of gambling, dog fighting, cock fighting, or prostitution, but also of state funding for the arts, or funding for public education, or for that matter, progressive taxation. The latter "positive" legislative acts are surely at least in part intended to promote a moral purpose and to inculcate a decent moral code in the citizenry, just as the prohibitions are intended to deter an immoral one, so long as "moral" and the "good" are given capacious meanings: literacy, appreciation of high culture, and a more rather than less egalitarian distribution of wealth all contribute to the formation of moral character. They all contribute, arguably, to an individual's abilities to intelligently and sympathetically engage, and feel, the interests of others, and incorporate those interests into his or her own "moral sentiments." Education, literacy, shared culture, and a just distribution of a community's resources might all be considered moral goals of government, intended to instill, reinforce, and encourage good moral character. They all contribute to a healthy body politic. They all contribute to a morally enriched environment for all citizens.

Furthermore, the morals of the citizenry have long been regarded, in constitutional law, as an appropriate end of state legislative action, *Lawrence* dicta to the contrary notwithstanding. No Supreme Court has ever definitively ruled to the contrary. Of the modern so-called privacy cases—*Griswold, Eisenstadt, Roe, Casey* and *Lawrence*—only *Lawrence* comes close to seriously contesting this point, and even *Lawrence* is somewhat limited in scope: as noted above, *Lawrence* dealt with the criminalization of consensual sodomitic behavior of gays and lesbians, where the state had failed to criminalize the same behavior of heterosexuals, and can be fairly read as resting on relatively narrow antipaternalist grounds pertaining to the legitimate reach of the state's criminal sanction. It might be a fairer reading of the *Griswold* to *Lawrence* line of decisions—it is certainly a permissible reading—as resting on the need to constrain the state's legitimate interest in moralistic legislation with a due regard for individual privacy, particularly where the state's interest in morals is expressed through the criminal code, rather than the broad basis that a state has no legitimate interest whatsoever in the moral well-being of the citizenry.

Nor is state neutrality toward morality a necessary feature of a liberal understanding of the state, if we look at "liberalism" as a three-centuries-old project, rather than just a product of the last forty years. Historically, classical liberals have not uniformly embraced state neutrality toward moral questions as constitutive of liberalism; a number of English nineteenth-century liberals, as well as American early twentieth-century liberals, have energetically debated and delineated various liberal conceptions of morality, and urged the state to promote them.[53] In the last few decades as well, the liberal insistence on state neutrality toward competing conceptions of morality and the nature of the good has been criticized not only from conservative theorists, but also from communitarians such as Harvard Philosophy Professor Michael Sandel,[54] and from dissenting liberals such as Professor (and advisor to President Clinton on domestic policy, including family policy) William Galston, as well.[55] State neutrality toward morality, both Sandel and Galston have argued, might be a starting assumption of libertarianism, and perhaps of laissez-faire free market policies—but it cannot be the fundamental assumption of robust liberalism. Liberalism, classically and today, in the United States if not elsewhere in the world, is associated not only with libertarian politics and free market ideology, but also with restraints on all of that: for liberals, perhaps foundationally, our distribution of resources, of power, of wealth, and of status must align with some minimal regard for the necessity of assuring access to the good life, to all citizens, equally. Such an aspiration is hard to reconcile with a sterile insistence that the state cannot contemplate, when ascertaining and pursuing legislative priorities, competing conceptions of a good and virtuous life to which all citizens must be given whatever access our aspirations for equality, equal worth, and equal dignity require.

Whatever might be the status of "neutrality" arguments within liberalism, however, in the context of the gay marriage debate, the practical limits of liberal arguments premised on state neutrality toward the good life are starkly laid bare. Liberal arguments in this context characteristically, and rigorously, eschew the need to articulate an understanding of both the moral good of marriage, and the moral value of gay sex and gay life. Rather, liberal arguments for gay marriage—and the Massachusetts decision in *Goodridge* is no exception—typically proceed by reference to individual rights, the imperative need for state neutrality on the nature of the good, and the dangers of moralistic legislation. The individual has a fundamental right to marriage, the argument proceeds (as it did in *Goodridge*), because of the structural nature of individual rights and the limits of legitimate state action—*not* because of the goodness of the institution, or the goodness of the individual who by virtue or his or her moral virtue is entitled to share in it. Rather, the state can legitimately take no stand with respect to the goodness of the individual or the goodness of marriage. As Marshall made clear in *Goodridge*, "civil marriage" is a legal construct, to which all individuals must have a fundamental right of access.[56]

Both philosophically and politically, however, it is not clear that such a morally sterile liberal understanding of both marriage and individual conduct is up to the task to which the liberal gay rights advocate puts it. Obviously, that individuals have a fundamental right to something doesn't mean they have a fundamental right to redefine it. (That you have a fundamental right to privacy does not give you a right to have sex in public places, on the grounds that privacy ought to be defined so as to include such performances.) But further, the state is not barred absolutely from engaging in moralistic legislation, and legislation opposing gay marriage, as well as definitions of marriage themselves, are almost always premised on moral assumptions about the nature of marriage and the morality of gay life and gay sex. The liberal rejoinder that everything the social conservative has to say, or might believe, on the morality of marriage and gay sex, whether true or false, is simply of no relevance seems to hit a wall of absurdity. The institution itself, and the conduct it enshrines, is now and has for recent history been virtually entirely justified as well as defined by reference to some such set of moral beliefs. The purpose and point of marriage, overwhelmingly, has been to promote morality—somehow defined—on the part of citizens.

Finally, and entirely aside from the philosophical and constitutional problems with liberal defenses of gay marriage, there lies a very serious political one: opposition to gay marriage, from legislator and citizen alike, is grounded in precisely the argument that the liberal argument put forward by the advocacy community on this issue explicitly—and even quite aggressively—refuses to join. This is not inconsequential: there is palpable political fallout. Liberal arguments premised on individual rights and state neutrality fail—or refuse—to provide any counter to conservative claims regarding the immorality of committed, monogamous, gay sex, leaving the actual basis of such legislation untouched, and second, by failing to do so, they squander an opportunity. There is a positive moral case to be made for gay sex, gay life, and gay unions. Insisting that the morality or immorality of these unions is irrelevant to the state's action is dangerously close to conceding their immorality. There's just no need for it, and it does real harm. Libertarian instincts among all but the most committed philosophical libertarians will only go so far—and the limits of those instincts likely lie in social institutions, the very point of which is perceived to be moral. And, the social institution that is moral par excellence, so to speak, is marriage.

Consequently, a second argument—along with a political campaign within the political campaign, dubbed, appropriately enough, "gay is good"—for gay marriage has developed among scholars less wedded than are contemporary liberals to the claim that the morality of conduct can never constitute grounds for legislative action. Professor Chai Feldblum of the Georgetown Law Center and Carlos Ball, of the University of Illinois, both longtime gay rights activists and advocates as well as scholars, have urged their fellow-traveling liberal defenders of gay marriage to "move past" neutrality, and to join two distinct and distinctly moral debates, their aversion to moralistic discourse notwithstanding: the first, over the moral good of marriage, and the second, over the moral good of gay sex.[57] On the first point, Feldblum and Ball, tracking arguments made more generally by Professors Milton Regan[58] and Mary Shanley,[59] urge that the moral good of marriage lies in the commitment that adults can make to the care and love of companions and dependents both, and that this moral good is equally availing of gay as straight individuals. Virtually all of the reasons that communitarians have given for the moral value of marriage—the importance of marriage as constitutive of identity, the centrality of marriage to our relational selves, the fragility of relationality in an overly atomized and commodified world, and the importance of relationships of dependence and interdependence in a liberal culture that valorizes independence and autonomy, can be made with respect to gay marriage, as traditional marriage. Briefly, if the communitarians are right regarding the moral point of marriage, there is simply no point in not extending it to same-sex couples, and a good bit of harm in refusing to do so. Moral arguments, and moral values, cut in favor of gay marriage, not against it.

Communitarian arguments for same-sex marriage also, though, attempt to engage social conservatives on the morality of gay sex and gay life itself. The claim is perfectly straightforward: gay sex is good. It is (or can be) good for some of the same reasons that nonprocreative straight sex is (or can be) good: giving pleasure to an intimate companion, and receiving pleasure from him or her, no less than giving and receiving gifts, is good, both intrinsically and extrinsically. Nonprocreative sex (with either same- or opposite-sex partners) contributes to intimacy, builds trust, encourages openness, and shared responsibility. It makes a couple already emotionally committed to each other all the more so. It's not called "making love" for nothing. None of this is to deny that nonprocreative sex, just like the procreative kind, can be destructive, exploitative, dehumanizing, violent, objectifying, boring, trivial, irritating, time consuming, or just massively inconsequential. It is very much to deny, however, that by virtue of not being procreative, sex is therefore immoral. Nonprocreative sex is indeed different, but it is for straight as well as gay couples. Gay sex is by definition nonprocreative. But with straight nonprocreative sex, it shares virtues, emotional dimensions, and moral qualities. It leaves participants closer, and builds trust. There is no reason, as liberal proponents of gay marriage rightly insist, to think that gay relationships are about nothing but sex: such relationships have all the moral potential of straight relationships, and much of that potential has nothing to do with any form of sexuality whatsoever. There is also no reason, however, to think that the sex in such relations is of no moral value: that "gay is good," implies that "gay sex is good." But the point needs to be broadened, to meet the breadth of the resistance to this claim: nonreproductive sex—"sex for pleasure"—between emotionally committed and responsible adults—is good. It is not the same moral good as procreative sex, but then, marriage is no longer, if it ever was, about nothing but the kids.

Social Utilitarian Arguments

A final cluster of arguments for gay marriage, made by both liberals and communitarians, but also by a number of influential gay conservatives, regard what we might call various externalities: the positive social utility that might be garnered from this change in our law, in addition to the positive effects the change might have on those most directly affected—gay and lesbian citizens. There are a number of benefits worth noting. First, the permissibility of gay marriage, some conservative gay men have long argued, might domesticate gay male sexual life, which is, they contend, considerably more promiscuous, and hence more dangerous, than either straight or lesbian sexual life, within or outside of marriage.[60] The availability of gay marriage to gay men would send a societal signal that marriage is not only a liberal right of all adults, but also a positive norm, or moral expectation, and that would well serve both the gay and straight community. With marriage available, gay men would be acculturated in the same way as straight men: marriage is to be expected. What one should do, as one enters adulthood, is settle down. The oversexed nature of some gay male life would be a thing of the past. Gay life would no longer be centered on sex, multiparty sex, nonmonogamous sex, and anonymous sex, were gay marriage to enter the picture, as not only a right but an expectation. The typical adult gay life might involve sexual experimentation, but as with straight life, the goal would be the fruition of a monogamous, long-term commitment to one other individual. Gay male prostitution, gay male promiscuity, gay male escort services, gay male bathhouses, and in general gay life overly committed to impersonal sexual pleasure would not disappear, obviously, but it would fade, and most important, would cease to be viewed, within the gay male community, as normative, unexceptional—normal. Monogamy would be understood within the gay community as good for gay men as it is for straight, although confining for both, and, something that, again like straight men, gay men don't take to naturally. Law, as elsewhere, would and should be an effective prod. Legal recognition of gay marriage, and then legal involvement in the promotion of gay marriage, would counter natural or cultural tendencies toward promiscuity with the carrots of social approval, as well the stick of social shame. Cheating, adultery, lying, and immoral sexual behavior that injures a trusting partner would become real restraints on behavior, with the same mechanisms of social control—gossip, social disapproval—that guides heterosexual conduct into narrowed, monogamous channels.

Second, law Professors Nan Hunter[61] and Robin West[62] have argued that gay marriage could have the salutary effect of challenging, by example, the gendered allocation of labor and power in married life, in a way that parallels, or simply extends, the sense in which gay life in general constitutes a challenge to what Adrienne Rich dubbed several decades back "compulsory heterosexuality."[63] This is not to say that same-sex relationships would be free of exploitation: there's no reason to think that would be the case. There's also no reason to think that the lines of exploitation would not track traditional gendered roles, where gender is decoupled from biological sex: one spouse might assume the role of the traditional wife, with less earning power and more household labor, and find him- or herself exploited—meaning his wishes ignored, his interests slighted, and his surplus labor value appropriated toward the ends of the stronger party—in a host of all too familiar ways. But there would not be the constant, repetitive, mind-numbing allocation of labor and power along lines of biological sex, with the biological woman assuming domestic chores, a subordinate political position, and economic weakness, while the biological man earns an income and assumes the role of domestic head of household. This alone would be a gain: there are real harms that come from the identification of biological women with the group best suited for domestic exploitation. The more household labor women disproportionately do, the less they earn in the wage labor market, the less they earn in the wage labor market, the less power they have in the household, the less power they have in the household, the more disproportionate household labor they perform—and so on. Same-sex marriages demonstrate, if nothing else, the non-necessity of private gendered subordination, along biological lines, within the household.

Finally, don't forget the kids. Children would benefit in at least three ways, likely more. First, there continues to be an adoption crisis in this country. There are many children that need adoptions, particularly African American children, and a shortage of families and couples qualified and willing to adopt. What could possibly be the downside of opening marriage to couples who seek it out precisely so as to publicly assert their willingness and desire to start a family? Second, the children of gay and lesbian couples who parent would benefit enormously from their parents' enhanced marital status, in material and psychic ways. Although there are few if any remaining explicit legal distinctions between legitimate and illegitimate children, the law continues to tolerate a host of private distinctions: the children of unmarried parents, for example, cannot qualify as an insured dependent on a health policy provided by the employer of the nonbiological parent. Likewise, children of unmarried parents suffer the delegitimacy of their parents' nonmarital status, as described above. Third, all children who might be themselves gay would benefit enormously from the legitimation of gay and lesbian marriage. If we can imagine a world with no disapproval of these unions, we are imagining a world in which children and teenagers don't learn to fear and hate their own emotional, sexual, and utterly biological longings and selves. All of these gains, in turn, would translate into saved dollars, and saved expenditures from the public purse.

The *Goodridge* decision, the formal equality argument it asserts, and more broadly the same-sex marriage movement itself, have generated enormous opposition, primarily from social conservatives, but also from some progressives and some queer theorists as well. Let's look at their most salient criticisms.

Social Conservative Arguments against Gay Marriage

While social conservatives have mounted a ferocious political movement against same-sex marriage, conservative scholars of the family and of marriage have raised a number of theoretical objections. First, the neonatural lawyers, as discussed above, see the "same-sex marriage movement" as nothing less than the destruction of marriage. Marriage, by definition, must consist of the conjoining of a man and a woman in marital reproductive sexual acts. "Same-sex marriage" is an oxymoron, or as it is sometimes put, a "moral impossibility."[64] Whatever might be the status of this claim in the context of religious marriage—marriage as defined and performed within communities of faith—it simply cannot hold sway as a serious objection to the expansion of civil marriage. Civil marriage is not defined as the neonatural lawyers wish to view it. Consummation of the marriage in acts of sexual intercourse of any sort is no longer necessary for a civil marriage. If there is a sexual relation between married partners, there is no requirement that those relations be of a "reproductive sort," nor is there any requirement that they be procreative. The use of birth control does not render the marriage null, nor does a sexual relationship between the parties that consists of nothing but noncoital sex acts. As Justice Marshall made clear in *Goodridge,* a marriage between two partners on their deathbeds, utterly incapable of lifting a finger, is as valid as a marriage between two partners in the throes of sexual passion.[65] The neonatural lawyers' account of the necessary relation between marriage and sex is both too narrow and too strict: too narrow, in that only sex of a procreative or at least reproductive sort can legitimate the marriage, and too strict, in that sex is indeed required. Neither prong tracks the state's understanding of marriage. The state truly isn't any longer in the business of requiring consummation of marriage, or of restricting marital sex to procreative or reproductive acts of coital intercourse.

Social conservatives of a more utilitarian, or simply more secular bent have added more germane arguments, generally focused on two empirical claims. These latter arguments, by contrast to those of the neonatural lawyers, tend to accept the secular and utilitarian claim that civil marriage must be defended, and defined, by reference to publicly accepted goals: that the institution of civil marriage, like all institutions constructed by law, must serve legitimate state ends. Likewise, they also accept the secular claim that civil marriage is best defended not by reference to the state's interest in protecting the morals of the citizenry, but rather, by reference to the state's interest in promoting and protecting the well-being of children and secondarily, to the state's interest in protecting the well-being of other dependents, such as the elderly. Heterosexual marriage and only heterosexual marriage, however, is facilitative of that end. Gay marriage, while not oxymoronic, is just counterproductive, and for basically two reasons.

First, on the basis of a small body of arguably ambiguous research, and on the basis of a much larger body of "common sense" and traditional understanding, a number of social scientists have argued that Justice Marshall's claim, in *Goodridge*, that there is no discernible difference between children raised in same-sex households and children raised in opposite-sex households, is simply false.[66] Rather, children in same-sex households tend to have different attitudes toward gender and sexual orientation both, with correspondingly different alignments of gender characteristics themselves. Thus, for example, boys of same-sex households are often more "nurturant," some of this research shows, while girls of egalitarian or same-sex households tend to be more aggressive, and both boys and girls are more accepting of same-sex life styles.[67] These are, the researchers posit, bad outcomes. Homosexuality is a dangerous and damaging lifestyle, and if same-sex marriage inculcates respect for it in the children of the household, that alone shows a significant and negative difference. Likewise and more broadly, traditional gender roles are both utile and moral: the specialization of work within the marriage that traditional gender roles facilitate contributes to familial wealth and overall familial happiness. Children who eschew those traditional roles are destined for impoverished and unhappy adulthoods. We should not be sanguine in the face of this threat. Even if these children are indistinguishable in terms of academic achievement, basic socialization, and employability, their attitudes toward gender and sex are markedly different—and in a way that imperils their future.

It is hard to know, at this point, how to evaluate this research, or what to make of the theoretical claims made on the basis of it. For many of us, that boys are more nurturant and girls more assertive in same-sex or egalitarian households than in their traditional counterpart is a plus, not a negative. There is also, however, at this point, just not enough research on either side of these questions to sway policy makers truly uncommitted on this issue, although there is plenty enough to lend a patina of empirical credence to conclusions already reached on other bases. Some of the most prominent researchers on both sides of this issue forthrightly acknowledge as much. Linda Waite and Mary Gallagher, for example, state clearly in their authoritative text on the utility of marriage that we simply won't know for some time whether there are any measurable and significant differences between children of same-sex and opposite-sex marriages.[68] We can't possibly know that until a good bit of time has passed between the passage of such a reform, as in Massachusetts or otherwise. The studies now being used to argue against same-sex marriage are not based on differences between children born of opposite-sex and same-sex marriages, but differences between children of legal marriage and same-sex unions, all of which are inconclusive in a pretty obvious way: there is no way to tell how much of the difference, or which differences, are a result of the lack of the marital option, or the result of the sexual orientation of the parent. And, there are also still only a handful of studies showing differences between same-sex unions of varying legal descriptions and children of legal marriage.

Finally, what little evidence there is, are of differences that are simply swamped by the much greater difference between children of two committed parents, no matter how their union is described, on the one hand, and single parents on the other. The latter alone should be enough to lead a reader to conclude, in context, that a concern for children should lead us to expand, not continue to limit, access to marriage, even if the differences between same-sex and opposite-sex unions hold up. But either way, this much seems fair to say: on the question of whether same-sex marriage leads to poorer outcomes—meaning, poorer, unhappier, less stable, less socialized, less educated children—than opposite-sex marriage, the data, at best, is inconclusive, open to wildly different interpretations, and paltry. It is nowhere near as robust as the remarkable body of research on the positive utility of marriage generally.

The second objection, made forcefully in dissent in *Goodridge*, in a decision by Justice Cordy,[69] and most recently in the majority decision in the New York same-sex marriage case *Hernandez*,[70] rests not on empirical data, but on a much more broadly interpretive and I think quite plausible if subtle claim about the function, if not the essential point, of civil marriage.[71] Civil marriage, according to Justice Cordy in *Goodridge* and the majority of the New York Court of Appeals in *Hernandez*, serves to both control heterosexual conduct, and to regulate the pregnancies, births, and children that are its inevitable product. The state has a legitimate interest, Justice Cordy argues, in sending the societal message that heterosexual intercourse should be confined to marriage and to marital partners, in part because of the needs of the children to which heterosexual intercourse leads. Heterosexuality within marriage is permitted and encouraged, because the children that result will benefit from a stable and enduring family structure. Heterosexuality outside of marriage is discouraged because the children that result will be deprived of these benefits, with the state picking up the tab for the resulting costs. Opening marriage to couples for whom sexuality does not result in pregnancy would muddle the message. It would put the state in the position of endorsing marriage and the sex within it, where there is no connection to possible conception, and therefore, in the position of endorsing sex without regard to reproduction. This in turn suggests the court's approval of nonreproductive sex—with the eventual implication being that the state turns a blind eye to heterosexuality outside of marriage as well. Some of that nonmarital heterosexuality will lead to children—thus the chaos that ensues, once the barriers are dropped.

Justice Cordy's argument has the notable virtue of addressing the crux of the issue, and that is the connection between what looks like a legitimate state interest in family life, namely, the well-being of children, and the otherwise inexplicable focus on the sexual behavior of consenting adults in marriage, who may or may not also parent children. The connection between these two things, Cordy opines, lies in the social message—what others in the academic literature refer to as the "social norm"—conveyed by the state's interest in marriage as currently constructed. Heterosexual marriage cabins heterosexual conduct, precisely because of the tendency of heterosexual conduct to result in live births—live births that in turn become a drain on the state's resources, if children are not adequately cared for. The interest in marriage, and the reason for the state's interest in funneling sex into marriage, then, is a consequence, albeit indirect, of the state's interest in children—with the spectre of unbound heterosexuality the missing middle premise. Without marriage, we would be awash in unregulated sex, which would lead to uncared-for babies and a drain on the public purse. With marriage opened up to gay couples, for whom children are not a natural product of sex, the social norm connecting sex to marriage, and child-raising to the family that results, is thereby weakened. With marriage opened to homosexual couples, heterosexual couples just won't get the message—the message, that is, that they should confine their sexual behavior, and therefore their tendency to create babies, to marriage, so that they might better thereby tend to those babies themselves. Promiscuous, heterosexual individuals, not committed homosexual couples, are the threat to social order, and it is heterosexuals, not homosexuals, that need to be reigned in by marriage. Opening marriage to homosexuals would stand in the way of the communication of this essential social norm.

No matter how nonromantic and calculating, this makes a lot of sense. It explains the state's interest in marriage in a way that connects its explicit and legitimate goal of protecting the well-being of children with its otherwise bizarre interest in the sexual conduct of adults: the interest in the sexual conduct of adults is a function of the state's legitimate goal of protecting the well-being of children to which heterosexuality leads. The problem with this pretty commonsensical understanding of marriage, I believe, is not its understanding of civil marriage itself. Nor does the argument—which some now dub the "reckless procreation argument"—seem like disguised homophobia, as has been recently charged.[72]

The problem, I believe, lies in its purported chain of causation. First, it is not at all clear that the social norm Justice Cordy identifies—if you want to have sex, and thereby risk the possibility that you will have children, then get married first—any longer has any positive effect on behavior. Birth control now does a far better job of regulating the social cost of unintended pregnancies—by preventing them—than the circuitous route of channeling sex into heterosexual marriage, with the hope that any unplanned children that result will be well cared for. Individuals can and do have sex outside of marriage, as well as inside of marriage, without risking pregnancies. Women who want to have children outside of marriage do so for complex reasons; refusing to extend marriage to include same-sex couples will not alter their thinking.

But second, it is not at all clear that extending marriage to include gay couples would weaken the social norm Cordy identifies, and in fact, it seems more likely that it would strengthen it. Go back to Cordy's understanding of the reason the state might want to channel sex into marriage: sex leads to babies, and marriage is an optimal environment for those babies. The first part of this understanding—that sex leads to babies—might not be such an ironclad rule any more, but the second part seems relatively unassailable. That is, even if parties can reliably have nonreproductive sex, such that there's no reason to discourage sex outside of marriage, it may still be true that when and if they engage in intentionally reproductive sex—when they do have sex in order to reproduce—they ought to do so within a familial, marital structure. That is, the state may still have an interest, post–birth control and post-*Griswold*, in channeling intentionally (or recklessly) reproductive, rather than nonreproductive, sex into marriage. Even if we're not societally threatened by the chaos that might ensue from out-of-wedlock births, due to reliable birth control, it might still be the case that marriage is an optimal environment within which to raise children. If so, there's good reason for the state to convey the social norm that if a couple contemplates parenting, they would be well advised to marry. If they contemplate heterosexual intercourse as the means by which to conceive, then likewise, they would be well advised to marry. Similarly, though, if they have in mind some *other* method by which to produce or acquire a child—adoption, surrogacy, IVF, sperm banks—they would also *be well advised to marry*. The conclusion one ought draw from these premises is precisely the opposite conclusion drawn by Justice Cordy in dissent in Massachusetts and the New York Court of Appeals: if the point of marriage is to ensure the well-being of children that might result from reckless heterosexual intercourse, then marriage should be expanded, not restricted, so as to facilitate responsible child-rearing by all couples that might wish to have children, regardless of the means by which they acquire or conceive them.

We can sum this up this way: it may be true that at one time, the only way to convey the social norm that protected the state's interest in the well-being of children, was, in essence, to discourage sex outside of marriage. The social norm, fully stated, was: "if you want to have sex, then marry first, so that the children that may be your issue will be well-provided for." Today, a sensible state norm might still convey a part of that, but heavily modified: "if you want and intend to raise children, then marry. If you want and intend to have uncontracepted sex with the expectation that children will result, or in reckless disregard of the possibility that children may result, then marry." The sex, though, is neither here nor there—it is one way, but not the only way, to produce the children that are the object of the state's legitimate concern. Note, though: if this revised social norm is the one that a sensible state might legitimately have an interest in communicating—if you want to have children, or if you want to engage in heterosexual behavior that carries a risk of children, then marry first, so that your children will be cared for—rather than, if you want to have sex, marry first, so that the children that may issue will be cared for—it clearly has nothing to do with sexual orientation, and indeed has nothing to do with sex. If that is the norm, we should leave sex out of the state's interest in marriage altogether. There's no reason to limit marriage to individuals with a particular sexual orientation, just as there's no reason to limit marriage to individuals with an interest in sex.

Progressive Arguments against Same-Sex Marriage

Social conservatives opposed to gay marriage find themselves with some surprising allies: feminists, queer theorists, and more than a few progressive legal and constitutional scholars have also registered a number of reservations about either the wisdom or coherence of the gay marriage movement. Some of this progressive resistance is a result of the *realpolitik* sorts of considerations raised above: whatever the merits of the argument made by gay marriage advocates, this might be the wrong time to be making the claim. The backlash brought on by this movement has led to massive electoral victories on the national level for opponents of gay marriage, and literally countless such victories at the local and state levels of government. For Democrats, progressives, liberals, and radicals, the loss of the presidency, Congress, the federal courts, the statehouses, and the city halls might just be too high a price to pay, both for progressive politics, and for the Democratic Party both. For many of us who are concerned about according equal respect and dignity to our gay and lesbian friends, partners, selves, and family members, but also are concerned about the health of the planet, with all due respect to Martin Luther King's insistence to the contrary, perhaps we really should just wait this one out. Al Gore might be right: the very earth might hang in the balance.

But not all of the objections from the political left to gay marriage are of this sort. Feminists, progressives, and queer theoretic scholars and activists concerned with various aspects of family and family law issues have put forward three separate arguments, or more mildly, perhaps, sets of concerns, about the direction of the same-sex marriage movement. The first concerns the overall justice of the institution. If marriage is a fundamentally unjust institution, making it more inclusive will not cure the injustice. Would the institution of slavery have been more just had married white women as well as married white men been allowed to buy and purchase black slaves? If marriage is fundamentally unjust, why is this so different? The second set of concerns regards equality itself. Will a gain in the equal treatment of gays and lesbians who wish to marry result in nothing but a net increase in the homophobic hatred, and the attendant harms, visited upon those gays and lesbians who don't, as well as an intensification, rather than diminishment, of the gendered allocation of work within marriage along traditionalist lines? The third concerns the quality of married life. Is married life really something to valorize? Will we have lost something of immeasurable value if we institutionalize gay marriage? Does the movement threaten to extinguish a gay culture that does not share mainstream values of monogamy, child-raising, and life-long commitment, and which has, and expresses other values worth cherishing? Is the price of this bland homogeneity too high to pay, not only for those gays and lesbians who once were a part of a vibrant and thriving—one might say throbbing—subculture, and will be no longer once they've been Ozzie and Harriet-ized, but for the rest of us as well?

Let me elaborate briefly upon each of these. First, surely, a formally equal legal institution might nevertheless be unjust. Reformed marriage that includes same-sex as well as opposite-sex couples nevertheless predicates the bestowal of state approval and legitimacy on some sort of monogamous, lifelong, sexual relationship. But what is the fairness, or even the rationality, of that? To reverse the song lyric, "what's sex got to do with it?" Presumably the state does have some interest in providing for, and bolstering, and encouraging, and protecting, families that care for one another and particularly those families whose members care for dependents: this is the most compelling reason a state can possibly give for having an interest in marriage and family life. A polity that consists of individuals embedded in families that provide care for one another will presumably be healthier, as well as less taxed, than a state that consists of rugged individuals with no interest in the well-being of anyone but themselves. Ruggedly successful individuals might save the state the cost of their own care in the short term, but over the long haul unbridled egoism has its costs: the savings from leaving the healthy twenty-year-old to make his own choices in life, would be more than offset by the huge investment of resources the state would have to pour into the project of feeding, nurturing, and diapering the infants; stimulating, loving and playing with the toddlers; educating and caring for the children; and then providing end-of-life care of his elderly parents that that rugged twenty-year-old individual will eventually leave in his wake. A society that consists of caregiving families, presumably, is a healthier, happier, and better functioning society than one in which family life has become dysfunctional, due to a hypervalorization of individualism. A state has an interest in protecting and promoting families, defined as such, that thrive.

But again, what does any of this have to do with the existence or nature of the sexual relation between the consenting adults that are providing this care? The objections noted above to the illogic of the state's interest in (and insistence on) the heterosexual conduct of married partners all apply, equally, to a state's potential interest in homosexual conduct. Why should it matter to the state whether committed partners, parents, or caregivers have a heterosexual relation or a gay one; whether they engage in coital, anal, or oral sexual play; whether they routinely, occasionally, or never have sexual relations with other consenting adults; or indeed, whether they have any sexual relationship at all? Might two sisters, two brothers, two neighbors, or three friends provide this care for each other, and each other's children? Why should the state have an interest in whether they're also having sex, and of what sort?

The state does seem to care, though, and the result is a dollop of irrationality, if not injustice, which the inclusion of "same-sex couples" within marriage's reach will not cure. Indeed, it might exacerbate it. Law Professor and gay rights activist Nancy Polikoff[73] has argued for some time now, that the same-sex marriage movement contributes to a celebratory rhetoric of marriage itself that further masks the uncompensated labor of caregivers both inside and outside of marriage, and, perhaps more significantly, further delegitimates the caregiving work of single mothers. The rhetoric of marriage makes it harder—sometimes, much harder—to direct societal attention to the pressing financial needs of unmarried parents: so long as marriage is touted as, and believed to be, the route out of poverty, it is all the harder to even articulate, much less successfully advocate for, social support for caregiving labor outside of marriage. Inclusion of gay couples within the circle of marriage has the unfortunate and undeniable effect of fully legitimating the privatization of caregiving (in a way that eerily parallels the sense in which the end of race and gender discrimination in the workplace had the effect of fully legitimating the "at will" employment regime): by removing one blatant injustice, the argument that marriage is the best way to create a family that can provide care for dependents seems all the more irrefutable. The greater legitimacy of marriage that might come in the wake of gay marriage, might thereby perversely contribute to the continuing impoverishment of single parents.

By the same token, it might also contribute to the continuing neglect of caregiving by the state within marriage as well as outside of it. As explored in Chapter 2, marriage, for many social conservatives, has become the preferred alternative to a robust safety net. In the United States, we don't provide for generous and paid maternity and paternity leaves, or universal day care for children under school age, or stipends for at-home paid care providers, or Social Security for housewives, or two-payee paychecks to the wage worker in one-worker households, or universal health care, or generous unemployment benefits, or a livable family wage. One reason we don't might be that we have collectively determined that these hedges against risk are better provided through the institution of marriage. The rhetoric of the current marriage movement—"Marriage Works"—is intended to convey the message that marriage is not only the way out of personal loneliness, and unhappiness, but also the way out of *poverty*. The institution of marriage obviates the need for a political, and public, solution to poverty: personal, responsible decisionmaking, through marriage, is the way to pull oneself and one's partner up by one's collective, marital bootstraps. The helping hand must be the hand of the man offering the marriage proposal, not that of a bureaucrat in a welfare office.

The "same-sex marriage" movement (or, as it is most often called, the "marriage equality movement") exists in considerable tension, of course, with the social conservative "marriage promotion" movement. Neither advocates marriage for the same reasons as the other, and both mean something very different by the "marriage" they so strongly support. Nevertheless, the rhetoric, and the arguments, of the marriage equality movement and the marriage promotion movement converge at significant points. The argument for the injustice of the same-sex ban is, in part, that denying the benefits of marriage to this class of worthy potential participants has the effect of impoverishing them. Marriage, so say the conservative marriage movement devotees, increases the sense of responsibility, and attentiveness to future risk, and hence the economic well-being of participants; likewise, so say same-sex marriage advocates permitting gay men and lesbians to marry would increase the future orientation and the economic well-being of gay and lesbian couples. By arguing for the inclusion of this class of presently excluded outsiders in this particular social institution, and on the grounds that the social institution confers benefits on participants, there is no denying the existence of those benefits. In this case, the "benefits" are largely economic. And, in this case, the very existence of those benefits is not overwhelmingly benign: the rhetoric behind them, particularly the morally charged rhetoric, works largely against the interest of those who still can't participate. They will continue to do so, when and if marriage extends its franchise.

The proposed reform in question—extend marriage to same-sex couples—removes an unfairness surrounding the institution that is itself a function of excluding a class of people who cannot possibly "choose" to participate or not participate. That would make the institution fairer and for many of us it would be perceived as fairer—because it would be more voluntary. What could be wrong with that? Well—post-reform, many of us will be more inclined than we presently are to believe that those who partake in the benefits and responsibilities of marriage, chose to, and that those who do not partake—and thus do not participate in the benefits, financial and otherwise—have chosen not to. The reformed institution will *also* look (counterfactually) more like one that *all* citizens either choose to participate in or not—and therefore, fair for all, participants and nonparticipants alike. But this is just not true, if it's the case that many who don't marry, can't do so, and not because of their sexual orientation. That group's needs, then, become further marginalized, delegitimated, as they increasingly and falsely come to be perceived as freely "chosen."

The same-sex marriage movement, in this way, becomes an unwitting ally of the attack on the social welfare net. If reformed, marriage will look all the more like a route out of poverty, entered into freely, and, particularly post-reform, available to all. Those who choose not to participate in it, therefore, must be choosing, for their own idiosyncratic, perhaps irresponsible, perhaps immoral, and certainly irrational, but nevertheless fully voluntary reasons, to opt for poverty. After all, we will have removed the one glaring injustice of marriage: its exclusion of persons who would marry but for a characteristic beyond their control. Therefore, it will be fair to assume that whoever doesn't marry, once the reform is in place, has made that decision of her "own free will." The bottom line consequence is that the poor really will get poorer—with the poor, here, being overwhelmingly single mothers and their children—as we feel all the more justified in our collective refusal to attend to their needs, while a group of already relatively well-off gay and lesbian partners will be marginally enriched.

There are other problems as well, from a broadly feminist perspective. The inclusion of gay couples within the marital circle underscores, rather than challenges, the continuing centrality of the sexual relation of two adults to the forms of permissible, valorized family life that will win the state's approval, solicitude, and considerable financial support. Even in post-reform Massachusetts, we might say, the state is still defining marriage by reference to the sexual relation between two adults, and still defining caregiving and family by virtue of marriage—and therefore, still defining the caregiving it legitimately might or will promote by reference to the quality of the adult sexual conduct between the two adults providing the care. This is not only irrational, and oddly ungenerous to poor people. Both the irrationality, and the unfairness, clearly have a gendered component as well. Contrary to the early and optimistic arguments—that gay marriage might by example stand as a counter to gendered distributions of both labor and sexual privilege in marriage—inclusion of gays and lesbians in the benighted circle of the married might serve to worsen, rather than better, women's overall role within this institution. Feminists should be worried over the direction of the same-sex marriage movement, and not only because of the message it has sent regarding the privatizing of care. It also sends a message, loud and clear, about *sex*, and its role in adult life that might not be conducive to women's overall well-being, economically and emotionally, but politically as well.

The message in reformed marriage states such as Massachusetts, generously construed, seems to be that sex of *some* sort is still an essential part of any relation between two adults that is actually strong enough to withstand the strains put on it by the demands of caregiving, particularly child-raising. Sex really is sticky. We just can't stick together without it—or at least, we can't stick together without it long enough to provide meaningful care to the next generation, or for our elders. But if that's right—if sex really is necessary to the formation of a relationship between two adults that will be strong enough to withstand the stress of child-raising—then the quality and nature of the sex might matter as well as the fact of it. And if *that's* right, feminists ought to be worried: we should worry about the possibility, so thoroughly explored by Catherine MacKinnon in her pathbreaking books on the political nature of heterosexuality, that our sexuality, as expressed in our sex, both reflects and constructs our political subordination. If MacKinnon is right about that, then to whatever degree sex itself—and particularly our sense of heterosexual normalcy—both reflects and constructs relations of male dominance and female subordination, then family life might well follow suit, and it might do so *regardless* of the biological sex or sexual orientation of the parties.[74] So long as sex is sex, meaning, so long as we leave its nature, patterns, contours, and politics unchallenged, then heterosexual women who are wives will continue to bear the brunt of this particular construction of its marital form. In a series of extraordinary articles exploring the risks of "gay rights" for gay people and for women, law professor and radical feminist Marc Spindelman, of Ohio Law School, concludes from these premises that if marriage, institutionally, has absorbed the lessons and hierarchies of such sex, then, if marriage is extended to gay men and women, some lesbians will share in the burden, as will some gay men. But that won't change the underlying distribution of either domestic labor or sexual subordination one whit. Our understanding of sex and our sexual practices must change, before the widening of marriage can be an egalitarian, as well as truly liberating movement.[75]

Last, literature Professor and queer theorist Michael Warner has argued against the gay marriage movement that marriage threatens to domesticate gay sex—and that should it do so, the value of not only the sex, but gay life will have been diminished.[76] Marriage, queer theorists point out, does indeed anchor the individual, order personal life, and calm the passions—but it is not for that reason something to celebrate; it is something to avoid. Of course, there is no compulsion to enter marriage, nor would there be, were marriage to expand its reach to include gay and lesbian couples wishing to marry. But personal choice is not the only thing at stake. Rather, gay marriage could threaten gay culture itself, and that would be a loss. Gay culture stands as an alternative and critique to mainstream culture, with decidedly nonmainstream values, mores, and forms of life. It is more accepting of physicality, whereas mainstream culture aims for the spiritual and mental; it is worldly where mainstream culture aspires for the transcendent; it celebrates sexuality whereas mainstream culture still stands in a posture of ambivalence; it embraces shame as an erotic, rather than a motivator for oppression. Queer culture eschews assimilation, and does so by choice, not just by necessity. Gay marriage threatens to co-opt not just queer culture per se, but more broadly, a rebellious way of life.

Like his natural law antagonists and bedfellows, Warner's queer theoretic arguments against same-sex marriage tend to be absolutist and anti-instrumentalist, but with pleasure, rather than marital coital sex, as the noninstrumental font of value. Whereas natural lawyers value marital sex for its own sake, and not for the affection, pleasure, intimacy, or even the reproduction to which it might lead, likewise, queer theorists value pleasureable, hedonistic sex for its own sake, and not for the affection, intimacy, or reproduction to which it might lead. Natural lawyers value the conjoining in coital marital sex acts of the reproductive sort absolutely, while queer theorists value nonmarital sex for pleasure absolutely. Both, however, disdain an instrumentalist account of the value of marriage, and the instrumental value of sex within it. Both oppose same-sex marriage accordingly: natural lawyers, because it is same-sex, and queer theorists, because it is marriage. They both view "same-sex" sex as definitionally outside the reach of marriage, and they both view same-sex marriage, accordingly, as a "moral impossibility."

Where does this leave us? Let me just register some reservations about the progressive, feminist, and queer reservations, and leave for the conclusion my own doubts about the current direction of the gay marriage movement. Basically, all three objections catalogued above, while giving good enough cause to put on the brakes, so to speak, rest on causal projections about the future—should gay marriage come to pass—that are pretty wildly speculative. Let me take them in reverse order. First, and most briefly, that same-sex marriage will threaten a gay culture committed to nonmonogamy, serial sexual relations, nonaffectionate plea-surable sex, and a sexual culture defined by a reveling in the physicality of it all, seems counterintuitive: Dionysian movements need Apollonian, counterpunctal movements against which to define themselves, and this one is no exception. A Playboy culture of willfully nonmonogamous men thrived during the heyday of traditional marriage, and one suspects that a willfully nonmonogamous and anti-marriage culture of gay men and lesbians would thrive as well, were marriage to expand to include those gay and lesbian citizens wishing to marry. It is not clear that same-sex marriage would do anything but heighten the contours of nonmarital gay culture. It would, likely, blur the lines between nonmarital gay and nonmarital straight culture: differences between married and unmarried might come to loom larger than differences between straight and gay. It is not clear, though, why that would be such a bad thing. It seems rather a good thing.

Nor is it at all clear, at least to me, why or how same-sex marriage would strengthen the identification of marital sexual submissiveness with subordina-tion—indeed it might undermine it. Even assuming that MacKinnon is right to argue that our current sexuality constructs women, wives, and female sexuality as submissive, there seems little harm in that bare fact alone: there's no good reason that a sexually submissive, passive, bottom partner in any consensual and mutually enjoyed and pleasurable sexual relation—marital, nonmarital, long term, short term, vanilla, nonvanilla, or a one-night stand—should also be the exploited party in the nonsexual realms of human interaction. There's no obvious connection between a taste for sexual submissiveness and a tendency or willingness or interest in having one's labor alienated. There may well be a connection—I think there is—between the appropriation or alienation of one's sexuality without one's pleasure or consent, and the appropriation and alienation of one's labor in nonsexual contexts, and of course there is a very strong connec-tion between the forced expropriation of sex, through violent or coercive rape, and subordination, or worse. I have argued as much, and feminists have argued something of this sort for hundreds of years. It was, for example, shared ground in nineteenth-century American and British feminism that women would have to gain control of their sexual and reproductive bodies within feminism before they could anticipate material gains in economic and political realms. But the expropriation or alienation of one's sexuality without one's consent, or even if consensual without one's desire, is (in my view) clearly a very different thing than consensual, voluntary submission to sex, complete with a wholehearted reveling in submissive or masochistic sex and sex roles, *when accompanied* by desire. The expropriation of women's sexuality within marriage and outside of marriage, and the alienation from one's own sexuality, one's own pleasure, one's own body and will that can accompany it, have done women tremendous harm, and part of the harm, no doubt, has been an induced willingness to devalue one's own interests, labor, and injuries, as well as one's desires, pleasures, and needs. There may well be a causal connection, in other words, between rape, sexual harassment, and subordination, including labor subordination both in the home and outside of it. There's no reason to conclude from that, however, that there is also a connection between a taste for sexual submission, and one's political subordination generally, either in the home or outside of it.[77] To whatever degree marriage is understood to be the institution within which women's sexual submissiveness (whether constructed or natural) justifies her subordination, it seems more likely that the perceived connection would be undermined, rather than strengthened, by same-sex marriage.

And lastly, it's just hard to assess whether the same-sex marriage movement would so strengthen the hand of the social conservative's marriage movement as to truly diminish our already *de minimis* societal concern for the well-being of unmarried caregivers. It might. But there's another "what if" story that can be told: the inclusion of gay and lesbian families, and their children, in the community's collective understanding of what it means to be a family could loosen the traditional understanding of family—complete with male and female parents, both of whom are genetically connected to their sons and daughters—on our collective sense of what families *are*. Central to the traditionalist conception of marriage is not only the male-female marriage at its head, but also the genetic vertical connection tying children to both parents. Adoption is the exceptional way to form a family, because the "normal" way is through sexual intercourse that leads to children that are genetic echoes of oneself and one's partner. The caregiving within families, as a result, has the feature of being caregiving among genetically linked individuals, and the valorization of family, accordingly, has the feature—I think unfortunately—of valorizing caregiving among genetically linked individuals. The care we give within families might be selfless, and admirable, but it is also care given to those who are as much like us as anyone on earth. This may or may not be a biological imperative. But it does not bode well for our sympathetic capacities beyond the familial circle. Indeed, it suggests a limit to the care we willingly and generously bestow on others: the beneficiaries of that care must be those who represent, in some way, an extension of ourselves.

Gay and lesbian parenting at least has the potential to move that image, if ever so slightly (as does opposite-sex adoptive parenting): if gay and lesbian parenting were to be embraced as full, equal, normal, ordinary parenting, it would demonstrate, by example, that it is possible to passionately care for children who are not genetic extensions of one's precious genetic self. Our social and culturally accepted understanding of who it is possible to care for—whom we routinely do and should express our altruism to, through the daily provision of selfless care—beyond one's self and genetic extensions of oneself, might be enlarged. If the idea that it is neither so difficult, nor so unnatural, to passionately care about and to routinely and daily care for children not one's biological own were to become commonplace, the sympathetic sentimental moral root of the social net might be strengthened.

I don't know that this "what if" story—that if we were to legalize gay marriage, and hence normalize gay parenting, we would become a more generous and caring society toward children who are not our own—is any more plausible than the "what if" story that envisions the same-sex movement lending unintended aid to the conservative marriage movement and thereby further impoverishing those who provide care outside of marital walls. Both stories are speculative—too speculative, I think, to ground political judgments. I suspect, although I'm not at all sure, that the conservative marriage movement needs to be answered on its own terms, and the same-sex marriage movement likewise, and without recourse to pretty far removed utopian or dystopian theoretical possibilities. On the other side of the balance, more familiarly liberal arguments supporting same-sex marriage are certainly ready at hand, as are ample grounds for skepticism regarding the claims of the conservative marriage movement. If same-sex couples are identically situated in all relevant respects as opposite-sex couples, then commonsense, as well as the demands of justice and the language of the Fourteenth Amendment of the Constitution, lead heavily toward expanding the institution for reasons powerfully spelt out in *Goodridge*. On the other hand, it's perfectly sensible to think that the conservative marriage movement is wrong—wrong on the facts, and wrong morally—to insist that civil marriage be understood, and undertaken, as a ticket out of poverty. Marriage is not a viable institutional substitute for our societal obligations to provide help for vulnerable people in times of great risk or hardship. There is no inconsistency in holding to both of these views, and the politics they generate. We can and likely should work toward rendering marriage more inclusive—and thereby more just—and at the same time, work toward a future in which remaining outside of it, by necessity or choice, matters much less, or not at all.

The Egalitarian Marriage Movement

Imagine Ozzie and Harriet, but with Harriet employed full time. They have three children and each makes a decent income. They're relatively happy with their lives and their marriage. There is, though, a problem. Harriet does virtually all of the housework—she shops for the family's groceries, plans the menus, does the cooking, does all the day-to-day cleaning, changes virtually all of the diapers for the baby, helps the older children with their homework, reads them nighttime stories, and disciplines them. She cleans up from breakfast and dinner, prepares the older children's bagged lunches, does all of the vacuuming, and does a load of laundry a night. She cleans the baby and younger child's rooms herself, and prods the older child to clean his. She makes all arrangements with the daytime babysitter for the baby, and gets the older children to their school bus stop in the morning. She takes one of her "sick leave" days when one of the children is sick or when the babysitter can't make it in to work. She takes the children to their doctor and dental appointments, and meets their teachers for teacher-parent conferences. Ozzie cuts the grass, tends to the needs of the family's two automobiles, takes out the garbage, and makes minor home repairs. He will on occasion help with cooking and dishwashing, and sometimes he takes the children to school. The family cannot afford a housecleaner, but occasionally they hire a cleaning team to do the hard cleaning in the house, and they routinely contract out for more serious home repairs and upkeep.

Harriet is working a "second shift," and because of it, she's tired, and more than a little resentful. She works from nine to five, or later, and then comes home and works an additional four to six hours at home. She doesn't find the work terribly obnoxious. She values the time with her children, and she wants a clean home. But she does regard it as work, and it is physically demanding. It also takes up time—a lot of time. She comes home around six, cooks until seven or so, eats with her family, cleans up, helps her children with homework, bathes the baby, puts the children to bed, does a load of laundry, and does enough cleaning to keep the house passably clean by her own standards. By then it's eleven o'clock and she goes to bed. She goes to sleep. She doesn't read. She doesn't watch *Lost, West Wing,* or *Twenty-Four.* Her weekends are filled with grocery shopping and household errands, and because of that, she socializes with her own friends less than she would like to. She's too tired at the end of the day to enjoy sex with her husband, and too preoccupied to do so during the mornings and weekends. Her house is not as clean as she would prefer, and her flower beds are overrun with weeds. She resents her husband's time spent on the living room couch watching sports, but she doesn't feel that there's anything she can do about it. She figures that he works hard at his job—maybe harder than she does, since, after all, he makes more money. At any rate, her marriage is pretty good. She loves her husband, and he loves her. They enjoy raising their children together. She puts up with it.

Harriet's life is not bad, and she knows it. She doesn't want a divorce, she doesn't think of herself as in an unhappy marriage. But it is unjust. Her husband has more leisure time than she. He does watch *Lost* and *Twenty-Four* and plenty of sports besides. He makes more money at his job, partly because he doesn't take the absences she takes in order to facilitate childcare: her own sick days when her children are sick, an afternoon here or there for parent-teacher conferences or school performances. He does no housecleaning, no cooking, and minimal child-care. He does play with the children, which she appreciates, but she also recognizes it for what it is: play. He doesn't do the work part of raising children—changing diapers, preparing meals, supervising homework, disciplining—perhaps because it just doesn't seem to occur to him to. He doesn't clean, he says, because the dust balls and the unmade beds just don't bother him. He has no interest in landscaping and gardening, and he has no talent for cooking. He's tired at the end of the day and wants to relax. It doesn't bother him that he relaxes by watching television and that his wife apparently relaxes by running a vacuum cleaner, planting flower beds, cooking meals, and tending to children. When he thinks about it at all, he figures that that must be what relaxes her.

The work distribution in Ozzie and Harriet's marriage is not atypical. Study after study after study has shown, with almost mind-numbing regularity, that working married women continue to do considerably more domestic work than their husbands—they do considerably more childcare and vastly more housework.[78] They work a "second shift,"[79] while their husbands do not: they come home from their paid job, as do their husbands, and put in another four, six, or eight hours of work at home, while their husbands do not. They have less leisure time, as a result, and they also earn less money in their paid work, as well: as mothers, these women take more time out of the paid labor force to accommodate their domestic and child-care duties. New mothers take several unpaid weeks, months, or years out of their jobs or careers after the birth of a child—with severe diminution in wages earned, as well as a serious diminution in wage-earning capacity in the future, when they return to the labor market. They also take hours and days off while employed, to accommodate childcare needs. They work shorter hours, if they can, with a drop in pay and often in benefits. As a result of all of this—the maternity leaves, the early departures from the wage labor market altogether, the time off, the shortened hours, the part-time jobs—there is now a far greater difference in the wages and earning capacities of mothers and nonmothers—both women and men who are nonmothers—than there is between women and men. Some researchers now call this the "maternal wage gap": mothers earn less over the course of their wage-earning career than either their husbands or their non-mothering female coworkers.[80] Mothers work less at work, and so they earn less. That alone, of course, doesn't seem odd, or particularly unfair. They also, however, work considerably more at home, and earn nothing for it. Overall, wives work more hours than husbands, and earn considerably less.

So—is this injustice a problem? Plenty of people think not. The whole arrangement is fully voluntary. Harriet could leave that marriage, and she doesn't. She doesn't want a divorce. Short of that, she could strike. She could quit cleaning the house, and she doesn't. She could be less attentive to the children. She could quit cooking. She could, in effect, go on strike, or at least work to rule. It might make a difference. But—she chooses not to. She wants a well-run household, some degree of cleanliness, and cared-for children. A strike doesn't seem to be in the cards. She didn't have to marry him in the first place, or have two more children after the first one, when it quickly became clear that he wasn't going to do his fair share. Yet, she did. She didn't have to enter this marriage, and she can always leave. At every point that brought her to this stage in her life, Harriet has had options. She wanted to get married, and she wanted to marry this man, and she obviously prefers to stay with him than to leave. So again, is this injustice a problem?

The short answer is that of course it is. Whether or not both consent to it—whether or not both view the arrangement as preferable to alternatives—it is transparently and flagrantly unfair for one of two adults living intimately and with a sense of shared mutual responsibility for the well-being of the other, to do the bulk of undesirable work from which they both benefit.[81] Any child knows this, including the children raised in these second-shift households, who nevertheless, over time, and for the most easily understood reasons, come to view both the distribution of labor, and the unfairness of it, as natural. The second shift represents a continual, day-to-day, gnawing, exhausting, self-denigrating injustice. Every load of laundry, every dirty dish, every changed diaper, every unmade bed, every overgrown flower bed, addressed by one partner with no help from the other, and with no anticipation of help, and with no eventual balancing of the books, is an injustice. It is also an injustice, or unfairness, with ripple effects. It has adverse effects on the woman herself; on our societal understanding of the value of caregiving labor, and on the children who absorb it, drink it, and breathe it in, along with the air and Gatorade that sustain them. All three effects have been explored in a large literature, much of which was triggered by the philosopher Susan Okin's pathbreaking book *Gender, Justice, and the Family*,[82] and by the social scientist Arlie Hochschild's book, *The Second Shift*.[83] Let me summarize these three effects here.

First, consider the psychic effect of the second shift on the woman herself. Think of your grandmother, your mother, your sister, yourself, your friend, or your neighbor whose marriage is a bit—or a lot—like Harriet's. What does the second shift do to her? If you're reflecting on your own life, what does it do to you? A man you love and trust and hold in high regard holds you in insufficiently high regard to treat you fairly. Either you're not deserving of fair treatment by a fair-minded individual, or you love an unjust man, and either way it's not only him, but you, that doesn't come off well. When you're treated unjustly day by day by day, the net effect will be not only rising and perfectly rational doubts about your own self-worth—you must not be deserving of basic justice—but also, an increasing willingness to be treated as subordinate. A lack of self-regard and a lack of due regard from others we hold in high esteem unsurprisingly results in a willingness to submit, a willingness to dispossess the self, to enlist the self in the service of others.

Second, consider the effect of the second shift on the larger society, and particularly on its valuation of caregiving and domestic labor. Wives work the second shift for nothing. Is it really surprising, given that brute fact, that we are not, socially, willing to pay much more than nothing for those same services, when, due to circumstance, we're forced to contract the work out to others? Nannies, babysitters, day-care workers, elder-care providers, and housecleaners earn the lowest wages going—except, of course, the wage rate for the housewife herself, which is zero. If a man can get a woman to do work for free by marrying her, it is not likely that he will choose to pay someone a substantial amount to do it for pay, when push comes to shove and he's forced to. The expectation that women will and should perform extra labors for free becomes habit forming, a part of the white noise of daily life: if women who are wives do it for free, it's hard to see why women who are not wives should be paid much to do it, and even easier to see why they can't command higher wages on an open market when they try to. Why should we give those who do this work for pay more than subsistence wages? That's what wives get, even if the subsistence is of a high quality. Once that message is internalized, it is likewise hard to see why we should provide tax dollars for childcare: children are ideally raised in two-parent marital homes, and wives in two-parent marital homes will and should do this work for free. And of course, it is very hard to see how any one man or cohort of men will decide, spontaneously, to relinquish the power, privilege, and benefit the second shift accords them, without being given a quid pro quo either from women themselves or other men. It is very hard to see how this cycle can be brought to heel, by private action, or market transactions, alone.

Third, consider the effect of the second shift on the children raised in the families that foster it. Children born into a family in which a mother but not a father works an uncompensated second shift are the direct beneficiaries—along with the father—of structural domestic injustice. They receive maternal love and nurturance from a woman who is herself visibly ill treated and the subject of an inequitable distribution of labor. Since mother's love is not only sweet, but necessary for survival, and since children tend to know this, it is hard to see how the injustice of home life could possibly be internalized by children as anything other than both natural and good: that injustice seems to be, after all, the precondition of the very nurturance and affection we all need to survive. This is not only demonstrably very bad for women—including the future girlfriends and wives of the boys so raised, as well as the future economic prospects of the girls. It is also just plain bad, across the board: it is a foundational lesson, to abstract from gender, in the naturalness and the inevitability and the goodness of injustice and inequality both.[84] It is not such a wonder that so many adults wrongly view even the most eminently changeable structures of injustice and inequality in their social world as both necessary and good. The necessity and goodness of injustice was learned at the mother's breast.

For all of these reasons, feminist social scientists, economists, moral philosophers, and legal scholars and activists have argued for some time now that the second shift is hardly insignificant. It does matter, in fact, who does the dishes; this is not a matter of making a "federal case out of nothing." Women's disproportionate and unpaid labor, particularly around child-raising, brings down women's wages on the labor market: women who take time out for sustained mothering, as well as women who take occasional afternoons off for teacher conferences and doctors appointments, take a sizeable hit in their earned income as well as their income potential. Thus, the "maternal wall": the disparity in labor market wages, not between women and men, so much, as between mothers and nonmothers. Beyond the workplace, the second shift also cuts into avocational time as well: it translates into a lesser quality of life, as pleasure is jettisoned for household chores. It increases rates of women's depression within marriage. It sends a powerful message to children regarding the inevitability and even the goodness of natural injustice. It depresses the wages paid for caregiving labor that is provided for pay. It severely depresses any sense of shared social responsibility for caregiving labor. The second shift is also hardy. It persists in the face of massive cultural and legal changes that one might have reasonably thought would have brought on its demise: equal pay for equal work laws, antidiscrimination and equal opportunity law, safe and accessible birth control, and easy exit from marriage through divorce. Women who can work good jobs for fair compensation, bring home half or more of a family's income, and have no serious impediment to separation or divorce should they so choose, nevertheless remain in marriages where they do a disproportionate amount of domestic labor. The alternatives for these women are obviously either worse or perceived to be worse: ending the marriage, loneliness, a losing struggle with one's mate that will diminish the quality of the marriage, or a filthy house and neglected children.

Hardy though it may be, however, the second shift is neither inevitable nor impervious to change. Men are no more inclined to injustice, or more inclined to wish themselves to benefit from it, than women. In point of fact, as women enter the workforce, the second shift at home is changing—as in fading—and there is no real reason to think it won't continue to do so. It's just changing *slowly*. The result is no small degree of paradox in our lived experience and our social science research both. On the one hand, husbands still do substantially less childcare than their wives, but on the other hand, they do far more than their own fathers did, and the same is true for housework. Studies show this, but baby boomer and generation X parents know it from experience. Many of us, as a consequence, are living out both truths simultaneously. In our own marriages, the wives do more domestic labor than our husbands, but at the same time, our husbands do more—even far more—domestic labor than did their own fathers. That these two lived realities are being experienced jointly, I think, is significant, both for our politics and for the quality of our lives. It suggests a straightforward explanation for what is otherwise puzzling, and that is that women in "second-shift" households often report themselves relatively satisfied with their marriages.[85] Perhaps that is not so odd. Our own marriages, in spite of their manifest injustice, are more just than the home environment in which we were ourselves raised. So, it's an improvement over the baseline, as social scientists like to say. It suggests—or goes some way toward suggesting—why women are satisfied with something less than 50/50: 30/70 is better than 10/90, and 10/90 is what we had good reason to expect.

That doubled experience might explain some degree of complacency, then. It also, though, suggests a moral imperative. We know, from the very fact of the distance between our own upbringing and the distribution of labor in our current marriages, that that distribution is both unjust and can be rectified. The second shift, like marriage generally, is a constructed institution. It can be changed. Thus, the imperative. Injustice that truly can't be changed perhaps should be tolerated—life's unfair, get over it—but injustice that can be changed, should be. The injustice within marriage is demonstrably of the latter sort. I reach this conclusion: contemporary civil marriage is very good for most participants, and it sure works for me. But marriage must also be made just—both the institution and my own. The injustice of this institution, even conceding its manifest social utility, should be addressed and rectified.

A nascent movement for egalitarian marriage—what is sometimes called the "just marriage" movement—seeks to do so, and to explore and remedy related injustices intertwined with marriage as well. Political philosopher Mary Shanley,[86] and law Professor Linda McClain,[87] now argue that the challenge facing us regarding contemporary marriage, both as an institution and as a legal structure, is to figure a way to retain it, but to remake it justly. This is a difficult claim. As Susan Okin's groundbreaking work three decades back showed, marriage and the family have not typically been regarded even as proper *subjects* for a theory of justice and even by the most generous and egalitarian of our liberal philosophers—hence their unfortunate omission from John Rawls's classic 1970s text, *A Theory of Justice,* on the demands of justice in liberal democracies.[88] Rather, marriage and family have more often—and for the most part are still—regarded as domains safely beyond the reach of the demands of justice. Our public institutions and work relations, we assume, should be regulated by norms that must themselves be just, and when they are not, they are properly criticized by reference to that virtue. In private intimate life, by contrast, it is widely believed that relations should be regulated not by reference to the virtue of justice, but rather, by reference to the domestic virtues of altruism, devotion, sacrifice, and love. This division of not only labor, but also of virtues, has been terrible for the public sphere: the public worlds of politics, commerce, and industry could use a healthy dollop of compassion, care, community responsibility, and altruism. But this same division of critical labor and virtue has also been a bad deal for women and family members in the private sphere: an unjust household is not particularly humane.[89] So long as the ideal of "just marriage" continues to strike many as odd, or paradoxical, marriage will be unjust, and so long as marriage is unjust, its participants will have lesser lives because of it.

So, what would just marriage entail? Minimally, it would mean an end to the undue privatization and underenforcement of criminal laws against domestic violence and marital rape. Ending violence within marriage would correct a double injustice: the injustice of the violence, and violation, itself, but second, the injustice of the state's neglect of it—it is the latter, rather than the former, that reflects women's debased status as secondary citizens. But second, just marriage would require an end to the undue privatization, the unjust distribution, and the undercompensation, of the caregiving and domestic labor that wives specifically, and women more generally, perform. It would require an end to the second shift. The labor at the heart of that shift is labor, not hobby or lifestyle. It is, well, laborious. Sometimes it is rewarding, occasionally gloriously so, but more often it is tedious, monotonous, physically demanding, and soul numbing. It cannot be borne by half the human family, at their expense, for the benefit of the other half. The structure of marriage renders this injustice invisible, but it also packages it as natural and good: as part of women's nature to perform, and to do so for the betterment of the human community. Participants in just marriages should not tolerate a second shift. Citizens in an equal and liberal democracy, likewise, should insist upon justice in marriage, quite generally, and in structural legal and political reforms that would facilitate it.

How to achieve that? Reform proposals proliferate. Paychecks in single-wage households could be required, by law, to be issued to both spouses as payees, rather than one, where a spouse is at home with children, and not in the wage market. Fathers could be either encouraged or required to take advantage of paternity and family leaves, upon the birth or adoption of a baby. Employers could be required to provide flexibility to workers who are parents, as well as to workers who are children of aging parents, as well as workers who are partners of sick or disabled loved ones, and who need hours in a week, or weeks in a year, or years over the course of a working career, to provide for the essential needs of dependents. Women who stay at home through substantial parts of their adulthood to care for small children or aging parents could be better protected through the Social Security system, by earning entitlements to their own Social Security through their own caregiving labor, rather than earning those entitlements only parasitically through their husbands. Most important, we could societally pick up part of the tab, through tax dollars, of some of the costs of caregiving, and we could do this either through compensating mothers or fathers who do this work for infants, in the form of paid family leaves, or by heavily subsidizing universal prekindergarten childcare. All of these proposals—but most dramatically the last—would evidence a society that has matured to the point where it can acknowledge that caregiving, as well as independence, ought to be valued, in public and private life both. All of it would also, however, evidence a society that has internalized the need to render marriage, and the intimate lives it structures, a fundamentally just institution.

Just marriage cannot possibly come to be solely through changing the internal work distribution within family. Rather, as Law Professor Joan Williams has amply demonstrated,[90] the workforce must undergo fundamental change as well. The modern workforce is designed to serve the interests of ideal breadwinning male employees: the nine-to-five workday; the heightened demands on workers in their twenties and thirties when women, but not men, are experiencing their years of greatest reproductive capacity; the now expanding expectation (because of technology that brings work home) that a worker will willingly devote undivided attention to an employer's needs and demands through the day, week, and year; the apparent inability—or simple refusal—of the work world and the public sector to jointly create a daily and yearly school schedule that accommodates working parents. These patterns of work life presuppose an ideal, male, breadwinning employee, freed from the demands of his dependents by virtue of having a nonworking wife at home. Such an ideal couple, consisting of a breadwinning husband and nonworking wife, of course, is no longer the norm, and was never particularly functional even when it was. What we now have, then, is a work life and home life structured by law, by social expectation, by custom, and by the economic- and market-driven demands of employers, to meet the needs of a dysfunctional and discarded norm. Changing it, while certainly within the realm of the possible, is no easy task. Employers are firms that respond to competitive pressures in order to survive in markets, that, we're constantly reminded, are now global in reach rather than national or local. Well-meaning husbands were once boys being raised by well-meaning but too often absent fathers. Firms don't want or need, and in many cases cannot internalize the additional expenses of providing for families' caregiving services, whether that be in the form of paid family leaves, employer-provided insurance, onsite day care, or flexible work policies. It is very hard, although not completely impossible, to imagine any combination of union-sector strikes and boycotts—or consumer-driven boycotts—that would make much of a dent in any of this.

It is easier to imagine legislation that would make a dent. There is, after all, a precedent for our national capacity to address, through law, massive, structural injustice in our employment markets. In the 1920s and 1930s, forward-looking states and eventually the federal government passed literally *thousands* of laws, all of them designed to provide working men and women protections against the risks to life and limb posed by unbridled, unregulated labor markets. Minimum-wage laws, maximum-hour laws, health and safety regulations, Social Security legislation, workers' compensation laws—collectively, what we came to call the "New Deal"—were all passed out of whole cloth—something from nothing—and within only a handful of years. Most to the point here, they were all passed in the face of a ferocious counterattack that relentlessly asserted the naturalness, the inevitability, the utility, and the goodness of what was in fact a constructed, contingent, disutile, and changeable regime of free contract—a regime of contractual laissez-faire, in labor markets, in which law was structured such that workers could rely on nothing but their own *de minimus* bargaining power—nil, if you're hungry—when negotiating terms of their work contracts. This changed when legislators took action, in the form of laws that structured those contracts, by delimiting mandatory terms—notably, minimum wages, maximum hours, and safety regulations. The entire country, in the wake of this experience, internalized the lesson that labor markets are not natural artifacts but are socially constructed through laws, and can be socially reconstructed so as to better suit human ends, if the democratic will is there to do so.

There's no reason to think that civil marriage is any different. If the political, democratic will is there to render civil marriage more just, law can be put to the task. Marriage in the year 2000 is no more a child of nature, divine providence, or intelligent design, than was the unregulated labor contract between capitalist and worker in 1900. We—meaning, "we humans"—created the common law of contract that made the worker's labor agreement look so misleadingly natural, benign, and mutually rewarding. Then, we remade our law to make it ever so slightly more rewarding, or at least less dangerous and dehumanizing, for workers. Likewise, here. We—"we humans"—created the laws of marriage, property, divorce, contract, and inheritance that have made the traditional marriage contract appear the same. We radically changed the labor contract, and we did it through law, democratically imposed, upon the will of capitalists and employees both. We can surely do the same thing here. Liberal scholars of the family, of marriage, and justice—Susan Okin and Molly Shanley in philosophy, Linda McClain and Joan Williams, in law—are showing us how.

Critics of Just Marriage

The just-marriage movement has not attracted the political resistance that the same-sex marriage movement has. It has, though, drawn a substantial critical response in the scholarly literature, and particularly by social scientists, ranging in disciplines from evolutionary biology, to economics, and most recently to behavioral psychology and sociology. Beginning with Gary Becker's Nobel Prize–winning effort in the early 1980s, *Treatise on the Family*,[91] some social scientists have argued, on various grounds, that just or egalitarian marriage is simply disutile. The disproportionate and unequal distribution of both labor and power within a traditional marriage and family, it is argued, is an overall good thing. It is such a good thing, in fact, that we should design civil marriage so as to facilitate and encourage and promote it, its possible injustice, as measured by abstract principle, notwithstanding. The second shift, they argue, is indeed unjust, but desirably so. It is at the heart, not the periphery, of marriage. We should understand its benefits to the human community, and do whatever is necessary to maintain it. Three principle arguments have emerged.

The first comes from sociobiology, or as it is sometimes called, evolutionary biology. The traditional breadwinning husband and domestic wife, and the allocation between them of the labor required to reproduce the species, whether fair or unfair, is grounded in evolutionary and biological mandates, some (not all) sociobiologists argue, that in the long run maximize the fitness of the individual for reproduction.[92] Men are biologically predisposed to impregnate as many women as widely and often as possible, basically so as to maximize their reproductive potential. Women, on the other hand, are biologically predisposed to put vastly greater resources into the completion of each pregnancy and the nurturance of each child. A woman cannot bring about the sheer quantity of pregnancies a man can, so to maximize her reproductive potential, she must do what needs to be done to ensure that each pregnancy will be successful, and each born child will mature to adulthood. Men and women thus have vastly different reproductive strategies. The man will seek to maximize the sheer number of pregnancies he causes, while the woman will spend her time and resources nurturing each born child. She nurtures; he impregnates. A woman's greater tendency toward childcare is thus grounded in genetic inclination. She cares for children to maximize her reproductive potential. He impregnates as many women as possible—by rape, seduction, or otherwise—to do the same.

That can't, however, be the end of the story. The mother, deserted by the father so that he can impregnate others, will find it extremely difficult to give birth, lactate, gather food, breastfeed, and then feed herself and her child without help. Other women will have no genetic interest in helping her, nor will men other than the father. The result of this picture will be sick and prematurely dead children—frustrating both the woman and man's reproductive quest. So, modify the picture. A woman's best bet at insuring both her own continuing well-being and her child's (and thereby maximize her reproductive success) is to create a sufficiently appealing nest, or home, so that the father will decide it is worth his time and energy to help her bring their child to maturity. The father's best bet might be to help with the raising and nurturing of a few of his offspring, rather than maximizing the number of pregnancies for which he's responsible. Of course, for him it's a tradeoff: the time he invests in assisting the mother in the raising of his child must be worth the loss to him of the further pregnancies he could be pursuing. If the mother is fit, however, and the child clearly his, it's not a bad deal. Random, chaotic impregnation of as many women as possible, but with other men doing likewise and hence with no guarantee, with respect to any particular child, of paternity, will result in little but a high rate of infant death and infanticide, his own offspring included. If he can keep his mate relatively sequestered, or at least protected against the sexual advances of other men, and his children healthy, he can thereby maximize his reproductive success. The mother can maximize her reproductive success by enticing the father to assist in the nurturance of their joint issue—although note that for her, there's also a tradeoff involved: it's a tradeoff between the time and resources invested in keeping the father at home, the time and resources invested in seeking and finding a more fit, and more complacent, future partner for her next pregnancy, and the time, and resources, invested in simply feeding and nurturing the newborn herself. For the most part, though, the traditional allocation of gendered labor represents the best bet for both. It is well suited to the reproductive strategies of both partners. The woman is inclined to nurture the newborns and babies; the father is inclined to assist by providing the means of sustenance. Both benefit from monogamy and a breadwinning, present father—although the mother benefits more than the father, if only because the opportunity costs for the father, as he adapts to monogamy, are so much greater. It's no wonder, then, that the mother is willing to put up with substantial injustice—the benefit of the sociobiological bargain, for her, is greater. Ergo—they both come out ahead. The second shift—domestic injustice—is simply the price exacted for his continuing presence. It's not a bad bargain for her. It's a pretty good one.

The economic argument against egalitarian marriage is similar, but with wealth—understood as enjoyed consumer surplus, not necessarily dollars and cents—maximized, rather than reproductive fitness. The traditional allocation of domestic labor, some economists have urged, is good because it maximizes the wealth of the parties through specialization.[93] Women tend to be better at domestic chores, including both keeping house and raising children, while men tend to be better suited for labor market competition. Therefore, although there may of course be exceptions, couples will be wealthier, in terms of enjoying the greatest amount of consumer surplus from their joint labor, if they specialize along traditional gender lines. A man will earn more value in the market than he could produce in comparable added value at home, while a woman will produce more value at home than she could produce in terms of wages on the market. Both will be better off if she focuses on the production of value at home and he on the production of wages in the market. The traditional allocation of labor in marriage accomplishes this specialization. So long as the traditional wife is well protected—through generous alimony payments and inheritance laws—against divorce and the death of her spouse, both will be enriched through this allocation. Law, then, is needed to ensure that she receives the economic benefit of her labor at the point of divorce or her husband's death. Beyond that, however, there is no further wealth-maximizing function for a legal regime to serve. The parties will tend to bargain themselves toward a maximization of the value of their specialized labor. Over time, custom will absorb the lesson of these bargains, developing roles that they can simply adopt, without the additional expense of experimentation. For the occasional couple for whom the traditional allocation is not wealth maximizing, equal opportunity laws and a cultural willingness to tolerate at-home dads will fill the gap, protecting each party and the nonconforming couple. For the most part though, the traditional allocation is more wealth maximizing, and to whatever degree wealth creates happiness, more desirable as well.

Finally, sociologist Stephen Nock and some of his colleagues have argued that traditional allocations of domestic labor, even if disproportionate and even when both spouses work outside the household as well, in fact leads to greater satisfaction than attempts at egalitarian distributions of work within the home.[94] Women who work, as well as women who don't work, proclaim themselves relatively satisfied in marriages in which they do the lion's share of the domestic and child-raising labor—even when that means women work a total of substantially more hours than their husbands. The exception to this trend, Nock suggests, is women in marriages in which the unfair allocation of labor between the parties is known by both and becomes a bone of contention between the two of them. In those marriages, wives suffer from the ill consequences of their own resentment, as they try unsuccessfully to change their husbands' behavior, and create considerable tension and eventually lower rates of satisfaction with the marriage. Otherwise, though, both wives and husbands happily adapt to the "social norm" expected of them, and as communicated to them through the medium of traditional marriage. Compliance with social norms is generally something that makes for high levels of satisfaction: it reduces uncertainty in life, regarding how we ought to behave; assures some measure of social acceptance; and involves us in a community, and a way of life, that transcends our individual egos. The conclusion Nock reaches is that married couples need to develop mechanisms to avoid "keeping the books." So long as the injustice of the allocation of labor is either not known or not dwelt on, it doesn't interfere with the parties' satisfaction with their marriage. Once known, and highlighted, it becomes an issue. Too much knowledge here, then, is a bad thing. A little obfuscation of the facts keeps the domestic peace.

Let me close this chapter with the suggestion that *even if these very interesting empirical claims are true* they don't imply much of anything, with respect to civil marriage and how we ought to structure it. The first thing to note, with respect to all three of these arguments, is that they are all loosely utilitarian in form, and utilitarianism is itself a controversial moral theory, not only for individual decisionmaking, but also for public policy. Even if traditional marriage does maximize reproductive fitness, wealth, and satisfaction, and even if the institution is utile, it doesn't follow that we ought to embrace it unchanged, or not seek its reform. A utilitarian institution might nevertheless be unjust, as moral philosophers have long argued, and might for that reason be morally objectionable, in spite of its utility. If we think, as a moral matter, that we ought not to embrace unjust social institutions, then the utility of marriage does not determinatively weigh in its favor.

Even from a utilitarian perspective, however, it is not clear that the conclusion that we ought to prefer traditional marriage to just marriage follows from any of this research. Reproductive fitness does not maximize happiness, it maximizes reproductive potential, and therefore, perhaps, population. But a miserable but large population living at subsistence level on an overcrowded globe fighting for survival is not a happy community. Wealth, we should all know by now, is not the same as happiness, and even quite committed "legal economists" rarely defend (any longer) the proposition that the law ought to single-mindedly pursue wealth when and wherever it conflicts with equity or happiness. In this context, the couple maximizing wealth and consumer surplus by specializing in the labor they best perform, may not be as happy as the less-well-off couple willing to mix it up a little, wealth consequences be damned. Lastly, satisfaction is not the same thing as happiness either: we may feel ourselves and report ourselves to be satisfied, because we have only a dim or no appreciation of the possibilities of other ways of organizing our lives or our social order. We may have acquiesced in what is at best the least bad of offered alternatives. We may have lowered our expectations, so as to reduce our bitterness and envy. We may suffer from false consciousness, or cognitive dissonance, or as Mill piquantly put the point, we may feel the satisfaction of a pig, because we have never been offered the resources necessary to appreciate the more robust (or as Mill put it, the "higher") happiness of a well-fed, well-nurtured, and well-educated human being.[95] More colloquially, we may not relish banging our head against a wall to improve our lives, and getting for our effort nothing but a headache. That we report ourselves to be satisfied—given bad alternatives—does not imply we shouldn't seek better alternatives. Just marriage might be a better alternative to traditional marriage, no matter how satisfied we are with the latter.

It is even less clear that the sociobiological story supports any particular form of social organization, marital or otherwise. That we are genetically predisposed to behave in a certain way, if true, only entails that we will have to be further motivated to act contrary to our disposition. It doesn't follow that we shouldn't act contrary to disposition, and it certainly doesn't follow that the state shouldn't take affirmative actions to deter us from acting as we are disposed to act. Thomas Hobbes famously opined that in a state of nature, men would be naturally inclined to pillage, murder, assault, and steal. He concluded from this not law's futility, but law's necessity: law, and the state, and a political order—a sovereign representing the commonwealth—are both necessary and desirable, given our natural rapaciousness. He did not conclude that a sovereign, or law, would be futile.[96] Likewise, even if, hypothetically, men or women have a "natural" or biological propensity to rape and pillage, it does not follow that we should decriminalize rape. It only follows that we will have to take some pretty serious steps to deter it. And, likewise here as well: if sociobiologists convince us that men are inclined to impregnate women, but are not naturally inclined to mother the born young, it doesn't follow that they shouldn't do it, or that we should not set up our institutions in such a way as to encourage them to. It only follows that we will have to make some collective effort to make it more likely than not that they will do so. It's also worth noting that even if we wish to draw a line from the sociobiologists' description of pre-civil life and some implied form of social organization—perhaps on the grounds that the form of social organization that best reflects our genetic predisposition will carry the lowest enforcement costs—it surely doesn't follow that the form of social organization we would turn to would be traditional marriage, rather than, say, lesbian-coupled parenting, assisted by IVF, or perhaps polygamy. The lesbian couple might be more stable, and might be better parents. There would be two committed, rather than one committed and one ambivalent parent, and perhaps, between the two of them, they could find time to earn a wage as well. Neither need worry that the other will be constantly weighing the advantages of staying, or leaving so as to impregnate a larger pool of women. Polygamous marriages look good from a sociobiological perspective as well, at least if we care about the quality of the parenting, although there is a huge cost paid by boys who find themselves without partners or spouses.

The wealth-maximization argument seems like a closer fit with traditional, monogamous marriage, than the argument from sociobiology, but it too fails to account for some of the features of traditional marriage, as well as some features of contractual marriage. That the traditional allocation of labor is wealth maximizing suggests a strong case, either for "wages for housework," or for paychecks to sole wage earners in a traditional marriage that are made out to both spouses, or at least, for much greater protection for the non-income-producing partner than that now provided for by Social Security, divorce, and inheritance law. To maximize the wealth that the traditional allocation of labor promises, without one of the two of them incurring so much undue risk as to nullify the value of the wealth, the partner who specializes in home care must be fully protected against desertion by being well compensated should it occur, or she will have too great an incentive to leave herself. The economic argument for marriage seemingly supports something like traditional marriage but with much more robust and heightened safeguards, rather than traditional marriage with easy exit. A number of legal economists, as well as some feminists, have, for reasons loosely tracking this logic, argued for greater, rather than lesser economic protection of traditional homemakers at the point of divorce through a number of imaginative reforms. Perhaps, for example, following divorce, the income that flows to the working partner, partly by virtue of the unpaid labor performed by the at-home partner, should continue to be equitably shared between them.[97]

Finally, Professor Nock's provocative argument that women are satisfied with marriages that require of them a second shift, so long as the injustice of the second shift does not become a salient feature of the marriage, and that we should therefore continue to encourage traditional marriage, could just as easily be re-stated in such a way as to lead to the opposite conclusion. Women are unhappy in inegalitarian marriages, unless they are kept in the dark about the injustice. Stated in this form, Nock's research is in line with earlier research showing very much the same thing. In one far-ranging study in the early nineties, women were asked an extensive series of questions about their happiness in their marriages, ranging from their happiness or unhappiness with their sex lives, their social lives as a couple and individually, their role as parents, their work aspirations, and so on. Much to the surprise, and somewhat to the consternation, of the interviewers, who expected something quite different, almost all the women cited household labor and child-raising—second shiftism—as the primary and in many cases the sole source of their dissatisfaction.[98] They also made clear the sort of psychological dynamic that fully explains the results that surprised Professor Nock: they were most unhappy when they tried to impress upon their husbands the unfairness of the allocation of labor. That way, they reported, lies divorce, and they did not want divorce. It doesn't follow from this that second-shift wives are happy with the second shift. It follows that they are happier with their marriages than they contemplate themselves being, should they end them.

Let me sum this up. Arguments for traditional marriage based on maximizing reproductive fit, wealth, or happiness all assume that utilitarian arguments are conclusive against justice-based claims, when they are not; assume that maximizing some one thing—satisfaction, or reproductive success, or wealth—is the same as maximizing happiness, when it is not, and assume that traditional rather than just marriage is entailed by their claims, when in each case, although for different reasons, it doesn't seem to be. The claims for egalitarian and just marriage look as strong today, after thirty years of utilitarian critique, as they did thirty years ago, when Susan Okin first suggested that marriage and family life ought to be constructed in such a way as to ensure that life within them can be lived justly. That said, the social science literature itself is illuminating, and ought to be central to the sensible construction of public policy. It just isn't as unidirectional in its "policy implications" as some of its users seemingly believe. That women are inclined to nurture the young, that given the nature of our species, that nurturance is demanding work over a long period of maturation, and that women cannot do this without substantial assistance from others and expect to survive, are indeed important sociobiological facts about our species. Those descriptive facts do strongly suggest the need for *some* sort of "social norm" calling for a network of postpartum support for mothers of newborns, infants, toddlers, and small children, whether it be from a husband, the father of the children, the mother's own mother, or friends, neighbors, or relatives. All of us, as children, need care, and a lot of it, to survive, and then to thrive. Caregivers that provide that essential care should not be impoverished by virtue of their caregiving. What follows from these facts? A tortured argument for traditional marriage, perhaps. But not necessarily. Perhaps what follows from the necessity of extended care of young and old to the survival of the species is the existence of a fundamental, human right of any caregiver to give care without risking impoverishment and a correlative duty of states, communities, or lawmakers to ensure she, or he, can do so.

Likewise, that women and men, when coupled, might be better off economically if they pool resources and specialize their labor to meet their skills seems true and important. What it suggests, though, is not necessarily traditional marriage for all, in lockstep form, but something considerably more pluralistic: alternating specialties, perhaps, and a good bit of experimentation. It suggests the value of recognizing unions, not only between a man and a woman that specialize in this way, but same-sex unions likewise, and nonsex couples as well. It doesn't follow that we should presuppose about ourselves or our children that we fit any set of generalized presumptions about who is better than who at doing what, and the view has been properly criticized for insisting to the contrary. But there's no reason to throw out the baby with the bath. Gary Becker and his colleagues have shown something important about human association. When we come together in intimate associations, no less than in the workplace, we might be better off tailoring our share of the labor needed to maintain the association to our individual proclivities, tastes, and abilities.

Finally, that working women report themselves satisfied in otherwise traditional marriages in spite of the inequality of labor surely doesn't suggest Nock's conclusion that we should therefore abandon the goal of just marriage. It does, though, suggest that there is something very sustaining about marriages, if women put up with such an awful lot of injustice to sustain them. We need to understand what it is about marriage that makes it worth it, as well as what it is about marriage that is unjust, and work to ensure that we preserve the former while dismantling the latter. We need to pursue the work of rendering marriage not only a just, but also a comfortable and happy home.

Reproductive success, the production and enjoyment of material wealth, security against risk, and individual happiness are important to people, and to many people they are more important than abstract justice. Utilitarian critique of just marriage does and should remind us of that fact. We want healthy, happy babies and children, we want to be economically successful in adult life and comfortable in old age, and we each want to achieve some measure of personal happiness. This is the stuff of life; these things matter hugely. At the same time, though, we need the institutions through which we attain these good things of life to be just, and we need to feel them to be such. There's no reason to conclude without far more evidence than the social norms theorists, the sociobiologists, and the behavioral economists have jointly produced, that these goals are mutually exclusive.

Conclusion: A Modest Proposal

*M*arriage, today, poses a political question requiring democratic resolution. It is no longer what it clearly was in the middle of the nineteenth century: a patriarchal institution, complete with delegated political authority from the state to husbands, with full authority to rule over their private and intimate sovereignties. Nor is it any longer what it was in the 1950s: a purely traditional institution, widely viewed as delineating gender roles, sexual mores, and a conception of the good life that jointly constitute the natural foundation of civil society. It is also no longer what it was in the 1970s: a matter of individual choice, with participants given full rein over its meaning.

Marriage today—marriage in the aughts—retains some threads of all of these, as well as an outsized dollop of the last. It is still somewhat patriarchal, although that is fading fast, and it is still intensely traditional for many people, although that too is changing rapidly. Most notably, the lessons of the 1970s have been completely absorbed, and incorporated, into contemporary marriage. Marriage today is more contractual than status based; a choice individuals make rather than a role they assume. Parties enter marriage when and if they want to and with partners of their own choice. They do so as adults, finished or nearing the finish of their education, with first jobs and rented apartments already under their belts, rather than as children just leaving their parents' nests. As adult individuals, they custom design their own marriage according to their own lights, free of gender "stereotypes." They sign premarital agreements reasonably expecting them to be enforceable by courts down the road, if need be. Cohabiting partners of both the same and opposite sex enter into "coparenting" agreements and powers of attorney to contractually mimic the benefits of marriage without actually entering the legal relationship. Separation agreements are routinely upheld unless they are a product of duress, and so on. Because of these changes and others, most of which began in the 1970s and has proceeded uninterruptedly since then, marriage has become far more individualized and far more "contractual" than it was earlier.

By virtue of this evolution from "patriarchy to tradition to contract," marriage has also become a much better deal for both sexes, but most profoundly, for women. There's no question but that the contractual marriage promise of the 1970s and beyond is a better deal than either the patriarchal promise of the 1850s or the traditional promise of the 1950s. Women have power to avoid marriage altogether, if they so desire, or to exit it, if need be. Women can mother outside of marriage if they wish, and can do so with very few legal impediments. Women also have more power within marriage that they did not have in earlier incarnations of that institution. They can more realistically insist on allocations of labor that are sensible for them, so as to combine marriage and child-raising with career and work, and so on. Marriage has not become fully equal, or fully just, as a result of all of this. But it has become a more liberal institution, and women are somewhat more equal, and much freer, as a result.

But marriage in the past decade has become something else as well: marriage has become a political question, and hence a matter for public deliberation. Because of that shift, we now need to look at marriage, and at the relationships it creates, fosters, and supports, not only as interested potential participants who might be inclined to fashion one of our own, and not only as scholars or "experts" with various family-related fields of expertise, but also as citizens, with an eye toward what might be best for us all. We have "opened marriage up" to political choice, in a way that echoes, but is nevertheless quite different from, what we did in the seventies, when we opened marriage up to individual choice. As individual participants, we can shape the norms of our own marriages to fit our individual predilections. The choices we face as citizens, though, reach beyond our individual households: it is the need for political judgment, not individual choice, which now presses upon us.

I have tried to show in this book that as citizens of a democratic, lawmaking polity, we are facing a three-tined fork in the road regarding this institution. We can preserve marriage as is, we can end it altogether, or we can amend it. No matter which way we go, we will make of marriage *what we will.* As we do so, we might be spurred on, occasionally, by legal process, judicial decisions, and the constitutional deliberations of United States Supreme Court justices. Eventually, however, and for better or worse, we are going to debate this question of marriage in the political realm and in the legislative branch, and we are going to do it, ultimately, state by state. We do not have, nor should we have, a federal marriage policy. The marriage wars will and should be resolved through the utterly ordinary and thoroughly political processes of state law: public debate, referendum, resolution, and state constitutional or legislative change.

Through that process, some of us might, as a community, strive to return marriage to its traditionalist roots. Toward that end, a state might roll back some of the reform movements of the twentieth century that pushed the evolution of marriage and marriage law from "status" to "contract." A state could, for example, through legislative reform, reverse the tide of the no-fault revolution. There'd be a fairly broad constituency of strange bedfellows that might applaud such a move. Traditionalists resist the basic premise of no-fault divorce: that morality should not be relevant to the legality, availability, or desirability of marital dissolution. Communitarians worry that no fault undercuts the commitment necessary to married life, and feminists worry that it impoverishes women at the point of divorce. We could go further in this direction still. Should the Supreme Court reverse *Roe v. Wade, Griswold,* and *Eisenstadt,* a state might seek to limit or eliminate the availability of birth control, even within marriage, but certainly outside of it. This position does not enjoy majority support in virtually any state, but it does enjoy the support of a core constituency of the Republican Party. This would reorient the nature and point of marriage, and in a profoundly traditional direction: without access to birth control, marriage itself might once again be viewed as an institution overwhelmingly concerned with the begetting of children—a "begetting" that inevitably follows from the noncontracepted heterosexual behavior of the adults that produce them. And of course, we could amend our federal Constitution, so that no state can experimentally expand marriage so as to include same-sex couples. We could enshrine in fundamental law, in other words, an understanding of marriage that no longer seems to be so enshrined in fundamental custom or tradition.

All of these changes would be important, and all of them in my view would be both regrettable and socially regressive. In one respect, however, they would not fundamentally "roll the clock back," in the ways their promoters hope or their opponents fear. If we use *law* to roll back reforms, in order to revert to a traditionalist understanding of marriage in this country, it will be with full knowledge that we are doing so as a matter of democratic choice. We will do so, if we do so, knowing full well that it could have been otherwise. We will do so knowing that other countries are pursuing a different path, and not committing social and legal suicide by so doing, and that particular local and state governments here might wish to do so as well. If we roll back no-fault divorce, encourage the Court to reverse *Roe v. Wade, Griswold v. Connecticut,* and *Eisenstadt,* recriminalize abortion and birth control, and amend the federal Constitution so as to limit marriage to committed heterosexuals, we will do all of that knowing that we have chosen this understanding of marriage rather than that one, that we have done so on the grounds that this one better serves our human interests rather than that one, and so on. Marriage will never again be perceived as having an essential core meaning as necessary to its identity as the institution is necessary to the survival of society. Once we've turned that corner—the corner from "necessity" to "contingency" in our thinking about marriage—we have moved marriage from the domain of nature to the domain of politics. No matter how "traditionalist" the institution we ultimately design, there's no returning mother nature herself to its core justification.

Why does this matter? What difference does it make whether marriage is limited to heterosexuals because of natural law, or because of foundational constitutional law? The difference is the difference between that which is seen as necessary, essential, and natural, and that which is undertaken with a full awareness of contingency.

Whatever we enshrine as law, even constitutional law, we can reverse. Law, including constitutional law, and including constitutional amendments, are man-made, changeable, positive enactments of will. We make law in statehouses, in Congress, and in city halls. If marriage is what we make through law, we—or those of us with political power—can unmake and remake it at will. And marriage is indeed what we make of it through law. Local, state, and federal laws, once passed, can be repealed, and state and federal constitutional amendments can be revoked, as our last ill-fated experience with constitutional moralism—the prohibition era—pretty starkly shows.[1] Marriage will be what it is as a matter of political choice. It will never again assume any particular shape, or have any particular content, as a matter of natural necessity. We've already turned that corner.

So, the important turn we have taken in the past twenty-five years is in the nature of the questions we ask about marriage. The question is not, any longer, "What is marriage?" and "What is its value?" as if we are discovering some truth of the matter that lies outside our own creation. Nor is the question "What is marriage, *for me*?" as if we are fashioning our own individual wardrobe. Rather, the question is "What should marriage be?" "How can we design an institution that best serves desirable human ends?" Not just "for me," but for my community.

In this conclusion, I would like to put forward a modest proposal regarding the direction of our equality practice. My long-range goal in doing so is to redirect the movement for same-sex marriage in a way that will not compromise its commitment to formal equality, but that will also address directly definitional and normative questions about the nature and point of marriage. I want to fashion a proposal for political reform of marriage that will turn the debate away from that of who may enter, and instead toward the question of the value of the house then occupied.

My short-term objective is to put another political possibility—another marriage proposal—on the table. I want to answer somewhat differently the question that Bill Eskridge, Chai Feldblum, and the many other constitutional and family law advocates and scholars all implicitly raise in their work on the "marriage equality" movement: with respect to marriage, to what end should we put our equality practice? I am not in the "defend marriage" camp, or the "end marriage" camp. My sympathies lie squarely with those who would reform it. My sense of how to do so, however, is different from that of the various "marriage equality" proposals I have seen. Before defending my own proposal, however, let me first explain my reservations regarding both the defense of marriage and the desirability of its demise.

Defending Marriage

Features of marriage, as currently configured, make it a fundamentally unjust institution, not only for gays and lesbians wishing to marry, but also for poor women and men who wish to care for dependents, but who, for various reasons, cannot partake of the array of economic and legal benefits marriage extends, and then find themselves objects of moral scorn for that failure. Martha Fineman and Nancy Polikoff are entirely right about this. Marriage rhetoric makes harder, rather than easier, the task of mustering the political will required to assemble a humane and truly helpful web of social resources to help people parent, give care to each other, or thrive on their own, outside as well as inside of marriage. So long as we continue to believe that marriage lifts individuals out of poverty, that children should be raised by married partners, that morally good people get married while bad people don't, and that all of this happens by virtue of free individual choice, we have a robust rationale for blaming, rather than helping, unmarried caregivers (and others) who find themselves in economic distress. The bottom line message of the current marriage initiative of the Bush administration is that poor people who cannot marry—whether for lack of resources or for lack of marriageable partners—should not parent, and can expect little assistance and a good deal of scorn, should they decide to do so anyway. The economic and legal benefits of marriage then work so as to further buttress the relatively more secure economic and social position of the married. That bare fact alone, in my view, and totally aside from the politics of gay and lesbian rights, ought to be enough to make both the hard-headed social utilitarian marriage enthusiast, as well as her more romantic, anticommodification-ist, anticonsumerist, softly Marxist, promarriage colleague, *pause.*

It ought to give them pause, furthermore, within the confines of their own arguments. Marriage, as an institution, is a good thing, the utilitarians and the neo-Marxist self-actualizers tell us, because of the wealth, health, and social utility it generates, or alternatively (or additionally), because of the countercommodifi-cationist and anti-atomistic relational self it valorizes. Both camps should worry, if it turns out to be the case that the institution of marriage, viewed socially, and from the perspective of nonparticipants as well as participants, does not produce wealth, and is destructive of rather than facilitative of healthy conceptions of the self, and for a substantial portion of the population.

Is it? First of all, on the individual level, for many poor people, marriage alone will not produce wealth, if the marriage partners are unemployed, underemployed, or employed at very low wages. Likewise, for some, marriage does not produce safety, if the marriage partner is violent, no matter the overall averages regarding violence within marriage as opposed to violence in cohabitating relationships. Second, for many people who nevertheless may wish to parent or find themselves giving care to dependents, marriage is just not a realistic option. For this group, marriage is obviously no solution to poverty. This alone, of course, is not an argu-ment for ending marriage. It is, though, an argument against relying upon mar-riage as a safety net. That safety net might well be required by social justice. If we are morally obligated, as a society, by norms of justice, to provide minimal social welfare for the least well off, we do not discharge that responsibility by relying upon an institution such as marriage to do so.

The damage done by the institution of marriage to poor people, both married and unmarried, and both parents and nonparents, is indeed largely rhetorical, but it is no less real by virtue of that fact. The moralistic and punitive rhetoric of the "marriage initiative," particularly in this decade, makes it less likely, rather than more likely, that the underlying causes of poverty, inequality, and private subordination will be meaningfully addressed. If we assume that marriage is the cure for poverty, and that the choice to marry is available to all, and that good people will opt for marriage while bad people won't, then we will have hidden economic inequality within a doubly obfuscating veil of legitimation: poverty is then legitimated by an economic system that assumes the voluntariness of economic choices in the labor market, and a moralistic domestic system that assumes both the voluntariness of choice in the marriage market, and the immorality of those who do not partake. Making marriage open to gays and lesbians won't change that.

And second, what of caregivers within marriage—still, overwhelmingly, women? Again, if we look at marriage rhetoric, and not just marriage itself, it is also clear that the institution of marriage makes it harder, not easier, to address the pressing needs of caregivers. To be sure, part of the point of marriage is to facilitate caregiving work, and to provide some public support for it. To a considerable degree it does just that: it is hard to make sense of the many economic benefits of marriage bestowed by government as anything other than subsidies for caregivers in the family structure proven over time as the optimal environment within which to provide such care. Nevertheless, the subsidies, such as they are, are misdirected and inadequate. Caregivers currently need far more than occasional tax breaks doled out to the marriage they may or may not be a part of. Caregivers in or out of marriage need paid leaves for childbirth and infant care, enhanced family wages for their wage-earning spouses or selves, enhanced Social Security protection for their old age, and universal health and child care for themselves and their dependents. The needs for these, the moral obligation of the state to ensure their availability, and the means by which the state might provide them, are all badly obfuscated by both the romantic gauze and the utilitarian justification of marriage. Marriage is the means by which we've privatized what ought to be to some degree public responsibilities. Caregivers inside as well as outside of marriage—overwhelmingly women—are the ones that are hurt by this.

Ending Marriage

It doesn't follow, though, that we should therefore "end marriage as we know it." Ending marriage is not a logical, or even sensible, response to the strongest case against marriage put forward by its critics. For example, it is true that marriage should not be viewed as the cure for poverty, and it is likewise true that the Bush administration's current "marriage initiative" should be faulted for insisting to the contrary. But marriage *is*, nevertheless, a significant hedge against poverty and its risks, for those who can and do avail themselves of it. *Ending* a hedge against poverty is not a response to the inadequacy of the hedge. Likewise, marriage does indeed obfuscate the needs of caregivers, inside as well as outside of marriage, and there is no question but that the victims of this obfuscation are overwhelmingly women. Nevertheless, the likely alternative to marriage—contract law—would be a step in the wrong direction. Marriage law is at least understood to be a part of our public law, if ambiguously so, implicating public goals and ends. Contract law is constructed so as to create a wall around private relations entirely. The obfuscation of injustice in and around marriages would become a part of the very point of the law that regulates them, were we to abandon marriage for individualized contracts, and subsume marriage law within contract law.

Nor have the marriage critics put forward fully convincing utilitarian arguments for ending marriage. First, of course, we cannot, as a practical matter, simply abandon marriage, and nor should we wish to. Most United States adults are married, will marry, wish to marry, intend to marry, or were married. Ending marriage would be an unbearably disruptive force for vast numbers of citizens. We also just know too much about marriage's utility, value, and importance in people's lives to simply end it. Marriage does work for people, for reasons easily articulable—economies of scale, specialization of labor, and so forth—and not so easily explicable—the authenticity of self, the need for relational commitment to a well led life. Marriage does leave its participants happier, and wealthier, and healthier. While some of this is because of legal privileges and economic entitlements that should be more widely shared, much of it is not: much of the marriage premium is a function of the sense of responsibility to the future, and the indebtedness to the past, that follows from knowing oneself to be absolutely essential to the well-being of another human being, and knowing that both of you are essential to the well-being, and even the existence, of others. And, not insignificantly, much of it comes from knowing that the community in which you live knows all of that—and applauds you for it—as well.

If we look at the various "interest groups" that might be affected by such a change, ending marriage looks like a lose-lose proposition. Men would not gain, but neither would women. Ending marriage would mean, in effect, that women who want to enter into long-term or for-life committed relationships with their male partners would have to depend on the rules of contract, and whatever contract terms, through their own cunning, foresight, and bargaining power they can manage to leverage. Even if they successfully negotiated favorable terms, they would then have to depend upon courts to uphold them—the same courts that have for two hundred years now been loathe to uphold private domestic contracts that allocate sexual, reproductive, and domestic labor among cohabiting couples. Even assuming the courts would be willing, however, are we really so certain that women would do *better* under a contract regime than a marital regime? Evidence doesn't support this: women in marriage are happier, better off financially, safer, and healthier than women in cohabitation. Prenuptial agreements even among the well off generally don't work in women's favor. Rather, they typically deprive women of property or assets they would otherwise be entitled to, upon divorce, under marriage and family laws. That is, in fact, their major function. It's hard to see how ending marriage and the obligations of support it imposes, through social norms, on married partners, and through legal norms, on divorced parties, would result in anything but the relative impoverishment of thousands of women, and their children, and very quickly.

Lastly, ending marriage would abolish the current point of intersection of the public sphere with this domain of private bargaining, private privilege, and private right, and would thus obliterate the window through which the justice or injustice of that domain can become visible—and hence changeable—to all. Civil marriage is the lens through which the state, through law and democratic process both, can evaluate, and reevaluate, the rules of private and intimate exchange. Ending marriage would indeed bring an end to the state's oddly prurient interest in the sexual behavior of consenting adults. It might bring about a greater level of enforcement of ordinary civil tort law and criminal law that are currently underenforced because of marital privileges—although it is not at all clear that it would. (The effect might be precisely the opposite: with marriage abolished, the old-fashioned "marital exemptions" and "marital privileges" might be simply extended, rather than wiped out, so as to affect an even broader range of private sexual and nonsexual relationships.) But even assuming that ending marriage would end the exemptions, and that would then lead to an increase in the enforcement of laws against violence and civil wrongs, it is still not clear the tradeoff would be a net gain. Ending marriage would bring an end to the state's, and the public's, and the community's, engagement with the utility or disutility, the justice or injustice, the humaneness or the inhumanness of our rules governing intimate and private association. Whatever might be the case elsewhere, at least in the United States, we need more, not less, state and public and community involvement in the justice of those relations, primarily because we need more, not less, social support for the care that is more often than not the point of those relations. This is clearly true when children, toddlers, and newborns are the objects of our familial caregiving, but it is also true of the care given by and bestowed upon the adult spouses themselves: spouses as well as parents could use more, not less, support in their caregiving of each other in times of crisis or stress. Ending marriage would be the logical extension of the very American tendency to overprivatize economic relations, and to overprivatize the process of compensating for the work that goes into maintaining them.

The danger, then, is that ending marriage would not cure the systemic injustice within or around marriage, but rather, would aggravate it. If we were to abolish marriage, the injustice of private, intimate relations would be taken off the table, so to speak, as an injustice of public concern; we would have literally no way to address it. Marriage would lose its "public" and "public law" dimension, and intimate life would lose whatever fragile status it now has, by virtue of marriage, as a domain of life that ought to be made just. Shrouded in the privacy that contract law so exquisitely protects, injustice within individual marriages would become next to impossible to even articulate, much less address.

This is not such a surprising conclusion. Ending a legal institution is not always the route to curing the injustice embedded within it. Laws, and legal institutions, including the flawed ones, and including even the unjust ones, often address injustice or violence that is pervasive in private action and interaction. The injustice in the law is often that it does so inadequately, or insufficiently. Wherever that's the case, repealing the law will leave the private violence, violation, or exploitation completely unattended, rather than just inadequately so. It will worsen, not improve, the underlying injustice.

Let me illustrate. Think of, first, marital rape exemptions: the state laws, criticized above, only recently reformed, that for centuries rendered rape within marriage a legal impossibility by defining rape as forced, nonconsensual intercourse with a woman "not one's wife."[2] Obviously, abolishing rape law entirely would eradicate the injustice of the exemption—marital rapes would be treated no differently than stranger rapes. But that gain in formal justice would be achieved only by creating a much worse problem, and a much worse injustice: the under-enforcement of laws against rape, as opposed to other crimes of violence. Here again, the injustice of treating rape differently from other crimes of violence could be cured by abolishing the Criminal Code. Rape would be treated no differently than murder—neither would be criminalized. We could keep this up until we're back to the state of nature, where there may not be a problem of formal injustice, but life for everyone would be brutish, nasty, and short. The moral of this story is simply that the problem with the original law—the marital rape exemption—was that it responded to the problem of rape inadequately. It is no cure of that injustice to simply repeal rape law.

Labor contracts, and the labor and contract law that inadequately regulate them, are another example. Many contracts between employers and employees, or in the old-fashioned language, between capitalists and workers, or masters and servants, are demonstrably unjust. The inequality in bargaining power between capitalist and worker makes exploitation of the laborer, and his alienation from his labor, so that the capitalist captures the surplus labor value, virtually inevitable. Nevertheless, the solution to this inequality is clearly not to repeal labor law, or even contract law. The inequalities that render so many labor contracts as well as contract law itself so unjust would be worsened, not improved, by abolishing the law that governs, regulates, and to some degree at least responds to the injustice of these relations. Labor law certainly, but even contract law (although to a much lesser extent) is the means, badly inadequate but nevertheless the means, of addressing that inequality in private bargaining power through the very public levers of law and regulation.

The moral from this is that law is potentially a public solution to private inequalities—a public answer to the injustice of subordination in the private sphere.

Of course it is also true that law often masks injustice, obfuscates it, and legitimates it. Nevertheless, in the aggregate, at least within systems minimally democratic, law is also almost always an improvement over what there would be in its absence. Sometimes—rape law is one such instance; labor contracts another—it is a substantial improvement. Where law is aimed at these privately subordinating, alienating relations, and is unjust, the injustice is oftentimes a function of the law's inadequate reach, or what I call "law's absence," not law's overbearing or intrusive presence. Where that's the case (again, it isn't always, but when it is the case), repealing the law will worsen, not improve or alleviate, the injustice.

Marriage law is almost paradigmatically of this nature. Rape law, labor law, and marriage law all have histories steeped in bitter inequalities, in more than a little private violence, in systematic subordination, and in sometimes thoroughly vicious exploitation. They all three bear the mark of those histories. Nevertheless, rape law, labor law, and marriage law have also, all three, become the means by which to address the private sphere subordination that manifests itself in widespread rape, in the exploitation of laborers, and the subordination of wives. There is no question but that law does, to some extent, and in all three cases, continue to exacerbate those inequalities. There is also no question, though, but that the presence of the law is a better bet than the private subordination, violence, and exploitation that we would confront were we to simply end them.

So, for all of these reasons, I'd put my money on reform. But what reform? Toward what end, as Bill Eskridge so helpfully puts the point, should we direct our "equality practice"?

The Justice of Civil Union Law

I propose that we should consider directing our "equality practice"—our litigating, our organizing, and our legislating around issues of marriage—toward the day when "civil unions"—roughly of the sort that the States of Vermont and Connecticut have created, but expanded, as explained below—become the norm. I mean "the norm" in two senses. First, every state, municipality, or jurisdiction should have a civil union law. It should become the "norm," then, in a statistical sense. It should become normal and ordinary, rather than extraordinary for a state to have such a law. It should become the "norm," however, in a second sense as well—a little closer to what the "social norms" theorists mean by the phrase. We should push for civil union laws, I believe, with the understanding and with the stated hope, that "civil union" should, and could, and would, over time, become the legal mechanism by which *any* two people—regardless of sexual orientation—who wish to commit themselves to the lifelong care of each other and their shared dependents, formalize and sanctify their intention and desire to do so. A couple so "civilly united" would then be entitled to the state's support, including those supports states now bestow upon married couples. Putting this the other way around, from the state's perspective, so to speak, "civil union" should be understood to be the institutional mechanism, provided by the state, through which the state, by law, expresses its support, both material and moral, for a particular form of intimate and social association—a form of intimate association that serves desirable social ends, and which the state accordingly has a not inconsiderable interest in promoting.

Civil union should then be open to any two individuals who wish to unite so as to form such an intimate and social association. It should be open to same-sex couples, or straight couples, or any other two individuals, regardless of the nature of the sexual relationship between them, and regardless of whether or not they have a sexual relationship—so long as the point of the union is to provide a lifetime of unconditional mutual care and support for each other and for their dependents. The criteria for entry would not be whether the two individuals are of any particular gender, sex, or sexual orientation. There would be no expectation that the relationships the state so sanctioned would pivot around sex at all, much less around any particular kind of sexual relationship. The criteria for entry would be whether the two individuals are seeking a public acknowledgement of a permanent union between them, and whether the union is sought in order to provide care to each other and others. If so, they can be civilly united, by a judge, clerk of the court, certified friend, priest, rabbi, or anyone else designated by the state as competent to perform such a ceremony. When so united, they are fully entitled to all the privileges, rights, and benefits currently given to married couples. Should marriage law change, civil union law would likewise.

There would, ideally, be no practical or legal difference between the two legal regimes, except that civil union would be considerably more "open" in terms of who might enter. There would, though, be symbolic differences and symbols do matter. A civil union law, so understood, unlike current marriage law, would align a state's legitimate interests with its positive law. A state has a legitimate interest in the health, well-being, and definition of families, including families that only consist of two civilly united or married adults, largely because it has a legitimate interest in the health and well-being of those of its citizens who are in states of dependency—whether because of their infancy, youth, advanced age, illness, or disability. This interest of states in the private affairs of citizens is not something to deplore, it is something to insist on. It is and should be absolutely central to the *raison d'etre* of the political state that it have some interest in the well-being of the weak. The state has a fully legitimate interest in the promotion of private associations that can promote the well-being of dependents; just as, presumably, it has an interest in the promotion of private associations that promote other legitimate state interests. For that reason, it seems to me, the state has an interest, as conservative marriage proponents have argued with respect to marriage, in doing whatever it can to promote civil unions of adults that promote the care of, and the well-being of, dependents, including, but not limited to, children.

The state does not, however, have any legitimate interest—at least that anyone has managed to well articulate in the last decade of the marriage wars—in the nature or existence of the sexual behavior of the two adults that have united in order to provide this care. There just isn't any good reason for the state to take an interest in whether that couple's sexual activity is contracepted or not; or whether it is coital, digital, anal, oral, or missionary; or whether it is masturbatory, coupled, or involves multiple partners; or whether it is monogamous, polygamous, polyamorous, or open; and so on. Likewise, the state surely has an interest in the well-being of the dependents the civil union is created to further (including the sometimes dependent status of the united individuals themselves). The state has no legitimate interest, however, in the means by which those dependents are created: noncontracepted heterosexual intercourse, adoption, assisted fertility, surrogacy contracts, and so on. The current oddity of our existing marriage law is that it combines a perfectly sensible point of entry for states to promote what is clearly a legitimate state interest—the well-being of children and other dependents—with a perfectly irrational point of entry for states to promote what clearly is not a legitimate state interest: the sexual behavior of consenting adults and the methods they use to procreate. An expanded civil union law would permit, encourage, and indeed require the state to continue, and expand upon, its legitimate interest in the well-being of children and other dependents. It would also require the state to jettison its apparent interest in the sexual and reproductive choices of competent adults—an interest that increasingly, today, looks nothing but prurient.

The goal of such a "civil union" movement (as opposed to a marriage movement, either same-sex or traditional) would be to become the norm *over time*—meaning eventually; not tomorrow, not today—and to become the norm, first by political action that would do nothing but expand choice, and then through the cumulative effect of many individual choices in turn guided by evolving social and cultural norms—not by judicial decree, and certainly not by constitutional mandate. The aim would *not* be to supplant, displace, or dislodge civil marriage through either legislative or judicial means. Rather, the goal would be to create a political system that includes both civil union and marriage, side by side, as civil union and marriage coexist today in Vermont, but with this major difference: we should aim to define civil union so that it is available not only to same-sex conjugal couples, but also as an option for straight couples, couples consisting of ambiguously sexed individuals, and nonconjugal couples of any combination of sexes and sexual orientations, as well. A heterosexual couple could either civilly marry, or civilly unite—the difference at the point of licensing might be (as Chai Feldblum has helpfully suggested in private conversation) nothing but the color of the form filled out. The choice between them also might, however, reflect the couple's view regarding the nature of the state's interest in their union. The civil union option would reflect the couple's endorsement of the state's interest in supporting and sanctioning and protecting the couple's declared intention to civilly unite, so that they might engage in caregiving labor, complete with all the responsibilities and joys attendant to that work, for each other and dependents. The marriage option does as well, but marriage additionally reflects the state's historical and to some degree ongoing interest in channeling heterosexual behavior into marital relations. The choice for heterosexual couples between marriage and civil union might be driven by personal beliefs, or by familial pressure, or by political solidarity with same-sex couples, or by nothing at all. The choice would not affect their legal relationship, or the relationship of their union or marriage to the state, however, in any way whatsoever.

What if, over time, we were to societally gravitate toward civil union, rather than civil marriage, as the norm for all couples? What would be the difference? First, civil union would be and would be understood to be an entirely secular, state-created institution, designed to promote individual and familial caregiving and to further the state interest in protecting the well-being of dependents. Religious or faith-based marriage might continue to thrive, but the difference between them would be clear-cut: faith-based marriage would serve and would be perceived to serve faith-based interests; state-based civil union would serve and would be perceived to serve state-based ends.

This would constitute a broadening and a clarification of an existing status quo. It would not require a sharp break from the past. There is, today, a difference between civil marriage and faith-based marriage; it is just not well understood. Thus, natural lawyers draw a distinction between civil marriage as a "mere legal convention" and the true idea of marriage for which they advocate—grounded in faith but enforced by states. They don't, however, confront the exclusionary consequences of defining true marriage basically by reference to its Judeo-Christian religious heritage. Reformers almost routinely make clear that the object of their reform is "civil marriage," as opposed to religious marriage, but they don't directly confront the seriousness of the conflation, or the extent of the identity, grounded in culture, between the two. This is not just the foreseeable consequence of an unfortunate trick of language: that we just happen to use the same word—marriage—to apply, blanket fashion, to different institutions, or ideas. It is rather the consequence of a centuries-long identification of the nature of the state's interest in the intimate affairs of adults with a particular religious conception of the good; or a set of such religious conceptions. Over time, the role of marriage and marriage law has changed: the state's legitimate interest in marriage is not in the intimate affairs of adults but in the caregiving work of families. A move to "civil union" and away from civil marriage would clarify, and finalize, that shift.

Second, and relatedly, civil union would be understood to be the ordinary, normal, accepted means by which the state involves itself in family life, and the institution through which its laws are brought to bear. This would have the laudable effect of opening "civil union" law to rational examination of its contours by democratically elected lawmakers, scholars, policy mavens, family experts, family health practitioners, and the like: the entire array of professionals and interested lay people who might have insight into the needs of dependents, the legal structure of familial relationships, and the relation between the two. We have well-developed and for the most part functional means for the crafting and recrafting of bodies of law, moved by democratic impulses and guided by expertise. Civil union law, like any body of law, needs to be examined with an eye toward its justice and its overall utility. Marriage law likewise, of course, should be so examined, and to a considerable extent this is happening now. But tradition, religion, and a near unmovable belief that marriage is somehow deeper than, older than, or just more basic than, the state, politics, or positive law that constitute it, puts it, for many people, and for some purposes, beyond the scope of rational deliberation and ordinary ethical judgment. A move from marriage to civil union might make our discussion of the purpose, the function, and the role of the state in our private lives less sexually and morally charged, and therefore more commendably ordinary.

It might by virtue of that "ordinariness" be a more fruitful discussion. We need to focus our attention on whether marriage or civil union well serves our happiness. We also need to focus on whether marriage law, as constituted, or civil union law, as envisioned, create just families, and whether they unjustly penalize or punish nonparticipants. We need to focus on whether marriage is a socially utile institution, and if the answer to that is an overwhelming yes—as it may be—we need to focus attention on how to preserve that social utility, while providing assistance and protection to nonparticipants who also wish or need to act as caregivers. We might engage these questions more fruitfully if the object of the inquiry is civil union, rather than marriage.

And possibly—although it's important not to overstate this possibility—a move toward civil union as the form of the caregiving relationship states have an interest in promoting *might* prompt the state, and the community, toward greater investment in caregiving labor. Today, the conservative marriage movement is quite explicitly designed so as to lessen the state's responsibility toward caregivers. The message is that marriage, not a welfare check, is the best way out of poverty: if you intend to have children, be sure to marry your children's father. Feminists, and antipoverty activists, are entirely right to worry that *any* promarriage movement—including the same-sex marriage movement in its current form—will further valorize marriage, and make more difficult, not less difficult, the already difficult task of securing state aid for unmarried mothers and their children who need it. Domestic violence victims and their advocates rightly worry that the consequence of an undue valorization of marriage will be to drive more of these women into violent, abusive marriages. Community activists correctly point out that the marriage promotion movement posits an unworkable and unavailable solution to the problem of poverty—presenting poor young people with the Hobson's choice of an unavailable marriage as a way to responsibly parent, or not parenting at all. All of these critics are right to worry that the marriage movement threatens to make parenting a privilege. If you have the means to responsibly marry, then you might become a parent. If you don't have the means to responsibly marry, then *don't parent.*

That is a cruel message. It reflects an unjustified degree of privatization of responsibility for dependents and for those who care for them. Its premise, though, is true. Parenting, or caring for one's own aging parents *with* a partner, is financially, physically, and practically easier than doing so on one's own. It is easier on the pocketbook, easier on the psyche, easier on the body, and better for the kids. How does a moral state respond to both of these truths—that the promotion of marriage can weaken our communal resolve to help people in need, while marriage itself can indeed make caregiving less risky? One response is to limit caregiving—parenting, and its joys—to those who have the means to first identify and then snag a partner with whom to share life's burdens. This seems unjust. Caregiving is a fundamental life activity; thrust upon many, chosen by some. It can consume a lifetime, whether joyously or not. It is labor that is essential to the perpetuation of community. To condition community support for it upon being "partnered" just seems wrong: a wrong to the individual, to the child, and to the community of which both are a part.

Another response, for which I have argued at length elsewhere,[3] would be to regard caregiving labor as something like what constitutional lawyers call a "fundamental interest," and then to construct the capacity to engage in such labor—and to do so without risking severe impoverishment—as a fundamental right of citizenship, and one that the state has a fundamental duty to promote. Anyone who cares for dependents—whether children, disabled, or the elderly—should have a right to do that caregiving work without risking life-threatening financial poverty by virtue of it. If that is right, then the state has a legitimate, indeed compelling, obligation to promote and protect families—whether headed by marriages or by civil unions—that come together to engage in that work. It also, though, has a fundamental duty to provide assistance to those caregivers who engage in this work *outside* marriage. The moral state response to both the efficacy and utility of civil union, and the injustice of abandoning those who give care outside of it to a life of relative misery, is for the state to both protect and promote civil unions, and to provide requisite material support to those caregivers who find themselves outside of it.

Currently, we do not regard parenting as a fundamental human interest, and we certainly don't regard individuals as having a basic human (or constitutional) right to engage in caregiving labor without risking impoverishment. We are as far from such an understanding as it is possible to be. To move toward a day when caregiving is regarded as essential human labor, deserving of communal respect and support, will require a reassessment of the value of this labor, to the community and to the individuals involved both. It will also, though, require demythologizing marriage. Marriage law and marriage rhetoric focuses the state's interest on the horizontal relation between the adults and their sexuality, rather than the vertical relation between the adult caregiver and the dependent. A movement away from marriage and toward civil union consciously constructed by state action, preserved through individual choice and action, might shift the state's attention, so as to better align it with the state's legitimate concern. It might, rhetorically, direct community concern toward the needs of caregivers, if our interest in families is identified exclusively as protecting the quality of care, rather than mixed with an interest in promoting a particular understanding of sexual morality. It might enliven our sense of caregiving as private and familial and individual labor in which we all have a profound interest.

Or—it might not. But the issue might be clarified. A state can and perhaps ought to promote marriage, or civil marriage, or civil union, or joint parenting, or same-sex marriage—marriage has a proven track record of improving the quality of contemporary men and women's lives. That promotion, however, must not and ought not come at the expense of efforts to end poverty, assist unmarried parents, find full employment for poor, unskilled, or only moderately skilled workers, increase the minimum wage so that it affords families a family wage, ensure health care for all, child care for those who need it, and so on. By shifting the debate from the morally charged questions that swirl around the "marriage wars" to a discussion of what states might or might not sensibly do to promote civil unions between would-be caregivers, we might rationalize the discussion. Even if we don't thereby redirect social resources toward the needs of those in economic need, we might at least redirect attention toward those needs, simply by putting our pitched battles over "marriage" in their proper place.

Civil Union and Marriage Equality: Some Contrasts

Let me briefly compare and then contrast the movement toward expanded civil union law that I am advocating with the current focus of our equality practice on the movement for same-sex marriage. A move toward an expansive civil union law, ideally, should also satisfy the demands of formal or legal justice that so strongly motivate the marriage equality movement. An expanded civil union law would take an even-handed and neutral approach to the sanctioning of our intimate associations that are dedicated toward the mutual provision of nurturant care. But a move toward universalized civil union, rather than universalized marriage, would also have the salutary effect of shedding sexuality from the state's sense of what it is that it's overseeing, when it oversees this institution. Otherwise, the quite real social utility of marriage would, and should, be borne by civil union as well. Marriage works, but so would civil union. A state-sanctified civil union would make participants as happy, healthy, and wealthy, as current marriage promotion advocates insist is true of marriage. The state could and should continue to send the message that this institution works. It would continue to have, as it currently has, a genuine and fully defensible interest in encouraging it, just as it has a legitimate interest in discouraging smoking and encouraging children to stay in school. Civil union law, though, unlike current marriage law and unlike even "equal marriage" open to gays and lesbians, could carry this message free of any moralistic and punitive punch. There would be no implicit argument that those who don't partake are immoral, by virtue of the sex they might enjoy outside the civil union. There would be no implicit argument that those who don't partake should be punished, or deterred from parenting, or in any other way marginalized. We can have socially utile institutions that don't penalize or shame nonparticipants. There's no reason civil union can't be such an institution.

The second reason for preferring civil union over marriage equality concerns the efficacy, and quality, of our critical *voice,* at least with respect to marriage law quite generally. Contrast, for a moment, the "civil union" arguments I've outlined above with the now-standard "formal rights" argument of the "marriage equality" movement. Gay and lesbian advocacy groups that have now identified gay marriage as the leading civil rights cause of our era are in a very particular historical moment: they can now see the right to marry as something that is *both* achievable and desirable—but note that for many, it is desirable, mainly, for the gain in formal justice it would constitute, rather than the value of the institution to which they would gain entrance.

The right to marry is being sought by these advocacy groups as a formal right to which they are entitled as a matter of justice. Same-sex relationships are functionally equivalent to heterosexual relationships, so there is just no good reason, albeit plenty of bad ones, to deny gay and lesbian couples wishing to marry the right to do so. As explored above, arguments for justice grounded in formal equality have a compelling necessity: the state *must* provide formal equality. There's a moral imperative behind these demands. There's no way *not* to comply with these demands, without denying equal respect and dignity to fully equal citizens of a commonwealth. However, the "full marriage equality" now being sought as a formal right, and so fervently by gay and lesbian advocates, comes at a huge cost to the coherence and the integrity of our critical practices. When advocates for gay marriage see the prize so close at hand, they lose—and so we all lose—their ability to think critically about the value of the prize that has so captured their gaze. It is hard to criticize the value of an institution, a practice, a school, or a marriage partner that one is so desperately trying to enter, or possess, particularly at the moment when the prize is finally within reach. The same may be true of the institution of marriage.

This is not peculiar to the campaign for same-sex marriage. In fact, it is such a recurrent pattern in legal reform movements that there is now a largely conventional explanation for its overall contours. An outgroup (blacks, women, sexual minorities, etc.) argues for their sameness to the ingroup so as to attain some right, benefit, or privilege. The argument rests on a claim of universality—the outgroup is just like the ingroup in all ways that should matter. The claim, though, is sometimes false and sometimes it really does come back to haunt you: the constitutional difficulties faced by affirmative action plans are a clear example. But that's not the only problem with formal equality arguments. The deeper problem is that arguments grounded in formal equality, virtually by necessity, rest on an assumption about the goodness, and even the overall fairness, of the institution, privilege, or benefit being sought—the fairness, that is, but for the challenged exclusion that itself, lo and behold, can be rectified by the stroke of the judicial pen. This assumption too, though, is often false, and can often—although it usually takes longer—come back to haunt all of us. The institution, benefit, privilege, etc., is "legitimated," "valorized," or more simply, just praised to high heaven by the outgroup seeking to rectify their unjust exclusion. At the end of the day, the end result of all this is that the outgroup may join the ingroup, but the institution's flaws—which may be thoroughgoing and deep—have become all the more hidden, all the more erased from public view; and the institution's victims all the more marginalized.

Let me illustrate this phenomenon with some examples, and then return to marriage. For decades, women sought entrance into Virginia Military Institute—a state-funded college for young men wishing to go into the military. The school excluded women. This practice was clearly unfair and unjust—there were plenty of women applicants as qualified as many of the male applicants. After years of arguing the point, the Supreme Court, in an opinion written by Justice Ruth Ginsburg, finally agreed with that simple proposition.[4] The school's exclusion of equally qualified young women was unconstitutional, she held; a violation of the Equal Protection Clause of the United States Constitution. This was a great victory, but again, look at the cost. What was lost, at least in the litigation and its aftermath, was the possibility of a sensible feminist critique of the value of a VMI education. There was such a critique circulating, and it did find its way into the litigation, but in the form of an amicus brief filed on behalf of the state, seeking to uphold the exclusion. Critique became regressive when it was so cojoined with, and put in service of, an end that was unappealing to both sides of this intrafeminist debate. The cost, then, of the VMI litigation was this: we lost the critique, when we gained access. The logic of formal equality—I'm like you, so I want access to whatever you have—virtually forced this result.

Take another gender-based example. Women are sometimes, allegedly, excluded from high-paying commission sales jobs on the basis of stereotypical assumptions about women's willingness to be on the road away from children for long periods of time, just as they are, allegedly, sometimes excluded from factory jobs on the basis of assumptions about purported harms that factory fumes or conditions might visit upon fetuses, should the workers happen to be pregnant. These sorts of exclusions seem unfair. Plenty of women would do quite well in high-commission sales jobs, and plenty of women factory workers are not pregnant and have no intention of becoming so. It is also a violation of the law to exclude women from these jobs on these grounds. What we lose, though, when we litigate cases that raise these sorts of issues, is the critical voice. *Is* it a good thing, for mothers or fathers, to take a high-paying commissioned job that forces long leaves from one's small children? Is it a good thing to incentivize sales jobs in this way in the first place? Is it okay for workers of either sex, pregnant or not, to work in factories that may be harmful to fetal life? More generally: by virtue of "formal equality" arguments, blacks and women have gained access to meritocratic workplaces and school institutions where human worth is measured by grades, or billable hours, claiming strenuously that women and blacks are as qualified as white men to be judged by comparable standards. But what is the worth of that meritocracy? Is it a good thing? It's hard to say it's a bad thing, or even question whether it's a good thing, while protesting the unfairness of one's own exclusion. Again—where we keep our eye on the prize, and the prize is access to jobs, military institutes, professional schools—it's just hard, maybe impossible, to also maintain a critical voice with respect to the value of the prize. Formal equality arguments are often worth their price. But it is important that we be cognizant of the price they exact. Sometimes, it might not be worth it.

Now, with respect to marriage. Is the price of this particular formal equality argument too high, if it comes at the sacrifice of our critical capacity? It might be. The prize might just not be all that worthy, and the critical voice we're tossing overboard in order to win might be just too valuable. Look at what the formal equality argument requires. "My committed, long-term, sexual relationship is just like your committed, long-term, sexual relationship. Whatever reason the state has for valorizing your relationship also extends to mine." Maybe that's true. But what if the state's reason for valorizing long-term committed heterosexual relationships is unjust in the first place? By including gays and lesbians within the circle of "good sexual relations" we will have corrected an injustice. But we will have further entrenched the habit of regarding "sexuality" as the key to the state's interest in families, rather than the quality of caregiving that occurs within them. It's not at all obvious that flame is worth the candle.

How much of a worry is this? It's hard to say. Concerns here about "legitimation costs" sound awfully precious and more than a little self-serving, from the perspective of gay and lesbian couples, socially reviled for most of their adulthoods, and on the verge of a symbolic success that could, over time, improve immeasurably the quality of their lives. Formal equality carries legitimation costs, but it also has an irreducible value. It really *is* wrong—in fact, it's too wrong to tolerate—to expel members of the community from the embrace of social acceptance on the facetious grounds that *their* sexuality, *their* relationships, *their* ability to parent, and so on, is just not quite up to snuff. That inequality—formal, substantive, or otherwise—causes real harms, leads to real insult and injury, and is grounded in centuries of hate. It can't be tolerated. It can be ended. Formal equality, constitutional argument, and so forth, is one sure-fire means of doing so.

But—to end this back-and-forth on a cliché—there's more than one way to skin a cat. We can provide formal equality by opening civil marriage to gay couples; or we can provide formal equality by opening civil union to straight couples. The latter, I believe, has to date unexplored potential for furthering a critically constructive conversation, while preserving the utility, and promoting the justice, of institutions that promote intimate associations. It might also provide a measure of formal equality, without at least some of the well-known costs that at least sometimes attach to such arguments.

A final and purely political reason for preferring a struggle over expanded civil union, rather than a struggle over marriage equality, concerns our priorities. Not only conservative marriage proponents, but the gay and lesbian advocacy community as well, may have oversold marriage. Yes, there are gains to be had from marriage. But they're not all *that* great. Much of the "marriage premium" touted by marriage proponents can be had through responsible, publicly recognized, celebrated cohabitation. Marriage can help bring some people out of poverty, but not all that far, and whatever modest gains it achieves in that regard might be outweighed by the considerable legitimation costs borne by those living in the poverty that remains. "Marriage equality now" would likely bring about a huge gain in the perceived social respectability and acceptance of same-sex couples—in fact, this might be the one clear gain to be had through this struggle, were it to be successful. But "marriage equality" is not going to happen "now," and it looks increasingly likely that the marriage equality movement might even prove counterproductive toward that end. A gradual, modest, grassroots, state-by-state, democratic, and individualized process of social reform might in fact be the faster route toward equal regard for gay and lesbian citizens. The marriage equality movement carries with it the danger of not only legitimating an awful lot of social injustice, but of actually rolling back progressive gains in a wide range of areas—including social and legal reforms directly aimed at improving the equality and liberties of gays and lesbians as well as persons of any or no sexual orientation in nonstandard family structures.

That might be a cost worth absorbing, if the prize is worthy. Here, though, the cost might not be worth absorbing, and the prize not quite so worthy. The prize might not be worthy, though, *not* because marriage—the prize—is fundamentally unjust. Marriage is indeed unjust, but it can and should be made just. Rather, the prize here might not be worth the costs of winning it, because the prize is just not sufficiently *consequential*. Marriage is good for participants. It is a good way to live, and it ought to be made more available. But it isn't all *that* good. It is not the be-all and end-all. It isn't as good as food, clothing, and shelter for the poorest among us, who have no right to any of those. It isn't as good as a quality education would be, for those without it. It isn't as good as a living family wage or universal health care. It isn't as good as a healthier environment, or a better foreign policy would be. If there are trade-offs between these goods, then those trade-offs matter in determining the preferred direction of our equality practice. A shift toward expanding civil union laws, where they exist, in a way that does not directly threaten traditional marriage but does provide an alternative to it, might bring our equality practice in line with defensible progressive politics more generally. It might also be a goal that is more proportional to the magnitude of the harm and the injustice that calls our attention.

On Civic Modesty

Let me end by defending the modesty of this proposal. There are two ways in which the proposal is a modest one. Both, I think, cut in its favor. First, the point of the civil union movement, like the point of the marriage equality movement, would be to democratize marriage, or civil union, or whatever we call the legal structures we design so as to facilitate caregiving. The methods used to achieve it, though, would be small-bore democratic—state-by-state legislative initiatives and individualistic—individual choice. It would not be through the high-profile, high-stakes, antimajoritarian route of individualistic rights, grounded in equality, liberty, and identity, articulated and enforced by the nondemocratic branch. The aim would not be to alter, forever, our foundational, constitutional law. The aim would be to resolve this political question in a direction that may be marginally fairer than the status quo.

Second, a debate that centers on civil union, rather than equal marriage, might be more civil in the most old-fashioned sense. The proposal is not that we abandon marriage and replace it with civil union. Rather, the proposal is that we provide all citizens who wish to civilly unite in a public ceremony that recognizes their desire to provide mutual care and support for each other and their dependents, the opportunity to do so. For heterosexual couples, then, there would be an option: they can marry, or they can civilly unite. The difference is that "civil union" would be open to all such couples, regardless of sexual orientation, regardless of the gender of the parties or the clarity of the parties' gender, and regardless of the presence of a sexual relationship. Marriage, by contrast, would retain whatever entrance requirements are currently in place.

Let me suggest an analogy. Today, a woman can choose to keep her surname, or adopt her husband's, when she marries. Women fifty years ago did not understand themselves as having such an option. The choice the modern bride makes regarding her name doesn't matter much, but the fact that she understands that she has a choice is of huge symbolic importance. Likewise, here, the proposal is that a heterosexual couple be able to choose marriage or civil union. The difference at the clerk's desk would be the difference between the yellow form or the blue form. The symbolic difference, however, might be substantial, as might be the impact of such a choice on our politics.

Why would a straight couple choose civil union over marriage? It would depend, I would imagine, on the direction of our "equality practice." They might do so out of a desire to express solidarity with their gay and lesbian friends, neighbors, and co-citizens. They might do so out of a desire to embrace what is right about marriage and distance themselves from what is wrong: this is what was behind the decisions so many of us made in the last quarter of the last century to keep our father's last name and not assume our husband's—and to do so in spite of the perfectly obvious political futility (this man's name or that man's name) and the equally obvious future practical difficulties involved in that choice. They might do so out of a desire to underscore the secularity of their union—civil union, unlike civil marriage, would have no linguistic connection to religiously organized marriage, and its quite different understanding of the point, meaning, and value of marriage. They might do so in recognition of the political nature of the private entity they are making: a union of the two of them, but a "civil" union, implicating, and facilitated by, the state, the community, and civil society.

Why would any of this help our civility? Primarily, because this is not a call to end marriage—or to change its meaning by changing its entrance requirements. It is, rather, a call to give people who can't marry but want to do so the right to civilly unite, and give people who can marry the civil union option as an alternative. The goal is for the "social norm" to evolve from civil marriage to civil union, but to do so in two major steps: first through the collective political act necessary to put civil union on the books as an option, but then, second, through the collective weight of many individual decisions made over time. Civil marriage would survive, and maybe for a very long time, but again, depending on the direction of our equality practice, it would eventually become something like a quaint option, really appealing only to highly "traditional" people. For other straight couples, the choice would be either inconsequential, or, maybe, quite important for its symbolic content—but in all cases, not fraught with fear, loathing, or deep anxiety.

Imagine newly married or united couples responding in these ways to the question: "Did you marry, or civilly unite?" "We got married rather than civilly united, but for the life of me I can't remember why." "I don't have the foggiest idea which we did. Which color form was which?" "Oh my parents married, and so did my sister, but I wanted a civil union. I don't really know why." "I wanted a civil union but my fiancé's parents would have been really upset, so just to reassure them, we married instead. But it's no big deal; it doesn't matter to us at all." "We married. We felt like that would connect us more with our parents and grandparents, and we wanted that." "We got a civil union, because we wanted to be married, but we didn't want all that historical baggage—yuck." "We civilly united because it just seems fairer. Marriage is sooooooo exclusionary." We have conversations much like these now, in fact, about our children's last names. "Oh they've got my husband's last name. It mattered to him hugely, but didn't really matter to me." "My name, all the way. Was he the one pregnant for nine months?" "They've got both our names, hyphenated." "My name—it's easier, dealing with schools and stuff." "His name, but we use mine, because he's on my insurance policy and it's easier." "My name—we've got to break this historical thing somehow!" "His name—I never really thought about it." And so on. Those conversations haven't swung national elections or perverted the mission and point of a major political party. But they are part of a substantial cultural evolution.

We could, possibly, diffuse the "marriage wars" in a similar way. You say potahto, I say potato. You say marriage, I say civil union. Some of us who civilly unite would have done so because we opted for it over marriage; some because marriage was not available. But many of us, over time, will be civilly united rather than married, and for virtually every transaction, virtually every day, it wouldn't matter all that much which. Over time, as the numbers of the civilly united increase, it might not matter why, either. It might, at that point, become the norm.

My modest proposal is only that we include this as an option in our ongoing deliberations over how best to press our equality practice. Rather than push for an expansion of marriage, so as to include gays and lesbians, push instead for an expansion of civil union, so as to include both nonconjugal unions and straight couples that opt for it. And—do it through local and national politics, not fundamental, constitutional law. Civil union, expanded for all, would give us a way to have a constructive and local conversation about the point of intimate association, and the basis for the state's interest. It would not be discriminatory. It would not be grounded in a religious and cultural institution, the point of which was historically the begetting of children, and the cabining of the heterosexual behavior that creates them. Once on the books, such a civil union law could eventually be expanded, if a community saw fit, to include partnerships of caregivers in units greater than two.[5] It would not have the punitive and moralistic undertow of civil marriage. It could be cleanly defined so as to make perfectly transparent the state's utter lack of interest in the sexuality and the sexual relations, or nonrelations, of the caregiving couple. It would have the utility of marriage but without the exclusionary and punitive sting for nonparticipants.

Civil union laws have already had these positive effects, to a limited degree. They have triggered a national conversation about the nature of the state's interest in marriage and union both, and what we, as citizens, ought to expect from that public institution. But we haven't gotten from them all they have to offer—and it is not only because they are still as rare as a bald eagle. We've not gotten their full promise in part because even those who have pushed so hard for them want them only as a temporary measure, and not an end in themselves. They're viewed by their supporters as the ultimate sunset laws: after we all wake up, smell the coffee, and extend marriage to same-sex couples, this ugly step-sibling will be retired. I think this conventional wisdom—or, the conventional wisdom in the quite unconventional world of GLBT legal advocacy—has it exactly backward. We could and should keep both these step-siblings around for a good long time. If we do so, I think we might discover that civil union, in the long run, is more just, more utile, and more civil, than civil marriage. It more perfectly expresses the true nature of the state's interest in our intimate and personal associations. It is open to change; it is intentionally malleable.[6] It is really *quite attractive,* as institutions go. Why would we want to view it as transitional? Maybe we should regard *marriage* as the "transitional institution": historically rooted in irrational traditions, imposed for centuries on unreflective boys and powerless girls, serving rarely explicated and never well-understood state needs for eugenics, population control, female subordination, and sexual discipline. A grown-up society can and should do better. By contrast to marriage, civil union law looks like a keeper.

Notes

Notes to the Introduction

1. The differences between fault-based divorce and the no-fault reform statutes that swept the country in the 1970s and early 1980s are critically discussed in Lenore Weitzman, *The Divorce Revolution* (New York: Free Press, 1985), pp. 1–51.

2. Ibid., pp. 16–17.

3. See generally Lynn D. Wardle, "Is Marriage Obsolete?" *Mich. J. Gender and L.* 10 (2003): 189–235, and the wealth of authorities cited therein. The major repositories of data pertaining to family, divorce, and remarriage include the Centers for Disease Control and Prevention; National Center for Health Statistics, Births, Marriages, Divorces, and Deaths; National Vital Statistics Report, available at http://www.cdc.gov/nchs/products/pubs/pubd/nvsr/nvsr.htm; and the U.S. Census Bureau, "America's Families and Living Arrangements," Current Population Reports, available at http://www.census.gov/main/www/cen2000.html. See also Lynn Wardle, "No-Fault Divorce and the Divorce Conundrum," *BYU L. Rev.* (1991): 79–142, 141; Stephen J. Bahr, "Social Science Research on Family Dissolution: What It Shows and How It Might Be of Interest to Family Law Reformers," *J.L. and Fam. Stud.* 4 (2002): 5–65; Andrew J. Cherlin, *Marriage, Divorce, Remarriage* (Cambridge: Harvard University Press, 1992).

Further data on the current statistical profile of marriage, as well as trends over the last four decades, can be found in *The State of Our Unions,* a yearly report generated by the National Marriage Project based at Rutgers University. *The State of Our Unions* reports annually on various topics of interest to researchers on marriage and the family, and includes current statistics regarding marriage, divorce, unmarried cohabitation, and the like. The National Marriage Project, in its own words, is a "nonpartisan, nonsectarian, and interdisciplinary initiative.... The project's mission is to provide research and analysis on the state of marriage in America and to educate the public on the social, economic, and cultural conditions affecting marital success and well-being." Its goals are to "(1) annually publish *the State of Our Unions* ... ; (2) investigate and report on younger adults' attitudes toward marriage; (3) examine the popular media's portrait of marriage; (4) serve as a clearinghouse resource of research and expertise on marriage; and (5) bring together marriage and family experts to develop strategies for revitalizing marriage." (Thus, the project is unabashedly promarriage.) Its report for 2006 contains essays chronicling the trends of the last four decades, including the overall decline in marriage rates, increase in divorce rates, increase in unmarried cohabitation, "loss of child centeredness," by which is meant the increased number of years married couples spend both before and after child-raising, thus leading to a change in the understanding of marriage as an institution centrally concerned with children to rather an institution centrally concerned with love and commitment, and lastly, the fragility of families with children in a society that is increasingly individualist and consumerist. Available at marriage@rci.rutgers.edu and http://marriage.rutgers.edu.

4. See generally Genaro C. Armas, "Cohabitation on the Rise: Unmarried Partner Households Increase by 72 Percent," May 15, 2001, available at http://cgi.jconline. com/cgi-bin/resend/printPage.pl?storypath=lafayettejc/Census/052004.shtml.

5. On New York's current status, see, Danny Hakim, "Panel Asks New York to Join the Era of No-Fault Divorce," *New York Times*, Feb. 7, 2006, p. A1. The move to no-fault divorce continues to spark debate, in part because it has had harmful consequences for many women, some of whom have been economically as well as psychically damaged by "divorce without cause." Women who have been traditional homemakers, and have no marketable skills, are arguably worse off in a no-fault regime than they are in a fault-based divorce system, where the amount of alimony was pegged to the fault of the nonmoving party. Professors Lenore Weitzman and Martha Fineman have both been longstanding critics of no-fault divorce from a feminist perspective. See Lenore Weitzman, *The Divorce Revolution: The Unexpected Economic Consequences for Women and Children in America* (New York: Free Press, 1985); Martha Fineman, *The Illusion of Equality: The Rhetoric and Reality of Divorce Reform* (Chicago: University of Chicago Press, 1994); Martha Fineman, *The Neutered Mother, the Sexual Family, and Other Twentieth-Century Tragedies* (New York: Routledge, 1995). But see Herbert Jacob, "Another Look at No-Fault Divorce and the Post-Divorce Finances of Women," *Law and Soc'y Rev.* 23 (1989): 95–115. Harvard law Professor Mary Ann Glendon has also been a critic of no-fault, on the grounds that it destroys a sense of moral responsibility, all in the name of individual "rights." See Mary Ann Glendon, *Rights Talk: The Impoverishment of Political Discourse* (New York: Free Press, 1989); Mary Ann Glendon, *The Transformation of Family Law* (Chicago: University of Chicago Press, 1989); Mary Ann Glendon, *Abortion and Divorce in Western Law* (Cambridge: Harvard University Press, 1989). Conservative family law scholars who are otherwise extremely critical of liberal divorce and its consequences, particularly for children, are, however, divided on the issue of whether we would be well advised to return to a fault-based system. For an enlightening debate on the topic between two critics of easy divorce, see Mary Gallagher and Barbara Whitehead, "End No-Fault Divorce?" *First Things* 75 (1997): 24–30.

6. See Margaret Brinig, "In Search of Prince Charming," *J. Gender Race and Just.* 4 (2001): 321–336; Douglas W. Allen and Margaret Brinig, "'These Boots Are Made for Walking': Why Most Divorce Filers Are Women," *Am. L. and Econ. Rev.* 2 (2000): 126–169; Douglas W. Allen and Margaret Brinig, "Sex, Property Rights, and Divorce," *Eur. J.L. and Econ.* 5 (1998): 211–233; June Carbone and Margaret Brinig, "Rethinking

Marriage: Feminist Ideology, Economic Change, and Divorce Reform," *Tul. L. Rev.* 65 (1991): 953–1010.

7. For a full discussion of this point, and a critique of the "clean break" theory of divorce that deemphasizes alimony payments in favor of property settlements, on the theory that it is best to give divorcing parties a clean break from the past, see Milton Regan, *Family Law and the Pursuit of Intimacy* (New York: New York University Press, 1993), pp. 38–39, 137–148.

8. *Griswold v. Connecticut*, 38 U.S. 479 (1965), pp. 485–486.

9. For a discussion of this development in its historical context, see Stephanie Coontz, *Marriage: A History: From Obedience to Intimacy or How Love Conquered Marriage* (New York: Viking Press, Penguin Group, 2005), pp. 253–257.

10. The Massachusetts Supreme Court held in *Goodridge v. Department of Public Health* that the State of Massachusetts could not foreclose the option of marriage to gay and lesbian couples under the Massachusetts Constitution. Statutory exclusion of gay and lesbian couples wishing to marry was therefore held to be unconstitutional. Consequently, same-sex marriage has been a feature of Massachusetts law and life since 2003. *Goodridge v. Department of Public Health*, 798 N.E.2d 941 (Mass. 2003).

11. Renwick McLean, "Spain Legalizes Same-Sex Marriage," *New York Times,* June 30, 2005.

12 By an act amending Book One of the Civil Code, December 21, 2000, concerning the opening up of marriage for persons of the same sex (Act on the Opening Up of Marriage); *Staatsblad van het Koninkrijk der Nederlanden* 9 (January 11, 2001).

13. The province of Ontario's highest court of appeals found the ban on same-sex marriage unconstitutional in *Halpern v. Canada*, 106 C.R.R.2d 329 (2003).

14. Partnership laws of one sort or another granting same-sex couples some of the same legal rights as married heterosexual couples are in place in Norway, Sweden, Greenland, Iceland, and Finland. For a good discussion of Scandinavia's step-by-step movement toward full recognition of the rights of same-sex couples, as well as that of a number of other European countries and Canadian provinces, see William Eskridge and Nan Hunter, *Sexuality, Gender, and the Law* (New York: West, 2003), pp. 1122–1138. William Eskridge argues elsewhere that the movement toward same-sex marriage (or, as it is often phrased by its advocates, "marriage equality") is and ought to be a part of a larger liberalizing movement in European and Western democracies toward giving individuals and couples a range of options from which to fashion their own, chosen, intimate relationships, and toward rationalizing the nature and extent of state involvement in those relationships. See William Eskridge, *Equality Practice: Civil Unions and the Future of Gay Rights* (New York: Routledge, 2002), pp. 121–126.

15. Thus, much of the Massachusetts Supreme Court decision was devoted to showing the nonexistence of meaningful differences between gay and lesbian couples wishing to marry and heterosexual couples wishing to do so. Finding no such sustainable difference (and no difference in the abilities of either set of couples to raise children), the court concluded:

> The marriage ban works a deep and scarring hardship on a very real segment of the community for no rational reason. The absence of any reasonable relationship between, on the one hand, an absolute disqualification of same-sex couples who wish to enter into civil marriage, and, on the other, protection of public health, safety, or

general welfare, suggests that the marriage restriction is rooted in persistent prejudices against persons who are (or who are believed to be) homosexual. The Constitution cannot control such prejudices but neither can it tolerate them. Private biases may be outside the reach of the law, but the law cannot, directly or indirectly give them effect.... Limiting the protections, benefits, and obligations of civil marriage to opposite-sex couples violates the basic premises of individual liberty and equality under law protected by the Massachusetts Constitution. (*Goodridge,* 798 N.E.3d, p. 968)

16. See *Loving v. Virginia,* 388 U.S. 1 (1967).

17. The contrast between these "formal equality" arguments for expanding marriage so as to include same-sex couples, and communitarian arguments for and against doing so, is detailed in William Eskridge, *Equality Practice: Civil Unions and the Future of Gay Rights* (New York: Routledge, 2002). I explore the difference in some detail in Chapter 4.

18. See Robert P. George, "Judicial Usurpation and Sexual Liberation: Courts and the Abolition of Marriage," *Regent U. L. Rev.* 17 (2004): 21–30; Robert P. George, "What's Sex Got to Do with It? Marriage, Morality, and Rationality," *Am. J. Juris.* 49 (2004): 63–85; John Finnis, "The Good Marriage and the Morality of Sexual Relations: Some Historical and Philosophical Observations," *Am. J. Juris.* 42 (1997): 97–134; Robert P. George, "Making Children Moral: Pornography, Parents, and the Public Interest," *Ariz. St. L.J.* 29 (1997): 569–580; Patrick Lee and Robert P. George, "What Sex Can Be: Self-Alienation, Illusion, or One-Flesh Union," *Am. J. Juris.* 42 (1997): 135–210; Robert P. George and Gerard V. Bradley, "Marriage and the Liberal Imagination," *Geo. L.J.* 84 (1995): 301–320.

19. See discussion and citations in Chapter 2.

20. *Loving v. Virginia,* 388 U.S. 1 (1967); *Griswold v. Connecticut,* 381 U.S. 479 (1965); *Poe v. Ullman,* 367 U.S. 497 (1961) (Harlan, J., dissenting); *Meyer v. Nebraska,* 262 U.S. 390 (1923).

21. Thus, it is significant that the first substantial claim made in Justice Marshall's decision in *Goodridge* is that civil marriage is entirely a creation of the state (*Goodridge,* 798 N.E.3d, pp. 954–955).

22. Justice Marshall made it clear in *Goodridge* that what was at stake was the fate and meaning of civil marriage, which she took pains to define as an institution completely created by state law rather than any particular religion's understanding of the meaning of marriage (*Goodridge,* 798 N.E.2d, pp. 954–955).

23. 42 U.S.C. § 2000(e)(2)(a) "It shall be an unlawful employment practice for an employer (1) to fail or refuse to hire or to discharge any individual, or otherwise to discriminate against any individual with respect to his compensation, terms, conditions, or privileges of employment, because of such individual's race, color, religion, *sex,* or national origin; or (2) to limit, segregate, or classify his employees or applicants for employment in any way which would deprive or tend to deprive any individual of employment opportunities or otherwise adversely affect his status as an employee, because of such individual's race, color, religion, *sex,* or national origin" (emphasis added).

24. The Court has found a number of state and federal laws that differentiate on the basis of sex to be unconstitutional, under what is called a "mid-level scrutiny" test: any such discriminating statute must be such as to meet a legitimate state goal, with the

"fit" judged by a fairly demanding test (not as rigid a test as racially discriminatory laws, but nevertheless, more rigorous than the test applied in adjudging the constitutionality of state or federal laws that do not touch on race or sex). See, for example, *Craig v. Boren*, 429 U.S. 190 (1976); *Geduldig v. Aiello*, 417 U.S. 484 (1974); *Frontiero v. Richardson*, 411 U.S. 677 (1973); and *Reed v. Reed*, 404 U.S. 71 (1971).

25. See the Supreme Court's infamous decision in *Bradwell v. Illinois*, a late nineteenth-century case upholding the constitutionality of an Illinois law barring women from the practice of law, for a succinct expression of this nineteenth-century view:

> The constitution of the family organization, which is founded in the divine ordinance, as well as in the nature of things, indicates the domestic sphere as that which properly belongs to the domain and functions of womanhood. The harmony, not to say identity, of interest and views which belong, or should belong, to the family institution is repugnant to the idea of a woman adopting a distinct and independent career from that of her husband. So firmly fixed was this sentiment in the founders of the common law that it became a maxim of that system of jurisprudence that a woman had no legal existence separate from her husband, who was regarded as her head and representative in the social state.... [A] married woman is incapable, without her husband's consent, of making contracts which shall be binding on her or him. ...
>
> It is true that many women are unmarried and not affected by any of the duties, complications, and incapacities arising out of the married state, but these are exceptions to the general rule. The paramount destiny and mission of woman are to fulfill the noble and benign offices of wife and mother. This is the law of the Creator. And the rules of civil society must be adapted to the general constitution of things, and cannot be based upon exceptional cases. (*Bradwell v. Illinois*, 83 U.S. 130, 141–42 [1873])

26. 42 U.S.C. § 2000(e)(2).

27. See, for example, *Price Waterhouse v. Hopkins*, 490 U.S. 228 (1989); *Rostker v. Goldberg*, 453 U.S. 57 (1981); *Craig v. Boren*, 429 U.S. 190 (1976); *Geduldig v. Aiello*, 417 U.S. 484 (1974); *Frontiero v. Richardson*, 411 U.S. 677 (1973); and *Reed v. Reed*, 404 U.S. 71 (1971).

28. In public life, the exclusion from combat in the military is the only significant remaining sex-linked distinction that the Supreme Court has not explicitly found unconstitutional. In employment, the only exceptions include those jobs where sex is in some sense biologically required for performance of the work, such as nursemaid or sperm donor.

29. As discussed elsewhere in this volume, this view of marriage continues to inform the natural law movement's understanding of marriage within Christianity, and also to guide its positions in the various debates over the meaning of civil marriage. See John Finnis, "Helping Enact Unjust Law without Complicity in Injustice," *Am. J. Juris.* 49 (2004): 11–42; John Finnis, "The Good of Marriage and the Morality of Sexual Relations: Some Philosophical and Historical Observations," *Am. J. Juris.* 42 (1997): 97–134; John Finnis, "Symposium: The Constitution and the Good Society: Virtue and the Constitution of the United States," *Fordham L. Rev.* 69 (2001): 1595–1602;

John Finnis, "On the Practical Meaning of Secularism," *Notre Dame L. Rev.* 73 (1998): 491–516.

30. For a good discussion of the importance of the evolving technology of contraception throughout the twentieth century to our understanding of marriage and contraception, see David J. Garrow, *Liberty and Sexuality: The Right to Privacy and the Making of Roe v. Wade*, updated with a new epilogue (Berkeley: University of California Press, 1998).

31. *Roe v. Wade,* 410 U.S. 113.

32. This is not to say that there are not dissenters from this view, only that the dissenters are far from the mainstream. Robert Bork famously argued against the liberty- or privacy-based right to noncontracepted sex that he saw in *Griswold,* as not warranted by the Constitution. Perhaps, he claimed, a law forbidding the use of contraception by married couples is unwise—he opined that he thought it was—but it is not for that reason alone unconstitutional. That single claim very likely cost Bork a seat on the Supreme Court. Since then, Bork's originalism has had a substantial comeback: there are more adherents to this view, and few if anyone treats originalism as a fringe view held only by other-worldly academics. Nevertheless, the specific claim Bork made regarding *Griswold* has not attracted contemporary supporters; indeed, that originalism means that *Griswold* is wrong, is now regarded as something of an embarrassment to originalists.

The literature on Robert Bork's confirmation hearing, and his failure to ascend to the High Court, is vast. For Bork's side of it, *see* Robert H. Bork, *The Tempting of America: The Political Seduction of the Law* (New York: Touchstone Books, 1990); for that of his antagonists, see, for example, Lawrence Tribe, *"Lawrence v. Texas:* The 'Fundamental Right' That Dare Not Speak Its Name," *Harv. L. Rev.* 117 (2004): 1893–1955; and Richard Posner, "Bork and Beethoven," *Stan. L. Rev.* 42 (1990): 1365–1382.

33. See Chapter 2 of this volume.

34. See Martha Fineman, *The Autonomy Myth: A Theory of Dependency* (New York: New Press, 2005); Martha Fineman, *The Neutered Mother, the Sexual Family, and Other Twentieth-Century Tragedies* (New York: New Press, 1995); Martha Fineman, *The Illusion of Equality: The Rhetoric and Reality of Divorce Reform* (Chicago: University of Chicago Press, 1994); Nancy Polikoff, "All Families Matter: What the Law Can Do about It," *Women's Rts. L. Rep.* 25 (2004): 205–209; Nancy Polikoff, "Making Marriage Matter Less: The ALI Domestic Partner Principles Are a Step in the Right Direction," *U. Chi. Legal F.* (2004): 353–379; Nancy Polikoff, "Ending Marriage as We Know It," *Hofstra L. Rev.* 32 (2003): 201–232; Martha Fineman, "Why Marriage?" *Va. J. Soc. Pol'y and L.* 9 (2001): 239–271; Nancy Polikoff, "We Will Get What We Ask for: Why Legalizing Gay and Lesbian Marriage Will Not 'Dismantle the Legal Structure of Gender in Every Marriage,'" *Va. L. Rev.* 79 (1993): 1535–1550.

35. See Chapter 2 of this volume.

36. See Kathryn Edin and Maria Kefalas, *Promises I Can Keep: Why Poor Women Put Motherhood before Marriage* (Berkeley: University of California Press, 2005).

37. See *Lawrence v. Texas,* 539 U.S. 558 (2003); *Eisenstadt v. Baird,* 405 U.S. 438 (1972); and *Griswold v. Connecticut,* 381 U.S. 479 (1965).

38. These arguments are catalogued and discussed in Chapter 3.

39. As I will discuss below in more detail, many family law scholars describe family law and marriage law as occupying a space "halfway between" "status" and "contract."

Much of our private law—meaning the law governing contract, tort, property, and so forth—went through a transformation in the nineteenth century, in which status-based norms were replaced by individualist "contract" norms. Family law, however, has been a holdout from this evolution. The law of "husband and wife" continues to be informed by "status"-type rules, and not solely by the contract or agreement entered into by the parties. This is changing somewhat: pre- and postnuptial agreements are now more enforceable than they were just twenty years ago; courts are more likely than they were thirty years ago to uphold surrogacy contracts; contracts between lovers for work and services, sometimes even sexual services, are occasionally upheld. Nevertheless, the transformation of "family law" from status to contract has been a good hundred years behind the rest of private law, leaving it an anomaly, in the eyes of many—the sole island of status-based legal obligations in a sea of responsibilities and rights otherwise determined solely by reference to contract, individual will, and parties' intent. For a full discussion, and a provocatively sympathetic reconstruction of the pure "status"-based marriage and family law regime of Victorian England and America, see Milton C. Regan, Jr., *Alone Together: Law and the Meanings of Marriage* (London: Oxford University Press, 1999), and Milton C. Regan, Jr., *Family Law and the Pursuit of Intimacy* (New York: New York University Press, 1993).

40. Jana Singer has long argued for a "partnership model" approach to the problem of the distribution of assets at the point of divorce. When couples divorce, courts should apply the principles and to some extent the rules governing the dissolution of a partnership, rather than the rules of alimony from divorce law. Among other things, she has argued, this would better protect the human capital women, and particularly traditional housewives, invest in marriage. That investment is still often not protected at the point of divorce, because of the rules of family law. It would be, however, under rules governing the dissolution of a partnership. See Jana Singer, "Husbands, Wives and Human Capital: Why the Shoe Won't Fit," *Fam. L.Q.* 31 (1997): 117; Jana Singer, "Divorce Obligations and Bankruptcy Discharge: Rethinking the Support/Property Distinction," *Harv. J. on Legis.* 30 (1993): 43–114; Jana Singer, "Divorce Reform and Gender Justice," *N.C. L. Rev.* 67 (1989): 1103–1121.

41. See Singer, note 40 *supra*.

42. See Edin and Kefalas, note 36 *supra*.

43. For an excellent discussion of the reliance of the gay and lesbian advocacy community on these liberal arguments of so-called formal equality, see William Eskridge, *Equality Practice: Civil Unions and the Future of Gay Rights* (New York: Routledge, 2002).

44. See Andrew Sullivan, *Virtually Normal: An Argument about Homosexuality* (New York: Vintage, 1995); William Eskridge, Jr., *The Case for Same-Sex Marriage: From Sexual Liberty to Civilized Commitment* (New York: Free Press, 1996); and Jonathan Rauch, *Gay Marriage: Why It Is Good for Gays, Good for Straights, and Good for America* (New York: Owl Books, 2004).

45. See Robin West, "Universalism, Liberal Theory, and the Problem of Gay Marriage," *Fla. St. U. L. Rev.* 25 (1998): 705–730; Nan Hunter, "Marriage, Law and Gender: A Feminist Inquiry," *Law and Sexuality* 1 (1991): 9–30.

46. See Linda McClain, *The Place of Families: Fostering Capacity, Equality, and Responsibility* (Cambridge: Harvard University Press, 2005).

Notes to Chapter One

1. Stephanie Coontz, *The Way We Never Were: American Families and the Nostalgia Trap* (New York: Basic Books, 1992); Stephanie Coontz, *The Way We Really Are: Coming to Terms with America's Changing Families* (New York: Basic Books, 1998); and Stephanie Coontz, *Marriage: A History* (London: Viking Press, 2005). See also Nancy Cott, *Public Vows: A History of Marriage and the Nation* (Cambridge: Harvard University Press, 2000); Dirk Hartog, *Man and Wife in America: A History* (Cambridge: Harvard University Press, 2000); Mary Shanley, *Feminism, Marriage, and the Law in Victorian England, 1850–1895* (Princeton, NJ: Princeton University Press, 1989).

2. Coontz, *The Way We Never Were*, note 1 *supra*, pp. 8–41.

3. Ibid., pp. 29–31.

4. Ibid., pp. 23–41.

5. Ibid., pp. 35–37. See generally Clare Dalton and Elizabeth Schneider, *Battered Women and the Law* (New York: Foundation Press, 2001), pp. 4–31 (summarizing work of historians of family violence of the twentieth century, including Linda Gordon, Elizabeth Pleck, Susan Schechter, and Reva Siegel).

6. See Susan Schechter, *Women and Male Violence: The Visions and Struggles of the Battered Women's Movement* (Cambridge: South End Press, 1982), pp. 20–24.

7. Not until well into the 1980s did women law students begin to protest the absence of rape and domestic violence from traditional criminal law and family law textbooks and courses. The case books and the courses began to change in the 1990s.

For examples of the change wrought in family law textbooks, compare Walter Wadlington et al., *Cases and Materials on Domestic Relations* (Menola, NY: Foundation Press, 1970), pp. 243–264 (hereinafter *Domestic Relations* [1970]) with Walter Wadlington, *Cases and Materials on Domestic Relations*, 3rd ed. (Westbury, NY: Foundation Press, 1995), pp. 238–264 (hereinafter *Domestic Relations* [1995]). In 1970, the casebook limited the discussion of violent crimes to spousal immunity and tort liability between spouses. The only mention of "rape" in the index refers to statutory rape and the only entry for "crimes between husband and wife" discusses a larceny charge (*Domestic Relations* [1970], p. 914). A more recent edition spends twenty-six pages discussing the erosion of spousal immunity and the increase in reported domestic violence (*Domestic Relations* [1995], pp. 238–264). Even the rare forward-looking casebooks that initially addressed domestic violence and rape have increased coverage over the past two decades. Compare Judith Areen, *Cases and Materials on Family Law* (Mineola, NY: Foundation Press, 1978), pp. 179–192 (hereinafter Areen [1978]) with Judith Areen and Milton C. Regan, Jr., *Family Law: Cases and Materials*, 5th ed. (New York: Foundation Press, 2006), pp. 281–345 (hereinafter Areen [2006]). Domestic violence spans sixty-four pages in Areen's fifth edition, while in the first edition it is covered in a then-impressive thirteen. Here the legal trends are more clearly seen: despite unusually long discussion of domestic violence in the first edition, marital rape is not explicitly mentioned. In the fifth edition marital rape is addressed through a lengthy excerpt from Jill Hasday's authoritative piece (ibid., pp. 281–288, excerpting Jill Elaine Hasday, "Contest and Consent: A Legal History of Marital Rape," *Cal. L. Rev.* 88 [2000]: 1373–1505).

For similar changes to criminal law textbooks, compare Sanford H. Kadish and Monrad G. Paulsen, *Criminal Law and Its Processes: Cases and Materials*, 2nd ed. (Boston:

Little, Brown, 1969) (hereinafter Kadish, *Criminal* [1969]) with Sanford H. Kadish and Stephen J. Schulhofer, *Criminal Law and Its Processes: Cases and Materials* 7th ed. (Gaithersburg, MD: Aspen, 2001) (hereinafter Kadish, *Criminal* [2001]). The 1969 edition spends one paragraph discussing a spousal rape case, *State v. Haines*, 25 So. 372, 372 (La. 1899), in a "problems" note to a larceny case (*State v. Hayes*, 16 S.W. 514 [Mo. 1891]), not so much for the crime of raping one's spouse but for illustrating culpability of a spouse in aiding and abetting. Nothing is mentioned of the court's decision to uphold spousal immunity (Kadish, *Criminal* [1969], p. 431). Earlier, when discussing the elements of rape, a lack of marital relationship is cited as the second element for rape, after "purpose to effect sexual relation" but before lack of consent (Kadish, *Criminal* [1969], p. 220). In the 2001 edition, however, the criminal category of rape covers over seventy pages: the first few pages discuss date rape, and five more pages are dedicated exclusively to the marital exemption (Kadish, *Criminal* [2001], pp. 313–366, 366–371). In addition to quoting the Model Penal Code commentary, Kadish cites the increasing number of reported marital rapes according to a well-known study from the mid-1980s. See Diana E. H. Russell, *Rape in Marriage* (New York: Macmillan, 1982).

8. See Elizabeth Schneider, *Battered Women and Feminist Lawmaking* (New Haven, CT: Yale University Press, 2000).

9. See, for example, 18 Pa. Cons. Stat. Ann. § 3121 (West 1984) "A person commits a felony of the first degree when he engages in sexual intercourse with another person not his spouse," repealed by Act of March 31, 1995, P.L. 985, No. 10, 1995 Pa. Legis. Serv. Sp. Sess. No. 1 10 (West 1995). Since the marital rape exception was a common-law rule, it was often only stated in court decisions and not statutes. Some of the more (in)famous court rulings are *Frazier v. State*, 86 S.W. 754, 755 (Tex. Crim. App. 1905) (finding no cause of action against the husband in a rape case); *State v. Haines*, 25 So. 372, 372 (La. 1899) (finding no charge against husband of raping his wife after he was found not to have aided and abetted her rape by a third party). See Kadish, *Criminal* (1969), note 7 *supra*, p. 220.

Rape is still defined in this way in the Model Penal Code, a criminal code authored by prominent lawyers and legal academics intended to serve as a model for state legislators. Model Penal Code § 213.1(1) note 8(c) (1980). Although in later editions the MPC claims to reject Hale's "generalized consent" argument relied upon by most courts, it nonetheless retains the exemption, reasoning that "the existence of a prior and continuing relation of intimacy ... is not irrelevant to the concerns of the law of rape." The commentary continues, appearing to contradict itself: "marriage or equivalent relationship ... does imply a kind of generalized consent that distinguishes *some versions* of the crime of rape from parallel behavior by a husband." Specifically, the code wishes to retain the exemption in cases where sexual intimacy would be considered statutory rape due to the age of the partners (ibid., p. 345). For responses to the Model Penal Code's inclusion of the marital rape exemption, see Deborah W. Denno, "Why the Model Penal Code's Sexual Offense Provisions Should Be Pulled and Replaced," *Ohio St. J. Crim. L.* 1 (2003): 207–218; Cassia C. Spohn, "The Rape Reform Movement: The Traditional Common Law and Rape Law Reforms," *Jurimetrics* 39 (1999): 119–130.

For a history of the marital rape exemption, see Jill Elaine Hasday, "Contest and Consent: A Legal History of Marital Rape," *Cal. L. Rev.* 88 (2000): 1373–1505. For critical commentary see Robin West, "Marital Rape and the Promise of the Fourteenth

Amendment," *Fla. L. Rev.* 42 (1990): 45–79; and Robin West, "Note: To Have and to Hold—The Marital Rape Exemption and the Fourteenth Amendment," *Harv. L. Rev.* 99 (1986): 1255–1273. See also Kelly C. Connerton, "Comment: The Resurgence of the Marital Rape Exemption—The Victimization of Teens by Their Statutory Rapists," *Alb. L. Rev.* 61 (1997): 237–283 (arguing that contemporary social services policies undermine attempts to prosecute statutory rape).

10. Betty Friedan, *The Feminine Mystique* (New York: W. W. Norton, 1963).

11. Ibid.

12. Coontz, *The Way We Never Were*, note 1 *supra*, pp. 10–15. Coontz's later work on the history of marriage spanning several centuries, rather than decades, emphatically makes this point. See Coontz, *A History of Marriage*, note 1 *supra*.

13. William Blackstone, *Commentaries* vol. 1, pp. 442–445.

14. See Hartog, note 1 *supra*.

15. Cott, note 1 *supra*.

16. See Hartog, note 1 *supra*, pp. 93–135; Cott, note 1 *supra*, pp. 7–8.

17. See Hartog, note 1 *supra*, pp. 103–115.

18. Ibid., pp. 115–122.

19. Ibid., p. 116.

20. Ibid.

21. See Hartog, note 1 *supra*, p. 116.

22. For reasons that are not entirely clear, Hartog does not examine chastisement in anything like the detail he gives to coverture, perhaps because he regards the chastisement doctrine as affecting only the relatively small number of marriages that we know to have been physically violent, but not so violent as to trigger criminal sanctions (whereas coverture affected, and profoundly, every marriage). From the cases Hartog does discuss, it seems that the U.S. courts were more hostile to the doctrine of chastisement than the English courts, rejecting, for example, the English rule that chastisement was reasonable so long as it was accomplished with a whip no wider than the breadth of a thumb. Nevertheless, Hartog argues, the U.S. courts and prosecutors were inclined to excuse husbands' abuse of their wives, if the abuse, in their eyes, was "provoked," or, particularly among the poor, if it was within the realm of the expected and unexceptional. This was often justified, though, not on the grounds of husbands' rights, but rather, on the more neutral-sounding grounds that the courts lacked institutional authority to intervene into the private sphere. See Hartog, note 1 *supra*, pp. 104–107.

Feminist legal historians over the last decade have given much greater prominence to both chastisement and to the marital rape exemption as constitutive of the meaning of Victorian marriage. Reva Siegel's work has been pioneering in this regard. See Reva Siegel, "The Rule of Love: Wife Beating as Prerogative and Privacy," *Yale L.J.* 105 (1996): 2117–2207. Jill Hasday has studied both the attempts of mid-nineteenth-century U.S. feminists to address women's physical disempowerment within their marriages, and the reasons that twentieth-century historians have for the most part failed to understand or credit that aspect of U.S. feminism. Hasday, note 9 *supra*. Mary Shanley has contributed a thorough treatment of domestic violence, marital rape, and chastisement in Victorian England, and the role of utilitarian and feminist reformers, such as John Stuart Mill and Harriet Taylor, in challenging it. Shanley, note 1 *supra*, pp. 156–188. According to Shanley, nineteenth-century English feminists clearly regarded both rape and domestic violence in marriage—meaning both marital rape and lawful chastisement as well as unlawful but unpoliced aggravated assault and murder—as central to the "subjection" of Victorian wives and to their political disempowerment. Those efforts, focused on establishing violence as sufficient grounds for divorce, relied heavily upon liberal principles of autonomy and individual respect (ibid.).

23. *Bradley v. State*, 1 Miss. (1 Walker) 156 (1824).

24. Ibid.

25. Siegel, note 22 *supra*, p. 2120.

26. Ibid.

27. Samuel D. Warren and Louis D. Brandeis, "The Right to Privacy," *Harv. L. Rev.* 4 (1890): 193–220, is widely regarded as the article that brought to the fore the newfound "right" to some measure of privacy. The article, however, sought to solidify and formalize a legal development that had been evolving for decades; the authors did not create something out of nothing (ibid., pp. 193–197).

28. Siegel, note 22 *supra*, pp. 2151–2161.

29. Women won the right to vote in the United States in 1920, when the last necessary state ratified the Nineteenth Amendment. Good histories of the struggle for suffrage, and of the feminist movement of Victorian America, include Joan Hoff, *Law, Gender, and Injustice: A Legal History of U.S. Women* (New York: New York University Press, 1991); Aileen S. Kraditor, *The Ideas of the Woman Suffrage Movement, 1890–1920* (New York: W. W. Norton, 1981 [1965]); and Anne F. Scott and Andrew M. Scott, *One Half the People: The Fight for Woman Suffrage* (Philadelphia: Lippincott, 1975).

30. The jury exclusion was not ruled unconstitutional until 1975. See *Taylor v. Louisiana*, 419 U.S. 522 (1975).

31. The executor rules were not challenged or ruled unconstitutional until 1971. See *Reed v. Reed*, 404 U.S. 71 (1971).

32. *Bradwell v. Illinois*, 83 U.S. (1 Wall.) 130, 141 (1872) (J. Bradley, concurring).

33. Ibid., pp. 141–142.

34. Ibid.

35. Married Women's Property Acts were passed in various states in the middle of the nineteenth century, partly as a result of concerted political efforts of organized feminists. Although, as Cott argues, the initial legislative purpose behind some of these acts was not so much to reverse the effects of the common-law rules of coverture, rather than to simply clarify the legal relations among and between different classes of men, nevertheless, they triggered an era of reform during which feminists had the coverture rules squarely in their sights, and coverture rules were indeed gradually eroded. See Cott, Public Vows, note 1 *supra*, pp. 52–55. A concise history of the acts can be found in Mary Becker, Cynthia Grant Bowman, and Morrison Torrey, *Cases and Materials on Feminist Jurisprudence: Taking Women Seriously* (St. Paul: West Group, 2001), pp. 6–9.

36. *Harris v. State*, 71 Miss. 462 (1894).

37. Reval Siegel, "Social Movement Conflict and Constitutional Change: The Case of the De Facto ERA," *Univ. of Cal. Law Review* 94 (2006): 1323–1419.

38. Stephanie Coontz, *Marriage: A History*, note 1 *supra*, pp. 222–228.

39. Nancy Cott, *Public Vows*, note 1 *supra*, pp. 174–179.

40. Siegel, note 22 *supra*, p. 2119.

41. See authorities cited in note 9 *supra*.

42. The Model Penal Code—a standard reference, consisting of model criminal laws drafted by legal academics, judges, and lawyers—has defined rape in such a way as to preserve the exemption, for its entire existence (see note 9 *supra*).

43. Many states that had criminalized abortion made exceptions for pregnancies that resulted from "rape," but those states also had marital rape exemptions. Therefore, pregnancy as a result of rape in marriage could not be terminated by abortion, where pregnancy as a result of rape outside of marriage could be. See generally Robin West, "West, J., Concurring in the Judgment," in *What Roe v. Wade Should Have Said* (New York: New York University Press, 2005).

44. Linda Gordon has provided the most thorough history, to date, of family violence and social responses to it. She identifies periods of social interest in domestic violence, as well as periods of relative lack of interest, or acquiescence. Briefly, she identifies the late nineteenth century, 1875–1910, as a period when family violence was construed as a moral problem, and charitable organizations, some of them influenced by feminism, organized movements against it. During the Progressive era, 1910–1930, family violence was understood as a social problem, and addressed by the then-nascent social work movement. During the Depression, family violence was deemphasized as economic hardship took center stage. During the 1940s and 1950s, profamily and promarriage values, combined with the rise of psychiatry, tended to either deemphasize violence out of a concern for family unity and harmony, or redefine it as a psychiatric problem. Not until the 1960s and 1970s, according to Gordon, did political pressures mount (mostly by feminists) to consider domestic violence as criminal, and the nonintervention of the state as a political problem, requiring a political solution (Linda Gordon, *Heroes of Their Own Lives: The Politics and History of Family Violence* [New York: Viking, 1988]). See also Susan Schechter, note 6 *supra*.

45. A good discussion of the history of intraspousal tort immunities—by virtue of which wives could not sue their husbands for compensation for the injuries inflicted on them—can be found in *Townsend v. Townsend*, 708 S.W. 2d 646 (Mo. 1986). In *Townsend*, the Supreme Court of Missouri overturned the immunity doctrine, thereby permitting a wife to sue her husband for the personal injuries she suffered when he shot her in the back with a shotgun, as he attempted to enter her home. The defendant had moved to dismiss the case, on the basis of the doctrine of intraspousal immunity. The court discussed the history of the doctrine, identifying it with the doctrine of coverture, marital union, and "identity of the spouses." The court then overturned the "archaic doctrine," permitting the suit to proceed.

46. See generally Wendy Williams, "Notes from a First Generation," *U. Chi. Legal. F.* (1989): 99–113, for an insider's autobiographical history of this development in the law, and the role of feminist litigators in bringing it to fruition.

47. See Susan Okin, *Gender, Justice and the Family* (New York: Basic Books, 1989). In this philosophical classic, Professor Okin famously asked how it is that families could be the seedbeds of virtue, when they were the sites of male dominance and female subordination. Okin opened up the question why it is that family life is not regarded as a fitting object of justice, and argued that it should be. Her claim has since been taken up, to great effect, by law professor and liberal feminist family law scholar Linda McClain,

among others. See Linda McClain, *The Place of Families: Fostering Capacity, Equality, and Responsibility* (Cambridge: Harvard University Press, 2006).

48. The exclusion of women from lists of potential jurors was ruled unconstitutional in *Taylor v. Louisiana*, 419 U.S. 522 (1975). See also *J.E.B. v. Alabama*, 511 U.S. 127 (1994).

49. This was ruled unconstitutional in *Reed v. Reed*, 404 U.S. 71 (1971).

50. The Supreme Court has generally upheld the power of Congress to hold an all-male draft, as well as the constitutionality of the exclusion of women from positions of combat. See *Rostker v. Goldberg*, 453 U.S. 57 (1981).

51. The Supreme Court has ruled that veterans' benefits statutes, which overwhelmingly favor men, are constitutional. See *Pers. Adm'r of Mass. v. Feeney*, 442 U.S. 256 (1979).

52. Private clubs and private schools enjoy First Amendment rights of association, which largely guarantee them the right to discriminate on the basis of gender, so long as they do not receive public funding. For a recent justification of this private discrimination, and the state's noninvolvement in it, see William Galston, "The Idea of Political Pluralism," *NOMOS* XLIX (New York: New York University Press, 2007); and for a response see Robin West, "Comment on William Galston's Liberal Pluralism," *NOMOS* XLIX (New York: New York University Press, 2007).

53. See Williams, note 46 *supra*.

54. For a full discussion of possible tensions between women's equality and religious liberty, see Mary Becker, "The Politics of Women's Wrongs and the Bill of Rights: A Bicentennial Perspective," *U. Chi. L. Rev.* 59 (1992): 453–517. For a more sympathetic description of the potential of religion to positively impact the quality of women's lives, but nevertheless with unmistakably oppressive dimensions, see Martha Nussbaum, *Women and Human Development: The Capabilities Approach* (Cambridge: Cambridge University Press, 2000), pp. 167–240.

55. Coontz, *Marriage: A History*, pp. 263–264; Coontz, *The Way We Never Were*, p. 15.

56. Coontz, *Marriage: A History*, p. 247.

57. Title IX of the Education Amendments of 1972, 20 U.S.C.A. § 1681(a)(1) (West 2006), prohibits most educational institutions receiving federal funds from discriminating on the basis of sex in regard to admissions and programmatic policies. The amendments require all grantor federal agencies to develop guidelines for the enforcement of this policy, and allow them to withhold funding from noncompliant institutions after notifying Congress and the noncompliant party (ibid., § 1682). The amendments also authorize suits to be filed under the APA (§1683).

58. This reform movement was led by Laura X, who founded the National Clearinghouse on Marital and Date Rape (NCMDR) as an advocacy and research group. Since Laura X has retired, the organization has been folded and the Web site is no longer updated. "Who We Are and What We Do" (2005), available at http://www.ncmdr.org (last visited August 1, 2006). For a brief autobiography of Laura X and a loose chronology of the reform movement, see Laura X, "Accomplishing the Impossible: An Advocate's Notes from the Successful Campaign to Make Marital and Date Rape a Crime in All Fifty U.S. States and Other Countries," *Violence Against Women* 9 (1999): 1064–1081, available at http://vaw.sagepub.com/content/vol5/issue9. For a more general historical

discussion of the reform movement and its implications, see Jill Hasday, note 9 *supra*; and Robin West, note 9 *supra*.

59. Coontz, *The Way We Never Were*, pp. 1–66, 148–179, and 254–288, presents, I believe, the best cultural and political history to date of the transformation in marriage from the 1950s to 1975. The themes explored in such detail in Coontz's texts are not at odds with accounts given by other historians as well. I have chosen to emphasize the changes in legal structure in part simply because Coontz, for the most part, does not. The cultural, political, and technological changes Coontz focuses on did not happen independently of changes in the law. Sometimes the legal changes merely reflected them, but sometimes they were conditions for them. Her discussion of the cultural transformation of the institution of marriage from the 1950s to the 1970s, in all other respects, is exhaustive. Nancy Cott's explanation of the differences in marriage between the 1950s and 1970s, albeit far more abbreviated than Coontz's, attends more closely to legal changes, and particularly to legal changes brought about through feminist legal reform. See Cott, *Public Vows*, pp. 194–211.

60. *Griswold v. Connecticut*, 381 U.S. 479 (1965), pp. 494–495.

61. *Eisenstadt v. Baird*, 405 U.S. 438 (1972).

62. *Roe v. Wade*, 410 U.S. 113 (1973).

63. 42 U.S.C. § 2000(e)(2).

64. *Roe v. Wade*, 410 U.S. 113 (1973).

65. Ibid.

66. 42 U.S.C. § 2000(e)(2).

67. Title IX of the Education Amendments of 1972, 20 U.S.C.A. § 1681(a)(1) (West 2006).

68. See, for example, *Reed v. Reed*, 404 U.S. 71 (1971) (statute creating preference for male executors struck as unconstitutional); *Frontiero v. Richardson*, 411 U.S. 677 (1973) (Air Force benefits rules that gave benefits to all wives of men, but only to economically dependent husbands of women in the Air Force struck as unconstitutional); *Stanton v. Stanton*, 421 U.S. 7 (1975) (statute creating different ages of majority for women and men struck as unconstitutional); *Craig v. Boren*, 429 U.S. 190 (1976) (statute creating gender-based rules regarding ability of young people to buy beer struck as unconstitutional); *Califano v. Goldfarb*, 430 U.S. 199 (1977) (Social Security provision giving benefits to widows automatically but requiring widowers to prove dependency on deceased wives, struck as unconstitutional); *Orr v. Orr*, 440 U.S. 268 (1979) (statute providing alimony for women but not men struck as unconstitutional); *United States v. Virginia*, 518 U.S. 515 (1996) (holding that the Virginia Military Institute must admit women).

69. Pregnancy Discrimination Act of 1978, Pub. L. No. 95-555, 92 Stat. 2076 (1978) (codified pp. 42 U.S.C.A. §2000e(k) (West 2006)), *Troupe v. May Department Stores Co.*, 20 F.3d 734 (7th Cir. 1994).

70. For critical views of the emphasis of second-wave feminists on antistereotyping and formal equality, see Mary Becker, "Prince Charming: Abstract Equality," *Sup. Ct. Rev.* 5 (1987): 201–247; and Christine Littleton, "Reconstructing Sexual Equality," *Cal. L. Rev.* 75 (1987): 1279–1337. For a sympathetic reconstruction of the reasons for this emphasis, see Wendy Williams, "Notes from a First Generation," *U. of Chi. Legal Forum* (1989): 99–113; and for an argument that in retrospect the strategy was a sound one,

see Wendy Williams, "Equality's Riddle: Pregnancy and the Equal Treatment/Special Treatment Debate," *Rev. of L. and Soc. Change* 13 (1984–1985): 325–380.

71. See, for example, Marjorie Maguire Shultz, "Reproductive Technology and Intent-Based Parenthood: An Opportunity for Gender Neutrality," *Wis. L. Rev.* (1990): 297–398.

Notes to Chapter Two

1. Contemporary advocates of this view include Robert P. George, professor of politics at Princeton, Gerard V. Bradley, professor of law at the University of Notre Dame, and John Finnis, professor of philosophy. *See* Robert P. George and Gerard V. Bradley, "Marriage and the Liberal Imagination," *Geo. L.J.* 84 (1995): 301–320; John Finnis, "Law, Morality, and Sexual Orientation," *Notre Dame L. Rev.* 69 (1994): 1049–1076; Gerard V. Bradley, "Life's Dominion: A Review Essay," *Notre Dame L. Rev.* 69 (1993): 29–91; Gerard V. Bradley, "Law and the Culture of Marriage," *Notre Dame J.L. Ethics and Pub. Pol'y* 18 (2004): 189–217; Gerard V. Bradley, "Same-Sex Marriage: Our Final Answer?" *Notre Dame J.L. Ethics and Pub. Pol'y* 14 (2000): 729–752; and Robert P. George, "Judicial Usurpation and Sexual Liberation: Courts and the Abolition of Marriage," *Regent U. L. Rev.* 17 (2004): 21–30.

2. The most prominent researchers on the effects of marriage on happiness, wealth, and health, who also unabashedly use this research to promote marriage as a social policy, are Linda Waite and Maggie Gallagher, *The Case for Marriage: Why Married People Are Happier, Healthier and Better off Financially* (New York: Doubleday, 2000). The literature, however, is vast, as discussed below.

3. The particular virtue theorists and communitarians I will discuss in this chapter also strongly support reform of marriage, so as to make it both more internally just and more inclusive. The arguments I will discuss in this chapter, however, are their defenses of marriage against various threats, and a caution that abandoning marriage because of its injustice or exclusivity would not be wise or justified. I take up their arguments and those of others for reforming marriage in Chapter 4 of this volume. *See* Mary Lyndon Shanley, ed., *Just Marriage* (Oxford: Boston Review Book, 2004); Milton Regan, Jr., *Alone Together: Law and the Meanings of Marriage* (New York: Oxford, 1999); and Milton Regan, Jr., *Family Law and the Pursuit of Intimacy* (New York: New York University Press, 1993).

4. William E. May, professor of moral theology at the Catholic University of America, explains in his essay "On the Impossibility of Same-Sex Marriage," available at http://www.christendom-awake.org/pages/may/homosex.htm, that magisterial teaching regarding the intrinsic, gravely immoral nature of homosexual acts, the impossibility of homosexual marriage, and the intrinsic goods of heterosexual marriage, is found, primarily in the *Catechism of the Catholic Church* (1993) and three documents of the Congregation for the Doctrine of the Faith: the "Vatican Declaration on Certain Questions of Sexual Ethics" (1975); "The Pastoral Care of the Homosexual Person" (1986); and "Considerations Regarding Proposals to Give Legal Recognition to Unions between Homosexual Persons" (2003).

5. See Robert P. George and Gerard V. Bradley, "Marriage and the Liberal Imagination," *Geo. L. J.* 84 (1995): 301–320.

6. Ibid., p. 301.

7. Ibid.

8. Ibid., p. 302.

9. Ibid.

10. Ibid., p. 305.

11. Ibid., p. 306.

12. Ibid., p. 314.

13. Ibid., p. 302.

14. Ibid., pp. 311–312 (quoting Germain Grisez, "The Christian Family as Fulfillment of Sacramental Marriage," paper presented at the Society of Christian Ethics Annual Conference, September 9, 1995 [unpublished manuscript, on file with the *Georgetown Law Journal*]).

15. George and Bradley, note 5 *supra*, p. 309.

16. Ibid., p. 309.

17. Ibid., p. 313.

18. Ibid., pp. 313–314.

19. Stephen Macedo, "Homosexuality and the Conservative Mind," *Geo. L. J.* 84 (1995): 261–300.

20. See Stephen Macedo, "Reply to Critics," *Geo. L. J.* 84 (1995): 329–337.

21. Ibid., pp. 331–334.

22. George and Bradley, note 5 *supra*, p. 307.

23. And, if such stimulative (rather than reproductive-type) acts are undertaken *for the purpose* of providing pleasure to the wife, they are immoral, as would be any other sodomitic act undertaken by even married partners (such as masturbation, mutual masturbation, or oral stimulation of either partner's genitalia):

> Now, this is by no means meant to suggest that pleasure is bad. Rather, its value depends on the moral quality of the acts in which pleasure is sought and taken. In morally good acts, pleasure is rightly sought as an experiential aspect of the perfection of persons' participation in the basic goods that provide reasons for their acts. Integrated with the good of marriage … pleasure is rightly sought and welcomed as part of the perfection of marital intercourse.… However, to simply instrumentalize intercourse to pleasure … is to vitiate its marital quality and damage the integrity of the genital acts even of spouses. (ibid., p. 315)

24. Mary Becker, "Women, Morality, and Sexual Orientation," *UCLA Women's L.J.* 8 (1998): 165–218, 188–191.

25. Chai Feldblum, "Gay Is Good: The Moral Case for Marriage Equality and More," *Yale J.L.and Feminism* 17 (2005): 139–184, 183–184.

26. See generally Jill Elaine Hasday, "Contest and Consent: A Legal History of Marital Rape," *Cal. L. Rev.* 88 (2000): 1373–1505; Reva B. Siegel, "The Rule of Love: Wife Beating as Prerogative and Privacy," *Yale L.J.* 105 (1996): 2117–2207.

27. On unwanted sex or sexual advances at work, see Catharine MacKinnon's groundbreaking work, *Sexual Harassment of Working Women: A Case of Sex Discrimination* (New Haven, CT: Yale University Press, 1979). On the marital rape exemption, see

Robin L. West, "Equality Theory, Marital Rape, and the Promise of the Fourteenth Amendment," *Fla. L. Rev.* 42 (1990): 45–79.

28. See, for example, the rich review of female sexuality in the encyclopedic *Our Bodies, Ourselves,* first published as a full length book in 1973 by the Boston Women's Health Book Collective, recently reissued in its twelfth edition. See also, for a range of essays on the value and importance of female sexual pleasure by a "sex positive feminist," Carol Vance, ed., *Pleasure and Danger: Exploring Female Sexuality* (New York: Thorsons Publishers, 1990).

29. Andrea Dworkin, *Intercourse* (New York: Free Press, 1987).

30. Dworkin emphasizes this point in *Intercourse,* note 29 *supra,* pp. 122–127.

31. Although the law on searches of bodily cavities is complex and conflicted, the Court has clearly stated that such searches implicate constitutional considerations. Thus, in *Schmerber v. California* the Court announced that the Fourth Amendment's "proper function is to constrain ... intrusions which are not justified in the circumstances, or which are made in an improper manner" (*Schmerber v. California,* 383 U.S. 757 [1966], p. 768). Though in *Schmerber* the Fourth Amendment did not protect the plaintiff's interest in bodily integrity from a blood test, the interest in bodily integrity and "human dignity" has protected individuals from "offensive" and "brutal" methods of evidence gathering, such as forcible expulsion of digestive material and from unwanted surgeries intended to reveal evidence (*Rochin v. California,* 342 U.S. 165 [1952], p. 174; *Winston v. Lee,* 470 U.S. 753 [1985]). *Winston* also articulated the Court's belief that physical intrusions implicate "[the] most personal and deep-rooted expectations of privacy" (p. 760).

32. One basic point of contention between Bradley and George, on the one hand, and Macedo on the other, regards the moral status of pleasure generally. For Bradley and George, pleasure should never be a basic reason for acting, although it may be innocent if integrated in other acts that are intrinsically moral. Macedo argues to the contrary. This has obvious implications for their views on the morality of nonreproductive sodomitic acts. See Bradley and George, note 5 *supra,* p. 315; and Macedo, note 19 *supra,* p. 335.

33. George and Bradley, note 5 *supra,* pp. 313–316.

34. See generally Robin West, "The Harms of Consensual Sex," *Am. Phil. Ass'n. Newsl.* 94 (1995): 52–53.

35. Waite and Gallager, note 2 *supra*; Maggie Gallager, "Why Marriage Is Good for You," *City Journal* (Autumn 2000): 76–82, available at http://www.city-journal.org/html/10_4_why_marriage_is.html. Linda Waite and Evelyn Lehrer, "The Benefits from Marriage and Religion in the United States: A Comparative Analysis," *Population and Dev. Rev.* 29, no. 2 (June 2003): 255–275; Linda Waite, "Does Marriage Matter?" *Demography* 32, no. 4 (November 1995): 483–507; John Witte, "The Goods and Goals of Marriage," *Notre Dame L. Rev.* 76 (2001): 1019–1071.

36. Waite and Gallager, note 2 *supra,* pp. 124–140.

37. Ibid., pp. 65–77. See also Allan V. Horwitz, Helen Raskin White, and Sandra Howell-White, "Becoming Married and Mental Health: A Longitudinal Study of a Cohort of Young Adults," *J. of Marriage and Fam.* 58, no. 4 (November 1996): 895–907; Steven Stack and Ross Eshleman, "Marital Status and Happiness: A 17 Nation Study," *J. of Marriage and Fam.* 60, no. 2 (May 1998): 527–536.

38. Waite and Gallager, note 2 *supra*, pp. 78–96.

39. Ibid., pp. 69–70.

40. Ibid., p. 75.

41. Ibid., pp. 107–109. See also Pamela Smock, Wendy Manning, and Sanjiv Gupta, "The Effect of Marriage and Divorce on Women's Economic Well-Being," *Am. Soc. Rev.* 64, no. 6 (December 2000): 794–812; Hao Lingxin, "Family Structure, Private Transfers, and the Economic Well-being of Families with Children," *Soc. Forces* 75, no. 1 (September 1996): 269–292.

42. Waite and Gallagher, note 2 *supra*, pp. 99–105. See also Joni Hersch and Leslie S. Stratton, "Household Specialization and the Male Marriage Wage Premium," *Indus. and Lab. Rel. Rev.* 54, no. 1 (October 2000); Stephen Nock, "Why Not Marriage?" *Va. J. Soc. Pol'y and L.* 9 (2001): 273–290.

43. Waite and Gallagher, note 2 *supra*, pp. 111–114.

44. Ibid., p. 111. See also L. Remez, "Married Mothers Fare the Best Economically, Even if They Were Unwed at the Time They Gave Birth," *Fam. Plan. Persp.* 31, no. 5 (October 1999): 258–259; and Steven Nock, "Why Not Marriage?" *Va. J. Soc. Pol'y and L.* 9 (2001): 273–290, 285.

45. Waite and Gallagher, note 2 *supra*, pp. 106, 108, 118–120. See also Pamela Smock, Wendy Manning, and Sanjiv Gupta, "The Effect of Marriage and Divorce on Women's Economic Well-Being," *Am. Soc. Rev.* 64, no. 6 (December 2000): 794–812; and Lenore J. Weitzman, *The Divorce Revolution: The Unexpected Social and Economic Consequences for Women and Children in America* (New York: Free Press, 1985).

46. Waite and Gallagher, note 2 *supra*, pp. 115–116.

47. Waite and Gallagher, note 2 *supra*, pp. 47–64. See also Robert H. Commbs, "Marital Status and Personal Well-Being: A Literature Review," *Fam. Rel.* 40 (1991): 97–102; Lee A. Lillard and Linda Waite, "'Til Death Do Us Part: Marital Disruption and Mortality," *Am. J. Sociol.* 100 (1995): 1131–1156; and Lynn Wardle, "Is Marriage Obsolete?" *Mich J. Gender and L.* 10 (2003): 189–235, for a review of studies.

48. Waite and Gallagher, note 2 *supra*, pp. 52–56. See also Linda Waite, "Does Marriage Matter?" *Demography* 32, no. 4 (November 1995): 483–507.

49. Waite and Gallagher, note 2 *supra*, pp. 53–57.

50. Ibid., pp. 59–61.

51. Ibid., pp. 150–160.

52. One researcher, Maggie Gallagher, has succinctly summarized on a Web page the benefits of marriage identified by her own and Linda Waite's research, in a Letterman-style "top ten" list of reasons that "marriage is good for you:"

Top Ten Reasons Why Marriage Is Good for You:

10. IT'S SAFER. Marriage lowers the risk that both men and women will become victims of violence, including domestic violence. A 1994 Justice Department report, based on the National Crime Victimization Survey, found that single and divorced women were four to five times more likely to be victims of violence in any given year than wives; bachelors were four times more likely to be violent-crime victims than husbands.

9. IT CAN SAVE YOUR LIFE. Married people live longer and healthier lives. ...

8. IT CAN SAVE YOUR KID'S LIFE. Children lead healthier, longer lives if parents get and stay married.

7. YOU WILL EARN MORE MONEY.... Married men make, by some estimates, as much as 40 percent more money than comparable single guys, even after controlling for education and job history. The longer a man stays married, the higher the marriage premium he receives. Wives' earnings also benefit from marriage, but they decline when motherhood enters the picture. Childless white wives get a marriage wage premium of 4 percent, and black wives earn 10 percent more than comparable single women.

6. DID I MENTION YOU'LL GET MUCH RICHER? Married people not only make more money, they manage money better and build more wealth together than either would alone.... On the verge of retirement, the average married couple has accumulated assets worth about $410,000, compared with $167,000 for the never-married and $154,000 for the divorced. Couples who stayed married in one study saw their assets increase twice as fast as those who had remained divorced over a five-year period.

5. YOU'LL TAME HIS CHEATIN' HEART (HERS, TOO). Marriage increases sexual fidelity. Cohabiting men are four times more likely to cheat than husbands, and cohabiting women are eight times more likely to cheat than wives. Marriage is also the only realistic promise of permanence in a romantic relationship. Just one out of ten cohabiting couples are still cohabiting after five years. By contrast, 80 percent of couples marrying for the first time are still married five years later, and close to 60 percent (if current divorce rates continue) will marry for life.

4. YOU WON'T GO BONKERS. Marriage is good for your mental health. Married men and women are less depressed, less anxious, and less psychologically distressed than single, divorced, or widowed Americans.... Married men are only half as likely as bachelors and one-third as likely as divorced guys to take their own lives. Wives are also much less likely to commit suicide than single, divorced, or widowed women. Married people are much less likely to have problems with alcohol abuse or illegal drugs. ...

3. IT WILL MAKE YOU HAPPY.... Overall, 40 percent of married people, compared with about a quarter of singles or cohabitors, say they are "very happy" with life in general. Married people are also only about half as likely as singles or cohabitors to say they are unhappy with their lives.

2. YOUR KIDS WILL LOVE YOU MORE. Divorce weakens the bonds between parents and children over the long run. Adult children of divorce describe relationships with both their mother and their father less positively, on average, and they are about 40 percent less likely than adults from intact marriages to say they see either parent at least several times a week.

1. YOU'LL HAVE BETTER SEX, MORE OFTEN.... Both husbands and wives are more likely to report that they have an extremely satisfying sex life than are singles or cohabitors. ...

Wives, for example, are almost twice as likely as divorced and never-married women to have a sex life that a) exists and b) is extremely satisfying emotionally. Contrary to popular lore, for men, having a wife beats shacking up by a wide margin: 50 percent of husbands say sex with their partner is extremely satisfying physically, compared with 39 percent of cohabiting men. (Maggie Gallager, "Why Marriage

Is Good for You," *City Journal* (Autumn 2000): 76–82, available at http://www. city-journal.org/html/10_4_why_marriage_is.html.)

53. Early critics hypothesized that the studies showing the utility of marriage may have been marred by self-selection problems: that they showed only that healthy, wealthy, and happy people tended to marry, not that marriage actually increases health, wealth, or happiness. At least with respect to happiness, this "self-selection hypothesis" seems to have been refuted. Robert Commbs, "Marital Status and Personal Well-Being: A Literature Review," *Fam. Rel.* 40 (1991): 97–102; and Nadine Marks, "Flying Solo at Midlife: Gender, Marital Status, and Psychological Well-being," *J. Marriage and Fam.* 58 (1996): 917–932, 930.

54. Waite and Gallagher, note 2 *supra*, pp. 124–140. See also Dean Byrd, "Gender Complementarity and Child-Rearing: Where Tradition and Science Agree," *J.L. and Fam. Stud.* 6 (2004): 213–235; Robin Fretwell Wilson, "Evaluating Marriage: Does Marriage Matter to the Nurturing of Children?" *San Diego L. Rev.* 42 (2005): 847–880; Wendy Manning and Kathleen A. Lamb, "Adolescent Well-Being in Cohabiting, Married, and Single-Parent Families," *J. Marriage and Fam.* 65, no. 4 (November 2003): 876–893; Wardle, "Is Marriage Obsolete?" *Mich. J. Gender and L.* 10 (2003): 189–235; Stephen Nock, "Why Not Marriage?" *Va. J. Soc. Pol'y and L.* 9 (2001): 273–290; Paul R. Amato, "Good Enough Marriages: Parental Discord, Divorce, and Children's Long-Term Well-Being," *Va. J. Soc. Pol'y and L.* 9 (2001): 71–93, 75–76; Paul Amato, "Children of Divorce in the 1990s: An Update of the Amato and Keith (1991) Meta-Analysis," *J. Fam. Psychol.* 15 (2001): 355–370.

55. For an excellent discussion of the contrast between the state law's protection of married women against domestic violence, and the law's protection of unmarried women (and men) against domestic violence, see Ruth Colker, "Marriage Mimicry: The Law of Domestic Violence," *Wm. and Mary L. Rev.* 47 (2006): 1841–1898.

56. Anita Bernstein, "For and Against Marriage: A Revision," *Mich. Law Rev.* 102 (2003): 129–212.

57. For example, married women suffer less domestic abuse than cohabiting women. As cohabiting women are *for the most part* the beneficiaries of the same level of protection against abuse than married women, this suggests that there is indeed something about marriage, rather than the protection we give those within it, that decreases the likelihood of domestic violence. Note, however, that as states pass constitutional amendments prohibiting all legal recognition of all nonmarital relations, as a part of an attempt to head off recognition of gay marriage, the protection nonmarried cohabiting women receive from the state by virtue of their "marriage-like" relationship is in increasing jeopardy. This is discussed in detail, with an appendix showing where each state stands, in Colker, note 55 *supra*.

58. Linda J. Waite, "Does Marriage Matter?" *Demography* 32, no. 4 (November 1995): 483–507. See also Waite and Gallagher, note 2 *supra*, pp. 13–35.

59. The most prominent is Steven Nock, "Why Not Marriage?" *Va. J. Soc. Pol'y and L.* 9 (2001): 273–290, and authorities cited therein. See also W. Bradford Wilcox and Steven L. Nock, "What's Love Got to Do With It? Equality, Equity, Commitment and Women's Marital Quality," *Soc. Forces* 84, no. 3 (March 2006): 1321–1345, 1339–1341. Although they do not explicitly label it as such, Waite and Gallagher also rely on the logic of social norms to explain the value of marriage, over that of cohabitation. Waite and Gallagher, note 2 *supra*, pp. 20–24.

60. Milton Regan, "Law, Marriage, and Intimate Commitment," *Va. J. Soc. Pol'y and L.* 9 (2001): 116–152.

61. The literature on domestic violence is vast, but congressional as well as scholarly authorities seemingly agree that battering by husbands, live-in male companions, and boyfriends—by intimates—is the largest source of violent injury women suffer. See generally Women's Action Coalition, "The Facts about Women: Developments in the Law—Legal Responses to Domestic Violence," *Harv. L. Rev.* 106 (1993): 1498, 1501; Mary P. Koss et al., *No Safe Haven: Male Violence Against Women at Home, at Work, and in the Community* (American Psychological Association, 1994), p. 44; Evan Stark and Anne Flitcraft, "Violence Against Intimates: An Epidemiological Review," in *Handbook of Family Violence* 293, ed. Alan S. Bellack, Michael Hersen, R. L. Morrison, and Vincent B. Van Hasselt (New York: Springer, 1987); "Women and Violence: Hearings on Legislation to Reduce the Growing Problem of Violent Crime against Women before the Senate Committee on the Judiciary," 101st Congress (1990); Majority Staff of Senate Committee on the Judiciary, 102nd Congress, "Violence against Women: A Week in the Life of America" (1992). These and other authorities are discussed in Catharine MacKinnon, *Sex Equality* (New York: Foundation Press, 2001), pp. 715–765.

62. This is a huge topic on which we will only briefly touch. A number of feminists now argue that the single greatest problem of "subordination" facing women is not the institution of marriage, but rather, the institution of mothering, and likewise, that the social issue regarding family to which we ought attend is not the marital franchise, but a crisis in our overly privatized system of caregiving. See generally Martha Fineman, *The Neutered Mother, the Sexual Family, and Other Twentieth-Century Tragedies* (New York: Routledge, 1995); Martha Fineman, "Why Marriage?" *Va. J. Soc. Pol'y and L.* 9 (2001): 239–271, 255–256; Joan C. Williams, *Unbending Gender: Why Family and Work Conflict and What to Do about It* (New York: Oxford University Press, 2000); Anne Alstott, *No Exit: What Parents Owe Their Children and Society Owes Parents* (New York: Oxford University Press, 2004); Eva Kittay, *Love's Labor: Essays on Women, Equality, and Dependency* (New York: Routledge, 1998); Eva Feder Kittay and Ellen K. Feder, eds., *The Subject of Care: Feminist Perspectives on Dependency* (Lanham, MD: Rowman and Littlefield, 2002); Mona Harrington, *Care and Equality: Inventing a New Family Politics* (New York: Knopf, 1999); Katha Pollitt, "Happy Mother's Day," *Nation* (May 28, 2001), available at http://www.thenation.com/doc/20010528/pollitt.

63. See, for example, Daniel N. Hawkins and Alan Booth, "Unhappily Ever After: Effects of Long-Term, Low-Quality Marriages on Well-Being," *Soc. Forces* 84, no. 1 (September 2005): 451–471; Laurie Culp and Steven R. H. Beach, "Marriage and Depressive Symptoms: The Role and Bases of Self-Esteem Differ by Gender," *Psychol. of Women Q.* 22 (1998): 647–663.

64. See Lenore Weitzman, *The Divorce Revolution*, pp. 371–374; Martha Fineman, *The Illusion of Equality: The Rhetoric and Reality of Divorce Reform* (Chicago: University of Chicago Press, 1991); Waite and Gallagher, note 2 *supra*, pp. 18–20. Waite and Gallagher find that although both men and women benefit from marriage, the benefits are different for each: men benefit more in terms of the wage premium and physical health, and women benefit more in terms of sexual satisfaction, financial well-

being, and protection from domestic violence. The gain in earned income, however, is far greater for men than for women. Women's financial gain in marriage is a result, primarily, of the fact that married men are more likely to share their higher income with their wives and children than are cohabitating men (Waite and Gallagher, note 2 *supra*, pp. 170–172). Although Waite and Gallagher don't draw this inference, it seems clearly implied that the "shared" income, and the greater financial benefit that results, combined with the economic impoverishment of divorced women, will keep women in bad marriages as well as good ones, so long as the danger or fear of losing the income support is greater than the unhappiness of the marriage itself.

65. Waite and Gallagher, note 2 *supra*, pp. 118–120.

66. Susan Okin, *Justice, Gender, and Family* (New York: Basic Books, 1989). See also Dorothy Dinnerstein, *The Mermaid and the Minotaur: Sexual Arrangements and Human Malaise* (New York: Harper and Row, 1976); Nancy Chodorow, *The Reproduction of Mothering: Psychoanalysis and the Sociology of Gender* (Berkeley: University of California Press, 1978); Nel Noddings, *Caring: A Feminine Approach to Ethics and Moral Education* (Berkeley: University of California Press, 1984); and Carol Gilligan, *In a Different Voice: Psychological Theory and Women's Development* (Cambridge: Harvard University Press, 1993).

67. Linda McClain, *The Place of Families: Fostering Capacity, Equality, and Responsibility* (Cambridge, MA: Harvard University Press, 2006).

68. A GAO Report prepared in response to a request by Senator Frist's office in 1997 lists 1,138 federal benefits that attach to the status of being married. See GAO OGC-97-16 Defense of Marriage Act (Washington, D.C., January 31, 1997). The list was updated, again by request from his office, in January of 2004. *See* GAO-04-353R Defense of Marriage Act (Washington, D.C., January 23, 2004). State benefits are even more extensive. For summaries of Oregon and Massachusetts marital benefits, see T. Dougherty, *Economic Benefits of Marriage under Federal and Oregon Law* (New York: National Gay and Lesbian Task Force Policy Institute, 2004); and T. Dougherty, *Economic Benefits of Marriage under Federal and Massachusetts Law* (New York: National Gay and Lesbian Task Force Policy Institute, 2004).

69. See authorities cited, note 68 *supra*.

70. Ibid.

71. Personal Responsibility and Work Opportunity Reconciliation Act of 1996, H.R. 3734, 104th Congress (1996); codified at 42 U.S.C. Sec. 601, et seq., available at http://thomas.loc.gov/cgi-bin/query/z?c104:H.R.3734.ENR:htm.

72. President William Jefferson Clinton, Address before a Joint Session of the Congress on the State of the Union (February 17, 1993).

73. PRWORA, 42 U.S.C. 601 et seq., Sec 408 Prohibitions: Requirements, Subsection (a)(Par. 7A).

74. See Rebekah J. Smith, "Family Caps in Welfare Reform: Their Coercive Effects and Damaging Consequences," *Harvard J. of L. and Gender* 29 (2006): 151–200.

75. 42 U.S. 601, § 408(b).

76. See 42 U.S.C. 601, 408(a)(7). The TANF Sixth Annual Report to Congress, Ch. VII-1, "Out of Wedlock Births," reviews Section 413(e) of the TANF Statute, which requires the Department of Health and Human Services to rank states according to the ratio of out-of-wedlock to total births among TANF recipients and to reward bonuses

to those states that achieve the greatest yearly reductions between fiscal years 1999 and 2003. As the report states, "An additional statutory purpose of TANF is to prevent and reduce the incidence of out-of-wedlock pregnancies and establish annual numerical goals for preventing and reducing the incidence of these pregnancies."

77. See Tom Zeller, "The Nation; Two Fronts: Promoting Marriage, Fighting Poverty," *New York Times,* January 18, 2004.

78. Erik Eckholm, "A Welfare Law Milestone Finds Many Left Behind," *New York Times,* August 22, 2006.

79. See Bill Clinton, op-ed., "How We Ended Welfare, Together," *New York Times,* August 22, 2006.

80. See generally Kathryn Edin and Laura Lein, *Making Ends Meet: How Single Mothers Survive Welfare and Low-Wage Work* (New York: Russell Sage Foundation, 1997); Barbara Ehrenreich, *Nickel and Dimed: On (Not) Getting By in America* (New York: Metropolitan Books, 2001); Peter Edelman, "Beyond Welfare Reform: Economic Justice in the Twenty-First Century," *Berkeley J. Emp. and Lab. L.* 24 (2003): 475–487, 482; Peter Edelman, "Poverty and Welfare Policy in the Post-Clinton Era," *Miss. L.J.* 70 (2001): 877–887, 883; Peter Edelman, "Responding to the Wake-Up Call: A New Agenda for Poverty Lawyers," *N.Y.U. Rev. L. and Soc. Change* 24 (1998): 547–561, 551–553; Pamela Loprest and Sheila Zedlewski, "Current and Former Welfare Recipients: How Do They Differ?" Urban Institute, Assessing the New Federalism Discussion Paper no. 99–17, 1999, available at http://www.urban.org/UploadedPDF/discussion99-17.pdf.

81. See Jill Duerr Berrick and Bruce Fuller, "Introduction: New Family Policy: How the State Shapes Parents' Lives"; and Jill Berrick and Bruce Fuller, "Implications for Families, Children, and Policy Makers," in *Good Parents or Good Workers?* ed. Jill Berrick and Bruce Fuller (New York: Palgrave MacMillan, 2005), pp. 3–6, 175–182.

82. See Robert Pear and Erik Eckholm, "A Decade after Welfare Overhaul, a Fundamental Shift in Policy and Perception," *New York Times,* August 21, 2006, p. A12, quoting statistics from the Congressional Research Service.

83. The complete findings, included as Section 101 of the act, read as follows:

SEC. 101. FINDINGS.
The Congress makes the following findings:

(1) Marriage is the foundation of a successful society.
(2) Marriage is an essential institution of a successful society which promotes the interests of children.
(3) Promotion of responsible fatherhood and motherhood is integral to successful child rearing and the well-being of children.
(4) In 1992, only 54 percent of single-parent families with children had a child support order established and, of that 54 percent, only about one-half received the full amount due. Of the cases enforced through the public child support enforcement system, only 18 percent of the caseload has a collection.
(5) The number of individuals receiving aid to families with dependent children (in this section referred to as 'AFDC') has more than tripled since 1965. More than two-thirds of these recipients are children. Eighty-nine percent of children receiving AFDC benefits now live in homes in which no father is present.
   (A)(i) The average monthly number of children receiving AFDC benefits—

(I) was 3,300,000 in 1965;

(II) was 6,200,000 in 1970;

(III) was 7,400,000 in 1980; and

(IV) was 9,300,000 in 1992.

  (ii) While the number of children receiving AFDC benefits increased nearly threefold between 1965 and 1992, the total number of children in the United States aged 0 to 18 has declined by 5.5 percent.

(B) The Department of Health and Human Services has estimated that 12,000,000 children will receive AFDC benefits within 10 years.

(C) The increase in the number of children receiving public assistance is closely related to the increase in births to unmarried women. Between 1970 and 1991, the percentage of live births to unmarried women increased nearly threefold, from 10.7 percent to 29.5 percent.

(6) The increase of out-of-wedlock pregnancies and births is well documented as follows:

(A) It is estimated that the rate of nonmarital teen pregnancy rose 23 percent from 54 pregnancies per 1,000 unmarried teenagers in 1976 to 66.7 pregnancies in 1991. The overall rate of nonmarital pregnancy rose 14 percent from 90.8 pregnancies per 1,000 unmarried women in 1980 to 103 in both 1991 and 1992. In contrast, the overall pregnancy rate for married couples decreased 7.3 percent between 1980 and 1991, from 126.9 pregnancies per 1,000 married women in 1980 to 117.6 pregnancies in 1991.

(B) The total of all out-of-wedlock births between 1970 and 1991 has risen from 10.7 percent to 29.5 percent and if the current trend continues, 50 percent of all births by the year 2015 will be out-of-wedlock.

(7) An effective strategy to combat teenage pregnancy must address the issue of male responsibility, including statutory rape culpability and prevention. The increase of teenage pregnancies among the youngest girls is particularly severe and is linked to predatory sexual practices by men who are significantly older.

(A) It is estimated that in the late 1980's, the rate for girls age 14 and under giving birth increased 26 percent.

(B) Data indicates that at least half of the children born to teenage mothers are fathered by adult men. Available data suggests that almost 70 percent of births to teenage girls are fathered by men over age 20.

(C) Surveys of teen mothers have revealed that a majority of such mothers have histories of sexual and physical abuse, primarily with older adult men.

(8) The negative consequences of an out-of-wedlock birth on the mother, the child, the family, and society are well documented as follows:

(A) Young women 17 and under who give birth outside of marriage are more likely to go on public assistance and to spend more years on welfare once enrolled. These combined effects of 'younger and longer' increase total AFDC costs per household by 25 percent to 30 percent for 17-year-olds.

(B) Children born out-of-wedlock have a substantially higher risk of being born at a very low or moderately low birth weight.

(C) Children born out-of-wedlock are more likely to experience low verbal cognitive attainment, as well as more child abuse, and neglect.

(D) Children born out-of-wedlock were more likely to have lower cognitive scores, lower educational aspirations, and a greater likelihood of becoming teenage parents themselves.

(E) Being born out-of-wedlock significantly reduces the chances of the child growing up to have an intact marriage.

(F) Children born out-of-wedlock are 3 times more likely to be on welfare when they grow up.

(9) Currently 35 percent of children in single-parent homes were born out-of-wedlock, nearly the same percentage as that of children in single-parent homes whose parents are divorced (37 percent). While many parents find themselves, through divorce or tragic circumstances beyond their control, facing the difficult task of raising children alone, nevertheless, the negative consequences of raising children in single-parent homes are well documented as follows:

(A) Only 9 percent of married-couple families with children under 18 years of age have income below the national poverty level. In contrast, 46 percent of female-headed households with children under 18 years of age are below the national poverty level.

(B) Among single-parent families, nearly 1/2 of the mothers who never married received AFDC while only 1/5 of divorced mothers received AFDC.

(C) Children born into families receiving welfare assistance are 3 times more likely to be on welfare when they reach adulthood than children not born into families receiving welfare.

(D) Mothers under 20 years of age are at the greatest risk of bearing low birth weight babies.

(E) The younger the single-parent mother, the less likely she is to finish high school.

(F) Young women who have children before finishing high school are more likely to receive welfare assistance for a longer period of time.

(G) Between 1985 and 1990, the public cost of births to teenage mothers under the aid to families with dependent children program, the food stamp program, and the Medicaid program has been estimated at $120,000,000,000.

(H) The absence of a father in the life of a child has a negative effect on school performance and peer adjustment.

(I) Children of teenage single parents have lower cognitive scores, lower educational aspirations, and a greater likelihood of becoming teenage parents themselves.

(J) Children of single-parent homes are 3 times more likely to fail and repeat a year in grade school than are children from intact 2-parent families.

(K) Children from single-parent homes are almost 4 times more likely to be expelled or suspended from school.

(L) Neighborhoods with larger percentages of youth aged 12 through 20 and areas with higher percentages of single-parent households have higher rates of violent crime.

(M) Of those youth held for criminal offenses within the State juvenile justice system, only 29.8 percent lived primarily in a home with both parents. In contrast to these incarcerated youth, 73.9 percent of the 62,800,000 children in the Nation's resident population were living with both parents. (10) Therefore, in light of this demonstration of the crisis in our Nation, it is the sense of the Congress that prevention of out-of-wedlock pregnancy and reduction in out-of-wedlock birth are very important Government interests and the policy contained in part A of title IV of the Social Security Act (as amended by section 103(a) of this Act) is intended to address the crisis.

There is now a substantial literature both on the promarriage movement that propelled the original Clinton-era welfare reform act and the even more intensified efforts of the Bush administration to promote marriage as the best way out of poverty, and the effects of all of this on the finances, the happiness, and the quality of mothering of poor mothers. On the former, see generally Linda McClain, *The Place of Families*, note 67 *supra*, pp. 117–154 (providing a history of the philosophical "marriage promotion" movement that propelled the welfare reform act during the Clinton years, and the "marriage initiative" during the Bush administration); Kathryn Edin and Maria Kefalas, *Promises I Can Keep: Why Poor Women Put Motherhood before Marriage* (Berkeley: University of California Press, 2005), pp. 4–6, 213–220 (seeking to explain, through poor women's words and stories why it is that poor women have retreated from marriage). On the latter, see generally Jill Duer Berrick and Bruce Fuller, eds., *Good Parents or Good Workers: How Policy Shapes Families' Daily Lives* (New York: Palgrave MacMillan, 2005) (reviewing quantitative studies examining effects of welfare reform on poor women and children). An ambitious, ongoing, and extremely illuminating "three-city study" has been undertaken over the past two years by a research group centrally located at Johns Hopkins University, reviewing the effects of welfare reform on poor women and children in Boston, Chicago, and San Antonio. This study has generated a substantial body of scholarly papers seeking to assess the impact of welfare reform on poor families. All information is available from the center's homepage, available at http://www.jhu.edu/~welfare, and a full description of the study, as well as an excellent summary of the history of welfare reform, is available at http://www.jhu.edu/~welfare/overviewanddesign.pdf, pp. 1–10. A full list of downloadable documents is available at http://www.jhu.edu/~welfare/welfare_publication.html. There is no simple way to summarize the findings of the three-city study.

For the most part, the authors of the papers included to date in the three-city study report that the impact of welfare reform has been more positive than many of its critics (including most participants in the study) initially believed it would be, when the idea was first proposed in the mid-1990s, but nevertheless far short of the goals of its legislative drafters. The work requirement, in particular, has indeed led a substantial number of women to leave welfare for full or at least partial reliance on wage income, and that has substantially increased these women's earned income, although those increases may be offset by the loss of the TANF grant and the loss of food stamps. See Robert A. Moffitt and Katie Winder, "Does It Pay to Move from Welfare to Work? A Comment on Danziger, Heflin, Corcoran, Oltmans, and Wang 13, 17" in *Welfare, Children, and Families: A Three City Study*, Johns Hopkins University Web site, April 2004, available at http://www.jhu.edu/~welfare/aclcrep8c_v3a.pdf; and Robert A. Moffitt and Katie Winder, "Does It Pay to Move from Welfare to Work? A Comment on Danziger, Heflin, Corcoran, Oltmans, and Wang 11" in *Welfare, Children, and Families: A Three City Study*, Johns Hopkins University Web site, revised August 2004. However, some researchers report, the high risk of not finding work at all, if one leaves TANF, creates serious hardships for those who leave and find themselves without any source of income at all, as well as disincentives to leaving the welfare rolls. Another group of researchers is more sympathetic to the reform, noting that the work requirement has indeed raised poor women's income, although they are careful to point out that "welfare leavers" are still very poor, and that their children continue to suffer the ill consequences of poverty. See Sheldon Danziger and Hui-chen Wang, "Does It Pay to Move from Welfare to Work? A Reply to Robert Moffitt and Katie Winder," available at http://www.jhu. edu/~welfare/danziger_wang_08_19_04.pdf#search=%22Wang%2C%20Does%20it% 20Pay%20to%20Move%20From%20Welfare%20to%20Work%3F%20A%20Reply%2 0to%20Robert%20Moffitt%20and%20Katie%20Winder%22. The effect on the quality of their mothering has been mixed, but again, not as negative as many of the authors themselves had feared it would be. See Andrew Cherlin, "The Consequences of Welfare Reform for Child Well-Being: What Have We Learned So Far and What Are the Policy Implications?" Paper presented at the annual meeting of the American Sociological Association, session on "The End of Welfare as We Knew It: What Now?" August 14, 2004, available at http://www.jhu.edu/~welfare. It is not at all clear, from any of the papers included in the three-city study, what effect, if any, the welfare reform act has had on incentives to marry or not marry. Marriage rates among poor women who leave welfare are not statistically different from those who stay. See Robert Moffitt and Katie Winder, "The Correlates and Consequences of Welfare Exit and Entry: Evidence from the Three City Study 9" in *Welfare, Children, and Families: A Three City Study*, Johns Hopkins University Web site, January 2003, available at http://www.jhu.edu/~welfare/ WebPub.pdf. According to Moffitt and Winder, the cohabitation rates of women on welfare have gone up modestly, but that is seemingly a function of women cohabitating with men who are not the biological fathers of their children. The same result is reached by Andrew Cherlin and Paula Fomby in their policy study. Andrew Cherlin and Paula Fomby, "A Closer Look at Changes in Children's Living Arrangements in Low-Income Families," policy brief 02-3 in *Welfare, Children and Families: A Three City Study*, John Hopkins University Web site, available at http://www.jhu.edu/~welfare. See generally Pamela Winston, Ronald Angel, Linda Burton, Andrew Cherlin, Robert Moffitt, and William Julius Wilson, *Welfare, Children, and Families: A Three-City Study, Overview, and Design Report*, Johns Hopkins University Web site, 1999, available at www.jhu. edu/~welfare. The marriage rates of those poor families who are entitled to TANF, but do not receive it, is higher than those who do receive it. For an excellent and succinct summary of the main results of this research in the discussion of the political debates surrounding marriage (and a word of caution regarding the degree to which empirical studies will settle what appears to the author to be a largely symbolic and moral debate over both marriage and women's roles), see Andrew Cherlin, "Should the Government Promote Marriage?" *Contexts* 2, no. 4 (Fall 2003): 30–35. For an up-to-date journalistic account of the overall effects of welfare reform, and the directions that reform might take over the remainder of the Bush administration years, see Robert Pear and Erik Eckhom, "A Decade after Welfare Overhaul, a Fundamental Shift in Policy and Perception," *New York Times*, August 21, 2006, p. A12. See also "Can Marriage Help Alleviate Poverty?" transcript from *News and Notes with Ed Gordon*, August 23, 2006; and "Promoting Marriage to Reduce Poverty" transcript from *Morning Edition with Steve Inskeep*, August 21, 2006.

84. See Personal Responsibility and Work Opportunity Reconciliation Act of 1996, H.R. 3734, 104th Congress § 101 (1996), codified at 42 U.S.C. 601 *et seq.*, note 71 *supra*.

85. See, for example, Rebekah Smith, "Family Caps in Welfare Reform," note 74 *supra*, p. 197.

86. See Robert A. Moffitt and Katie Winder, "Does It Pay to Move from Welfare to Work? A Comment on Danziger, Heflin, Corcoran, Oltmans, and Wang 13, 17," in *Welfare, Children, and Families: A Three City Study*, Johns Hopkins University Web site, April 2004, available at http://www.jhu.edu/~welfare/aclcrep8c_v3a.pdf. For anecdotal accounts skeptical of the efficacy of marriage as a poverty-fighting measure, see Katherine Boo, "The Marriage Cure: Is Wedlock Really a Way Out of Poverty?" *New Yorker*, August 18, 2003, p. 105; and Sharon Hays, *Flat Broke with Children: Women in the Age of Welfare Reform* (New York: Oxford University Press, 2003). See generally Andrew Cherlin, "Should the Government Promote Marriage?" *Contexts* 2, no. 4 (Fall 2003): 30–35.

87. Erik Eckholm, "A Welfare Law Milestone Finds Many Left Behind," *New York Times*, August 22, 2006; Erik Eckholm, "For the Neediest of the Needy, Welfare Reforms Still Fall Short, Study Says," *New York Times*, May 17, 2006. For a balanced account of the welfare reform movement and its effects on the lives of poor women and their children, see Jason DeParle, *American Dream: Three Women, Ten Kids, and a Nation's Drive to End Welfare* (New York: Viking Press, 2004).

88. For a summary of the evidence of this, see Laura Frame, "Where Poverty and Parenting Intersect: The Impact of Welfare Reform on Caregiving," in *Good Parents or Good Workers? How Policy Shapes Families' Daily Lives*, ed. Jill Berrick and Bruce Fuller (New York: Palgrave MacMillan, 2005), pp. 63–84.

89. Ibid., pp. 76–77.

90. Ibid.

91. It has, however, seemingly increased cohabitation rates, but generally not with the biological father. See Andrew Cherlin and Paula Fomby, "A Closer Look at Changes in Children's Living Arrangements in Low-Income Families," Policy Brief 02-3 in *Welfare, Children, and Families: A Three City Study*, available at http://www.jhu.edu/~welfare.

92. Ibid.

93. Kathryn Edin and Maria Kefalas, *Promises I Can Keep: Why Poor Women Put Motherhood before Marriage* (Berkeley: University of California Press, 2005).

94. See Jill Berrick and Bruce Fuller, note 88 *supra*; and Peter Edelman, "Beyond Welfare Reform: Economic Justice in the Twenty-First Century," *Berkeley J. Emp. and Lab. L.* 24 (2003): 475–487, 482; Peter Edelman, "Poverty and Welfare Policy in the Post-Clinton Era," *Miss. L.J.* 70 (2001): 877–887, 883; Peter Edelman, "Responding to the Wake-Up Call: A New Agenda for Poverty Lawyers," *N.Y.U. Rev. L. and Soc. Change* 24 (1998): 547–561, 551–553.

95. In some ways, for some children, and for some mothers, this is a plus: subsidized childcare contributes to children's well-being in numerous ways. Even high quality childcare, however, induces considerable anxiety and self doubts in mothers, and poor child-care even more so. For adolescents, the picture is more mixed: in some years, drop-out rates from high school have risen, as well as truancy rates, post–welfare reform. See Andrew Cherlin and Paula Fomby, note 91 *supra*.

96. Linda Waite and Evelyn Lehrer, "The Benefits from Marriage and Religion in the United States: A Comparative Analysis," *Population and Dev. Rev.* 29, no. 2 (June 2003): 255–275, 266–267.

97. Perhaps the best history to date of the welfare reform movement's promotion of marriage is Linda McClain, *The Place of Families*, note 67 *supra*, pp. 117–154.

98. See, for a general account of the role of the marriage initiative in the Bush administration's welfare policy, and a discussion of the split this has caused between social conservatives and libertarians within his administration, Tom Zeller, "Two Fronts: Promoting Marriage, Fighting Poverty," New York Times, January 18, 2004.

99. Jason DeParle, *American Dream: Three Women, Ten Kids, and a Nation's Drive to End Welfare* (New York: Viking Press, 2004), pp. 329–330.

100. Kathryn Edin and Maria Kefalas, *Promises I Can Keep: Why Poor Women Put Motherhood before Marriage* (Berkeley: University of California Press, 2005), p. 5.

101. See authorities cited in notes 54 and 59 *supra*.

102. See Lenore Weitzman, *The Divorce Revolution: The Unexpected Social and Economic Consequences for Women and Children in America* (New York: Free Press, 1985); Karen Holden and Pamela Smock, "The Economic Costs of Marital Dissolution: Why Do Women Bear a Disproportionate Cost?" *Ann. Rev. Soc.* 17 (1991): 52–74.

103. See generally Arlie Hochschild, *The Second Shift: Working Parents and the Revolution at Home* (New York: Viking, 1989); and Roberta Sigel, *Ambition and Accommodation: How Women View Gender Relations* (Chicago: University of Chicago Press, 1996).

104. Hochschild, note 103 *supra*, pp. 1–21.

105. This is borne out by some research. The subjects in the focus groups assembled by Roberta Sigel seem to suggest something like the hypothesis presented in the text. Their reaction to the second shift, primarily, was one of anger, hurt, and resignation, not indignation or a sense that they were victims of injustice. Roberta Sigel, note 103 *supra*, pp. 167–168.

106. Steven Nock, "Why Not Marriage," note 44 *supra*, p. 285.

107. J. S. Mill, "Utilitarianism," in *Utilitarianism: With Critical Essays*, ed. Samuel Gorovitz (Indianapolis: Bobbs-Merril, 1971), pp. 19–21.

108. Prominent communitarian theorists of marriage include Mary Shanley, Milton Regan, and Amitai Etzioni. See, for example, Mary Shanley, ed., *Just Marriage*, note 3 *supra*; Milton Regan, Jr., *Family Law and the Pursuit of Intimacy*, note 3 *supra*; Milton Regan, Jr., *Alone Together: Law and the Meaning of Marriage*, note 3 *supra*; and Amitai Etzioni, "A Communitarian Position for Civil Unions," in *Just Marriage*, ed. Mary Shanley (Oxford: Boston Review Book, 2004), pp. 63–67.

109. The argument that follows is a synthesis of communitarians' and virtue theorists' writing on marriage. I have tried to capture those parts of the argument that sound distinctly anti-utilitarian or at least contain nonutilitarian themes, although there is obviously a great deal of overlap. Much of my account draws on the scholarship of Milton Regan, Jr. and Mary Shanley. See Milton Regan, Jr., "Law, Marriage, and Intimate Commitment," *Va. J. Soc. Pol'y and L.* 9 (2001): 116–152, and Mary Shanley, *Just Marriage*, note 3 *supra*.

110. Anne Alstott, *No Exit: What Parents Owe Their Children and What Society Owes Parents* (New York: Oxford University Press, 2004).

111. For a full argument to the effect that this relatively unwilled quality of the caregiving is a central characteristic of it, and that its value to the individual and therefore to society is not well accounted for in liberal theories of the state, see Eva Kittay, *Love's Labor: Essays on Women, Equality and Dependency* (New York: Routledge, 1999).

112. Both Regan and Shanley make identitarian and care-based arguments, but Regan emphasizes the former, and Shanley, the latter. A number of feminists have also argued both that the caregiving labor women do is societally undervalued, and that women are unjustly subordinated because of it. See, for example, Martha Fineman, *The Neutered Mother, the Sexual Family, and Other Twentieth-Century Tragedies* (New York: Routledge, 1995); Eva Kittay, *Love's Labor: Essays on Women, Equality, and Dependency* (New York: Routledge, 1999); and Robin West, *Caring for Justice* (New York: New York University Press, 1997). Only Shanley, however, to the best of my knowledge, has derived from the insight regarding care an argument for marriage. More typically, feminists who are concerned about the undervaluation of care worry that marriage serves to unjustly allocate that work to women, and to completely privatize it within private and intimate relations, and thereby render invisible the injustice of the allocation. See, for example, Fineman, "Why Marriage?" note 62 *supra*, and discussion in Chapter 3 of this volume.

113. See Robin West, "Do We Have a Right to Care?" in *The Subject of Care: Feminist Perspectives on Dependency*, ed. Eva Feder Kittay and Ellen K. Feder (Lanham, MD: Rowman and Littlefield, 2002), pp. 88–114.

114. Mary Shanley, *Just Marriage*, note 3 *supra*, p. 25.

115. See, for example, Martha Fineman, "Why Marriage?" note 62 *supra*, pp. 239–271, 255–256.

116. Robert Putnam, *Bowling Alone: The Collapse and Revival of American Community* (New York: Simon and Schuster, 2001).

Notes to Chapter Three

1. See, for example, *Zablocki v. Redhail*, 434 U.S. 374 (1978), in which the Court invalidated a Wisconsin law that prevented noncustodial parents with child support obligations from remarrying without court approval. See also *Turner v. Salfey*, 482 U.S. 78 (1978), in which the Court invalidated a prison regulation denying inmates the right to marry.

2. *Loving v. Virginia*, 388 U.S. 1 (1967).

3. *Michael H. v. Gerald D.*, 491 U.S. 110 (1989).

4. The right to privacy upon which *Roe v. Wade* relied for the right to abortion was originally a right pertaining to marital couples. See *Griswold v. Connecticut*, 381 U.S. 479 (1965).

5. This is a somewhat controversial claim, but if the Constitution is to have any meaning at all, independent of judicial interpretation, it must be true. The Court itself, of course, recognizes its own fallibility when it reverses prior decisions, as it has done on many occasions. *Dred Scott v. Sanford*, 60 U.S. (19 How.) 393, striking as unconstitutional state laws that purported to give rights to freed slaves, and *Plessy v. Ferguson*, 163 U.S. 537 (1896), upholding de jure segregation on the basis of race, are just the two most notorious examples of constitutional mistakes. See generally Ronald Dworkin, *Taking Rights*

Seriously (Cambridge, MA: Harvard University Press, 2005), for a sustained argument to the effect that the Constitution does not mean "whatever the Court says it means," and that because of that the Court can be, and often is, mistaken.

6. A cottage industry of scholarship has developed over the last twenty years to this effect. See Lawrence G. Sager, *Justice in Plainclothes: A Theory of American Constitutional Practice* (New Haven, CT: Yale University Press, 2004); Lawrence G. Sager, "Foreword: State Courts and the Strategic Space between the Norms and Rule of Constitutional Law," *Tex. L. Rev.* 63 (1985): 959–976; Lawrence G. Sager, "Fair Measure: The Legal Status of Underenforced Constitutional Norms," *Harv. L. Rev.* 91 (1978): 1212–1264; Larry Kramer, *The People Themselves: Popular Constitutionalism and Judicial Review* (New York: Oxford University Press, 2004); Mark Tushnet, *Taking the Constitution Away from the Courts* (Princeton, NJ: Princeton University Press, 1999).

7. Constitutional argument of this sort, in the face of conceded judicial recalcitrance, is not uncommon in our constitutional history. Constitution-minded abolitionists long argued that the institution of slavery—which itself could be understood as consisting of nothing but state laws delineating distinctions between classes of persons—was unconstitutional, under the *original* Constitution (interpreted through the lens of the Declaration of Independence). See generally Randy E. Barnett, "Was Slavery Unconstitutional before the 13th Amendment? Lysander Spooner's Theory of Interpretation," *Pac. L.J.* 28 (1977): 977–1014; Frederick Douglass, "The Meaning of July Fourth for the Negro, Speech Delivered at Rochester, New York (July 5, 1882)," in *The Life and Writings of Frederick Douglass,* ed. Philip S. Foner (New York: International, 1950), pp. 181–204; Frederick Douglass, "The Constitution of the United States: Is It Pro-Slavery or Anti-Slavery? Speech Delivered in Glasgow, Scotland (March 26, 1860)," in *The Life and Writings of Frederick Douglass,* ed. Philip S. Foner (New York: International, 1950), pp. 467–480. Even given the implicit constitutional recognition of the institution of slavery in a number of specific provisions, Spooner, Douglass, and other activists urged, the Constitution, best read as against the backdrop of the Declaration and the document's most general and most generous phrases, taken in its entirety, clearly contemplated the institution's demise. These arguments did not sway courts, but they may well have swayed fence-sitters who were neither squarely in the abolitionist camp or opposed to it. See generally William M. Wiecek, *The Sources of Antislavery Constitutionalism in America, 1760–1848* (Ithaca, NY: Cornell University Press, 1977); Daniel R. Ernst, "Legal Positivism, Abolitionist Litigation, and the New Jersey Slave Case of 1845," *Law and Hist. Rev.* 4 (1986): 337–365. Likewise, extrajudicial "equality practice" of this sort has been hugely important to the development of both nineteenth- and twentieth-century feminism. See generally Reva Siegel, "Constitutional Culture, Social Movement Conflict and Constitutional Clange: The Case of the de facto ERA," *Cal. L. Rev.* 94 (2006): 1323–1419. Nineteenth-century feminists developed detailed arguments regarding the unconstitutionality of coverture, of chastisement, of disenfranchisement, and of the barring of women from the public sphere of civic life and wage-earning employment—long before courts began to seriously consider the arguments. The labor movement likewise, during the aftermath of the industrial movement, engaged in something I call in this chapter (borrowing from Bill Eskridge) "equality practice": the use of "popular" rather than judicial constitutional arguments to sway public opinion. See William E. Forbath, "The Ambiguities of Free Labor: Labor and the Law in the Guilded Age," *Wis. L. Rev.* (1985): 767–817,

794 (arguing that the labor movement redefined liberty as a "free market to work" and equal access to work); William E. Forbath, "The Shaping of the American Labor Movement," *Harv. L. Rev.* 102 (1989): 1109–1159 (tracing the judicial acceptance of Populist constitutional interpretations in response to claims that trade union ideals were higher than the Constitution). There are many other examples of "equality practice" effecting our political beliefs (on the political right as well as the political left). To take just one other example that I will look at in considerably more detail in the following chapter, beginning in the 1970s, advocates for "same-sex marriage" devised arguments for the unconstitutionality of the exclusion of same-sex couples from marriage rights decades before any court, in Massachusetts or elsewhere, even imagined that there could possibly be such arguments on the horizon. See William Eskridge, Jr., *Equality Practice: Civil Unions and the Future of Gay Rights* (New York: Routledge, 2002). The lawyers that put these arguments forward, again, decades before there was any hope that a court would view them seriously, did so, not only so as to predict where the court would one day go. Rather, they did so in the not unreasonable hope that the arguments themselves would prove persuasive to many people—and hence hasten the day when, either through adjudication or through lawmaking, political actors would change the law so as to match the constitutional aspiration. The Constitution articulates, albeit imperfectly and with a good deal of ambivalence, egalitarian, libertarian, and communitarian political ideals, or moral ideals, against which state law can be judged—regardless of what particular, temporal courts do or don't do, will or won't do, can or can't do. There is no reason not to examine current state law, or laws, or institutions, including social institutions, in the light of those principles. Whatever courts might do with these claims, citizens might well be swayed by them.

8. The Equal Protection Clause is not the only possible source of conflict between marriage and constitutionalism; the First Amendment may present another. Marriage is largely a religious institution, and it is hard, perhaps impossible, to understand it in fully secular terms. I have also argued elsewhere that we should recognize a fundamental "right to give care" under the Fourteenth Amendment's so-called substantive Due Process Clause, that would explicitly recognize the centrality and importance of caregiving—meaning both parental care for children, and care for the elderly and disabled. Were we to do so, a good number of our current welfare laws, and perhaps some of our marriage laws as well, might be constitutionally problematic. In this discussion, I focus only on the Equal Protection Clause, and the possibility that distinction between married and unmarried persons effectuated by them are "insidious" and therefore unconstitutional. The arguments, however, intersect. See Robin West, "Do We Have a Right to Care?" in *The Subject of Care,* ed. Eva Kittay and Ellen Feder (Lanham, MD: Rowman and Littlefield, 2003), pp. 88–114.

9. The Fourteenth Amendment to the U.S. Constitution states in relevant part, "No state shall make or enforce any law which shall abridge the privileges or immunities of citizens of the United States, nor shall any State deprive any person of life, liberty, or property, without due process of law; nor deny to any person within its jurisdiction the equal protection of the laws." U.S. Const. Amend. XIV.

10. The Court's modern equal protection law is widely understood as beginning with *Brown v. Board of Education,* 347 U.S. 483 (1954), in which de jure segregation laws were found unconstitutional, roughly on the grounds that they rested on impermissibly

subordinating and false views about the differences between white and black citizens, and secondarily on the grounds that they caused harm to black children for no good, publicly regarding reason.

11. Of course, anyone can (and should) write a will, but some forms of property, such as the entitlement to a rent-controlled rental property, cannot be bequeathed by will, while they can be part of an estate, passed on to beneficiaries through the intestacy laws. See Jennifer Jaff, "Wedding Bell Blues," *Ariz. L. Rev.* 30 (1988): 207–242, 215. See generally Nancy Polikoff, "Ending Marriage as We Know It," *Hofstra L. Rev.* 32 (2003): 201–232; Nancy Polikoff, "All Families Matter: What the Law Can Do about It," *Women's Rts. L. Rep.* 25 (2004): 205–209; Nancy Polikoff, "Making Marriage Matter Less: The ALI Domestic Partner Principles Are One Step in the Right Direction," *U. Chi. Legal F.* (2004): 353–379.

12. See *Michael H. v. Gerald D.*, 491 U.S. 110 (1989) (holding that a state law establishing an irrebuttable presumption that the husband of a mother is the father of a child born during the duration of a marriage, against a challenge by the biological father, is constitutional).

13. Jaff, note 11 *supra*, p. 216. The Arkansas Supreme Court recently invalidated a state law precluding gay persons from becoming foster parents, leaving only Missouri with a flat ban. Nevertheless, the practice of preferring married, heterosexual couples over both single and same-sex couples, persists. For a summary of the GAO's 2004 list of marital benefits, see the National Gay and Lesbian Task Force Policy Institute, *The Issues—Marriage and Partnership Recognition* (2006), available at www.thetaskforce.org/theissues/issue.cfm?issueID=14.

14. See Gen. Accounting Office, GAO OGC-97-16, Defense of Marriage Act (Washington, D.C., January 31, 1997), available at http://www.gao.gov/archive/1997/og97016.pdf. The list was updated, again by request from his office, in January of 2004. See Gen. Accounting Office, GAO-04-353R, Defense of Marriage Act (Washington, D.C., January 23, 2004), available at http://www.gao.gov/new.items/d04353r.pdf. State benefits are even more extensive. For summaries of Oregon and Massachusetts marital benefits, see Terence Dougherty, National Gay and Lesbian Task Force Policy Institute, *Economic Benefits of Marriage under Federal and Oregon Law* (2004), available at http://www.thetaskforce.org/downloads/OregonTaxStudy.pdf; Terence Dougherty, National Gay and Lesbian Task Force Policy Institute, *Economic Benefits of Marriage under Federal and Massachusetts Law* (2004), available at http://www.thetaskforce.org/downloads/EconomicCosts.pdf.

15. See generally the National Gay and Lesbian Task Force Policy Institute, *The Issues—Marriage and Partnership Recognition* (2006), available at www.thetaskforce.org/theissues/issue.cfm?issueID=14.

16. William Eskridge, *Equality Practice: Civil Practice and the Future of Gay Rights* (New York: Routledge, 2002).

17. The "insular and discrete" language stems from a footnote in a case that arose during the Great Depression, in which the Court limited the powers of its own review of economic legislation, but indicated in dicta a willingness to look more closely at cases involving statutes "directed at particular religious, ... or racial minorities, ... [where] prejudice against discrete and insular minorities may be a special condition, which tends seriously to curtail the operation of those political processes ordinarily to be relied upon

to protect minorities, and which may call for a correspondingly more searching judicial inquiry" (*United States v. Carolene Products Co.*, 304 U.S. 144 [1938]).

18. See generally John Ely, *Democracy and Distrust* (Cambridge, MA: Harvard University Press, 1980).

19. For general discussions of the equal protection test, as developed by the Supreme Court and briefly summarized in the text, see Gerald Gunther, "Foreword: In Search of Evolving Doctrine on a Changing Court: A Model for a Newer Equal Protection," *Harv. L. Rev.* 86 (1972): 1–48; and John Hart Ely, *Democracy and Distrust* (Cambridge, MA: Harvard University Press, 1980), pp. 135–170. For a succinct but exhaustive presentation of the Equal Protection Clause, as it has developed through case law, see Gerald Gunther and Kathleen Sullivan, *Constitutional Law*, 13th ed. (New York: Foundation Press, 1997), pp. 628–917.

20. The Court's earliest clear statement of this principle came in *Korematsu v. United States*, 323 U.S. 214 (1944), in which the Court made clear that racial classifications must be held to the highest, most demanding standard, but then notoriously upheld the racial classification at issue in that case: a World War II–era military order excluding all persons of Japanese ancestry from certain areas in the West Coast, resulting in their incarceration, on the grounds of military necessity. For an excellent overview of the structure of equal protection doctrine, see Gunther and Sullivan, note 19 *supra*, pp. 628–635.

21. *Brown v. Board of Education*, 347 U.S. 483 (1954).

22. See, for example, *Harper v. Va. State Bd. of Elections*, 383 U.S. 663 (finding a poll tax an unconstitutional infringement on the fundamental interest in voting); *Griffin v. Illinois*, 351 U.S. 12 (1956) (finding a fundamental interest in access to the courts); *Douglas v. California*; 372 U.S. 353 (1963) (finding a fundamental interest in access to the courts); and *Shapiro v. Thompson*, 394 U.S. 618 (1968) (finding a fundamental interest in interstate travel).

23. The relevant authorities are collected and discussed in Gunther and Sullivan, note 19 *supra*, pp. 910–916.

24. Gunther and Sullivan, note 19 *supra*, pp. 635–663.

25. Ibid., pp. 648–663.

26. *Reed v. Reed*, 404 U.S. 71 (1971) (finding that statute creating preference for male estate executors is unconstitutional); *Frontiero v. Richardson*, 411 U.S. 677 (1973) (finding that statutory scheme giving benefits to spouses of men but only to economically dependent spouses of women in the Air Force ruled unconstitutional); *Craig v. Boren*, 429 U.S. 190 (1976) (finding that different rules on ability of young people to buy beer was unconstitutional); *Michael M.* v. *Superior Court*, 450 U.S. 464 (1981) (upholding statutory rape law as constitutional); *Mississippi Univ. for Women v. Hogan*, 458 U.S. 718 (1982) (nursing school open only to women ruled unconstitutional); and *United States v. Virginia*, 518 U.S. 515 (1996) (holding Virginia Military Institute's male-only admissions policy unconstitutional).

27. *Rostker v. Goldberg*, 453 U.S. 57 (1981) (upholding selective service registration limited to males as constitutional); and *Geduldig v. Aiello*, 417 U.S. 484 (1974) (upholding state disability plan covering all but pregnancy-related disabilities as constitutional).

28. *Goodridge v. Dept of Public Health*, 798 N.E.2d 941 (Mass. 2003).

29. Ibid., pp. 958–968.

30. Ibid., pp. 954–957.

31. Ibid., pp. 962–964.

32. Ibid., pp. 962–963.

33. Ibid., pp. 959–967.

34. As of July 18, 2006, forty-five states have either constitutional amendments or state laws precluding same-sex marriage, some number of which also closes the door on civil union and domestic partnership acts as well. See Jill Abrams, "Gay Marriage Amendment Faces Uphill Battle," Associated Press, July 18, 2006. However, the tide might be turning, even at the state level. See T. R. Reid, "Optimism on Both Sides of Gay Marriage Debate," *Washington Post,* July 18, 2006, p. A04. See also http://www.thetaskforce.org/theissues/issue.cfm?issueID=14.

35. For a review and discussion of the quantitative and qualitative studies that suggest this, see Kathryn Edin and Maria Kefalas, *Promises I Can Keep: Why Poor Women Put Motherhood before Marriage* (Berkeley: University of California Press, 2005).

36. Ibid., pp. 201–220. Edin and Kefalas also emphasize some noneconomic factors in the "retreat from marriage" among poor people, such as the very high value poor women place on children and mothering (ibid., pp. 204–207). Generally, though, their analysis supports the centrality of economic factors to the resistance to marriage among poor mothers.

37. The most important of these is likely poverty, and the Court has held repeatedly that "poverty" is not an immutable characteristic that triggers strict scrutiny. Put differently, the "poor" are not a suspect classification, so the Court has never seen fit to strike legislation that adversely affects poor people on equal protection grounds. See, for example, *San Antonio School District v. Rodriguez,* 411 U.S. 1 (1973) (holding that Equal Protection Clause does not require a public education, much less a high quality or an equal one). The literature by commentators, overwhelmingly critical of the Court's refusal to view poverty as raising constitutional issues, is vast. See Charles Black, *A New Birth of Freedom: Human Rights, Named and Unnamed* (New York: Grosset/Putnam, 1997); Frank Michelman, "Foreword: On Protecting the Poor through the Fourteenth Amendment," *Harv. L. Rev.* 83 (1969): 7–59; Frank Michelman, "In Pursuit of Constitutional Welfare Rights: One View of Rawls' Theory of Justice," *U. Pa. L. Rev.* 121 (1973): 962–1019; Peter Edelman, "The Next Century of Our Constitution: Rethinking Our Duty to the Poor," *Hastings L.J.* 39 (1987): 1–61; Peter Edelman, "Welfare and the Politics of Race, Same Tune, New Lyrics?" *Geo. J. of Poverty L. and Pol'y.* 11 (2004): 389–403; Lawrence G. Sager, *Justice in Plainclothes: A Theory of American Constitutional Practice* (New Haven, CT: Yale University Press, 2004); Lawrence Sager, "Fair Measure: The Legal Status of Underenforced Constitutional Norms," *Harv. L. Rev.* 91 (1978): 1212–1264; Lawrence Sager, "Foreword: State Courts and the Strategic Space between the Norms and Rule of Constitutional Law," *Tex. L. Rev.* 63 (1985): 959–976; Robin West, "Is Progressive Constitutionalism Possible?" *Widener L. Symp. J.* 4 (1999): 1–18; Robin West, "Rights, Capabilities, and the Good Society," *Fordham L. Rev.* 69 (2001): 1901–1932; Robin West, "Katrina, the Constitution, and the Legal Question Doctrine," *Chi.-Kent L. Rev.* 81 (2006): 1127–1172.

38. See West, "Do We Have a Right to Care?" in *The Subject of Care,* ed. Eva Kittay and Ellen Feder (Lanham, MD: Rowman and Littlefield, 2003), pp. 88–114.

39. *Goodridge,* pp. 954–957.

40. *Roe v. Wade,* 410 U.S. 113 (1972); *Griswold v. Connecticut,* 381 U.S. 479 (1965); and *Eisenstadt v. Baird,* 405 U.S. 438 (1972).

41. One researcher indicates that marriage alone would boost poor women's income by as much as 25 percent. See R. Lerman, "Marriage as a Protective Force against Economic Hardship," paper presented at the 23rd Annual Research Conference of the Association for Public Policy Analysis and Management, Washington, D.C., November 1–3, 2001. See generally Chapter 2 of this volume.

42. For a wonderful discussion of the social history of the gendered assumptions of the Social Security laws, and the impact of those assumptions on social views of marriage well into the twentieth century, see Nancy Cott, *Public Vows: A History of Marriage and the Nation* (Cambridge, MA: Harvard University Press, 2000), pp. 174–179.

43. See Chapter 2 of this volume.

44. *Goodridge,* pp. 962–964.

45. Ibid.

46. Martha Fineman, *The Neutered Mother, the Sexual Family and Other Twentieth-Century Tragedies* (New York: Routledge, 1995); Martha Fineman, "Why Marriage?" *Va. Soc. Pol. and the Law* 9 (2001): 239–271.

47. Fineman, *The Neutered Mother,* pp. 219–222 (reviewing work of Weitzman and others showing the economically damaging consequences for women of divorce). See generally Lenore Weitzman, *The Divorce Revolution: The Unexpected Social and Economic Consequences for Women and Children in America* (New York: Free Press, 1985).

48. Martha Fineman, "Why Marriage?" note 46 *supra,* pp. 247–251.

49. Ibid., pp. 254–255.

50. Ibid., pp. 257–268.

51. Ibid., pp. 244–246, 267–270.

52. Ibid., p. 257. Fineman's acknowledgement of the limits of contractualism as a way toward social justice with respect to children, render her preference for contract law over marriage law, even with ameliorating doctrines, somewhat puzzling. See "Why Marriage?" pp. 266–267.

53. This was one consequence of "coverture," the legal doctrine by which a wife's identity was presumed to be "covered" by that of the husband. See Chapter 1 of this volume.

54. Although nineteenth-century U.S. feminists were keenly aware of the need to end husbands' authority over women's sexual and reproductive bodies—as had been earlier Victorian feminists, from Mary Wollstonecraft to Harriet Taylor and John Stuart Mill—they made little headway on the issue. Perhaps for strategic reasons, according to one legal historian, nineteenth-century U.S. feminists quite consciously decided to push forward not on marital rights of physical integrity, but on economic and political fronts instead. Thus, nineteenth-century feminism concertedly pursued married women's property acts, which, broadly, gave wives control over property, empowered them to enter contracts, and allowed them to keep wages earned during the course of their marriage in their own name—and for political enfranchisement. Returning control of women's sexual bodies and reproductive lives to wives, and to women generally, was felt keenly as a political and moral imperative, but as the more difficult of the three political battles (for property rights, physical autonomy, or political power). According to law Professor Jill Hasday's research, they spoke of the issues in a virtual code, fearing to alienate natural

allies who would be morally offended by a frank discussion of sexual and reproductive issues. They forged alliances where they could be forged, but were generally limited in that regard to churchmen, who urged "restraint" on married men as a matter of personal and religious duty. They were also hampered by the felt sheer impossibility of a full-scale frontal assault on separate spheres ideology, to which the doctrine of husbands' control, and sovereignty, over wives' sexual and reproductive bodies was so central. *See* Jill Elaine Hasday, "Contest and Consent: A Legal History of Marital Rape," *Cal. L. Rev.* 88 (2000): 1373–1505.

For whatever reasons, though, feminists did not agitate for wives' control of their bodies in marriage until well into the twentieth century. Feminists well understood that domestic violence in marriage was a major result, cause of, and manifestation of women's inequality, and at the turn of the century began to address it—but typically as an analogue to the less controversial topic of violence perpetrated against children. At mid-century, domestic violence came to be viewed as caused by various sorts of psychological disorders in some marriages, typically involving wives who either could not, because of their own naiveté, or would not, because of their own character flaws, undertake the work necessary to learn how to cool their husbands' tempers without occasioning a brawl. It was not until well into the 1960s that domestic violence was squarely posed as a political problem facing wives, but one that could be attributed to state abdication of responsibility rather than female neurosis, and as one that the state, through the criminal law, had the primary responsibility for addressing. It was not until well into the 1980s that marital rape "exemptions" began to be challenged—initially in a few judicial cases, and then eventually in a wave of legislative enactments. That work, it should be noted, is ongoing—there are still fairly major differences in the way that rape is treated in and out of marriage. For the most part, though, nonconsensual forced sex, within marriage, is now a crime. In the 1970s, it generally was not.

55. Stephanie Coontz, *Marriage: A History: From Obedience to Intimacy or How Love Conquered Marriage* (New York: Viking, 2005).

56. Ibid., pp. 145–247.

57. Sigmund Freud, *Civilization and Its Discontents,* trans. and ed. James Strachey (New York: W. W. Norton, 1989).

58. Michael Warner, *The Trouble with Normal: Sex, Politics, and the Ethics of Queer Life* (New York: Free Press, 1999).

59. Ibid., pp. 81–147.

60. Ibid., p. 147.

61. Fineman, "Why Marriage?" note 43 *supra*, p. 262.

62. More broadly the centuries-long legality of marital rape has normalized, to some degree, both date rape and acquaintance rape: the more a "rape" looks like sex between husband and wife, the less likely it is to be viewed as criminal, by perpetrator, victim, police, and prosecutor alike.

63. Fineman, "Why Marriage?" pp. 262–263.

64. Ibid., p. 263.

65. Ibid.

66. Ibid., p. 267.

67. For example, the poverty and racism that were so strikingly on display in the aftermath of Katrina struck me as raising constitutional questions about state neglect,

in spite of the clear reality that no court will ever hold poverty itself to be unconstitutional. The failure of states to criminalize marital rape, likewise, might well have been a constitutional failing—although no federal court ever squarely so held.

68. Cass Sunstein, "Words, Conduct, Caste," *U. Chi. L. Rev.* 60 (1993): 795–845.

69. William Eskridge, *Equality Practice: Civil Unions and the Future of Gay Rights* (New York: Routledge, 2002), p. 126.

70. Stephen Nock, "Why Not Marriage?" *Va. J. Soc. Pol'y and L.* 9 (2001): 273–290.

71. Linda Waite and Mary Gallagher, *The Case for Marriage: Why Married People Are Happier, Healthier, and Better off Financially* (New York: Broadway Books, 2001). p. 155.

Notes to Chapter Four

1. *Goodridge v. Department of Public Health,* 798 N.E.2d 941 (MA 2003).

2. See generally "2006 Proposed State Amendments Limiting Marriage," for an up-to-the-minute survey of state laws limiting marriage to man-woman unions, Human Rights Campaign Web site, available at http://hrc.org/Template.cfm?Section=CenterandTemplate=/TaggedPage/TaggedPageDisplay.cfmandTPLID=63andContentID=17353.

3. 28 U.S.C.A. § 1738C states that no state shall be required to give full faith and credit to "any public act, record, or judicial proceeding of any other State respecting a relationship between persons of the same sex that is treated as a marriage under the laws of such other State, ... or a right or claim arising from such relationship." 1 U.S.C.A. § 7 defines the term "marriage" to mean "only a legal union between one man and one woman as husband and wife," and the term "spouse" to mean "a person of the opposite sex who is a husband or a wife."

4. *Hernandez v. Robles,* 2006 N.Y. Slip Op. 05239 (N.Y., July 6, 2006).

5. In 2006, this proposed amendment failed to gain even a bare majority in the Senate, and was far from the two-thirds needed in the House, to send a proposed constitutional amendment to the states for ratification. See Shailagh Murray, "Gay Marriage Amendment Fails in Senate," *Washington Post,* June 8, 2006, p. A01.

6. In a few states, adoption by gay or lesbian individuals is still flatly prohibited, on the grounds of the immorality of their sexual conduct. See *In re Appeal in Pima County Juvenile Action B—10489,* 727 P.2d 839, 835 (Ariz. Ct. App. 1986), and Miss Code Sec. 93-17-3(2). Other states bar adoption by gay and lesbian individuals or couples on the grounds that children should be raised in the optimal environment, and a same-sex household is suboptimal (see, e.g., Florida Stat. Sec 63.042[3]).

7. This is changing, but it is still the case that most partners in same-sex couples are not covered by their partner's employer-provided health insurance. Fortune 500 couples have been the most forward in providing such coverage, and many state and local governmental employers do likewise. Neither employers nor their insurance providers, however, are under any obligation to extend coverage to nonmarital partners of their employees.

8. A GAO Report prepared in response to a request by Senator Frist's office in 1997 lists 1,138 federal benefits that attach to the status of being married. See GAO OGC-97-16 Defense of Marriage Act (Washington, D.C., January 31, 1997). The list was updated, again by request from his office, in January of 2004. See GAO-04-353R Defense of Marriage Act (Washington, D.C., January 23, 2004). State benefits are even more extensive. For summaries of Oregon and Massachusetts marital benefits, see Terrence Dougherty, *Economic Benefits of Marriage under Federal and Oregon Law* (New York: National Gay and Lesbian Task Force Policy Institute, 2004); and Terrence Dougherty, *Economic Benefits of Marriage under Federal and Massachusetts Law* (New York: National Gay and Lesbian Task Force Policy Institute, 2004), Appendix B. National Gay and Lesbian Taskforce Web site, available at www.thetaskforce.org.

9. GAO Report, note 8 *supra*, pp. 1–3.

10. Ibid., p. 4.

11. For a relatively recent decision denying visitation rights to a nonbiological lesbian parent, after a separation, on the grounds that the word "parent" in the state's Domestic Relations Law that authorizes either parent of a child to bring suit for determination of custody or visitation rights does not include a nonbiological parent, see *In the Matter of Alison D. v. Virginia M.*, 77 N.Y. 2d 651 (1991). Other states have declined to follow suit, relying on the "best interest of the child" standard, as well as academic research on "attachment theory," to reason that a nonbiological lesbian parent who has actively parented a child should be treated as such when determining visitation rights postseparation. A good collection and discussion of relevant case law and statutory authority are collected and discussed in Eskridge and Hunter, *Sexuality, Gender and the Law*, 2d ed. (New York: Foundation Press, 2004), pp. 1198–1210.

12. Courts have generally declined to extend the divorce rules governing the distribution of property to cohabiting couples. See, for example, *Hewitt v. Hewitt*, 77 Ill.2d 49 (1979); and *Marvin v. Marvin*, 18 Cal. 3d 550 (1976).

13. Although courts today typically enforce agreements between nonmarried persons engaged in a sexual relationship, they only do so if it is clear from the agreement that "sexuality" is not a part of the consideration for which the bargain was struck. To do otherwise would be tantamount to upholding contracts for prostitution. At the same time, such agreements are more regularly enforced than contracts between married persons for the distribution of property between them. For a thorough discussion of the case law, and an attempt to make sense of its underlying normative premises, see Jill Elaine Hasday, "Intimacy and Economic Exchange," *Harv. L. Rev.* 119 (2005): 491–530, 499–511.

14. GAO Report, note 8 *supra*, p. 5.

15. Ibid.

16. Contrast *Moore v. East Cleveland*, 431 U.S. 494 (1977) (striking a zoning ordinance as unconstitutional because it so narrowly defined "family" as to exclude a grandmother and her grandsons) with *Belle Terre v. Boraas*, 416 U.S. 1 (1974) (upholding a "families only" ordinance against a privacy rights challenge brought by unrelated individuals).

17. For a general discussion of this and other noneconomic but tangible benefits of marital status, see *Goodridge*, 798 N.E.2d, pp. 955–956.

18. Married partners cannot be compelled to testify against each other in criminal proceedings; other intimately related persons, such as a mother and child, can be so compelled. See generally 8 Wigmore, Evidence Sec 2232 (1961). For a good critical discussion of the privilege, and a revealing contrast with the forced testimony of Monica Lewinsky's mother to the grand jury during the Clinton years, see Nancy Polikoff, "Ending Marriage as We Know It," *Hofstra L. Rev.* 32 (2003): 201–232, 201–204. For a defense, of the privilege, see Milton Regan, Jr., *Alone Together: Law and the Meanings of Marriage* (New York: Oxford University Press, 1999), pp. 89–135.

19. So long as an organization is truly "private," and does not depend upon state-provided funding, and so long as it is not a "public accommodation" (and therefore within the scope of federal law prohibiting discrimination by public accommodations facilities on the basis of race or sex), and so long as it has some expressive purpose, it has broad associational rights and free speech rights to discriminate against individuals or groups. A minority of states and the District of Columbia have enacted laws prohibiting discrimination on the basis of sexual orientation by public accommodations. See generally *NAACP v. Alabama*, 357 U.S. 449 (1958) (finding a broad right to associate under the First Amendment); *Roberts v. United States Jaycees*, 468 U.S. 509 (1984) (finding that the Jaycees are a public accommodation, and that their speech and associational rights were not infringed upon by a public accommodations law forbidding them from discriminating on the basis of gender); *Hurley v. Irish-American Gay, Lesbian and Bisexual Group of Boston*, 515 U.S. 557 (1995) (finding that the War Veterans Council is not a public accommodation, distinguishing *Roberts*, and that they have First Amendment rights to exclude the Irish American Gay, Lesbian and Bisexual Group from a St. Patrick's Day march); and *Boy Scouts of America et al. v. James Dale*, 530 U.S. 640 (2000) (finding that the Boy Scouts have an expressive, First Amendment interest in excluding gay men from positions of leadership).

20. GAO report, note 8 *supra*.

21. See "Protections, Benefits, and Obligations of Marriage under Massachusetts and Federal Law: Some Key Provisions of a Work-in-Progress" (GLAAD study, June 21, 2001), Appendix: Additional Legal Benefits, Protections, and Obligations of Marriage, p. 16.

22. Ibid., p. 15.

23. Ibid.

24. Ibid.

25. Ibid., p. 16.

26. GAO Report, note 8 *supra*, pp. 3–4.

27. Ibid.

28. GAO Report, note 8 *supra*.

29. *Goodridge*, 798 N.E.2d, pp. 955–956.

30. See, for example, Linda Waite and Maggie Gallagher, *The Case for Marriage: Why Married People Are Happier, Healthier, and Better off Financially* (New York: Broadway Books, 2000), pp. 18–23; Stephen Nock, "Why Not Marriage?" *Va J. L. Soc. Pol.* 9 (2001): 273–290, 288–290.

31. Communitarians tend to emphasize this understanding of the point of marriage more than do utilitarians. See, for example, Mary Shanley, *Just Marriage* (New York: Oxford University Press, 2004), p. 26 ("when people marry they become part of an entity

that is not reducible to or identical with its individual components."). See generally Milton Regan, Jr., *Alone Together* (New York: Oxford University Press, 1999), pp. 22–29.

32. See, for example, *Mayor of Baltimore v. Dawson*, 350 U.S. 877 (1955) (holding that segregated beaches are unconstitutional); *Gayle v. Browder*, 352 U.S. 903 (1956) (holding that segregated buses are unconstitutional); *Holmes v. Atlanta*, 350 U.S. 879 (1955) (holding that segregated golf courses are unconstitutional); and *New Orleans City Park Improvement Assoc'n v. Detiege*, 358 U.S. 54 (1958) (holding that segregated parks are unconstitutional).

33. See, for example, *Reed v. Reed*, 404 U.S. 71 (1971) (finding a statute creating a preference for male executors to be unconstitutional); *Frontiero v. Richardson*, 411 U.S. 677 (1973) (holding that Air Force benefits rules that gave benefits to all wives of men, but only to economically dependent husbands of women in the Air Force as unconstitutional); *Stanton v. Stanton*, 421 U.S. 7 (1975) (finding a statute creating different ages of majority for women and men to be unconstitutional); *Craig v. Boren*, 429 U.S. 190 (1976) (holding a statute creating gender-based rules regarding the ability of young people to buy beer struck unconstitutional); *Califano v. Goldfarb*, 430 U.S. 199 (1977) (holding a Social Security provision giving benefits to widows automatically but requiring widowers to prove dependency on deceased wife to be unconstitutional); *Orr v. Orr*, 440 U.S. 268 (1979) (finding a statute providing alimony for women but not men to be unconstitutional); and *United States v. Virginia*, 518 U.S. 515 (1996) (requiring the Virginia Military Institute to admit women).

34. *Goodridge*, 798 N.E.2d, pp. 957–967.

35. There are other equal protection arguments that could be and have been pressed toward the conclusion that the limits on marriage to opposite-sex couples are unconstitutional beyond the one focused on in the text. Notably, the Hawaii Supreme Court, in 1991, put forward the argument that had then gained considerable currency in the academic community; that the limit to opposite-sex couples renders marriage an instance of sex (or gender) discrimination: allowing a woman to marry a man, but not a woman, treats women differently from men for no apparent reason. There are surely differences between this claim and the claim that the same law violates constitutional principle because it treats same-sex couples differently than opposite-sex couples. Nevertheless, for purposes of this discussion, the arguments are more similar than dissimilar: they both focus attention on the irrationality of conferring marital benefits on the basis of the gender, and hence the nature of the sexual relation, of the parties to the union. See *Baehr v. Lewin*, 852 P. 2d 44 (Ha. 1993).

36. *Brown v. Board of Education*, 347 U.S. 483 (1954).

37. See George and Bradley, "Marriage and the Liberal Imagination," *Geo. L. J.* 84 (1995): 301–320, 301.

38. Ibid.

39. A number of studies reach this conclusion—which is in turn often cited both by supporters and critics of same-sex marriage. See Judith Stacey and Timothy Biblarz, "How Does the Sexual Orientation of Parents Matter?" *Am. Soc. Rev.* 88 (April 2001): 159–183 (boys and girls raised by lesbian couples are more open to gender-nonconforming play activities and related gender prescriptions); Fiona Tasker and Susan Golombok, *Growing Up in a Lesbian Family: Effects on Child Development* (New York: Guilford, 1997) (girls raised in lesbian families are more sexually adventurous and less chaste, boys are

less adventurous and more chaste, but no difference in degree to which girls self-identify as lesbian).

40. William Eskridge, *Equality Practice: Civil Unions and the Future of Gay Rights* (New York: Routledge, 2002).

41. The empirical literature finding no significant differences, save greater tolerance for homosexuality and greater flexibility regarding gender roles, is thoroughly reviewed in Charlotte Patterson, "Adoption of Minor Children by Lesbian and Gay Adults: A Social Science Perspective," *Duke J. Gender L. and Pol'y* 2 (1995): 191–205. Professor Lynn Wardle has criticized the Patterson article and the sources she discusses primarily on the grounds that the sample sizes in the studies Patterson discusses were small. Lynn Wardle, "The Potential Impact of Homosexual Parenting on Children," *U. Ill. L. Rev.* (1997): 833–920. Wardle does not introduce substantial empirical evidence of his own to the effect that the children of lesbian and gay parents are harmed, and relies heavily on only one study by Paul Cameron and Kirk Cameron (ibid.); Paul Cameron and Kirk Cameron, "Homosexual Parents," *Adolescence* 31 (1996): 757–776. Rather, Wardle's arguments are speculative (e.g., gay men are likely to sexually abuse their children) and readily refuted by well-established empirical studies. Carlos Ball and Janice Pea have responded to Wardle in "Warring with Wardle: Morality, Social Science, and Gay and Lesbian Parents," *U. Ill. L. Rev.* (1998): 253–339. See also Mike Allen and Nancy Burrell, "Comparing the Impact of Homosexual and Heterosexual Parents on Children: Meta-Analysis of Existing Research," *J. Homosexuality* 32 (1996): 19–35; Judith Stacey and Timothy Biblarz, "How Does Sexual Orientation of Parents Matter?" *Am. Soc. Rev.* 66 (2001): 159–183.

One recent article argues that contrary to conventional wisdom, there are indeed differences in the outcome of children raised by homosexual and heterosexual parents. The differences actually cited turn out to be slim, primarily revolving around the increased femininity of boys and assertiveness of girls raised by lesbians. Dean Byrd, "Gender Complementarity and Child-Rearing: Where Tradition and Science Agree," *J. L. and Fam. Stud.* 6 (2004): 213–235. Otherwise, the evidence cited is primarily that gays and lesbians are vulnerable to health problems that do not beset straight individuals, that their relationships are more transient, and that they present poor "modeling" of the importance of traditional family arrangements. However, Byrd does not present evidence to the effect that lesbian and gay parents, as opposed to lesbians and gays generally, have more transient relationships or more health problems, and whether the lack of modeling for traditional family relations is or isn't a problem obviously depends upon the value placed on those traditional family relations.

42. Byrd, note 41 *supra*.

43. *Goodridge*, 798 N.E.2d, pp. 959–961.

44. *Lawrence v. Texas*, 539 U.S. 558 (2003).

45. Ibid.

46. *Griswold v. Connecticut*, 381 U.S. 479 (1965) (holding a state's criminalization of the possession of birth control by married couples an unconstitutional infringement of the right to privacy).

47. *Eisenstadt v. Baird*, 405 U.S. 438 (1972) (state law criminalizing possession of birth control by unmarried individuals held an unconstitutional infringement of the right to privacy).

48. *Roe v. Wade*, 410 U.S. 113 (1973) (state criminalization of abortion unconstitutional violation of the right to privacy).

49. *Planned Parenthood of Southeast Pennsylvania. v. Casey*, 505 U.S. 833 (1992) (*Roe* upheld, at least with respect to the previability stages of pregnancy, but postviability, a state's interest in the developing life of the fetus may be weighed against the woman's interest in terminating the pregnancy).

50. *Lawrence*, 539 U.S. 558 (2003).

51. Ibid.

52. Ibid.

53. For a general discussion, see Robin West, "Liberalism Rediscovered: A Pragmatic Definition of the Liberal Vision," *U. Pitt. L. Rev.* 46 (1985), pp. 673–738.

54. Michael Sandel, *Democracy's Discontent: America in Search of a Public Philosophy* (Cambridge, MA: Harvard University Press, 1996).

55. See, for example, William Galston, *Liberal Pluralism: The Implication of Value Pluralism for Political Theory and Practice* (New York: Cambridge University Press, 2002); Martha Nussbaum, *Women and Human Development* (New York: Cambridge University Press, 2000); and Richard Rorty, *Philosophy and Social Hope* (New York: Penguin, 1999).

56. *Goodridge*, 798 N.E.2d, p. 954 ("We begin by considering the nature of civil marriage itself. Simply put, the government creates civil marriage. In Massachusetts, civil marriage is, and since precolonial days has been, precisely what its name implies: a wholly secular institution.... No religious ceremony has ever been required to validate a Massachusetts marriage").

57. See Chai Feldblum, "Gay Is Good: The Moral Case for Marriage Equality and More," *Yale J.L. and Feminism* 17 (2005): 139–184; and Carlos Ball, *The Morality of Gay Rights: An Exploration of Political Philosophy* (New York: Routledge, 2003).

58. Milton Regan, Jr., *Alone Together: Law and the Meanings of Marriage* (New York: Oxford Press, 1999); and Milton Regan, Jr., *Family Law and the Pursuit of Intimacy* (New York: New York University Press, 1993).

59. Mary Shanley, *Just Marriage* (New York: Oxford University Press, 2004).

60. Andrew Sullivan, *Virtually Normal: An Argument about Homosexuality* (New York: Knopf, 1995); Andrew Sullivan, "Here Comes the Groom: A (Conservative) Case for Gay Marriage," *New Republic*, August 28, 1989; William Eskridge, *The Case for Same-Sex Marriage: From Sexual Liberty to Civilized Commitment* (New York: Free Press, 1996); Jonathan Rauch, *Gay Marriage: Why It's Good for Straights, and Good for America* (New York: Times Books/Henry Holt, 2004); and Jonathan Rauch, "Who Needs Marriage?" in *Beyond Queer: Challenging Gay Left Orthodoxy*, ed. Bruce Bawer, 1996, p. 296.

61. Nan Hunter, "Marriage, Law, and Gender: A Feminist Inquiry," *L. and Sexuality* 1 (1991): 9–30.

62. Robin West, "Universalism, Liberal Theory, and the Problem of Gay Marriage," *Fla. St. U. L. Rev.* 25 (1998): 705–730.

63. Adrienne Rich, "Compulsory Heterosexuality and Lesbian Existence," *Signs: J. Women in Culture and Soc'y* 5, no. 4 (1980): 631–660.

64. See Robert P. George and Gerard V. Bradley, "Marriage and the Liberal Imagination," *Geo. L. J.* 84 (1995): 301–320; John Finnis, "Law, Morality, and Sexual Orientation," *Notre Dame L. Rev.* 69 (1994): 1049–1076; Gerard V. Bradley, "Life's Dominion:

A Review Essay," *Notre Dame L. Rev.* 69 (1993): 329–391; Gerard V. Bradley, "Law and the Culture of Marriage," *Notre Dame J.L. Ethics and Pub. Pol'y* 18 (2004): 189–217; Gerard V. Bradley, "Same-Sex Marriage: Our Final Answer?" *Notre Dame J. L. Ethics and Pub. Pol'y* 14 (2000): 729–752; and Robert P. George, "Judicial Usurpation and Sexual Liberation: Courts and the Abolition of Marriage," *Regent U.L. Rev.* 17 (2004): 21–30. See generally Chapter 2 of this volume.

65. *Goodridge,* 798 N.E.2d, p. 961.

66. *Hernandez v. Robles,* 2006 N.Y. Slip Op. 05239 (N.Y. July 6, 2006); Lynn Wardle, "Is Marriage Obsolete?" *Mich. J. Gender and L.* 10 (2003): 189–235; Lynn Wardle, "The Potential Impact of Homosexual Parenting on Children," *U. Ill. L. Rev.* 1997 (1997): 833–906; and Dean Byrd, "Gender Complementarity and Child-Rearing: Where Tradition and Science Agree," *J.L. and Fam. Stud.* 6 (2004): 213–235.

67. Byrd, note 66 *supra,* p. 218.

68. Waite and Gallagher, *The Case for Marriage,* note 30 *supra,* pp. 200–201.

69. *Goodridge,* 798 N.E.2d, p. 983.

70. *Hernandez v. Robles,* 2006 N.Y. Slip Op. 05239 (N.Y., July 6, 2006).

71. *Goodridge,* 798 N.E.2d, pp. 996–1004.

72. Kenji Yoshino, "Too Good for Marriage," *New York Times,* July 14, 2006, p. A19.

73. Nancy Polikoff, "Ending Marriage as We Know It," *Hofstra L. Rev.* 32 (2003): 201–232; Nancy Polikoff, "Why Lesbians and Gay Men Should Read Martha Fineman," *Am. U. J. Gender Soc. Pol'y and L.* 8 (2000): 167–176; Ruthann Robson, "The State of Marriage," *Y.B.N.Z. Jurisprudence* 1 (1997): 1.

74. Catharine MacKinnon, *Toward a Feminist Theory of the State* (Cambridge, MA: Harvard University Press, 1989); and MacKinnon, *Feminism UnModified: Discourses on Life and Law* (Cambridge, MA: Harvard University Press, 1987).

75. Marc Spindelman has made this argument most explicitly, in two major articles: one criticizing what he sees as the sexual libertarianism of the *Lawrence* decision, and the second, criticizing the valorization of marriage in the *Goodridge* decisions. He criticizes *Lawrence* and *Goodridge* on both feminist and gay rights grounds, but his political concern, in both articles, is primarily with male-on-male gay sexual violence. His worry is that the libertarian, prosex, constitutional privacy thrown around gay sex in *Lawrence,* and the praise heaped upon marriage, in *Goodridge,* will further shield gay rape from prosecution, and even from critique. See Marc Spindelman, "Surviving *Lawrence v. Texas,*" *Mich. L. Rev.* 102 (2004): 1615–1667; and Marc Spindelman, "Homosexuality's Horizon," *Emory L. Rev.* 54 (2005): 1361–1406.

76. Michael Warner, *The Trouble with Normal* (Cambridge, MA: Harvard University Press, 2000).

77. I have argued this at some length in a series of recent articles. See Robin West, "Law's Nobility," *Yale J.L. and Feminism* 17 (2006): 385; West, "Desperately Seeking a Moralist," *Harv. J.L. and Gender* 29 (2006): 1–150. See generally West, "The Difference in Women's Hedonic Lives: A Phenomenological Critique of Liberal and Radical Feminism," *Wisc. Women's L.J.* 3 (1988): 81.

78. See, for example, Arlie Hochschild, *The Second Shift: Working Parents and the Revolution at Home* (New York: Viking, 1989); Philip Blumstein and Pepper Schwartz, *American Couples: Money, Work, Sex* (New York: Morrow, 1983); Roberta Sigel, *Ambition*

and Accommodation: How Women View Gender Relations (Chicago: University of Chicago Press, 1996); and Janice Steil, *Marital Equality: Its Relationship to the Well-being of Husbands and Wives* (Thousand Oaks, CA: Sage, 1997).

79. Hochschild, note 78 *supra*.

80. See Joan Blades and Kristin Rowe-Finkbeiner, "The Motherhood Manifesto," *Nation*, May 4, 2006, available at http://www.thenation.com/doc/20060522/blades.

81. See Susan Moller Okin, *Justice, Gender, and the Family* (New York: Basic Books, 1989) for an early feminist argument that the injustice of family life undercuts liberal aspirations for a just society.

82. Ibid.

83. See Arlie Hochschild, *The Second Shift: Working Parents and the Revolution at Home* (New York: Viking, 1989).

84. Object psychologists influenced by feminism have explored this issue in depth, touching off, perhaps inadvertently, a large movement as well as scholarly agenda. See Nancy Chodorow, *The Reproduction of Mothering* (Berkeley: University of California Press, 1978); Nancy Dinnerstein, *The Mermaid and the Minotaur: Sexual Arrangements and Human Malaise* (New York: Other Press, 1999); Carol Gilligan, *In a Different Voice: Psychological Theory and Women's Development* (Cambridge, MA: Harvard University Press, 1982).

85. Stephen Nock, "Why Not Marriage?" *Va. J. Soc. Pol'y and L.* 9 (2001): 273–290, 276–277.

86. Shanley, *Just Marriage* (Oxford: Boston Review Book, 2004).

87. Linda McClain, *The Place of Families: Fostering Capacity, Equality, and Responsibility* (Cambridge, MA: Harvard University Press, 2006).

88. Susan Moller Okin, *Justice, Gender, and the Family* (New York: BasicBooks, 1991).

89. See Robin West, *Caring for Justice* (New York: New York University Press, 1997), for an extended argument to this effect.

90. Joan C. Williams, *Unbending Gender* (New York: Oxford University Press, 2000); Joan C. Williams, "Deconstructing the Maternal Wall: Strategies for Vindicating the Civil Rights of 'Carers' in the Workplace," *Duke J. Gender L. and Pol'y* 13 (2006): 31–53; Joan C. Williams, "Hibbs as a Federalism Case; Hibbs as a Maternal Wall Case," *U. Cin. L. Rev.* 72 (2004): 365–398; Joan C. Williams, "Better on Balance? The Corporate Counsel Work/Life Report," *Wm. and Mary J. Women and L.* 10 (2004): 367–457; and Joan C. Williams, "The Family-Hostile Corporation," *Geo. Wash. L. Rev.* 70 (2002): 921–930.

91. Gary Becker, *A Treatise on the Family*, enlarged ed. (Cambridge, MA: Harvard University Press, 2005).

92. Classic treatments include Jerome Barkow, Leda Cosmides, and John Tooby, *The Adapted Mind: Evolutionary Psychology and the Generation of Culture* (New York: Oxford University Press, 1992); Richard Dawkins, *The Selfish Gene* (New York: Oxford University Press, 1976); George Williams, *Sex and Evolution* (Princeton, NJ: Princeton University Press, 1975); Edward O. Wilson, *Sociobiology: The New Synthesis* (Cambridge, MA: Belknap Press of Harvard University Press, 2000); Robert Wright, *The Moral Animal: Why We Are the Way We Are—The New Science of Evolutionary Psychology* (New York: Vintage, 1994); and Richard Posner, *Sex and Reason* (Cambridge, MA: Harvard University Press, 1992).

93. Gary Becker, *A Treatise on the Family* (Cambridge, MA: Harvard University Press, 2005).

94. Stephen Nock, "Why Not Marriage?" *Va. J. of Soc. Pol. and L.* 9 (2001): 273–290.

95. John Stuart Mill, *Utilitarianism*, ed. George Sher (Indianapolis: Hackett, 1979).

96. Thomas Hobbes, *Leviathan*, ed. Richard Tuck (New York: Cambridge University Press, 1996).

97. Lenore Weitzman, *The Divorce Revolution: The Unexpected Social and Economic Consequences for Women and Children in America* (New York: Free Press, 1985); Martha Fineman, "Feminist Legal Theory," *Am. U.J. Gender Soc. Pol'y and L.* 13 (2005): 13–23; Martha Fineman, "The Social Foundations of Law," *Emory L.J.* 54 (2005): 201–237; Martha Fineman, "Gender and Law: Feminist Legal Theory's Role in New Legal Realism," *Wis. L. Rev.* (2005): 405–431; Mary Becker, "Care and Feminists," *Wis. Women's L.J.* 17 (2002): 57–110; Mary Becker, "Caring for Children and Care-Takers," *Chi.-Kent L. Rev.* 76 (2001): 1495–1540; Jana Singer, "Husbands, Wives, and Human Capital: Why the Shoe Won't Fit," *Fam. L.Q.* 31 (1997): 119–131; and Jana Singer, "Alimony and Efficiency: The Gendered Costs and Benefits of the Economic Justification for Alimony," *Geo. L.J.* 82 (1994): 2423–2460.

98. See Roberta S. Sigel, *Ambition and Accommodation*, pp. 96–98, 167–168. See generally Mary Becker et al., *Taking Women Seriously* (St. Paul, MN: West, 2001), pp. 616–628.

Notes to the Conclusion

1. U.S. Constitution, Amendment XVIII, repealed by U.S. Constitution, Amendment XXI, 1.

2. See Jill Elaine Hasday, "Contest and Consent: A Legal History of Marital Rape," *Cal. L. Rev.* 88 (2000): 1373–1505; and Robin West, "The Harms of Consensual Sex," *Am Phil. Ass'n. Newsl.* 94 (Spring 1995): 52–53.

3. See Robin West, "Do We Have a Right to Care?" in *The Subject of Care*, ed. Eva Kittay and Ellen Feder (Lanham, MD: Rowman and Littlefield, 2003), pp. 88–114.

4. *United States v. Virginia*, 518 U.S. 515 (1996).

5. I have not explicitly advocated expanding civil union to embrace unions of persons in numbers greater than two. I have not done so, however, only in the interest of keeping this "modest proposal" both modest and simple: the limited goal here is to urge that marriage equality advocates shift their attention from marriage equality to civil union equality, for gay and straight couples. I don't mean to suggest, however, that there is any reason inherent in the nature of polygamous relationships, or nonconjugal groups of three or more adults, that preclude state recognition of the validity and potential of such relations, for purposes of raising children or caring for dependents. Polygamy, as currently practiced in the United States, is surely often harmful to participants, but usually because of the violation of various criminal laws, not the polygamous form of marriage itself. It is or ought to be criminal to force a girl to marry someone not of her own choice, to participate in such a wedding, to expel adolescent boys from a community because of

the threat they pose to middle-aged men, and so forth. It doesn't follow from the immorality or the criminality of that conduct, that polygamy itself is a terrible way to live, for those who opt for it as adults. Surely, with a civil union law on the books, it would be a desirable next step for a conscientious legislature to ask whether there is any sense in restricting civil union to intimate unions of two, rather than to larger groupings.

6. Civil union laws of this sort, passed in a large number of states, might also, ideally, tip the weight of opinion regarding federal law as well. For federal marriage benefits, rather than just state marriage benefits, to extend to unconventional couples (whether same sex, nonconjugal, or heterosexuals opting for civil union rather than marriage) not only would federal laws such as DOMA have to be repealed, and liberal state laws enacted, but federal law would also have to define the scope of the marriages affected by statutory schemes such as Social Security laws. Ideally, this could focus attention on the need to define those benefits rationally, with an eye toward the needs of all citizens, rather than simply incorporating definitions, with their many-gendered assumptions, from the past. This important point is explored at some length in Nancy Cotts, *Public Vows: A History of Marriage and Union* (Cambridge, MA: Harvard University Press, 2000), pp. 174–179.

Bibliography

Abrams, Jill. "Gay Marriage Amendment Faces Uphill Battle." Associated Press, July 18, 2006.

Allen, Douglas W., and Margaret Brinig. "Sex, Property Rights, and Divorce." *Eur. J.L. and Econ.* 5 (1998): 211–233.

———. "'These Boots Are Made for Walking:' Why Most Divorce Filers Are Women." *Am. L. and Econ. Rev.* 2 (2000): 126–169.

Allen, Mike, and Nancy Burrell. "Comparing the Impact of Homosexual and Heterosexual Parents on Children: Meta-Analysis of Existing Research." *J. Homosexuality* 32 (1996): 19–35.

Alstott, Anne. *No Exit: What Parents Owe Their Children and Society Owes Parents.* New York: Oxford Univ. Press, 2004.

Amato, Paul. "Children of Divorce in the 1990s: An Update of the Amato and Keith (1991) Meta-Analysis." *J. Fam. Psychol.* 15 (2001): 355–370.

———. "Good Enough Marriages: Parental Discord, Divorce, and Children's Long-Term Well-Being." *Va. J. Soc. Pol'y and L.* 9 (2001): 71–93.

Areen, Judith. *Cases and Materials on Family Law.* Mineola, NY: Foundation Press, 1978.

Areen, Judith, and Milton C. Regan, Jr. *Family Law: Cases and Materials*, 5th ed. New York: Foundation Press, 2006.

Armas, Genaro C. "Cohabitation on the Rise: Unmarried Partner Households Increase by 72 Percent." May 15, 2001, available at http://cgi.jconline.com/cgi-bin/resend/printPage.pl?storypath=lafayettejc/Census/0520104.shtml.

Bahr, Stephen J. "Social Science Research on Family Dissolution: What It Shows and How It Might Be of Interest to Family Law Reformers." *J.L. and Fam. Stud.* 4 (2002): 5–65.

Ball, Carlos. *The Morality of Gay Rights: An Exploration of Political Philosophy.* New York: Routledge, 2003.

Ball, Carlos, and Janice Pea. "Warring with Wardle: Morality, Social Science, and Gay and Lesbian Parents." *U. Ill. L. Rev.* 1998 (1998): 253–339.

Barkow, Jerome, Leda Cosmides, and John Tooby. *The Adapted Mind: Evolutionary Psychology and the Generation of Culture.* New York: Oxford University Press, 1992.

Barnett, Randy E. "Was Slavery Unconstitutional Before the 13th Amendment? Lysander Spooner's Theory of Interpretation." *Pac. L.J.* 28 (1977): 977–1014.

Becker, Gary. *A Treatise on the Family,* enlarged ed. Cambridge, MA: Harvard University Press, 2005.

Becker, Mary. "Prince Charming: Abstract Equality." *Sup. Ct. Rev.* 5 (1987): 201–247.

———. "The Politics of Women's Wrongs and the Bill of Rights: A Bicentennial Perspective." *U. Chi. L. Rev.* 59 (1992): 453–517.

———. "Women, Morality, and Sexual Orientation." *UCLA Women's L.J.* 8 (1998): 165–218.

———. "Caring for Children and Care-Takers." *Chi.-Kent L. Rev.* 76 (2001): 1495–1540.

———. "Care and Feminists" *Wis. Women's L.J.* 17 (2002): 57–110.

Becker, Mary, Cynthia Grant Bowman, and Morrison Torrey. *Cases and Materials on Feminist Jurisprudence: Taking Women Seriously.* St. Paul, MN: West Group, 2001.

Bernstein, Anita. "For and Against Marriage: A Revision." *Mich. Law Rev.* 102 (2003): 129–210.

Berrick, Jill Duerr, and Bruce Fuller. "Implications for Families, Children, and Policy Makers." Pp. 3–6 in Jill Berrick and Bruce Fuller, eds., *Good Parents or Good Workers? How Policy Shapes Families' Daily Lives.* New York: Palgrave Macmillan, 2005.

———. "Introduction: New Family Policy: How the State Shapes Parents' Lives." Pp. 175–182 in Jill Berrick and Bruce Fuller, eds., *Good Parents or Good Workers? How Policy Shapes Families' Daily Lives.* New York: Palgrave Macmillan, 2005.

Berrick, Jill Duer, and Bruce Fuller, eds. *Good Parents or Good Workers: How Policy Shapes Families' Daily Lives.* New York: Palgrave Macmillan, 2005.

Black, Charles. *A New Birth of Freedom: Human Rights, Named and Unnamed.* New York: Grosset/Putnam, 1997.

Blackstone, William. *Commentaries* 1, pp. 442–445.

Blades, Joan, and Kristin Rowe-Finkbeiner. "The Motherhood Manifesto." *Nation* (May 4, 2006), available at http://www.thenation.com/doc/20060522/blades.

Blumstein, Philip, and Pepper Schwartz. *American Couples: Money, Work, Sex.* New York: Morrow, 1983.

Boo, Katherine. "The Marriage Cure: Is Wedlock Really a Way Out of Poverty?" *New Yorker* (August 18, 2003): 105.

Bork, Robert H. *The Tempting of America: The Political Seduction of the Law.* New York: Touchstone, 1990.

Boston Women's Health Book Collective. *Our Bodies Ourselves: A New Edition for a New Era.* New York: Simon and Schuster, 2005.

Bradley, Gerard V. "Life's Dominion: A Review Essay." *Notre Dame L. Rev.* 69 (1993): 29–91.

———. "Same Sex Marriage: Our Final Answer?" *Notre Dame J.L. Ethics and Pub. Pol'y* 14 (2000): 729–752.

———. "Law and the Culture of Marriage." *Notre Dame J.L. Ethics and Pub. Pol'y* 18 (2004): 189–217.

Brinig, Margaret. "In Search of Prince Charming." *J. Gender Race and Just.* 4 (2001): 321–336.

Byrd, Dean. "Gender Complementarity and Child-Rearing: Where Tradition and Science Agree." *J.L. and Fam. Stud.* 6 (2004): 213–235.

Cameron, Paul, and Kirk Cameron. "Homosexual Parents." *Adolescence* 31 (1996): 757–776.

Carbone, June, and Margaret Brinig. "Rethinking Marriage: Feminist Ideology, Economic Change, and Divorce Reform." *Tul. L. Rev.* 65 (1991): 953–1010.

Centers for Disease Control and Prevention. "Births, Marriages, Divorces, and Deaths." National Vital Statistics Report, available at http://www.cdc.gov/nchs/products/pubs/pubd/nvsr/nvsr.htm.

Cherlin, Andrew. *Marriage, Divorce, Remarriage.* Cambridge, MA: Harvard University Press, 1992.

———. "Should the Government Promote Marriage?" *Contexts* 2, no. 4 (Fall 2003): 30–35.

———. "The Consequences of Welfare Reform for Child Well-Being: What Have We Learned So Far and What Are the Policy Implications?" Paper presented at the 2004 Annual Meeting of the American Sociological Association, session "The End of Welfare as We Knew It: What Now?" August 14, 2004, available at http://www.jhu.edu/~welfare.

Cherlin, Andrew, and Paula Fomby. "A Closer Look at Changes in Children's Living Arrangements in Low-Income Families." Policy Brief 02-3 of *Welfare, Children and Families: A Three City Study*, available at http://www.jhu.edu/~welfare.

Cherlin, Andrew, et al. *Welfare, Children and Families: A Three City Study*, available at http://www.jhu.edu/~welfare; http://www.jhu.edu/~welfare/welfare_publication.html.

Chodorow, Nancy. *The Reproduction of Mothering: Psychoanalysis and the Sociology of Gender.* Berkeley: University of California Press, 1978.

Clinton, William Jefferson. "Address before a Joint Session of the Congress on the State of the Union." February 17, 1993.

———. "How We Ended Welfare, Together." *New York Times*, August 22, 2006.

Colker, Ruth. "Marriage Mimicry: The Law of Domestic Violence." *Wm. and Mary L. Rev.* 47 (2006): 1841–1898.

Combs, Robert H. "Marital Status and Personal Well-Being: A Literature Review." *Fam. Rel.* 40 (1991): 97–102.

Congregation for the Doctrine of the Faith. "Vatican Declaration on Certain Questions of Sexual Ethics." (1975).

———. "The Pastoral Care of the Homosexual Person." (1986).

———. "Catechism of the Catholic Church." (1993).

———. "Considerations Regarding Proposals to Give Legal Recognition to Unions Between Homosexual Persons." (2003).

Connerton, Kelly C. "Comment: The Resurgence of the Marital Rape Exemption: The Victimization of Teens by Their Statutory Rapists." *Alb. L. Rev.* 61 (1997): 237–283.

Coontz, Stephanie. *The Way We Never Were: American Families and the Nostalgia Trap.* New York: Basic Books, 1992.

———. *The Way We Really Are: Coming to Terms with America's Changing Families.* New York: Basic Books, 1998.

———. *Marriage: A History: From Obedience to Intimacy or How Love Conquered Marriage.* New York: Viking/Penguin, 2005.

Cott, Nancy. *Public Vows: A History of Marriage and the Nation.* Cambridge, MA: Harvard University Press, 2000.

Culp, Laurie, and Steven R. H. Beach. "Marriage and Depressive Symptoms: The Role and Bases of Self-Esteem Differ by Gender." *Psychol. of Women Q.* 22 (1998): 647–663.

Dalton, Clare, and Elizabeth Schneider. *Battered Women and the Law.* New York: Foundation Press, 2001.

Danziger, Sheldon, and Hui-chen Wang. "Does It Pay to Move from Welfare to Work? Reply to Robert Moffitt and Katie Winder." available at http://www.jhu.edu/~welfare/danziger_wang_08_19_04.pdf.

Dawkins, Richard. *The Selfish Gene.* New York: Oxford University Press, 1976.

Denno, Deborah W. "Why the Model Penal Code's Sexual Offense Provisions Should Be Pulled and Replaced." *Ohio St. J. Crim. L.* 1 (2003): 207–218.

DeParle, Jason. *American Dream: Three Women, Ten Kids, and a Nation's Drive to End Welfare.* New York: Viking Press, 2004.

Dinnerstein, Dorothy. *The Mermaid and the Minotaur: Sexual Arrangements and Human Malaise.* New York: Harper and Row, 1976.

Dougherty, Terrance. "Economic Benefits of Marriage under Federal and Massachusetts Law." New York: National Gay and Lesbian Task Force Policy Institute, 2004, available at http://www.thetaskforce.org/downloads/EconomicCosts.pdf.

———. "Economic Benefits of Marriage under Federal and Oregon Law." New York: National Gay and Lesbian Task Force Policy Institute, 2004.

Douglass, Frederick. "The Constitution of the United States: Is it Pro-Slavery or Anti-Slavery?" Speech delivered in Glasgow, Scotland, March 26, 1860. Pp. 467–480 in Philip S. Foner, ed., *The Life and Writings of Frederick Douglass.* New York: International, 1950.

———. "The Meaning of July Fourth for the Negro." Speech delivered in Rochester, New York, July 5, 1882. Pp. 181–204 in Philip S. Foner, ed., *The Life and Writings of Frederick Douglass.* New York: International, 1950.

Dworkin, Andrea. *Intercourse.* New York: Free Press, 1987.

Dworkin, Ronald. *Taking Rights Seriously.* Cambridge, MA: Harvard University Press, 2005.

Eckholm, Erik. "For the Neediest of the Needy, Welfare Reforms Still Fall Short, Study Says." *New York Times,* May 17, 2006.

———. "A Welfare Law Milestone Finds Many Left Behind." *New York Times,* August 22, 2006.

Edelman, Peter. "The Next Century of Our Constitution: Rethinking Our Duty to the Poor." *Hastings L.J.* 39 (1987): 1–61.

———. "Responding to the Wake-Up Call: A New Agenda for Poverty Lawyers." *N.Y.U. Rev. L. and Soc. Change* 24 (1998): 547–561.

———. "Poverty and Welfare Policy in the Post-Clinton Era." *Miss. L.J.* 70 (2001): 877–887.

———. "Beyond Welfare Reform: Economic Justice in the 21st Century." *Berkeley J. Emp. and Lab. L.* 24 (2003): 475–487.

———. "Welfare and the Politics of Race, Same Tune, New Lyrics?" *Geo. J. of Poverty L. and Pol'y* 11 (2004): 389–403.

Edin, Kathryn, and Laura Lein. *Making Ends Meet: How Single Mothers Survive Welfare and Low-Wage Work*. New York: Russell Sage Foundation, 1997.

Edin, Kathryn, and Maria Kefalas. *Promises I Can Keep: Why Poor Women Put Motherhood before Marriage*. Berkeley: University of California Press, 2005.

Ehrenreich, Barbara. *Nickel and Dimed: On (Not) Getting By in America*. New York: Metropolitan Books, 2001.

Ely, John Hart. *Democracy and Distrust*. Cambridge, MA: Harvard University Press, 1980.

Ernst, Daniel R. "Legal Positivism, Abolitionist Litigation, and the New Jersey Slave Case of 1845." *Law and Hist. Rev.* 4 (1986): 337–365.

Eskridge, William, Jr. *The Case for Same-Sex Marriage: From Sexual Liberty to Civilized Commitment*. New York: Free Press, 1996.

———. *Equality Practice: Civil Unions and the Future of Gay Rights*. New York: Routledge Press, 2002.

Eskridge, William, Jr., and Nan Hunter. *Sexuality, Gender, and the Law*. St. Paul, MN: West, 2003.

Etzioni, Amitai. "A Communitarian Position for Civil Unions." Pp. 63–67 in Mary Shanley, ed., *Just Marriage*. New York: Oxford University Press, 2004.

Feldblum, Chai. "Gay Is Good: The Moral Case for Marriage Equality and More." *Yale J.L. and Feminism* 17 (2005): 139–184.

Fineman, Martha. *The Illusion of Equality: The Rhetoric and Reality of Divorce Reform*. Chicago: University of Chicago Press, 1994.

———. *The Neutered Mother, the Sexual Family and Other Twentieth Century Tragedies*. New York: Routledge, 1995.

———. "Why Marriage?" *Va. J. Soc. Pol'y and L.* 9 (2001): 239–271.

———. *The Autonomy Myth: A Theory of Dependency*. New York: New Press, 2005.

———. "Feminist Legal Theory." *Am. U.J. Gender Soc. Pol'y and L.* 13 (2005): 13–23.

———. "Gender and Law: Feminist Legal Theory's Role in New Legal Realism." *Wis. L. Rev.* 2005 (2005): 405–431.

———. "The Social Foundations of Law." *Emory L.J.* 54 (2005): 201–237.

Finnis, John. "Law, Morality, and Sexual Orientation." *Notre Dame L. Rev.* 69 (1994): 1049–1076.

———. "The Good Marriage and the Morality of Sexual Relations: Some Historical and Philosophical Observations." *Am. J. Juris.* 42 (1997): 97–134.

———. "On the Practical Meaning of Secularism." *Notre Dame L. Rev.* 73 (1998): 491–516.

———. "Symposium: The Constitution and the Good Society: Virtue and the Constitution of the United States." *Fordham L. Rev.* 69 (2001): 1595–1602.

———. "Helping Enact Unjust Law without Complicity in Injustice." *Am. J. Juris.* 49 (2004): 11–42.

Forbath, William E. "The Ambiguities of Free Labor: Labor and the Law in the Guilded Age." *Wis. L. Rev.* 1985 (1985): 767–817.

———. "The Shaping of the American Labor Movement." *Harv. L. Rev.* 102 (1989): 1109–1159.

Frame, Laura. "Where Poverty and Parenting Intersect: The Impact of Welfare Reform on Caregiving." Pp. 63–84 in Jill Berrick and Bruce Fuller, eds., *Good Parents or Good Workers? How Policy Shapes Families' Daily Lives*. New York: Palgrave MacMillan, 2005.

Freud, Sigmund. *Civilization and Its Discontents*. Translated and edited by James Strachey. New York: W. W. Norton, 1989.

Friedan, Betty. *The Feminine Mystique*. New York: W. W. Norton, 1963.

Gallagher, Maggie. "Why Marriage Is Good for You." *City Journal* (Autumn 2000):76–82, available at http://www.city-journal.org/html/10_4_why_marriage_is.html.

Gallagher, Mary, and Barbara Whitehead. "End No-Fault Divorce?" *First Things* 75 (1997): 24–30.

Galston, William. *Liberal Pluralism: The Implication of Value Pluralism for Political Theory and Practice*. New York: Cambridge University Press, 2002.

———. "On Liberal Pluralism." *NOVA* (forthcoming).

Garrow, David J. *Liberty and Sexuality: The Right to Privacy and the Making of* Roe v. Wade, updated with a new epilogue. Berkeley: University of California Press, 1998.

Gay and Lesbian Alliance against Defamation (GLAAD). *Protections, Benefits, and Obligations of Marriage under Massachusetts and Federal Law: Some Key Provisions of a Work-in-Progress*. New York: GLAAD, 2001.

General Accounting Office, GAO OGC-97-16, Defense of Marriage Act, January 31, 1997, available at http://www.gao.gov/archive/1997/og97016.pdf.

———. GAO-04-353R, Defense of Marriage Act, January 23, 2004, available at http://www.gao.gov/new.items/d04353r.pdf.

George, Robert P. "Making Children Moral: Pornography, Parents, and the Public Interest." *Ariz. St. L.J.* 29 (1997): 569–580.

———. "Judicial Usurpation and Sexual Liberation: Courts and the Abolition of Marriage." *Regent U. L. Rev.* 17 (2004): 21–30.

———. "What's Sex Got to Do With It? Marriage, Morality, and Rationality." *Am. J. Juris.* 49 (2004): 63–85.

George, Robert P., and Gerard V. Bradley. "Marriage and the Liberal Imagination." *Geo. L.J.* 84 (1995): 301–320.

Gilligan, Carol. *In a Different Voice: Psychological Theory and Women's Development*. Cambridge, MA: Harvard University Press, 1993.

Glendon, Mary Ann. *Abortion and Divorce in Western Law*. Cambridge, MA: Harvard University Press, 1989.

———. *Rights Talk: The Impoverishment of Political Discourse*. New York: Free Press, 1989.

———. *The Transformation of Family Law*. Chicago: University of Chicago Press, 1989.

Gordon, Ed. "Can Marriage Help Alleviate Poverty?" Transcript from August 23, 2006, *News and Notes with Ed Gordon*.

Gordon, Linda. *Heroes of Their Own Lives: The Politics and History of Family Violence*. New York: Viking, 1988.

Grisez, Germain. "The Christian Family as Fulfillment of Sacramental Marriage." Paper presented at the Society of Christian Ethics Annual Conference, September 9, 1995 (unpublished manuscript, on file with *Georgetown Law Journal*).

Gunther, Gerald. "Foreword: In Search of Evolving Doctrine on a Changing Court: A Model for a Newer Equal Protection." *Harv. L. Rev.* 86 (1972): 1–48.

Gunther, Gerald, and Kathleen Sullivan. *Constitutional Law.* 13th ed. New York: Foundation Press, 1997.

Hakim, Danny. "Panel Asks New York to Join the Era of No-Fault Divorce." *New York Times,* February 7, 2006, p. A1.

Harrington, Mona. *Care and Equality: Inventing a New Family Politics.* New York: Alfred A. Knopf, 1999.

Hartog, Dirk. *Man and Wife in America: A History.* Cambridge, MA: Harvard University Press, 2000.

Hasday, Jill Elaine. "Contest and Consent: A Legal History of Marital Rape." *Cal. L. Rev.* 88 (2000): 1373–1505.

———. "Intimacy and Economic Exchange." *Harv. L. Rev.* 119 (2005): 491–530.

Hawkins, Daniel N., and Alan Booth. "Unhappily Ever After: Effects of Long-Term, Low-Quality Marriages on Well-Being." *Soc. Forces* 84, no. 1 (September 2005): 451–471.

Hays, Sharon. *Flat Broke with Children: Women in the Age of Welfare Reform.* New York: Oxford University Press, 2003.

Hersch, Joni, and Leslie S. Stratton. "Household Specialization and the Male Marriage Wage Premium." *Indus. and Lab. Rel. Rev.* 54, no. 1 (October 2000).

Hobbes, Thomas. *Leviathan.* Edited by Richard Tuck. New York: Cambridge University Press, 1996.

Hochschild, Arlie. *The Second Shift: Working Parents and the Revolution at Home.* New York: Viking, 1989.

Hoff, Joan. *Law, Gender, and Injustice: A Legal History of U.S. Women.* New York: New York University Press, 1991.

Holden, Karen, and Pamela Smock. "The Economic Costs of Marital Dissolution: Why Do Women Bear a Disproportionate Cost?" *Ann. Rev. Soc.* 17 (1991): 52–74.

Horwitz, Allan V., Helen Raskin-White, and Sandra Howell-White. "Becoming Married and Mental Health: A Longitudinal Study of a Cohort of Young Adults." *J. of Marriage and Fam.* 58, no. 4 (November 1996): 895–907.

Hunter, Nan. "Marriage, Law and Gender: A Feminist Inquiry." *Law and Sexuality* 1 (1991): 9–30.

Inskeep, Steve. "Promoting Marriage to Reduce Poverty." Transcript from August 21, 2006, *Morning Edition,* Steve Inskeep, host.

Jacob, Herbert. "Another Look at No-Fault Divorce and the Post-Divorce Finances of Women." *Law and Soc'y Rev.* 23 (1989): 95–115.

Jaff, Jennifer. "Wedding Bell Blues." *Ariz. L. Rev.* 30 (1988): 207–242.

Kadish, Sanford H., and Monrad G. Paulsen. *Criminal Law and Its Processes: Cases and Materials,* 2nd ed. Boston: Little, Brown, 1969.

Kadish, Sanford H., and Stephen J. Schulhofer, 7th ed. *Criminal Law and Its Processes: Cases and Materials.* Gaithersburg, MD: Aspen, 2001.

Kittay, Eva Feder. *Love's Labor: Essays on Women, Equality, and Dependency.* New York: Routledge, 1998.

Kittay, Eva Feder, and Ellen K. Feder, eds. *The Subject of Care: Feminist Perspectives on Dependency.* Lanham, MD: Rowman and Littlefield, 2002.

Koss, Mary P., Lisa A. Goodman, and Angela Browne. *No Safe Haven: Male Violence against Women at Home, at Work, and in the Community.* American Psychological Association, 1994.

Kraditor, Aileen S. *The Ideas of the Woman Suffrage Movement, 1890–1920.* New York: Norton, 1981 (1965).

Kramer, Larry. *The People Themselves: Popular Constitutionalism and Judicial Review.* New York: Oxford University Press, 2004.

Lee, Patrick, and Robert P. George. "What Sex Can Be: Self-Alienation, Illusion, or One-Flesh Union." *Am. J. Juris.* 42 (1997): 135–210.

Lerman, R. "Marriage as a Protective Force against Economic Hardship." Paper presented at the 23rd Annual Research Conference of the Association for Public Policy Analysis and Management, Washington, D.C., November 1–3.

Lillard, Lee A., and Linda Waite. "'Til Death Do Us Part: Marital Disruption and Mortality." *Am. J. Sociol.* 100 (1995): 1131–1156.

Lingxin, Hao. "Family Structure, Private Transfers, and the Economic Well-being of Families with Children." *Soc. Forces* 75, no. 1 (September 1996): 269–292.

Littleton, Christine. "Reconstructing Sexual Equality." *Cal. L. Rev.* 75 (1987): 1279–1337.

Loprest, Pamela, and Sheila Zedlewski. "Current and Former Welfare Recipients: How Do They Differ?" Urban Institute, Assessing the New Federalism 9, Discussion Paper No. 99-17, 1999, available at http://www.urban.org/UploadedPDF/discussion99-17.pdf.

Macedo, Stephen. "Homosexuality and the Conservative Mind." *Geo. L. J.* 84 (1995): 261–300.

———. "Reply to Critics." *Geo. L. J.* 84 (1995): 329–337.

MacKinnon, Catherine. *Sexual Harassment of Working Women: A Case of Sex Discrimination.* New Haven, CT: Yale University Press, 1979.

———. *Feminism Unmodified: Discourses on Life and Law.* Cambridge, MA: Harvard University Press, 1987.

———. *Toward a Feminist Theory of the State.* Cambridge, MA: Harvard University Press, 1989.

———. *Sex Equality.* New York: Foundation Press, 2001.

Majority Staff of Senate Committee on the Judiciary, 102d Cong., *Violence against Women: A Week in the Life of America.* Washington, DC: Government Printing Office, 1992.

Manning, Wendy, and Kathleen A. Lamb. "Adolescent Well-Being in Cohabiting, Married, and Single-Parent Families." *J. Marriage and Fam.* 65, no. 4 (November 2003): 876–893.

Marks, Nadine. "Flying Solo at Midlife: Gender, Marital Status and Psychological Well-being." *J. Marriage and Fam.* 58 (1996): 917–932.

May, William E. "On the Impossibility of Same-Sex Marriage." available at http://www.christendom-awake.org/pages/may/homosex.htm.

McClain, Linda. *The Place of Families: Fostering Capacity, Equality, and Responsibility.* Cambridge, MA: Harvard University Press, 2005.

McLean, Renwick. "Spain Legalizes Same-Sex Marriage." *New York Times,* June 30, 2005.

Michelman, Frank. "Foreword: On Protecting the Poor through the Fourteenth Amendment." *Harv. L. Rev.* 83 (1969): 7–59.

———. "In Pursuit of Constitutional Welfare Rights: One View of Rawls' Theory of Justice." *U. Pa. L. Rev.* 121 (1973): 962–1019.

Mill, John Stuart. "Utilitarianism." Pp. 19–21 in Samuel Gorovitz, ed., *Utilitarianism: With Critical Essays.* Indianapolis: Bobbs-Merril, 1971.

Moffitt, Robert, and Katie Winder. "The Correlates and Consequences of Welfare Exit and Entry: Evidence from the Three-City Study." In *Welfare, Children, and Families: A Three-City Study* (January 2003), available at the Johns Hopkins University Web site, http://www.jhu.edu/~welfare/WebPub.pdf.

———. "Does It Pay to Move from Welfare to Work? A Comment on Danziger, Heflin, Corcoran, Oltmans, and Wang." In *Welfare, Children, and Families: A Three-City Study* (April 2004, revised August 2004), available at the Johns Hopkins University Web site, http://www.jhu.edu/~welfare/moffitt_winder_v4c.pdf.

Murray, Shailagh. "Gay Marriage Amendment Fails in Senate." *Washington Post*, June 8, 2006, p. A01.

National Clearinghouse on Marital and Date Rape. "Who We Are and What We Do." available at http://www.ncmdr.org/who.html (accessed August 1, 2006).

National Gay and Lesbian Task Force Policy Institute. "The Issues—Marriage and Partnership Recognition" (2006), available at www.thetaskforce.org/theissues/issue.cfm?issueID=14.

National Marriage Project. "The State of Our Unions." available at http://marriage.rutgers.edu.

Nock, Stephen. "Why Not Marriage?" *Va. J. Soc. Pol'y and L.* 9 (2001): 273–290.

Noddings, Nel. *Caring: A Feminine Approach to Ethics and Moral Education.* Berkeley: University of California Press, 1984.

"Note: To Have and to Hold: The Marital Rape Exemption and the Fourteenth Amendment." *Harv. L. Rev.* 99 (1986): 1255–1273.

Nussbaum, Martha. *Women and Human Development.* New York: Cambridge University Press, 2000.

Okin, Susan. *Justice, Gender, and the Family.* New York: Basic Books, 1989.

"Out of Wedlock Births." TANF Sixth Annual Report to Congress, Ch. VII-1.

Patterson, Charlotte. "Adoption of Minor Children by Lesbian and Gay Adults: A Social Science Perspective." *Duke J. Gender L. and Pol'y* 2 (1995): 191–205.

Paulsen, Monrad G., and Walter Waddlington. *Cases and Other Materials on Domestic Relations.* Menola, NY: Foundation Press, 1970.

Pear, Robert, and Erik Eckholm. "A Decade after Welfare Overhaul, a Fundamental Shift in Policy and Perception." *New York Times*, August 21, 2006, p. A12.

Pitcher, J. William. "Rape and Other Sexual Offense Law Reform in Maryland, 1976–1977." *U. Balt. L. Rev.* 7 (1977): 151–170.

Polikoff, Nancy. "We Will Get What We Ask For: Why Legalizing Gay and Lesbian Marriage Will Not 'Dismantle the Legal Structure of Gender in Every Marriage.'" *Va. L. Rev.* 79 (1993): 1535–1550.

———. "Why Lesbians and Gay Men Should Read Martha Fineman." *Am. U. J. Gender Soc. Pol'y and L.* 8 (2000): 167–176.

———. "Ending Marriage as We Know It." *Hofstra L. Rev.* 32 (2003): 201–232.

———. "All Families Matter: What the Law Can Do about It." *Women's Rts. L. Rep.* 25 (2004): 205–209.

———. "Making Marriage Matter Less: The ALI Domestic Partner Principles Are a Step in the Right Direction." *U. Chi. Legal F.* 2004 (2004): 353–379.

Pollitt, Katha. "Happy Mother's Day." *Nation* (May 28, 2001), available at http://www. thenation.com/doc/20010528/pollitt.

Posner, Richard. "Bork and Beethoven." *Stan. L. Rev.* 42 (1990): 1365–1382.

———. *Sex and Reason.* Cambridge, MA: Harvard University Press, 1992.

Putnam, Robert. *Bowling Alone: The Collapse and Revival of American Community.* New York: Simon and Schuster, 2001.

Rauch, Jonathan. "Who Needs Marriage?" P. 296 in Bruce Bawer, ed., *Beyond Queer: Challenging Gay Left Orthodoxy.* New York: Free Press, 1996.

———. *Gay Marriage: Why It Is Good for Gays, Good for Straights, and Good for America.* New York: Owl Books, 2004.

Regan, Milton C., Jr. *Family Law and the Pursuit of Intimacy.* New York: New York University Press, 1993.

———. *Alone Together: Law and the Meanings of Marriage.* London: Oxford University Press, 1999.

———. "Law, Marriage, and Intimate Commitment." *Va. J. Soc. Pol'y and L.* 9 (2001): 116–152.

Reid, T. R. "Optimism on Both Sides of Gay Marriage Debate." *Washington Post,* July 18, 2006, p. A04.

Remez, L. "Married Mothers Fare the Best Economically, Even If They Were Unwed at the Time They Gave Birth." *Fam. Plan. Persp.* 31, no. 5 (October 1999): 258–259.

Rich, Adrienne. "Compulsory Heterosexuality and Lesbian Existence." *Signs: J. Women in Culture and Soc'y* 5, no. 4 (1980): 631–660.

Robson, Ruthann. "The State of Marriage." *Y.B.N.Z. Jurisprudence* 1 (1997): 1.

Rorty, Richard. *Philosophy and Social Hope.* New York: Penguin Books, 1999.

Russell, Diana E. H. *Rape in Marriage.* New York: Macmillan, 1982.

Sager, Lawrence G. "Fair Measure: The Legal Status of Under-enforced Constitutional Norms." *Harv. L. Rev.* 91 (1978): 1212–1264.

———. "Foreword: State Courts and the Strategic Space between the Norms and Rule of Constitutional Law." *Tex. L. Rev.* 63 (1985): 959–976.

———. *Justice in Plainclothes: A Theory of American Constitutional Practice.* New Haven, CT: Yale University Press, 2004.

Sandel, Michael. *Democracy's Discontent: America in Search of a Public Philosophy.* Cambridge, MA: Harvard University Press, 1996.

Schechter, Susan. *Women and Male Violence: The Visions and Struggles of the Battered Women's Movement.* Cambridge, MA: South End Press, 1982.

Schneider, Elizabeth. *Battered Women and Feminist Lawmaking.* New Haven, CT: Yale University Press, 2000.

Scott, Anne F., and Andrew M. Scott. *One Half the People: The Fight for Woman Suffrage.* Philadelphia: Lippincott, 1975.

Shanley, Mary. *Feminism, Marriage, and the Law in Victorian England, 1850–1895.* Princeton, NJ: Princeton Press, 1989.

Shanley, Mary, ed. *Just Marriage.* Oxford: Boston Review Book, 2004.

Shultz, Marjorie Maguire. "Reproductive Technology and Intent-Based Parenthood: An Opportunity for Gender Neutrality." *Wis. L. Rev.* 1990 (1990): 297–398.

Siegel, Reva. "The Rule of Love: Wife Beating as Prerogative and Privacy." *Yale L.J.* 105 (1996): 2117–2207.

———. "Constitutional Culture, Social Movement Conflict and Constitutional Change: The Case of the de facto ERA." *Cal. L. Rev.* (forthcoming).

Sigel, Roberta. *Ambition and Accommodation: How Women View Gender Relations.* Chicago: University of Chicago Press, 1996.

Singer, Jana. "Divorce Reform and Gender Justice." *N.C. L. Rev.* 67 (1989): 1103–1121.

———. "Divorce Obligations and Bankruptcy Discharge: Rethinking the Support/Property Distinction." *Harv. J. on Legis.* 30 (1993): 43–114.

———. "Alimony and Efficiency: The Gendered Costs and Benefits of the Economic Justification for Alimony." *Geo. L.J.* 82 (1994): 2423–2460.

———. "Husbands, Wives, and Human Capital: Why the Shoe Won't Fit." *Fam. L.Q.* 31 (1997): 117.

Smith, Rebekah J. "Family Caps in Welfare Reform: Their Coercive Effects and Damaging Consequences." *Harvard J. L. and Gender* 29 (2006): 151–200.

Smock, Pamela, Wendy Manning, and Sanjiv Gupta. "The Effect of Marriage and Divorce on Women's Economic Well-Being." *Am. Soc. Rev.* 64, no. 6 (December 2000): 794–812.

Spindelman, Marc. "Surviving *Lawrence v. Texas.*" *Mich. L. Rev.* 102 (2004): 1615–1667.

———. "Homosexuality's Horizon." *Emory Law Review* 54 (2005): 1361–1406.

Spohn, Cassia C. "The Rape Reform Movement: The Traditional Common Law and Rape Law Reforms." *Jurimentrics* 39 (1999): 119–130.

Staatsblad van het Koninkrijk der Nederlanden (Official Journal of the Netherlands) 9 (January 11, 2001).

Stacey, Judith, and Timothy Biblarz. "(How) Does the Sexual Orientation of Parents Matter?" *Am. Soc. Rev.* 88 (April 2001): 159–183.

Stack, Steven, and Ross Eshleman. "Marital Status and Happiness: A 17-Nation Study." *J. of Marriage and Fam.* 60, no. 2 (May 1998): 527–536.

Stark, Evan, and Anne Flitcraft. "Violence Against Intimates: An Epidemiological Review." P. 293 in Alan S. Bellack, Michael Hersen, R. L. Morrison, and Vincent B. Van Hasselt, eds., *Handbook of Family Violence.* New York: Springer, 1987.

Steil, Janice. *Marital Equality: Its Relationship to the Well-being of Husbands and Wives.* Thousand Oaks, CA: Sage Publications, 1997.

Sullivan, Andrew. "Here Comes the Groom: A (Conservative) Case for Gay Marriage." *New Republic* (August 28, 1989).

———. *Virtually Normal: An Argument about Homosexuality.* New York: Vintage, 1995.

Sunstein, Cass. "Words, Conduct, Caste." *U. Chi. L. Rev.* 60 (1993): 795–845.

Tasker, Fiona, and Susan Golombok. *Growing Up in a Lesbian Family: Effects on Child Development.* New York: Guilford, 1997.

Tribe, Lawrence. "*Lawrence v. Texas:* The 'Fundamental Right' that Dare Not Speak Its Name." *Harv. L. Rev.* 117 (2004): 1893–1955.

Tushnet, Mark. *Taking the Constitution away from the Courts.* Princeton, NJ: Princeton University Press, 1999.

U.S. Census Bureau. "America's Families and Living Arrangements." Current Population Reports, available at http://www.census.gov/main/www/cen2000.html.

Vance, Carol, ed. *Pleasure and Danger: Exploring Female Sexuality*. New York: Thorsons, 1990.

Wadlington, Walter. *Cases and Materials on Domestic Relations*, 3rd ed. Westbury, NY: Foundation Press, 1995.

Waite, Linda. "Does Marriage Matter?" *Demography* 32, no. 4 (November 1995): 483–507.

Waite, Linda, and Evelyn Lehrer. "The Benefits from Marriage and Religion in the United States: A Comparative Analysis." *Population and Dev. Rev.* 29, no. 2 (June 2003): 255–275.

Waite, Linda, and Maggie Gallagher. *The Case for Marriage: Why Married People Are Happier, Healthier, and Better off Financially*. New York: Doubleday, 2000.

Wardle, Lynn D. "No-Fault Divorce and the Divorce Conundrum." *BYU L. Rev.* 1991 (1991): 79–142.

———. "The Potential Impact of Homosexual Parenting on Children." *U. Ill. L. Rev.* (1997): 833–920.

———. "Is Marriage Obsolete?" *Mich. J. Gender and L.* 10 (2003): 189–235.

Warner, Michael. *The Trouble with Normal: Sex, Politics, and the Ethics of Queer Life*. New York: Free Press, 1999.

Warren, Samuel D., and Louis D. Brandeis. "The Right to Privacy." *Harv. L. Rev.* 4 (1890): 193–220.

Weitzman, Lenore J. *The Divorce Revolution: The Unexpected Social and Economic Consequences for Women and Children in America*. New York: Free Press, 1985.

West, Robin. "Liberalism Rediscovered: A Pragmatic Definition of the Liberal Vision." *U. Pitt. L. Rev.* 46 (1985): 673–738.

———. "The Difference in Women's Hedonic Lives: A Phenomenological Critique of Liberal and Radical Feminism." *Wis. Women's L.J.* 3 (1988): 81–145.

———. "Equality Theory, Marital Rape, and the Promise of the Fourteenth Amendment." *Fla. L. Rev.* 42 (1990): 45–79.

———. "Marital Rape and the Promise of the Fourteenth Amendment." *Fla. L. Rev.* 42 (1990): 45–79.

———. "The Harms of Consensual Sex." *Am. Phil. Ass'n. Newsl.* 94 (1995): 52–53.

———. *Caring for Justice*. New York: New York University Press, 1997.

———. "Universalism, Liberal Theory, and the Problem of Gay Marriage." *Fla. St. U. L. Rev.* 25 (1998): 705–730.

———. "Is Progressive Constitutionalism Possible?" *Widener L. Symp. J.* 4 (1999): 1–18.

———. "Rights, Capabilities and the Good Society." *Fordham L. Rev.* 69 (2001): 1901–1932.

———. "Do We Have A Right to Care." Pp. 88–114 in Eva Feder Kittay and Ellen K. Feder, eds., *The Subject of Care: Feminist Perspectives on Dependency*. Lanham, MD: Rowman and Littlefield, 2002.

———. "West, J., Concurring in the Judgment." Pp. 121–147 in Jack M. Balkin, ed., *What Roe v. Wade Should Have Said*. New York: New York University Press, 2005.

———. "Law's Nobility." *Yale J.L. and Feminism* 17 (2006): 385–458.

———. "Desperately Seeking a Moralist." *Harvard J.L. and Gender* (forthcoming).

———. "Comment on William Galston's Liberal Pluralism." *NOVA* (forthcoming).

———. "Katrina, Poverty, and the Constitution." *Chi.-Kent L. Rev.* 74 (forthcoming).

Wiecek, William M. *The Sources of Antislavery Constitutionalism in America, 1760–1848.* Ithaca, NY: Cornell University Press, 1977.

Wigmore, Evidence 8 § 2232 (1961).

Wilcox, W. Bradford, and Steven L. Nock. "What's Love Got to Do With It? Equality, Equity, Commitment, and Women's Marital Quality." *Soc. Forces* 84, no. 3 (March 2006).

Williams, George. *Sex and Evolution.* Princeton, NJ: Princeton University Press, 1975.

Williams, Joan C. *Unbending Gender: Why Family and Work Conflict and What to Do about It.* New York: Oxford University Press, 2000.

———. "The Family-Hostile Corporation." *Geo. Wash. L. Rev.* 70 (2002): 921–930.

———. "Better on Balance? The Corporate Counsel Work/Life Report." *Wm. and Mary J. Women and L.* 10 (2004): 367–457.

———. "Hibbs as a Federalism Case; Hibbs as a Maternal Wall Case." *U. Cin. L. Rev.* 72 (2004): 365–398.

———. "Deconstructing the Maternal Wall: Strategies for Vindicating the Civil Rights of 'Carers' in the Workplace." *Duke J. Gender L. and Pol'y* 13 (2006): 31–53.

Williams, Wendy. "Equality's Riddle: Pregnancy and the Equal Treatment/Special Treatment Debate." *Rev. of L. and Soc. Change* 13 (1984–1985): 325–380.

———. "Notes from a First Generation." *U. Chi. Legal. F.* 1989 (1989): 99–113.

Wilson, Edward O. *Sociobiology: The New Synthesis.* Cambridge, MA: Belknap Press of Harvard University Press, 2000.

Wilson, Robin Fretwell. "Evaluating Marriage: Does Marriage Matter to the Nurturing of Children?" *San Diego L. Rev.* 42 (2005): 847–880.

Winston, Pamela, Ronald Angel, Linda Burton, Andrew Cherlin, Robert Moffitt, and William Julius Wilson. *Welfare, Children, and Families: A Three-City Study—Overview and Design Report* (1999), available at Johns Hopkins University Web site, www.jhu.edu/~welfare.

Witte, John. "The Goods and Goals of Marriage." *Notre Dame L. Rev.* 76 (2001): 1019–1071.

"Women and Violence: Hearings on Legislation to Reduce the Growing Problem of Violent Crime against Women before the Senate Comm. on the Judiciary." 101st Cong. (1990).

Women's Action Coalition. "The Facts about Women; Developments in the Law: Legal Responses to Domestic Violence." *Harv. L. Rev.* 106 (1993): 1498–1501.

Wright, Robert. *The Moral Animal: Why We Are the Way We Are—The New Science of Evolutionary Psychology.* New York: Vintage Books, 1994.

X, Laura/National Clearinghouse on Marital and Date Rape. "Accomplishing the Impossible: An Advocate's Notes from the Successful Campaign to Make Marital and Date Rape a Crime in All 50 U.S. States and Other Countries." *Violence against Women* 9 (1999): 1064–1081, available at http://vaw.sagepub.com/content/vol5/issue9.

Yoshino, Kenji. "Too Good for Marriage." *New York Times,* July 14, 2006, p. A19.

Zeller, Tom. "The Nation: Two Fronts—Promoting Marriage, Fighting Poverty." *New York Times,* January 18, 2004.

Index

About the Author

Robin West is Professor of Law at Georgetown University Law Center. She teaches and writes in the fields of constitutional law and theory, jurisprudence, law and humanities, and feminist and gender studies. Her most recent book is *Re-Imagining Justice* (Ashgate Press 2003).